ENGLISH / KOREAN
영어 / 한국어

OXFORD
PICTURE
DICTIONARY

SECOND EDITION

OPD

Jayme Adelson-Goldstein

Norma Shapiro

OXFORD
UNIVERSITY PRESS

198 Madison Avenue
New York, NY 10016 USA

Great Clarendon Street, Oxford OX2 6DP UK

Oxford University Press is a department of the University of Oxford.
It furthers the University's objective of excellence in research, scholarship,
and education by publishing worldwide in

Oxford New York

Auckland Cape Town Dar es Salaam Hong Kong Karachi
Kuala Lumpur Madrid Melbourne Mexico City Nairobi
New Delhi Shanghai Taipei Toronto

With offices in

Argentina Austria Brazil Chile Czech Republic France Greece
Guatemala Hungary Italy Japan Poland Portugal Singapore
South Korea Switzerland Thailand Turkey Ukraine Vietnam

OXFORD and OXFORD ENGLISH are registered trademarks of
Oxford University Press.

© Oxford University Press 2009

Library of Congress Cataloging-in-Publication Data

Adelson-Goldstein, Jayme.
    The Oxford picture dictionary. Monolingual /
Jayme Adelson-Goldstein and Norma Shapiro.– 2nd ed.
       p. cm.
    Includes index.
    ISBN-13: 978-0-19-474016-6

    1. Picture dictionaries, English. 2. English
language–Textbooks for foreign speakers.
I. Shapiro, Norma. II. Title.
PE1629.S52 2008
423'.1–dc22

                        2007041017

Database right Oxford University Press (maker)

Executive Publishing Manager: Stephanie Karras
Managing Editor: Sharon Sargent
Development Editors: Glenn Mathes II, Bruce Myint, Katie La Storia
Associate Development Editors: Olga Christopoulos, Hannah Ryu, Meredith Stoll
Design Manager: Maj-Britt Hagsted
Project Manager: Allison Harm
Senior Designers: Stacy Merlin, Michael Steinhofer
Designer: Jaclyn Smith
Senior Production Artist: Julie Armstrong
Production Layout Artist: Colleen Ho
Cover Design: Stacy Merlin
Senior Image Editor: Justine Eun
Image Editors: Robin Fadool, Fran Newman, Jenny Vainisi
Manufacturing Manager: Shanta Persaud
Manufacturing Controller: Faye Wang
Translated by: Techno-Graphics & Translations, Inc.

ISBN: 978 0 19 474016 6

Printed in China

20 19 18 17 16 15

This book is printed on paper from certified and well-managed sources.

The OPD team thanks the following artists for their storyboarding and sketches:
Cecilia Aranovich, Chris Brandt, Giacomo Ghiazza, Gary Goldstein, Gordan Kljuc
Vincent Lucido, and Glenn Urieta

Illustrations by: Lori Anzalone: 13, 70-71, 76-77; Joe "Fearless" Arenella/Will Sump
178; Argosy Publishing: 66-67 (call-outs), 98-99, 108-109, 112-113 (call-outs), 152
193, 194-195, 196, 197, 205; Barbara Bastian: 4, 15, 17, 20-21, 162 (map), 198, 21
(map), 220-221; Philip Batini/AA Reps: 50; Thomas Bayley/Sparks Literary Agenc
158-159; Sally Bensusen: 211, 214; Annie Bissett: 112; Peter Bollinger/Shannon
Associates: 14-15; Higgens Bond/Anita Grien: 226; Molly Borman-Pullman: 116,
117; Jim Fanning/Ravenhill Represents: 80-81; Mike Gardner: 10, 12, 17, 22, 132,
114-115, 142-143, 174, 219, 228-229; Garth Glazier/AA Reps: 106, 118-119; Dennis
Godfrey/Mike Wepplo: 204; Steve Graham: 124-125, 224; Graphic Map & Chart Co.:
200-201, 202-203; Julia Green/Mendola Art: 225; Glenn Gustafson: 9, 27, 48, 76,
100, 101, 117, 132, 133, 136, 155, 161, 179, 196; Barbara Harmon: 212-213, 215; Ben
Hasler/NB Illustration: 94-95, 101, 148-149, 172, 182, 186-187; Betsy Hayes: 134,
138-139; Matthew Holmes: 75; Stewart Holmes/Illustration Ltd.: 192; Janos Jantner/
Beehive Illustration: 5, 13, 82-83, 122-123, 130-131, 146-147, 164-165, 184, 185; Ken
Joudrey/Munro Campagna: 52, 68-69, 177, 208-209; Bob Kaganich/Deborah Wolfe:
10, 40-41, 121; Steve Karp: 230, 231; Mike Kasun/Munro Campagna: 218; Graham
Kennedy: 27; Marcel Laverdet/AA Reps: 23; Jeffrey Lindberg: 33, 42-43, 92-93, 133,
160-161, 170-171, 176; Dennis Lyall/Artworks: 198; Chris Lyons:/Lindgren & Smith:
173, 191; Alan Male/Artworks: 210, 211; Jeff Mangiat/Mendola Art: 53, 54, 55, 56, 57,
58, 59, 66-67; Adrian Mateescu/The Studio: 188-189, 232-233; Karen Minot: 28-29;
Paul Mirocha/The Wiley Group: 194, 216-217; Peter Miserendino/P.T. Pie Illustrations:
198; Lee Montgomery/Illustration Ltd.: 4; Roger Motzkus: 229; Laurie O'Keefe: 111,
216-217; Daniel O'Leary/Illustration Ltd.: 8-9, 26, 34-35, 78, 135, 136-137, 238; Vilma
Ortiz-Dillon: 16, 20-21, 60, 98-99, 100, 211; Terry Pazcko: 46-47, 144-145, 152, 180,
227; David Preiss/Munro Campagna: 5; Pronk & Associates: 192-193; Tony Randazzo/
AA Reps: 156, 234-235; Mike Renwick/Creative Eye: 126-127; Mark Riedy/Scott Hull
Associates: 48-49, 79, 140, 153; Jon Rogers/AA Reps: 112; Jeff Sanson/Schumann &
Co.: 84-85, 240-241; David Schweitzer/Munro Campagna: 162-163; Ben Shannon/
Magnet Reps: 11, 64-65, 90, 91, 96, 97, 166-167, 168-169, 179, 239; Reed Sprunger/
Jae Wagoner Artists Rep.: 18-19, 232-233; Studio Liddell/AA Reps: 27; Angelo Tillar
108-109; Ralph Voltz/Deborah Wolfe: 50-51, 128-129, 141, 154, 175, 236-237;
Jeff Wack/Mendola Art: 24, 25, 86-87, 102-103, 134-135, 231; Brad Walker: 104-10
150-151, 157, 206-207; Wendy Wassink: 110-111; John White/The Neis Group: 19
Eric Wilkerson: 32, 138; Simon Williams/Illustration Ltd.: 2-3, 6-7, 30-31, 36, 38-39
44-45, 72-73; Lee Woodgate/Eye Candy Illustration: 222-223; Andy Zito: 62-23; Craig
Zuckerman: 14, 88-89, 112-113, 120-121, 194-195.

Chapter icons designed by Von Glitschka/Scott Hull Associates

Cover Art by CUBE/Illustration Ltd (hummingbird, branch); Paul Mirocha/The Wiley
Group (cherry); Mark Riedy/Scott Hull Associates (stamp); 9 Surf Studios (lettering).

Studio photography for Oxford University Press done by Dennis Kitchen Studio: 37,
61, 72, 73, 74, 75, 95, 96, 100, 180, 181, 183, 226.

Stock Photography: Age FotoStock: 238 (flute; clarinet; bassoon; saxophone; violin; cello;
bass; guitar; trombone; trumpet; xylophone; harmonica); Comstock, 61 (window);
Morales, 221 (bat); Franco Pizzochero, 98 (cashmere); Thinkstock, 61 (sink); Alamy:
Corbis, 61 (table); Gary Crabbe, 220 (park ranger); The Associated Press: 198 (strike;
soldiers in trench); Joe Rosenthal, 198 (Iwo Jima); Neil Armstrong, 198 (Buzz Aldrin
on Moon); CORBIS: Philip Gould, 198 (Civil War); Photo Library, 220 (Yosemite Falls);
Danita Delimont: Greg Johnston, 220 (snorkeling); Jamie & Judy Wild, 220 (El Capitan);
Getty Images: 198 (Martin Luther King, Jr.); Amana Images, 61 (soapy plates), The
Granger Collection: 198 (Jazz Age); The Image Works: Kelly Spranger, 220 (sea turtle);
Inmagine: 238 (oboe; tuba; French horn; piano; drums; tambourine; accordion);
istockphoto: 61 (oven); 98 (silk), 99 (suede; lace; velvet); Jupiter Images: 61 (tiles); 98
(wool); 99 (corduroy); Foodpix: 98 (linen); Rob Melnychuk/Brand X Pictures, 61 (glass
shower door); Jupiter Unlimited: 220 (seagulls); 238 (electric keyboard); Comstock, 99
(denim); Mary Evans Picture Library: 198 (women in factory); NPS Photo: Peter Jones, 221
(Carlsbad Cavern entrance; tour; cavern; spelunker); OceanwideImages.com: Gary Bell,
220 (coral); Photo Edit, Inc: David Young-Wolff, 220 (trail); Picture History: 198 (Hiram
Rhodes); Robertstock: 198 (Great Depression); Punchstock: 98 (t-shirt), Robert Glusic,
31 (Monument Valley); Roland Corporation: 238 (organ); SuperStock: 99 (leather); 198
(Daniel Boone); Shutterstock: Marek Szumlas, 94 (watch); United States Mint: 126;
Veer: Brand X Pictures, 220 (deer); Photodisc, 220 (black bear); Yankee Fleet, Inc.: 220
(Fort Jefferson; Yankee Freedom Ferry), Emil von Maltitz/Lime Photo, 37 (baby carrier).

This second edition of
the Oxford Picture Dictionary
is lovingly dedicated to
the memory of Norma Shapiro.

Her ideas, her pictures, and
her stories continue to teach,
inspire, and delight.

Acknowledgments

The publisher and authors would like to acknowledge the following individuals for their invaluable feedback during the development of this program:

Dr. Macarena Aguilar, Cy-Fair College, Houston, TX

Joseph F. Anselme, Atlantic Technical Center, Coconut Creek, FL

Stacy Antonopoulos, Monterey Trail High School, Elk Grove, CA

Carol Antunano, The English Center, Miami, FL

Irma Arencibia, Thomas A. Edison School, Union City, NJ

Suzi Austin, Alexandria City Public School Adult Program, Alexandria, FL

Patricia S. Bell, Lake Technical Center, Eustis, FL

Jim Brice, San Diego Community College District, San Diego, CA

Phil Cackley, Arlington Education and Employment Program (REEP), Arlington, VA

Frieda Caldwell, Metropolitan Adult Education Program, San Jose, CA

Sandra Cancel, Robert Waters School, Union City, NJ

Anne Marie Caney, Chula Vista Adult School, Chula Vista, CA

Patricia Castro, Harvest English Institute, Newark, NJ

Paohui Lola Chen, Milpitas Adult School, Milpitas, CA

Lori Cisneros, Atlantic Vo-Tech, Ft. Lauderdale, FL

Joyce Clapp, Hayward Adult School, Hayward, CA

Stacy Clark, Arlington Education and Employment Program (REEP), Arlington, VA

Nancy B. Crowell, Southside Programs for Adults in Continuing Education, Prince George, VA

Doroti da Cunha, Hialeah-Miami Lakes Adult Education Center, Miami, FL

Paula Da Silva-Michelin, La Guardia Community College, Long Island City, NY

Cynthia L. Davies, Humble I.S.D., Humble, TX

Christopher Davis, Overfelt Adult Center, San Jose, CA

Beverly De Nicola, Capistrano Unified School District, San Juan Capistrano, CA

Beatriz Diaz, Miami-Dade County Public Schools, Miami, FL

Druci J. Diaz, Hillsborough County Public Schools, Tampa, FL

Marion Donahue, San Dieguito Adult School, Encinitas, CA

Nick Doorn, International Education Services, South Lyon, MI

Mercedes Douglass, Seminole Community College, Sanford, FL

Jenny Elliott, Montgomery College, Rockville, MD

Paige Endo, Mt. Diablo Adult Education, Concord, CA

Megan Ernst, Glendale Community College, Glendale, CA

Elizabeth Escobar, Robert Waters School, Union City, NJ

Joanne Everett, Dave Thomas Education Center, Pompano Beach, FL

Jennifer Fadden, Arlington Education and Employment Program (REEP), Arlington, VA

Judy Farron, Fort Myers Language Center, Fort Myers, FL

Sharyl Ferguson, Montwood High School, El Paso, TX

Dr. Monica Fishkin, University of Central Florida, Orlando, FL

Nancy Frampton, Reedley College, Reedley, CA

Lynn A. Freeland, San Dieguito Union High School District, Encinitas, CA

Cathy Gample, San Leandro Adult School, San Leandro, CA

Hillary Gardner, Center for Immigrant Education and Training, Long Island City, NY

Martha C. Giffen, Alhambra Unified School District, Alhambra, CA

Jill Gluck, Hollywood Community Adult School, Los Angeles, CA

Carolyn Grimaldi, LaGuardia Community College, Long Island City, NY

William Gruenholz, USD Adult School, Concord, CA

Sandra G. Gutierrez, Hialeah-Miami Lakes Adult Education Center, Miami, FL

Conte Gúzman-Hoffman, Triton College, River Grove, IL

Amanda Harllee, Palmetto High School, Palmetto, FL

Mercedes Hearn, Tampa Bay Technical Center, Tampa, FL

Robert Hearst, Truman College, Chicago, IL

Patty Heiser, University of Washington, Seattle, WA

Joyce Hettiger, Metropolitan Education District, San Jose, CA

Karen Hirsimaki, Napa Valley Adult School, Napa, CA

Marvina Hooper, Lake Technical Center, Eustis, FL

Katie Hurter, North Harris College, Houston, TX

Nuchamon James, Miami Dade College, Miami, FL

Linda Jennings, Montgomery College, Rockville, MD

Bonnie Boyd Johnson, Chapman Education Center, Garden Grove, CA

Fayne B. Johnson, Broward County Public Schools, Fort Lauderdale, FL

Stavroula Katseyeanis, Robert Waters School, Union City, NJ

Dale Keith, Broadbase Consulting, Inc. at Kidworks USA, Miami, FL

Blanche Kellawon, Bronx Community College, Bronx, NY

Mary Kernel, Migrant Education Regional Office, Northwest Educational Service District, Anacortes, WA

Karen Kipke, Antioch High School Freshman Academy, Antioch, TN

Jody Kirkwood, ABC Adult School, Cerritos, CA

Matthew Kogan, Evans Community Adult School, Los Angeles, CA

Ineza Kuceba, Renton Technical College, Renton, WA

John Kuntz, California State University, San Bernadino, San Bernadino, CA

Claudia Kupiec, DePaul University, Chicago, IL

E.C. Land, Southside Programs for Adult Continuing Education, Prince George, VA

Betty Lau, Franklin High School, Seattle, WA

Patt Lemonie, Thomas A. Edison School, Union City, NJ

Lia Lerner, Burbank Adult School, Burbank, CA

Krystyna Lett, Metropolitan Education District, San Jose, CA

Renata Lima, TALK International School of Languages, Fort Lauderdale, FL

Luz M. Lopez, Sweetwater Union High School District, Chula Vista, CA

Osmara Lopez, Bronx Community College, Bronx, NY

Heather Lozano, North Lake College, Irving, TX

Betty Lynch, Arlington Education and Employment Program (REEP), Arlington, VA

Meera Madan, REID Park Elementary School, Charlotte, NC

Ivanna Mann Thrower, Charlotte Mecklenburg Schools, Charlotte, NC

Michael R. Mason, Loma Vista Adult Center, Concord, CA

Holley Mayville, Charlotte Mecklenburg Schools, Charlotte, NC

Margaret McCabe, United Methodist Cooperative Ministries, Clearwater, FL

Todd McDonald, Hillsborough Adult Education, Tampa, FL

Nancy A. McKeand, ESL Consultant, St. Benedict, LA

Rebecca L. McLain, Gaston College, Dallas, NC

John M. Mendoza, Redlands Adult School, Redlands, CA

Bet Messmer, Santa Clara Adult Education Center, Santa Clara, CA

Christina Morales, BEGIN Managed Programs, New York, NY

Lisa Munoz, Metropolitan Education District, San Jose, CA

Mary Murphy-Clagett, Sweetwater Union High School District, Chula Vista, CA

Jonetta Myles, Rockdale County High School, Conyers, GA

Marwan Nabi, Troy High School, Fullerton, CA

Dr. Christine L. Nelsen, Salvation Army Community Center, Tampa, FL

Michael W. Newman, Arlington Education and Employment Program (REEP), Arlington, VA

Rehana Nusrat, Huntington Beach Adult School, Huntington Beach, CA

Cindy Oakley-Paulik, Embry-Riddle Aeronautical University, Daytona Beach, FL

Acknowledgments

Janet Ochi-Fontanott, Sweetwater Union High School District, Chula Vista, CA

Lorraine Pedretti, Metropolitan Education District, San Jose, CA

Isabel Pena, BE/ESL Programs, Garland, TX

Margaret Perry, Everett Public Schools, Everett, WA

Dale Pesmen, PhD, Chicago, IL

Cathleen Petersen, Chapman Education Center, Garden Grove, CA

Allison Pickering, Escondido Adult School, Escondido, CA

Ellen Quish, LaGuardia Community College, Long Island City, NY

Teresa Reen, Independence Adult Center, San Jose, CA

Kathleen Reynolds, Albany Park Community Center, Chicago, IL

Melba I. Rillen, Palmetto High School, Palmetto, FL

Lorraine Romero, Houston Community College, Houston, TX

Eric Rosenbaum, BEGIN Managed Programs, New York, NY

Blair Roy, Chapman Education Center, Garden Grove, CA

Arlene R. Schwartz, Broward Community Schools, Fort Lauderdale, FL

Geraldyne Blake Scott, Truman College, Chicago, IL

Sharada Sekar, Antioch High School Freshman Academy, Antioch, TN

Dr. Cheryl J. Serrano, Lynn University, Boca Raton, FL

Janet Setzekorn, United Methodist Cooperative Ministries, Clearwater, FL

Terry Shearer, EDUCALL Learning Services, Houston, TX

Elisabeth Sklar, Township High School District 113, Highland Park, IL

Robert Stein, BEGIN Managed Programs, New York, NY

Ruth Sutton, Township High School District 113, Highland Park, IL

Alisa Takeuchi, Chapman Education Center, Garden Grove, CA

Grace Tanaka, Santa Ana College School of Continuing Education, Santa Ana, CA

Annalisa Te, Overfelt Adult Center, San Jose, CA

Don Torluemke, South Bay Adult School, Redondo Beach, CA

Maliheh Vafai, Overfelt Adult Center, San Jose, CA

Tara Vasquez, Robert Waters School, Union City, NJ

Nina Velasco, Naples Language Center, Naples, FL

Theresa Warren, East Side Adult Center, San Jose, CA

Lucie Gates Watel, Truman College, Chicago, IL

Wendy Weil, Arnold Middle School, Cypress, TX

Patricia Weist, TALK International School of Languages, Fort Lauderdale, FL

Dr. Carole Lynn Weisz, Lehman College, Bronx, NY

Desiree Wesner, Robert Waters School, Union City, NJ

David Wexler, Napa Valley Adult School, Napa, CA

Cynthia Wiseman, Borough of Manhattan Community College, New York, NY

Debbie Cullinane Wood, Lincoln Education Center, Garden Grove, CA

Banu Yaylali, Miami Dade College, Miami, FL

Hongyan Zheng, Milpitas Adult Education, Milpitas, CA

Arlene Zivitz, ESOL Teacher, Jupiter, FL

The publisher, authors, and editors would like to thank the following people for their expertise in reviewing specific content areas:

Ross Feldberg, Tufts University, Medford, MA

William J. Hall, M.D. FACP/FRSM (UK), Cumberland Foreside, ME

Jill A. Horohoe, Arizona State University, Tempe, AZ

Phoebe B. Rouse, Louisiana State University, Baton Rouge, LA

Dr. Susan Rouse, Southern Wesleyan University, Central, SC

Dr. Ira M. Sheskin, University of Miami, Coral Gables, FL

Maiko Tomizawa, D.D.S., New York, NY

Table of Contents 목차

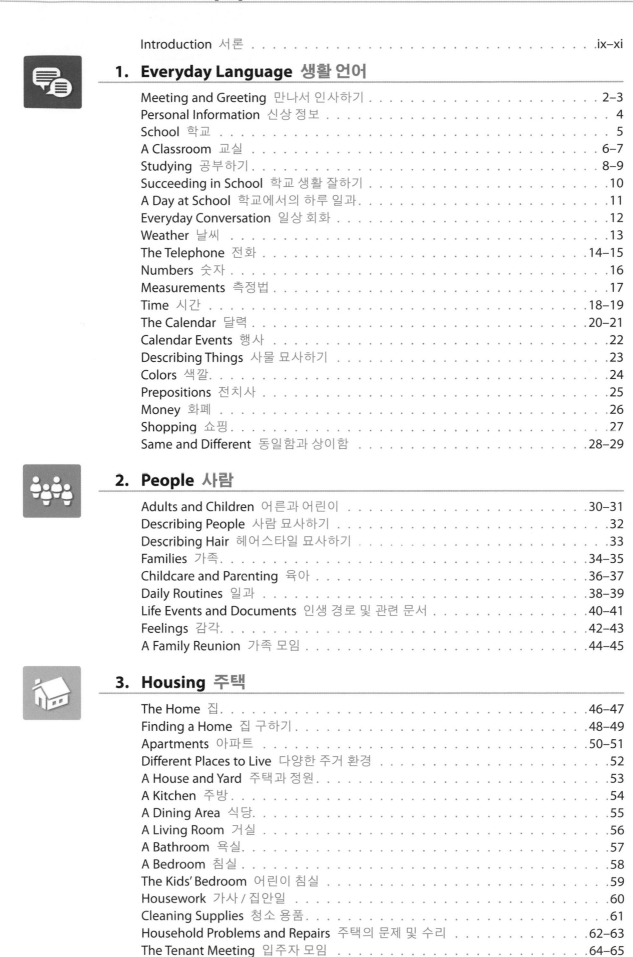

Introduction 서론 . . . . ix–xi

1. Everyday Language 생활 언어

Meeting and Greeting 만나서 인사하기 2–3
Personal Information 신상 정보 4
School 학교 5
A Classroom 교실 6–7
Studying 공부하기 8–9
Succeeding in School 학교 생활 잘하기 10
A Day at School 학교에서의 하루 일과 11
Everyday Conversation 일상 회화 12
Weather 날씨 13
The Telephone 전화 14–15
Numbers 숫자 16
Measurements 측정법 17
Time 시간 18–19
The Calendar 달력 20–21
Calendar Events 행사 22
Describing Things 사물 묘사하기 23
Colors 색깔 24
Prepositions 전치사 25
Money 화폐 26
Shopping 쇼핑 27
Same and Different 동일함과 상이함 28–29

2. People 사람

Adults and Children 어른과 어린이 30–31
Describing People 사람 묘사하기 32
Describing Hair 헤어스타일 묘사하기 33
Families 가족 34–35
Childcare and Parenting 육아 36–37
Daily Routines 일과 38–39
Life Events and Documents 인생 경로 및 관련 문서 40–41
Feelings 감각 42–43
A Family Reunion 가족 모임 44–45

3. Housing 주택

The Home 집 46–47
Finding a Home 집 구하기 48–49
Apartments 아파트 50–51
Different Places to Live 다양한 주거 환경 52
A House and Yard 주택과 정원 53
A Kitchen 주방 54
A Dining Area 식당 55
A Living Room 거실 56
A Bathroom 욕실 57
A Bedroom 침실 58
The Kids' Bedroom 어린이 침실 59
Housework 가사 / 집안일 .60
Cleaning Supplies 청소 용품 61
Household Problems and Repairs 주택의 문제 및 수리 62–63
The Tenant Meeting 입주자 모임 64–65

Contents 목차

4. Food 음식

Back from the Market 시장을 보고 돌아와서. .66–67
Fruit 과일 68
Vegetables 야채 69
Meat and Poultry 고기류. 70
Seafood and Deli 해산물 및 가공 식품 .71
A Grocery Store 식료품점 72–73
Containers and Packaging 용기와 포장 .74
Weights and Measurements 무게와 단위 75
Food Preparation and Safety 음식 준비와 안전 76–77
Kitchen Utensils 주방 용품 78
Fast Food Restaurant 패스트 푸드점 79
A Coffee Shop Menu 커피 숍 메뉴 80–81
A Restaurant 식당 82–83
The Farmers' Market 농산물 시장 84–85

5. Clothing 의복

Everyday Clothes 평상복. 86–87
Casual, Work, and Formal Clothes 캐주얼, 근무복 및 정장 88–89
Seasonal Clothing 계절별 의복 90
Underwear and Sleepwear 속옷과 잠옷 .91
Workplace Clothing 직업별 의복. 92–93
Shoes and Accessories 신발과 액세서리 94–95
Describing Clothes 의복 묘사 96–97
Making Clothes 옷 만들기 98–99
Making Alterations 옷 수선 100
Doing the Laundry 세탁하기 101
A Garage Sale 차고 세일 102–103

6. Health 건강

The Body 신체 104–105
Inside and Outside the Body 신체 내외부 106–107
Personal Hygiene 개인 위생 108–109
Symptoms and Injuries 증상 및 부상. 110
Illnesses and Medical Conditions 질병과 의료 상황 111
A Pharmacy 약국. 112–113
Taking Care of Your Health 건강 관리 114–115
Medical Emergencies 응급 의료 상황 116
First Aid 응급 치료 117
Medical Care 진료 118
Dental Care 치과 진료 119
Hospital 병원. 120–121
A Health Fair 건강 박람회 122–123

7. Community 지역사회

Downtown 시내 124–125
City Streets 시가지 126–127
An Intersection 교차로 128–129
A Mall 쇼핑센터 130–131
The Bank 은행 132
The Library 도서관 133
The Post Office 우체국 134–135
Department of Motor Vehicles (DMV) 운전 면허국 . . . 136–137
Government and Military Service 정부 및 군 복무 138–139
Civic Rights and Responsibilities 시민권과 의무 140
The Legal System 법제도 141
Crime 범죄 142
Public Safety 공공 안전 143
Emergencies and Natural Disasters 비상사태와 천재지변 . 144–145
Emergency Procedures 응급 상황 대비 절차 146–147
Community Cleanup 지역사회 청소 148–149

8. Transportation 교통

Basic Transportation 기본 교통 수단 150–151
Public Transportation 대중 교통 152
Prepositions of Motion 동작 관련 전치사 153
Traffic Signs 교통 표지판 154
Directions and Maps 방향 및 지도 155
Cars and Trucks 자동차와 트럭 156
Buying and Maintaining a Car 자동차 구입 및 유지관리 . . 157
Parts of a Car 자동차 부품 158–159
An Airport 공항 160–161
Taking a Trip 여행하기 162–163

9. Work 일

The Workplace 직장 164–165
Jobs and Occupations A-C 직업 (A~C, 영어순) 166
Jobs and Occupations C-H 직업 (C~H, 영어순) 167
Jobs and Occupations H-P 직업 (H~P, 영어순) 168
Jobs and Occupations P-W 직업 (P~W, 영어순) 169
Job Skills 직업 특기 170
Office Skills 사무실에서 필요한 기술들 171
Career Planning 진로 계획 172
Job Search 직업 찾기 173
Interview Skills 면접 기술 174
A Factory 공장 175
Landscaping and Gardening 조경 및 정원 관리 176
Farming and Ranching 농사일과 목장일 177
Construction 건축 178
Job Safety 작업 안전 179
Tools and Building Supplies 공구 및 건물 보수 용품 180–181
An Office 사무실 182–183
A Hotel 호텔 184
Food Service 음식 서비스 185
A Bad Day at Work 직장에서의 불운한 하루 186–187

Contents 목차

10. Areas of Study 학과

Schools and Subjects 학교 및 과목 188–189
English Composition 영작문 190–191
Mathematics 수학 192–193
Science 과학 194–195
Computers 컴퓨터 196
The Internet 인터넷 197
U.S. History 미국 역사 198
World History 세계사 199
North America and Central America 북아메리카 및 중앙 아메리카 . . . 200–201
World Map 세계 지도 202–203
Geography and Habitats 지형 및 서식지 204
The Universe 우주 205
A Graduation 졸업 206–207

11. Plants and Animals 식물과 동물

Nature Center 자연 센터 208–209
Trees and Plants 나무와 식물 210
Flowers 꽃 211
Marine Life, Amphibians, and Reptiles 바다생물, 양서류 그리고 파충류 . . . 212–213
Birds, Insects, and Arachnids 새, 곤충 그리고 거미류 214
Domestic Animals and Rodents 가축과 설치류 동물 215
Mammals 포유동물 216–217
Energy and Conservation 에너지와 보존 218–219
U.S. National Parks 미국 국립 공원 220–221

12. Recreation 레크리에이션

Places to Go 놀러갈 곳 222–223
The Park and Playground 공원과 놀이터 224
The Beach 해변 225
Outdoor Recreation 야외 활동 226
Winter and Water Sports 동계 스포츠와 수중 스포츠 227
Individual Sports 개인 스포츠 228
Team Sports 팀 스포츠 229
Sports Verbs 스포츠 동사 230
Sports Equipment 운동기구 231
Hobbies and Games 취미와 게임 232–233
Electronics and Photography 전자제품과 사진 234–235
Entertainment 엔터테인먼트 236–237
Music 음악 238
Holidays 축제일 239
A Birthday Party 생일 파티 240–241

Verb Guide 동사 가이드 242–244
How to Use the Index 색인을 사용하는 방법 245
English Index 영어 색인 246–281
Geographical Index 지리 색인 282–284
Korean Index 한국어 색인 285–304
Research Bibliography 참고 문헌 목록 305

Teaching with the *Oxford Picture Dictionary* Program

The following general guidelines will help you prepare single and multilevel lessons using the OPD program. For step-by-step, topic-specific lesson plans, see *OPD Lesson Plans*.

1. Use Students' Needs to Identify Lesson Objectives

- Create communicative objectives based on your learners' needs assessments (*see OPD 2e Assessment Program*).
- Make sure objectives state what students will be able to do at the end of the lesson. For example: *Students will be able to respond to basic classroom commands and requests for classroom objects.* (pp. 6–7, A Classroom)
- For multilevel classes, identify a low-beginning, high-beginning, and low-intermediate objective for each topic.

2. Preview the Topic

Identify what your students already know about the topic.

- Ask general questions related to the topic.
- Have students list words they know from the topic.
- Ask questions about the picture(s) on the page.

3. Present the New Vocabulary

Research shows that it is best to present no more than 5–7 new words at a time. Here are a few presentation techniques:

- Say each new word and describe it within the context of the picture. Have volunteers act out verbs and verb sequences.
- Use Total Physical Response commands to build vocabulary comprehension.
- For long or unfamiliar word lists, introduce words by categories or select the words your students need most.
- Ask a series of questions to build comprehension and give students an opportunity to say the new words. Begin with *yes/no* questions: *Is #16 chalk?* Progress to *or* questions: *Is #16 chalk or a marker?* Finally, ask *Wh-* questions: *What can I use to write on this paper?*
- Focus on the words that students want to learn. Have them write 3–5 new words from each topic, along with meaning clues such as a drawing, translation, or sentence.

More vocabulary and **Grammar Point** sections provide additional presentation opportunities (see p. 5, School). For multilevel presentation ideas, see *OPD Lesson Plans*.

4. Check Comprehension

Make sure that students understand the target vocabulary. Here are two activities you can try:

- Say vocabulary words, and have students point to the correct items in their books. Walk around the room, checking if students are pointing to the correct pictures.
- Make true/false statements about the target vocabulary. Have students hold up two fingers for true, three for false.

5. Provide Guided and Communicative Practice

The exercise bands at the bottom of the topic pages provide a variety of guided and communicative practice opportunities and engage students' higher-level thinking.

6. Provide More Practice

OPD Second Edition offers a variety of components to facilitate vocabulary acquisition. Each of the print and electronic materials listed below offers suggestions and support for single and multilevel instruction.

OPD Lesson Plans Step-by-step multilevel lesson plans feature 3 CDs with multilevel listening, context-based pronunciation practice, and leveled reading practice. Includes multilevel teaching notes for *The OPD Reading Library*.

OPD Audio CDs or Audio Cassettes Each word in OPD's word list is recorded by topic.

Low-Beginning, High-Beginning, and Low-Intermediate Workbooks Guided practice for each page in OPD features linked visual contexts, realia, and listening practice.

Classic Classroom Activities A photocopiable resource of interactive multilevel activities, grammar practice, and communicative tasks.

The OPD Reading Library Readers include civics, academic content, and workplace themes.

Overhead Transparencies Vibrant transparencies help to focus students on the lesson.

OPD Presentation Software A multilevel interactive teaching tool using interactive whiteboard and LCD technology. Audio, animation, and video instructional support bring each dictionary topic to life.

The OPD CD-ROM An interactive learning tool featuring four-skill practice based on OPD topics.

Bilingual Editions OPD is available in numerous bilingual editions including Spanish, Chinese, Vietnamese, Arabic, Korean, and many more.

My hope is that OPD makes it easier for you to take your learners from comprehension to communication. Please share your thoughts with us as you make the book your own.

Jayme Adelson-Goldstein

Jayme Adelson-Goldstein

OPDteam.us@oup.com

Welcome to the
OPD SECOND EDITION

The second edition of the *Oxford Picture Dictionary* expands on the best aspects of the 1998 edition with:

- New artwork presenting words within meaningful, real-life contexts
- An updated word list to meet the needs of today's English language learners
- 4,000 English words and phrases, including 285 verbs
- 40 new topics with 12 intro pages and 12 story pages
- Unparalleled support for vocabulary teaching

Subtopics present the words in easy-to-learn "chunks."

Color coding and icons make it easy to navigate through *OPD*.

Public Transportation

A Bus Stop

BUS 10 Northbound

Main	Elm	Oak
6:00	6:10	6:13
6:30	6:40	6:43
7:00	7:10	7:13
7:30	7:40	7:43

A Subway Station

1. bus route
2. fare
3. rider
4. schedule
5. transfer

6. subway car
7. platform
8. turnstile
9. vending machine
10. token
11. fare card

New art and rich contexts improve vocabulary acquisition.

A Train Station

Airport Transportation

12. ticket window
13. conductor
14. track
15. ticket
16. one-way trip
17. round trip

18. taxi stand
19. shuttle
20. town car
21. taxi driver
22. taxi license
23. meter

More vocabulary

hail a taxi: to raise your hand to get a taxi
miss the bus: to get to the bus stop after the bus leaves

Ask your classmates. Share the answers.

1. Is there a subway system in your city?
2. Do you ever take taxis? When?
3. Do you ever take the bus? Where?

152

Revised practice activities help students from low-beginning through low-intermediate levels.

Each intro page teaches key vocabulary items within the unit theme.

Practice activities make it easy to manage multilevel classrooms.

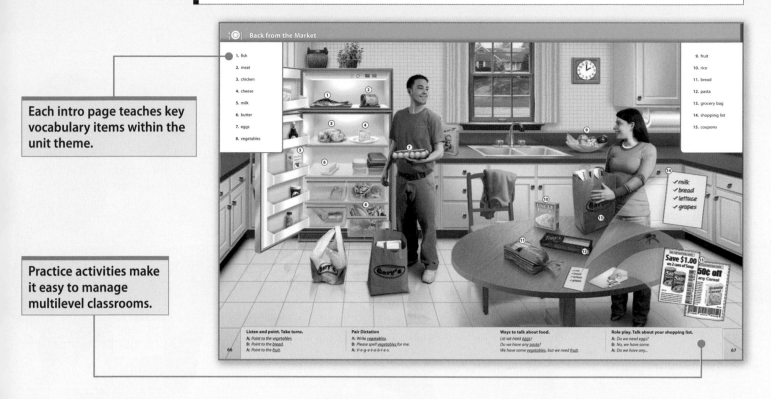

Pre-reading questions build students' previewing and predicting skills.

High-interest readings promote literacy skills.

Post-reading questions and role-play activities support critical thinking and encourage students to use the language they have learned.

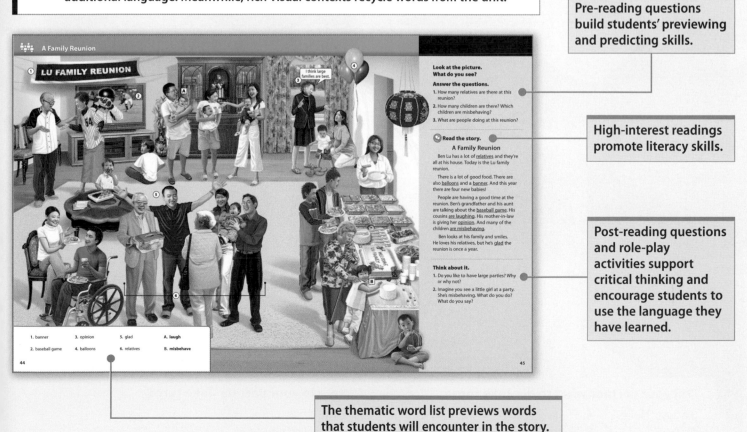

The thematic word list previews words that students will encounter in the story.

A. **Say**, "Hello."
"안녕하세요." 라고
말하기.

B. **Ask**, "How are you?"
"잘 지내세요?" 라고
묻기.

C. **Introduce** yourself.
자기 **소개하기**.

D. **Smile**.
미소 짓기.

E. **Hug**.
안아 주기.

F. **Wave**.
손을 흔들기.

Tell your partner what to do. Take turns.

1. *Say, "Hello."*
2. *Bow.*
3. *Smile.*
4. *Shake hands.*
5. *Wave.*
6. *Say, "Goodbye."*

Dictate to your partner. Take turns.

A: *Write smile.*
B: *Is it spelled s-m-i-l-e?*
A: *Yes, that's right.*

G. **Greet** people.
사람들에게 **인사하다**.

H. **Bow**.
머리 숙여 인사하다.

I. **Introduce** a friend.
친구를 **소개하다**.

J. **Shake** hands.
악수 하다.

K. **Kiss**.
키스하다.

L. **Say**, "Goodbye."
"안녕히 가세요"
라고 **말하다**.

Ways to greet people

Good morning.
Good afternoon.
Good evening.

Ways to introduce yourself

I'm Tom.
My name is Tom.

Pair practice. Make new conversations.

A: *Good morning. My name is Tom.*
B: *Nice to meet you, Tom. I'm Sara.*
A: *Nice to meet you, Sara.*

A. Say your name.
이름을 말하다.

B. Spell your name.
이름의 **철자를 말하다**.

C. Print your name.
이름을 **쓰다**.

D. Sign your name.
서명하다.

Filling Out a Form 양식에 기입하기

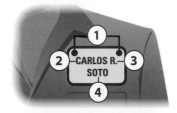

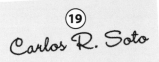

School Registration Form 학교 등록 양식

1. name:
   성명:

2. first name   3. middle initial   4. last name   5. address   6. apartment number
   이름   중간 이름   성   주소   아파트 호수

                                                   (   )

7. city   8. state   9. ZIP code   10. area code   11. phone number
   시   주   우편 번호   지역 번호   전화 번호

(   )

12. cell phone number   13. date of birth (DOB)   14. place of birth
    휴대 전화   생년월일   출생지

    -    -   16. sex: 17. male ☐
15. Social Security number   성별: 남
    사회보장번호   19. signature
                           18. female ☐   서명
                                    여

Pair practice. Make new conversations.

A: *My first name is Carlos.*
B: *Please spell Carlos for me.*
A: *C-a-r-l-o-s*

Ask your classmates. Share the answers.

1. Do you like your first name?
2. Is your last name from your mother? father? husband?
3. What is your middle name?

Campus 캠퍼스

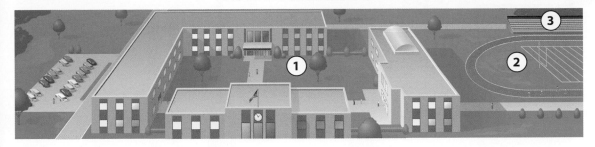

Administrators 교직원

Around Campus 교내 시설

1. quad
   안뜰
2. field
   운동장
3. bleachers
   야외 관람석
4. principal
   교장
5. assistant principal
   교감
6. counselor
   상담 교사
7. classroom
   교실
8. teacher
   교사
9. restrooms
   화장실
10. hallway
    복도
11. locker
    사물함
12. main office
    주 사무실
13. clerk
    사무원
14. cafeteria
    학교 식당
15. computer lab
    컴퓨터실
16. teacher's aide
    보조 교사
17. library
    도서관
18. auditorium
    강당
19. gym
    체육관
20. coach
    코치
21. track
    트랙

More vocabulary

Students do not pay to go to a **public school**.
Students pay to go to a **private school**.
A church, mosque, or temple school is a **parochial school**.

Grammar Point: contractions of the verb be

He + is = He's   *He's a teacher.*
She + is = She's   *She's a counselor.*
They + are = They're   *They're students.*

5

1. chalkboard
   칠판

2. screen
   스크린

3. whiteboard
   화이트보드

4. teacher / instructor
   선생님 / 교사

5. student
   학생

6. LCD projector
   LCD 프로젝터

7. desk
   책상

8. headphones
   헤드폰

A. **Raise** your hand.
손을 **들다**.

B. **Talk** to the teacher.
선생님과 **이야기하다**.

C. **Listen** to a CD.
CD를 **듣다**.

D. **Stand up**.
일어 서다.

E. **Write** on the board.
칠판에 **쓰다**.

F. **Sit down.** / **Take** a seat.
앉다. / 자리에 **앉다**.

G. **Open** your book.
책을 **펴다**.

H. **Close** your book.
책을 **덮다**.

I. **Pick up** the pencil.
연필을 **들다**.

J. **Put down** the pencil.
연필을 **내려 놓다**.

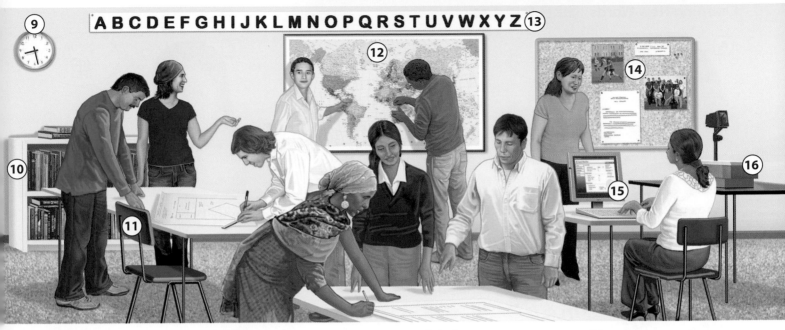

9. clock
시계

10. bookcase
책장

11. chair
의자

12. map
지도

13. alphabet
알파벳

14. bulletin board
게시판

15. computer
컴퓨터

16. overhead projector
오버헤드 프로젝터

17. dry erase marker
화이트보드용 마커

18. chalk
분필

19. eraser
지우개

20. pencil
연필

21. (pencil) eraser
(연필) 지우개

22. pen
펜

23. pencil sharpener
연필 깎이

24. marker
마커

25. textbook
교과서

26. workbook
연습장

27. 3-ring binder / notebook
3링 바인더 / 공책

28. notebook paper
공책 속지

29. spiral notebook
스프링 노트

30. dictionary
사전

31. picture dictionary
그림 사전

Look at the picture.
Describe the classroom.

A: There's a chalkboard.
B: There are fifteen students.

Ask your classmates. Share the answers.

1. Do you like to raise your hand in class?
2. Do you like to listen to CDs in class?
3. Do you ever talk to the teacher?

7

Learning New Words 새로운 단어 학습

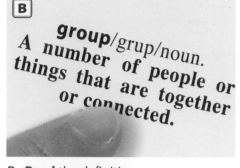

A. Look up the word.
단어를 **찾는다**.

B. Read the definition.
뜻을 **읽는다**.

C. Translate the word.
단어를 **번역한다**.

D. Check the pronunciation.
발음을 **확인한다**.

E. Copy the word.
단어를 **베껴 쓴다**.

F. Draw a picture.
그림을 **그린다**.

Working with Your Classmates 반 친구와 함께 학습하기

G. Discuss a problem.
문제에 대해 **토의한다**.

H. Brainstorm solutions /
answers.
해결책 / 답을 **함께 생각해
본다**.

I. Work in a group.
그룹으로 **공부한다**.

J. Help a classmate.
반 친구를 **도와준다**.

Working with a Partner 짝과 함께 공부하기

K. Ask a question.
질문을 **한다**.

L. Answer a question.
질문에 **대답한다**.

M. Share a book.
책을 **같이 본다**.

N. Dictate a sentence.
문장을 **받아 쓴다**.

Following Directions 지시 사항 따르기

O. **Fill in** the blank.
빈 칸을 **채우세요**.

P. **Choose** the correct answer.
맞는 답을 **고르세요**.

Q. **Circle** the answer.
답에 **동그라미 하세요**.

R. **Cross out** the word.
단어에 **줄을 그어 지우세요**.

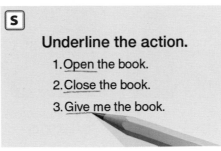

S. **Underline** the word.
단어에 **밑줄 치세요**.

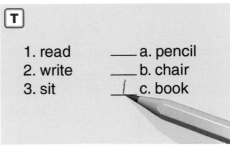

T. **Match** the items.
맞는 항목끼리 **짝지우세요**.

U. **Check** the correct boxes.
정답란을 **확인하세요**.

V. **Label** the picture.
그림에 **이름을 붙이세요**.

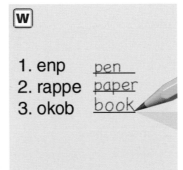

W. **Unscramble** the words.
단어의 철자 배열을 **맞게 고치세요**.

X. **Put** the sentences in order.
문장을 순서대로 **놓으세요**.

Y. **Take out** a piece of paper.
종이 한 장을 **빼세요**.

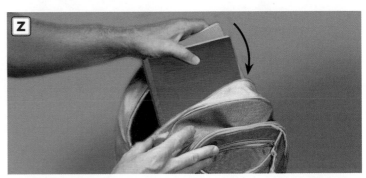

Z. **Put away** your books.
책을 **치우세요**.

Ask your classmates. Share the answers.

1. Do you like to work in a group?
2. Do you ever share a book?
3. Do you like to answer questions?

Think about it. Discuss.

1. How can classmates help each other?
2. Why is it important to ask questions in class?
3. How can students check their pronunciation? Explain.

Succeeding in School

학교 생활 잘하기

Ways to Succeed 학교 생활을 잘하는 방법

A. **Set** goals.
목표를 **세운다**.

B. **Participate** in class.
학급 활동에 **참여한다**.

C. **Take** notes.
노트에 필기**한다**.

D. **Study** at home.
집에서 **공부한다**.

E. **Pass** a test.
시험에 **통과한다**.

F. **Ask** for help.
도움을 **요청한다**.

G. **Make** progress.
향상시킨다.

H. **Get** good grades.
좋은 성적을 **받는다**.

Taking a Test 시험치기

1. test booklet
시험 책자

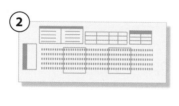

2. answer sheet
답안지

3. score
점수

A	90%-100%	Outstanding
B	80%-89%	Very good
C	70%-79%	Satisfactory
D	60%-69%	Barely passing
F	0%-59%	Fail

4. grades
성적

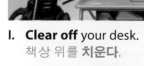

I. **Clear off** your desk.
책상 위를 **치운다**.

J. **Work** on your own.
혼자서 문제를 **푼다**.

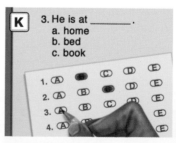

K. **Bubble in** the answer.
답을 **표시한다**.

L. **Check** your work.
표시한 답을 **확인 한다**.

M. Erase the mistake.
잘못 표시한 것을 **지운다**.

N. Correct the mistake.
잘못 표시한 것을 **고친다**.

O. Hand in your test.
시험지를 **제출한다**.

A. **Enter** the room.
교실에 **들어가다**.

B. **Turn on** the lights.
불을 **켜다**.

C. **Walk** to class.
교실로 **걸어가다**.

D. **Run** to class.
교실로 **뛰어가다**.

E. **Lift / Pick up** the books.
책을 **들다 / 집다**.

F. **Carry** the books.
책을 **나르다**.

G. **Deliver** the books.
책을 **전달하다**.

H. **Take** a break.
휴식을 **취하다**.

I. **Eat**.
먹다.

J. **Drink**.
마시다.

K. **Buy** a snack.
과자를 **사다**.

L. **Have** a conversation.
대화**하다**.

M. **Go back** to class.
교실로 돌**아가다**.

N. **Throw away** trash.
쓰레기를 **버리다**.

O. **Leave** the room.
교실에서 **나가다**.

P. **Turn off** the lights.
불을 **끄다**.

Grammar Point: present continuous

Use **be** + verb + **ing**
He **is** walk**ing**. They **are** enter**ing**.
Note: He is run**ning**. They are leav**ing**.

Look at the pictures.
Describe what is happening.

A: *They are <u>entering the room</u>*.
B: *He is <u>walking</u>*.

A. **start** a conversation
대화 **시작하기**

B. **make** small talk
간단한 대화 **나누기**

C. **compliment** someone
상대방을 **칭찬하기**

D. **offer** something
무언가를 **제공하기**

E. **thank** someone
감사의 뜻을 **전하기**

F. **apologize**
사과하기

G. **accept** an apology
사과 **받아들이기**

H. **invite** someone
상대방 **초대하기**

I. **accept** an invitation
초대 **받아들이기**

J. **decline** an invitation
초대 **거절하기**

K. **agree**
동의하기

L. **disagree**
동의하지 않기

M. **explain** something
무언가를 **설명하기**

N. **check** your understanding
제대로 알아 들었는지
확인하기

More vocabulary

request: to ask for something
accept a compliment: to thank someone for a compliment

Pair practice. Follow the directions.

1. Start a conversation with your partner.
2. Make small talk with your partner.
3. Compliment each other.

Temperature 기온

1. Fahrenheit
   화씨
2. Celsius
   섭씨
3. hot
   더운
4. warm
   따뜻한
5. cool
   시원한
6. cold
   추운
7. freezing
   매우 추운
8. degrees
   도

A Weather Map 일기도

9. sunny / clear
   맑은
10. cloudy
    흐린
11. raining
    비가 오는
12. snowing
    눈이 오는

Weather Conditions 기상 조건

13. heat wave
    열기
14. smoggy
    스모그가 낀
15. humid
    습한

16. thunderstorm
    천둥
17. lightning
    번개
18. windy
    바람이 부는

19. dust storm
    먼지 바람
20. foggy
    안개 낀
21. hailstorm
    우박을 동반한 폭풍

22. icy
    얼은
23. snowstorm / blizzard
    눈보라

Ways to talk about the weather

It's <u>sunny</u> in <u>Dallas</u>.
What's the temperature?
It's <u>108</u>. They're having <u>a heat wave</u>.

Pair practice. Make new conversations.

A: *What's the weather like in <u>Chicago</u>?*
B: *It's <u>raining</u> and it's <u>cold</u>. It's <u>30</u> degrees.*

PARTS OF A PHONE

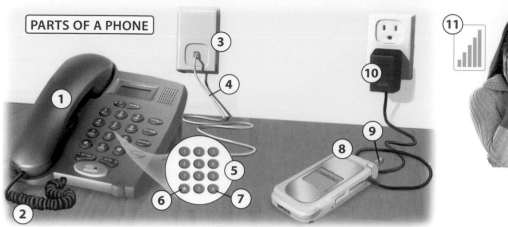

I'll be home by 6:00.

Hello? Hello? Can you hear me?

1. receiver / handset 수화기	**4.** phone line 전화선	**7.** pound key 우물정 버튼	**10.** charger 충전기
2. cord 코드	**5.** key pad 키패드	**8.** cellular phone 휴대 전화	**11.** strong signal 수신 상태 양호
3. phone jack 전화 잭	**6.** star key 별표 버튼	**9.** antenna 안테나	**12.** weak signal 수신 상태 불량

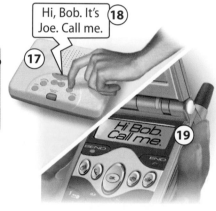

Hi, Bob. It's Joe. Call me.

1531-5471-2923-889

$50 Rechargeable Phone Card

International calling made easy

Hi Bob. Call me.

13. headset 헤드셋	**15.** calling card 전화 카드	**17.** answering machine 자동 응답기	**19.** text message 문자 메시지
14. wireless headset 무선 헤드셋	**16.** access number 접속 번호	**18.** voice message 음성 메시지	

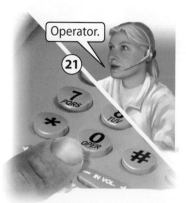

Hi, Grandpa.

Hello, Jun.

Operator.

City and state, please.

For customer service, please press 2.

20. Internet phone call 인터넷 전화	**21.** operator 교환원	**22.** directory assistance 전화번호 안내	**23.** automated phone system 자동 응답 시스템

24. cordless phone
무선 전화

25. pay phone
공중 전화

26. TDD*
청각 장애자용 전화기

27. smart phone
스마트폰

Reading a Phone Bill 전화 요금 청구서 확인하기

28. phone bill
전화요금 청구서

29. area code
지역 번호

30. phone number
전화 번호

31. local call
시내 전화/단거리 전화

32. long distance call
장거리 전화

33. country code
국가 번호

34. city code
지역 번호

35. international call
국제 전화

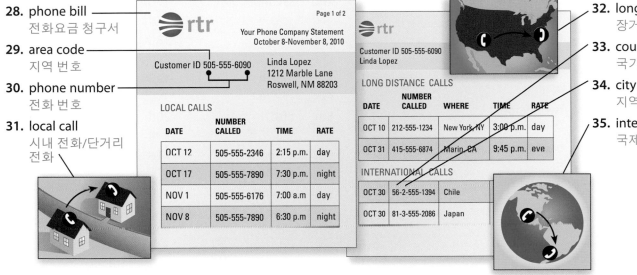

Making a Phone Call 전화 걸기

A. Dial the phone number.
전화 번호를 **누른다**.

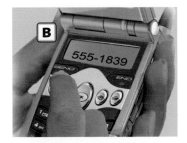

B. Press "send".
"통화" 버튼을 **누른다**.

C. Talk on the phone.
통화 한다.

D. Hang up. / Press "end".
전화를 **끊는다**.
"종료"를 **누른다**.

Making an Emergency Call 비상 전화 걸기

E. Dial 911.
911을 **누른다**.

F. Give your name.
이름을 **말한다**.

G. State the emergency.
응급 상황에 대해 **설명한다**.

H. Stay on the line.
수화기를 들고 **기다린다**.

*telecommunication device for the deaf

Cardinal Numbers 기수

0	zero 영	20	twenty 이십
1	one 일	21	twenty-one 이십 일
2	two 이	22	twenty-two 이십 이
3	three 삼	23	twenty-three 이십 삼
4	four 사	24	twenty-four 이십 사
5	five 오	25	twenty-five 이십 오
6	six 육	30	thirty 삼십
7	seven 칠	40	forty 사십
8	eight 팔	50	fifty 오십
9	nine 구	60	sixty 육십
10	ten 십	70	seventy 칠십
11	eleven 십일	80	eighty 팔십
12	twelve 십이	90	ninety 구십
13	thirteen 십삼	100	one hundred 백
14	fourteen 십사	101	one hundred one 백일
15	fifteen 십오	1,000	one thousand 천
16	sixteen 십육	10,000	ten thousand 만
17	seventeen 십칠	100,000	one hundred thousand 십만
18	eighteen 십팔	1,000,000	one million 백만
19	nineteen 십구	1,000,000,000	one billion 십억

Ordinal Numbers 서수

1st	first 첫번째	16th	sixteenth 열여섯번째
2nd	second 두번째	17th	seventeenth 열일곱번째
3rd	third 세번째	18th	eighteenth 열여덟번째
4th	fourth 네번째	19th	nineteenth 열아홉번째
5th	fifth 다섯번째	20th	twentieth 스무번째
6th	sixth 여섯번째	21st	twenty-first 스물한번째
7th	seventh 일곱번째	30th	thirtieth 서른번째
8th	eighth 여덟번째	40th	fortieth 마흔번째
9th	ninth 아홉번째	50th	fiftieth 쉰번째
10th	tenth 열번째	60th	sixtieth 예순번째
11th	eleventh 열한번째	70th	seventieth 일흔번째
12th	twelfth 열두번째	80th	eightieth 여든번째
13th	thirteenth 열세번째	90th	ninetieth 아흔번째
14th	fourteenth 열네번째	100th	one hundredth 백번째
15th	fifteenth 열다섯번째	1,000th	one thousandth 천번째

Roman Numerals 로마 숫자

I = 1	VII = 7	XXX = 30
II = 2	VIII = 8	XL = 40
III = 3	IX = 9	L = 50
IV = 4	X = 10	C = 100
V = 5	XV = 15	D = 500
VI = 6	XX = 20	M = 1,000

A. divide
나누다

B. calculate
계산하다

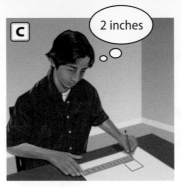

C. measure
측정하다

D. convert
환산하다

Fractions and Decimals 분수와 소수

1. one whole
1 = 1.00
전체

2. one half
1/2 = .5
이분의 일

3. one third
1/3 = .333
삼분의 일

4. one fourth
1/4 = .25
사분의 일

5. one eighth
1/8 = .125
팔분의 일

Percents 퍼센트

6. calculator
계산기

7. decimal point
소수점

8. 100 percent — 100%
9. 75 percent — 75%
10. 50 percent — 50%
11. 25 percent — 25%
12. 10 percent — 10%

0% 10% 20% 30% 40% 50% 60% 70% 80% 90% 100%

8. 100 percent
100 퍼센트

9. 75 percent
75 퍼센트

10. 50 percent
50 퍼센트

11. 25 percent
25 퍼센트

12. 10 percent
10 퍼센트

Measurement 측정

13. ruler
자

14. centimeter [cm]
센티미터(cm)

15. inch [in.]
인치(in)

Dimensions 치수

16. height
높이

17. length
길이

18. depth
깊이

19. width
너비

Equivalencies

12 inches = 1 foot
3 feet = 1 yard
1,760 yards = 1 mile
1 inch = 2.54 centimeters
1 yard = .91 meters
1 mile = 1.6 kilometers

Telling Time 시간 말하기

1. hour
시각

2. minutes
분

3. seconds
초

4. a.m.
오전

5. p.m.
오후

6. 1:00
one o'clock
한시

7. 1:05
one-oh-five
five after one
1시 5분
한시 오분

8. 1:10
one-ten
ten after one
1시 10분
한시 십분

9. 1:15
one-fifteen
a quarter after one
1시 15분
한시 십오분

10. 1:20
one-twenty
twenty after one
1시 20분
한시 이십분

11. 1:30
one-thirty
half past one
1시 30분
한시 삼십분

12. 1:40
one-forty
twenty to two
1시 40분
한시 사십분

13. 1:45
one-forty-five
a quarter to two
1시 45분
한시 사십오분

Times of Day 하루 중의 때

14. sunrise
일출

15. morning
아침

16. noon
정오

17. afternoon
오후

18. sunset
일몰

19. evening
저녁

20. night
밤

21. midnight
자정

Ways to talk about time

I wake up at 6:30 a.m.
I wake up at 6:30 in the morning.
I wake up at 6:30.

Pair practice. Make new conversations.

A: *What time do you wake up on weekdays?*
B: *At 6:30 a.m. How about you?*
A: *I wake up at 7:00.*

22. early
이른

23. on time
정시에

24. late
늦은

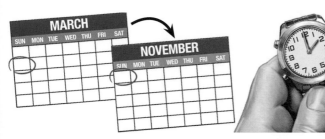

25. daylight saving time
일광 절약 시간(서머타임)

26. standard time
표준 시간

Time Zones 시간대

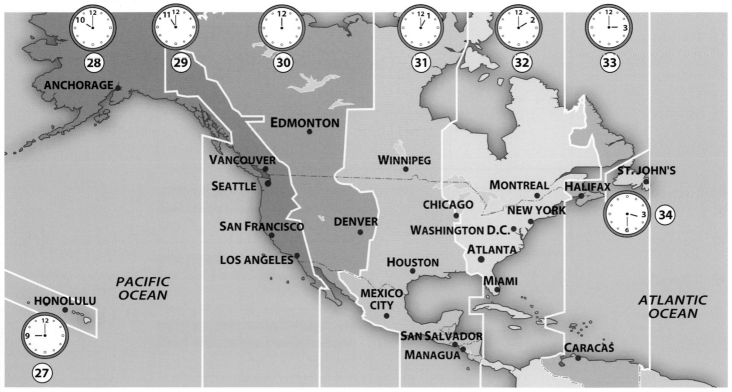

27. Hawaii-Aleutian time
하와이-알류샨 표준시

28. Alaska time
알래스카 표준시

29. Pacific time
태평양 표준시

30. Mountain time
마운틴 표준시

31. Central time
미국 중부 표준시

32. Eastern time
미국 동부 표준시

33. Atlantic time
대서양 표준시

34. Newfoundland time
뉴펀들랜드 표준시

Ask your classmates. Share the answers.

1. When do you watch television? study? relax?
2. Do you like to stay up after midnight?
3. Do you like to wake up late on weekends?

Think about it. Discuss.

1. What is your favorite time of day? Why?
2. Do you think daylight saving time is a good idea? Why or why not?

1. date
   날짜
2. day
   요일
3. month
   월
4. year
   년

5. today
   오늘
6. tomorrow
   내일
7. yesterday
   어제

Days of the Week 요일

8. Sunday
   일요일
9. Monday
   월요일
10. Tuesday
    화요일
11. Wednesday
    수요일
12. Thursday
    목요일
13. Friday
    금요일
14. Saturday
    토요일

MAY

(8) SUN	(9) MON	(10) TUE	(11) WED	(12) THU	(13) FRI	(14) SAT
1	2	3	4	5	6	7
8	9	10	11	12	13	14
15	16	17	18	19	20	21
22	23	24	25	26	27	28
29	30	31				

15. week
    주
16. weekdays
    평일
17. weekend
    주말

Frequency 빈도

18. last week
    지난 주
19. this week
    이번 주
20. next week
    다음 주

SUN	MON	TUE	WED	THU	FRI	SAT
✓	✓	✓	✓	✓	✓	✓ (21)

SUN	MON	TUE	WED	THU	FRI	SAT
	✓					(22)

SUN	MON	TUE	WED	THU	FRI	SAT
	✓		✓			(23)

SUN	MON	TUE	WED	THU	FRI	SAT
	✓	✓		✓		(24)

21. every day / daily
    매일 / 매일의
22. once a week
    일주일에 한 번
23. twice a week
    일주일에 두 번
24. three times a week
    일주일에 세 번

Ways to say the date

Today is <u>May 10th</u>. It's the <u>tenth</u>.
Yesterday was <u>May 9th</u>.
The party is on <u>May 21st</u>.

Pair practice. Make new conversations.

A: *The <u>test</u> is on <u>Friday</u>, <u>June 14th</u>.*
B: *Did you say <u>Friday</u>, the <u>fourteenth</u>?*
A: *Yes, the <u>fourteenth</u>.*

㉕ JAN

SUN	MON	TUE	WED	THU	FRI	SAT
					1	2
3	4	5	6	7	8	9
10	11	12	13	14	15	16
17	18	19	20	21	22	23
24/31	25	26	27	28	29	30

㉖ FEB

SUN	MON	TUE	WED	THU	FRI	SAT
	1	2	3	4	5	6
7	8	9	10	11	12	13
14	15	16	17	18	19	20
21	22	23	24	25	26	27
28						

㉗ MAR

SUN	MON	TUE	WED	THU	FRI	SAT
	1	2	3	4	5	6
7	8	9	10	11	12	13
14	15	16	17	18	19	20
21	22	23	24	25	26	27
28	29	30	31			

㉘ APR

SUN	MON	TUE	WED	THU	FRI	SAT
				1	2	3
4	5	6	7	8	9	10
11	12	13	14	15	16	17
18	19	20	21	22	23	24
25	26	27	28	29	30	

㉙ MAY

SUN	MON	TUE	WED	THU	FRI	SAT
						1
2	3	4	5	6	7	8
9	10	11	12	13	14	15
16	17	18	19	20	21	22
23/30	24/31	25	26	27	28	29

㉚ JUN

SUN	MON	TUE	WED	THU	FRI	SAT
		1	2	3	4	5
6	7	8	9	10	11	12
13	14	15	16	17	18	19
20	21	22	23	24	25	26
27	28	29	30			

㉛ JUL

SUN	MON	TUE	WED	THU	FRI	SAT
				1	2	3
4	5	6	7	8	9	10
11	12	13	14	15	16	17
18	19	20	21	22	23	24
25	26	27	28	29	30	31

㉜ AUG

SUN	MON	TUE	WED	THU	FRI	SAT
1	2	3	4	5	6	7
8	9	10	11	12	13	14
15	16	17	18	19	20	21
22	23	24	25	26	27	28
29	30	31				

㉝ SEP

SUN	MON	TUE	WED	THU	FRI	SAT
			1	2	3	4
5	6	7	8	9	10	11
12	13	14	15	16	17	18
19	20	21	22	23	24	25
26	27	28	29	30		

㉞ OCT

SUN	MON	TUE	WED	THU	FRI	SAT
					1	2
3	4	5	6	7	8	9
10	11	12	13	14	15	16
17	18	19	20	21	22	23
24/31	25	26	27	28	29	30

㉟ NOV

SUN	MON	TUE	WED	THU	FRI	SAT
	1	2	3	4	5	6
7	8	9	10	11	12	13
14	15	16	17	18	19	20
21	22	23	24	25	26	27
28	29	30				

㊱ DEC

SUN	MON	TUE	WED	THU	FRI	SAT
			1	2	3	4
5	6	7	8	9	10	11
12	13	14	15	16	17	18
19	20	21	22	23	24	25
26	27	28	29	30	31	

Months of the Year
월

25. January
1월

26. February
2월

27. March
3월

28. April
4월

29. May
5월

30. June
6월

31. July
7월

32. August
8월

33. September
9월

34. October
10월

35. November
11월

36. December
12월

Seasons
계절

37. spring
봄

38. summer
여름

39. fall / autumn
가을

40. winter
겨울

Dictate to your partner. Take turns.

A: *Write* <u>*Monday*</u>*.*
B: *Is it spelled* <u>*M-o-n-d-a-y*</u>*?*
A: *Yes, that's right.*

Ask your classmates. Share the answers.

1. What is your favorite day of the week? Why?
2. What is your busiest day of the week? Why?
3. What is your favorite season of the year? Why?

21

1. birthday
생일

2. wedding
결혼

3. anniversary
기념일

4. appointment
약속

5. parent-teacher conference
학부모회

6. vacation
휴가

7. religious holiday
종교적 휴일

8. legal holiday
법정 공휴일

Legal Holidays 법정 공휴일

Happy New Year!

I have a dream.

PROUD TO WORK

DEC 25

9. New Year's Day
신정 / 새해 첫날

10. Martin Luther King Jr. Day
마틴 루터 킹 주니어 기념일

11. Presidents' Day
대통령의 날

12. Memorial Day
전몰장병 기념일

13. Fourth of July /
Independence Day
독립기념일 / 7월 4일

14. Labor Day
노동절

15. Columbus Day
컬럼버스 기념일

16. Veterans Day
재향군인의 날

17. Thanksgiving
추수감사절

18. Christmas
크리스마스

Pair practice. Make new conversations.

A: *When is your <u>birthday</u>?*
B: *It's on <u>January 31st</u>. How about you?*
A: *It's on <u>December 22nd</u>.*

Ask your classmates. Share the answers.

1. What are the legal holidays in your native country?
2. When is Labor Day in your native country?
3. When do you celebrate the New Year in your native country?

1. **little** hand
작은 손

2. **big** hand
큰 손

3. **fast** driver
빠른 운전사

4. **slow** driver
느린 운전사

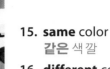
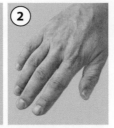

5. **hard** chair
딱딱한 의자

6. **soft** chair
부드러운 의자

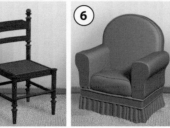

7. **thick** book
두꺼운 책

8. **thin** book
얇은 책

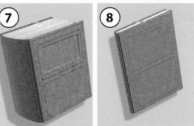

9. **full** glass
가득 찬 잔

10. **empty** glass
빈 잔

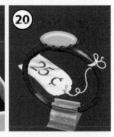

11. **noisy** children /
loud children
시끄러운 아이들

12. **quiet** children
조용한 아이들

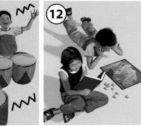

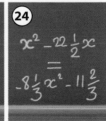

13. **heavy** box
무거운 상자

14. **light** box
가벼운 상자

15. **same** color
같은 색깔

16. **different** colors
다른 색깔들

17. **good** dog
착한 개

18. **bad** dog
나쁜 개

19. **expensive** ring
비싼 반지

20. **cheap** ring
싼 반지

21. **beautiful** view
아름다운 경치

22. **ugly** view
보기 흉한 광경

23. **easy** problem
쉬운 문제

24. **difficult** problem /
hard problem
어려운 문제

Ask your classmates. Share the answers.

1. Are you a slow driver or a fast driver?
2. Do you prefer a hard bed or a soft bed?
3. Do you like loud parties or quiet parties?

Use the new words.
Look at page 150–151. Describe the things you see.

A: *The street* is *hard*.
B: *The truck* is *heavy*.

23

Basic Colors 기본색

1. red
빨강

2. yellow
노랑

3. blue
파랑

4. orange
주황

5. green
초록

6. purple
자주

7. pink
분홍

8. violet
보라

9. turquoise
청록

10. dark blue
암청색

11. light blue
하늘색

12. bright blue
밝은 청색

Neutral Colors 중간색

13. black
검정

14. white
흰색

15. gray
회색

16. cream / ivory
크림색 / 아이보리

17. brown
갈색

18. beige / tan
베이지색

Ask your classmates. Share the answers.

1. What colors are you wearing today?
2. What colors do you like?
3. Is there a color you don't like? What is it?

Use the new words. Look at pages 86–87.
Take turns naming the colors you see.

A: *His shirt is <u>blue</u>.*
B: *Her shoes are <u>white</u>.*

1. The yellow sweaters are **on the left**.
노란색 스웨터는 **왼쪽에** 있습니다.

2. The purple sweaters are **in the middle**.
자주색 스웨터는 **가운데** 있습니다.

3. The brown sweaters are **on the right**.
갈색 스웨터는 **오른쪽에** 있습니다.

4. The red sweaters are **above** the blue sweaters.
빨간색 스웨터는 파란색 스웨터 **위에** 있습니다.

5. The blue sweaters are **below** the red sweaters.
파란색 스웨터는 빨간색 스웨터 **아래에** 있습니다.

6. The turquoise sweater is **in** the box.
청록색 스웨터는 상자 **안에** 있습니다.

7. The white sweater is **in front of** the black sweater.
흰색 스웨터는 검정색 스웨터 **앞에** 있습니다.

8. The black sweater is **behind** the white sweater.
검정색 스웨터는 흰색 스웨터 **뒤에** 있습니다.

9. The orange sweater is **on** the gray sweater.
주황색 스웨터는 회색 스웨터 **위에** 있습니다.

10. The violet sweater is **next to** the gray sweater.
보라색 스웨터는 회색 스웨터 **옆에** 있습니다.

11. The gray sweater is **under** the orange sweater.
회색 스웨터는 주황색 스웨터 **아래에** 있습니다.

12. The green sweater is **between** the pink sweaters.
초록색 스웨터는 분홍색 스웨터 **사이에** 있습니다.

More vocabulary

near: in the same area
far from: not near

Role play. Make new conversations.

A: *Excuse me. Where are the <u>red</u> sweaters?*
B: *They're <u>on the left</u>, <u>above</u> the <u>blue</u> sweaters.*
A: *Thanks very much.*

25

Coins 동전

1. $.01 = 1¢
a penny / 1 cent
페니 / 1 센트

2. $.05 = 5¢
a nickel / 5 cents
니켈 / 5 센트

3. $.10 = 10¢
a dime / 10 cents
다임 / 10 센트

4. $.25 = 25¢
a quarter / 25 cents
쿼터 / 25 센트

5. $.50 = 50¢
a half dollar
해프 달러

6. $1.00
a dollar coin
1 달러 동전

Bills 지폐

7. $1.00
a dollar
1 달러

8. $5.00
five dollars
5 달러

9. $10.00
ten dollars
10 달러

10. $20.00
twenty dollars
20 달러

11. $50.00
fifty dollars
50 달러

12. $100.00
one hundred dollars
100 달러

Do you have change for a dollar?

Yes, I do.

A

A. Get change.
거스름돈을 **받다**.

Can I borrow a dollar?

Sure. Here you go.

B

C

B. Borrow money.
돈을 **빌리다**.

C. Lend money.
돈을 **빌려주다**.

Thanks.

D

D. Pay back the money.
돈을 **갚다**.

Pair practice. Make new conversations.

A: *Do you have change for a dollar?*
B: *Sure. How about two quarters and five dimes?*
A: *Perfect!*

Think about it. Discuss.

1. Is it a good idea to lend money to a friend? Why or why not?
2. Is it better to carry a dollar or four quarters? Why?
3. Do you prefer dollar coins or dollar bills? Why?

Ways to Pay 지불 방법

A. pay cash
현금으로 **지불한다**

B. use a credit card
신용 카드를 **사용한다**

C. use a debit card
직불 카드를 **사용한다**

D. write a (personal) check
개인 수표를 **쓴다**

E. use a gift card
상품 카드를 **사용한다**

F. cash a traveler's check
여행자 수표로 **지불한다**

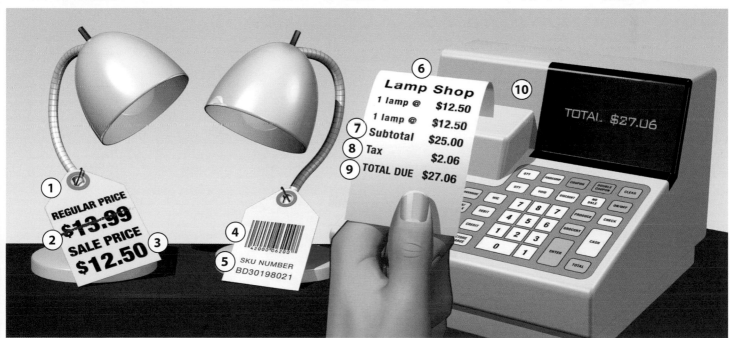

1. price tag 가격표	**3.** sale price 특매가 / 세일가격	**5.** SKU number SKU 번호	**7.** price / cost 가격 / 비용	**9.** total 총액
2. regular price 정상가	**4.** bar code 바코드	**6.** receipt 영수증	**8.** sales tax 판매세	**10.** cash register 금전 등록기

G. buy / pay for
사다 / 지불하다

H. return
환불하다

I. exchange
교환하다

27

1. twins
쌍둥이

2. sweater
스웨터

3. matching
잘 어울리는

4. disappointed
실망한

5. navy blue
남색

6. happy
기쁜

A. shop
쇼핑하다

B. keep
보관하다

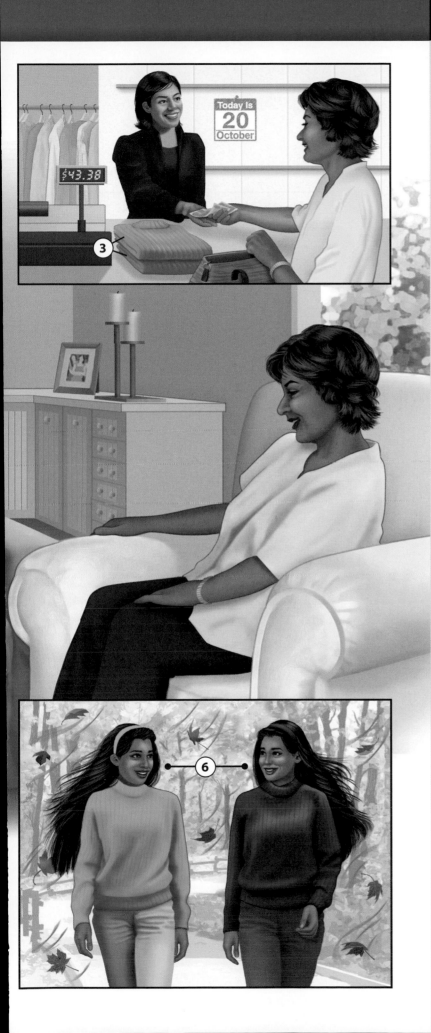

**Look at the pictures.
What do you see?**

Answer the questions.

1. Who is the woman shopping for?

2. Does she buy matching sweaters or different sweaters?

3. How does Anya feel about her green sweater? What does she do?

4. What does Manda do with her sweater?

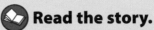 **Read the story.**

Same and Different

Mrs. Kumar likes to <u>shop</u> for her <u>twins</u>. Today she's looking at <u>sweaters</u>. There are many different colors on sale. Mrs. Kumar chooses two <u>matching</u> green sweaters.

The next day, Manda and Anya open their gifts. Manda likes the green sweater, but Anya is <u>disappointed</u>. Mrs. Kumar understands the problem. Anya wants to be different.

Manda <u>keeps</u> her sweater. But Anya goes to the store. She exchanges her green sweater for a <u>navy blue</u> sweater. It's an easy answer to Anya's problem. Now the twins can be warm, <u>happy</u>, and different.

Think about it.

1. Do you like to shop for other people? Why or why not?

2. Imagine you are Anya. Would you keep the sweater or exchange it? Why?

1. man
   (성인)남자
2. woman
   (성인)여자
3. women
   여자들
4. men
   남자들
5. senior citizen
   노인

Listen and point. Take turns.

A: *Point to a <u>woman</u>.*
B: *Point to a <u>senior citizen</u>.*
A: *Point to an <u>infant</u>.*

Dictate to your partner. Take turns.

A: *Write <u>woman</u>.*
B: *Is that spelled <u>w-o-m-a-n</u>?*
A: *Yes, that's right, <u>woman</u>.*

6. infant
갓난 아기

7. baby
아기

8. toddler
유아

9. 6-year-old boy
6세 소년

10. 10-year-old girl
10세 소녀

11. teenager / teen
10대 청소년

Ways to talk about age

1 month – 3 months old = **infant**	13 – 19 years old = **teenager**
18 months – 3 years old = **toddler**	18+ years old = **adult**
3 years old – 12 years old = **child**	62+ years old = **senior citizen**

Pair practice. Make new conversations.

A: *How old is Sandra?*
B: *She's thirteen years old.*
A: *Wow, she's a teenager now!*

31

Age 나이

1. young
   젊은
2. middle-aged
   중년의
3. elderly
   노년의

Height 신장

4. tall
   키가 큰
5. average height
   평균 신장
6. short
   키가 작은

Weight 몸무게

7. heavy / fat
   체중이 많이 나가는 / 살찐
8. average weight
   평균 체중
9. thin / slender
   마른 / 날씬한

Disabilities 장애

10. physically challenged
    신체 장애가 있는
11. sight impaired / blind
    시각 장애가 있는 / 맹인
12. hearing impaired / deaf
    청각 장애가 있는 / 귀가 먼

Appearance 외양

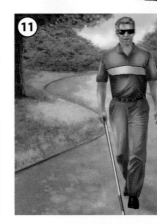

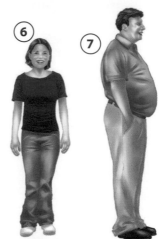

13. attractive   14. cute
    매력적인   귀여운

15. pregnant
    임신한

16. mole
    점

17. pierced ear
    귀를 뚫은 귀
18. tattoo
    문신

Ways to describe people

He's a <u>heavy</u>, <u>young</u> man.
She's a <u>pregnant</u> woman with <u>a mole</u>.
He's <u>sight impaired</u>.

Use the new words. Look at pages 2–3.
Describe the people and point. Take turns.

A: He's a <u>tall</u>, <u>thin</u>, <u>middle-aged</u> man.
B: She's a <u>short</u>, <u>average-weight</u> <u>young</u> woman.

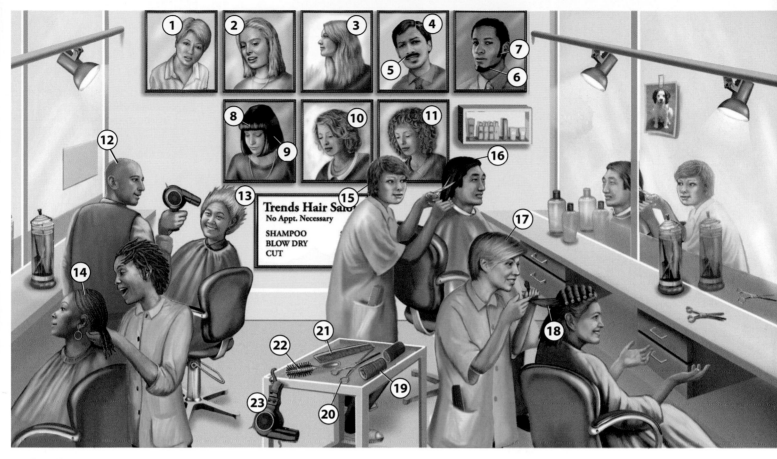

1. **short hair**
   짧은 머리

2. **shoulder-length hair**
   어깨에 닿을 정도의 머리

3. **long hair**
   긴 머리

4. **part**
   가르마

5. **mustache**
   콧수염

6. **beard**
   턱수염

7. **sideburns**
   짧은 구레나룻

8. **bangs**
   앞머리

9. **straight hair**
   곧은 머리

10. **wavy hair**
    웨이브가 있는 머리

11. **curly hair**
    곱슬 머리

12. **bald**
    대머리

13. **gray hair**
    백발

14. **corn rows**
    콘로

15. **red hair**
    빨강 머리

16. **black hair**
    검은 머리

17. **blond hair**
    금발 머리

18. **brown hair**
    갈색 머리

19. **rollers**
    롤러

20. **scissors**
    가위

21. **comb**
    빗

22. **brush**
    브러쉬

23. **blow dryer**
    헤어 드라이기

Style Hair 머리 손질

A. cut hair
머리를 **자르다**

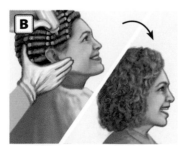

B. perm hair
파마하다

C. set hair
머리를 **세팅하다**

D. color hair / **dye** hair
머리를 **염색하다**

Ways to talk about hair

Describe hair in this order: length, style, and then color.
She has long, straight, brown hair.

Role play. Talk to a stylist.

A: *I need a new hairstyle.*
B: *How about short and straight?*
A: *Great. Do you think I should dye it?*

33

1. grandmother
   할머니
2. grandfather
   할아버지
3. mother
   어머니
4. father
   아버지
5. sister
   여자 형제
6. brother
   남자 형제
7. aunt
   숙모 / 이모 / 고모
8. uncle
   삼촌
9. cousin
   사촌

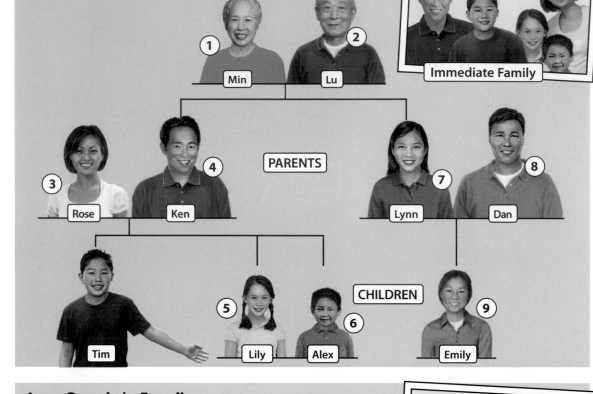

Tim Lee's Family

GRANDPARENTS
① Min   ② Lu

Immediate Family

PARENTS
③ Rose   ④ Ken   ⑦ Lynn   ⑧ Dan

CHILDREN
Tim   ⑤ Lily   ⑥ Alex   ⑨ Emily

10. mother-in-law
    시어머니 / 장모
11. father-in-law
    시아버지 / 장인
12. wife
    아내
13. husband
    남편
14. daughter
    딸
15. son
    아들
16. sister-in-law
    시누이 / 올케
17. brother-in-law
    매형 / 처남
18. niece
    여자 조카
19. nephew
    남자 조카

Ana Garcia's Family

⑩ Eva   ⑪ Sam

Extended Family

⑫ Ana   ⑬ Tito   ⑯ Marta   ⑰ Carlos

⑭ Sara   ⑮ Felix   ⑱ Alice   ⑲ Eddie

More vocabulary

Tim is Min and Lu's **grandson**.
Lily and Emily are Min and Lu's **granddaughters**.
Alex is Min's youngest **grandchild**.

Ana is Tito's **wife**.
Ana is Eva and Sam's **daughter-in-law**.
Carlos is Eva and Sam's **son-in-law**.

Carol, Bruce, and Lisa

Lisa, Age 4

Lisa Green's Family

Lisa, Age 7

Rick   Carol   Bruce   Sue

Lisa, Today

Mary   David   Kim   Bill

20. married couple
결혼한 부부

21. divorced couple
이혼한 부부

22. single mother
아이를 혼자 키우는 엄마

23. single father
아이를 혼자 키우는 아빠

24. remarried
재혼

25. stepfather
계모

26. stepmother
계모

27. half sister
이복 / 이부 여자 형제

28. half brother
이복 / 이부 남자 형제

29. stepsister
이붓 자매

30. stepbrother
의붓 형제

More vocabulary

Bruce is Carol's **former husband** or **ex-husband**.
Carol is Bruce's **former wife** or **ex-wife**.
Lisa is the **stepdaughter** of both Rick and Sue.

Look at the pictures.
Name the people.

A: *Who is Lisa's half sister?*
B: *Mary is. Who is Lisa's stepsister?*

35

A. hold
안다

B. nurse
수유하다

C. feed
먹이다

D. rock
흔들다

E. undress
옷을 벗기다

F. bathe
목욕 시키다

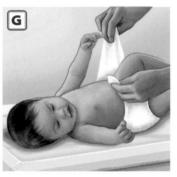

G. change a diaper
기저귀를 갈다

H. dress
옷을 입히다

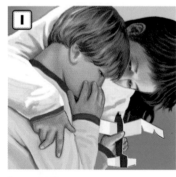

I. comfort
달래다

Good job!

J. praise
칭찬하다

No!

K. discipline
가르치다

L. buckle up
벨트를 채우다

M. play with
함께 **놀아주다**

N. read to
책을 읽어주다

O. sing a lullaby
자장가를 **부르다**

P. kiss goodnight
잘자라고 **키스하다**

Look at the pictures.
Describe what is happening.

A: *She's <u>changing her baby's diaper</u>*.
B: *He's <u>kissing his son goodnight</u>*.

Ask your classmates. Share the answers.

1. Do you like to take care of children?
2. Do you prefer to read to children or play with them?
3. Can you sing a lullaby? Which one?

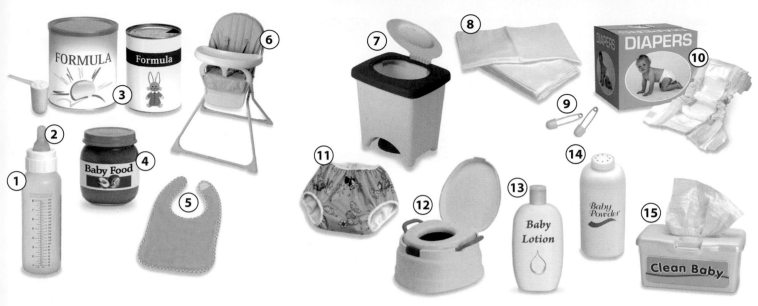

1. bottle
젖병

2. nipple
젖꼭지

3. formula
분유

4. baby food
이유식

5. bib
턱받이

6. high chair
하이 체어

7. diaper pail
기저귀 통

8. cloth diaper
헝겊 기저귀

9. safety pins
안전핀

10. disposable diaper
1회용 기저귀

11. training pants
배변 연습 팬티

12. potty seat
유아용 변기 의자

13. baby lotion
베이비 로션

14. baby powder
베이비 파우더

15. wipes
물티슈

16. baby bag
기저귀 가방

17. baby carrier
아기 캐리어

18. stroller
유모차

19. car safety seat
안전 시트

20. carriage
아기용 유모차

21. rocking chair
흔들 의자

22. nursery rhymes
유아용 책

23. teddy bear
곰인형

24. pacifier
고무 젖꼭지

25. teething ring
고리 모양의 물리개

26. rattle
딸랑이

27. night light
야간등

Dictate to your partner. Take turns.

A: *Write pacifier.*
B: *Was that pacifier, p-a-c-i-f-i-e-r?*
A: *Yes, that's right.*

Think about it. Discuss.

1. How can parents discipline toddlers? teens?
2. What are some things you can say to praise a child?
3. Why are nursery rhymes important for young children?

A. wake up
잠에서 깨다

B. get up
일어나다

C. take a shower
샤워하다

D. get dressed
옷 입다

E. eat breakfast
아침 식사를 하다

F. make lunch
점심을 만들다

G. take the children to school /
drop off the kids
아이들을 학교에 **데려다 주다** /
아이들을 **내려주다**

H. take the bus to school
버스를 **타고** 학교에 가다

I. drive to work / **go** to work
차로 **출근하다** / **출근하다**

J. go to class
수업에 출석하다

K. work
일하다

L. go to the grocery store
시장을 보러 **가다**

M. pick up the kids
아이들을 **데려오다**

N. leave work
퇴근하다

Grammar Point: third person singular

For *he* and *she*, add -s or -es to the verb:
He wakes up.   *He watches TV.*
He gets up.   *She goes to the store.*

These verbs are different (irregular):
*Be: She **is** in school at 10:00 a.m.*
*Have: He **has** dinner at 6:30 p.m.*

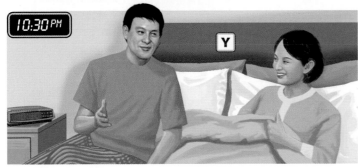

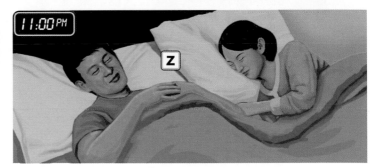

O. **clean** the house
집을 **청소하다**

P. **exercise**
운동하다

Q. **cook** dinner / **make** dinner
저녁 식사를 **요리하다**

R. **come** home / **get** home
집에 **오다** / 집에 **도착하다**

S. **have** dinner / **eat** dinner
저녁을 **먹다**

T. **do** homework
숙제 **하다**

U. **relax**
쉬다

V. **read** the paper
신문을 **읽다**

W. **check** email
이메일을 **확인하다**

X. **watch** TV
텔레비전을 **보다**

Y. **go** to bed
잠자리에 **들다**

Z. **go** to sleep
자다

Pair practice. Make new conversations.

A: *When does he go to work?*
B: *He goes to work at 8:00 a.m. When does she go to class?*
A: *She goes to class at 10:00 a.m.*

Ask your classmates. Share the answers.

1. Who cooks dinner in your family?
2. Who goes to the grocery store?
3. Who goes to work?

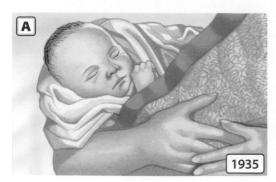

A. be born
태어나다

B. start school
학교를 다니기 **시작하다**

1. birth certificate
출생 증명서

C. immigrate
이주하다

D. graduate
졸업하다

2. Resident Alien card / green card
영주권 / 그린카드

E. learn to drive
운전을 **배우다**

F. get a job
직장을 **구하다**

3. diploma
졸업 증서

4. driver's license
운전 면허증

G. become a citizen
시민이 **되다**

H. fall in love
사랑에 빠지다

5. Social Security card
사회 보장 카드

6. Certificate of Naturalization
귀화 증명서

Grammar Point: past tense

start		immigrate	retire	
learn	+ed	graduate	die	+d
travel				

These verbs are different (irregular):

be – was	go – went	buy – bought
get – got	have – had	
become – became	fall – fell	

I. go to college
대학에 **들어가다**

J. get engaged
약혼**하다**

7. college degree
대학 학위

K. get married
결혼하다

L. have a baby
아기를 **낳다**

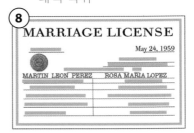

8. marriage license
결혼 증서

M. buy a home
집을 **사다**

N. become a grandparent
조부모가 **되다**

9. deed
증서

O. retire
퇴직하다

P. travel
여행하다

10. passport
여권

Q. volunteer
자원 봉사하다

R. die
죽다

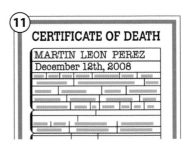

11. death certificate
사망 증명서

More vocabulary
When a husband dies, his wife becomes a **widow**.
When a wife dies, her husband becomes a **widower**.

Ask your classmates. Share the answers.
1. When did you start school?
2. When did you get your first job?
3. Do you want to travel?

1. hot
더운

2. thirsty
목마른

3. sleepy
졸린

4. cold
추운

5. hungry
배고픈

6. full / satisfied
배부른 / 만족한

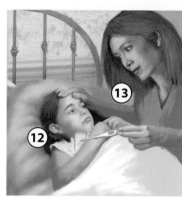

7. disgusted
역겨운

8. calm
침착한

9. uncomfortable
불편한

10. nervous
불안한

11. in pain
아픈

12. sick
병든

13. worried
염려되는

14. well
건강한

15. relieved
안도

16. hurt
다친

17. lonely
외로운

18. in love
사랑에 빠진

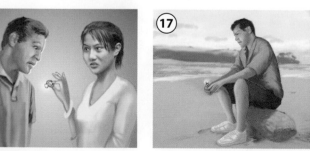

Pair practice. Make new conversations.

A: *How are you doing?*
B: *I'm hungry. How about you?*
A: *I'm hungry and thirsty, too!*

Use the new words.
Look at pages 40–41. Describe what each person is feeling.

A: *Martin is excited.*
B: *Martin's mother is proud.*

19. sad
슬픈

20. homesick
향수병에 걸린

21. proud
자랑스러운

22. excited
흥분한

23. scared / afraid
겁에 질린 /
두려워하는

24. embarrassed
당황한

25. bored
지루한

26. confused
혼란스러운

27. frustrated
낙심힌

28. upset
당황스러운

29. angry
화가 난

30. surprised
놀란

31. happy
기쁜

32. tired
피곤한

Ask your classmates. Share the answers.

1. Do you ever feel homesick?
2. What makes you feel frustrated?
3. Describe a time when you were very happy.

More vocabulary

exhausted: very tired
furious: very angry
humiliated: very embarrassed

overjoyed: very happy
starving: very hungry
terrified: very scared

43

1. banner
배너

2. baseball game
야구 경기

3. opinion
의견

4. balloons
풍선

5. glad
기쁜

6. relatives
친척

A. **laugh**
웃다

B. **misbehave**
잘못된 행동을 하다

I think large families are best.

Look at the picture. What do you see?

Answer the questions.

1. How many relatives are there at this reunion?

2. How many children are there? Which children are misbehaving?

3. What are people doing at this reunion?

Read the story.

A Family Reunion

Ben Lu has a lot of <u>relatives</u> and they're all at his house. Today is the Lu family reunion.

There is a lot of good food. There are also <u>balloons</u> and a <u>banner</u>. And this year there are four new babies!

People are having a good time at the reunion. Ben's grandfather and his aunt are talking about the <u>baseball game</u>. His cousins <u>are laughing</u>. His mother-in-law is giving her <u>opinion</u>. And many of the children <u>are misbehaving</u>.

Ben looks at his family and smiles. He loves his relatives, but he's <u>glad</u> the reunion is once a year.

Think about it.

1. Do you like to have large parties? Why or why not?

2. Imagine you see a little girl at a party. She's misbehaving. What do you do? What do you say?

1. roof
   지붕

2. bedroom
   침실

3. door
   문

4. bathroom
   화장실

5. kitchen
   주방

6. floor
   바닥

7. dining area
   식당

Listen and point. Take turns.

A: *Point to <u>the kitchen</u>.*
B: *Point to <u>the living room</u>.*
A: *Point to <u>the basement</u>.*

Dictate to your partner. Take turns.

A: *Write <u>kitchen</u>.*
B: *Was that <u>k-i-t-c-h-e-n</u>?*
A: *Yes, that's right, <u>kitchen</u>.*

8. attic
   다락방

9. kids' bedroom
   어린이 침실

10. baby's room
    아기 방

11. window
    창문

12. living room
    거실

13. basement
    지하

14. garage
    차고

Ways to give locations

I'm home.
I'm in <u>the kitchen</u>.
I'm on <u>the roof</u>.

Pair practice. Make new conversations.

A: *Where's the man?*
B: *He's in the attic. Where's the teenager?*
A: *She's in the laundry room.*

1. Internet listing
인터넷 게시물

2. classified ad
광고물

3. furnished apartment
가구가 딸린 아파트

4. unfurnished apartment
가구가 딸리지 않은 아파트

Gas   Water   Electricity   Phone   Cable   DSL

5. utilities
설비

Renting an Apartment 아파트 임대하기

A. Call the manager.
매니저에게 **전화하다**.

Are utilities included?

No, they aren't.

B. Ask about the features.
조건을 **물어보다**.

C. Submit an application.
신청서를 **제출하다**.

D. Sign the rental agreement.
임대 계약서에 **서명하다**.

E. Pay the first and last month's rent.
첫번째 달과 마지막 달 임대료를 **지불하다**.

F. Move in.
이사하다.

More vocabulary

lease: a monthly or yearly rental agreement

redecorate: to change the paint and furniture in a home

move out: to pack and leave a home

Ask your classmates. Share the answers.

1. How did you find your home?
2. Do you like to paint or arrange furniture?
3. Does gas or electricity cost more for you?

Buying a House 집 구매 하기

G. Meet with a realtor.
부동산 중개인을 **만나다**.

H. Look at houses.
집을 **보다**.

I. Make an offer.
제의**하다**.

J. Get a loan.
대출 **받다**.

K. Take ownership.
소유권을 **가지다**.

L. Make a mortgage payment.
모기지를 **지불하다**.

Moving In 이사하기

M. Pack.
짐을 **싸다**.

N. Unpack.
짐을 **풀다**.

O. Put the utilities in your name.
공공 요금 지불자로 자신의 이름으로 **올리다**.

P. Paint.
페인트하다 .

Q. Arrange the furniture.
가구를 **배치하다**.

R. Meet the neighbors.
이웃을 **만나다**.

Ways to ask about a home's features

Are utilities included?
Is the kitchen large and sunny?
Are the neighbors quiet?

Role play. Talk to an apartment manager.

A: *Hi. I'm calling about the apartment.*
B: *OK. It's unfurnished and rent is $800 a month.*
A: *Are utilities included?*

49

Fourth Floor

Third Floor

Second Floor

First Floor

1. **apartment building**
   아파트 건물
2. **fire escape**
   비상 계단
3. **playground**
   놀이터
4. **roof garden**
   옥상 정원

Entrance 출입구

Lobby 로비

5. **intercom / speaker**
   인터콤 / 스피커
6. **tenant**
   거주자
7. **vacancy sign**
   빈 방 광고문
8. **manager / superintendent**
   지배인 / 관리인

9. **elevator**
   엘리베이터
10. **stairs / stairway**
    계단 / 층계
11. **mailboxes**
    우편함

Basement 지하

LAUNDRY ROOM

RECREATION ROOM

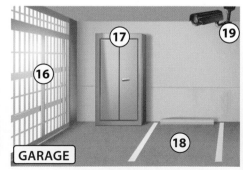

GARAGE

12. **washer**
    세탁기
13. **dryer**
    건조기
14. **big-screen TV**
    대형스크린 TV
15. **pool table**
    당구대
16. **security gate**
    보안용 문
17. **storage locker**
    보관함
18. **parking space**
    주차 공간
19. **security camera**
    보안 카메라

Grammar Point: *there is / there are*

singular: there is   **plural:** there are
There is a recreation room in the basement.
There are mailboxes in the lobby.

Look at the pictures.
Describe the apartment building.

A: *There's <u>a pool table</u> in the recreation room.*
B: *There are <u>parking spaces</u> in the garage.*

APARTMENT COMPLEX

20. balcony
발코니

21. courtyard
안뜰

22. swimming pool
수영장

23. trash bin
쓰레기통

24. alley
골목

Hallway 복도

25. emergency exit
비상구

26. trash chute
쓰레기 낙하장치

Rental Office 사무실

27. landlord
집주인

28. lease / rental agreement
임대 계약서

An Apartment Entryway 아파트 통로

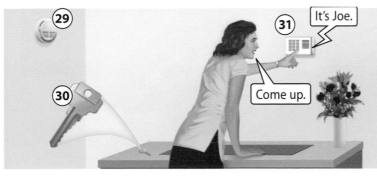

It's Joe.

Come up.

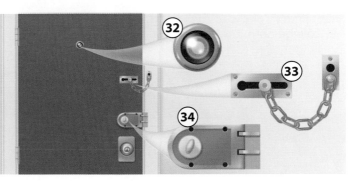

29. smoke detector
연기 탐지기

30. key
열쇠

31. buzzer
버저

32. peephole
내다 보는 구멍

33. door chain
도어 체인

34. dead-bolt lock
강력 잠금장치

More vocabulary

upstairs: the floor(s) above you
downstairs: the floor(s) below you
fire exit: another name for emergency exit

Role play. Talk to a landlord.

A: Is there <u>a swimming pool</u> in this <u>complex</u>?
B: Yes, there is. It's near <u>the courtyard</u>.
A: Is there…?

51

1. the city / an urban area
도시 / 도회 지역

2. the suburbs
교외

3. a small town / a village
작은 마을

4. the country / a rural area
시골 / 전원 지역

5. condominium / condo
콘도

6. townhouse
연립주택

7. mobile home
이동식 주택

8. college dormitory / dorm
대학 기숙사

9. farm
농장

10. ranch
목장

11. senior housing
노인 거주 시설

12. nursing home
요양원

13. shelter
보호소

More vocabulary

co-op: an apartment building owned by residents
duplex: a house divided into two homes
two-story house: a house with two floors

Think about it. Discuss.

1. What's good and bad about these places to live?
2. How are small towns different from cities?
3. How do shelters help people in need?

Front Yard and House 앞마당과 주택

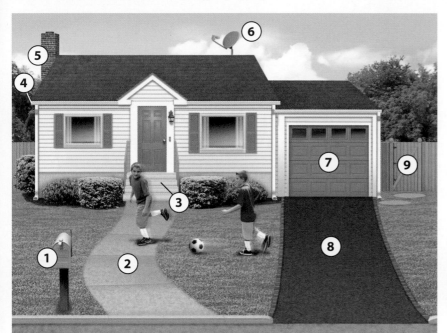

1. mailbox 우편함	**4.** gutter 홈통	**7.** garage door 차고 문
2. front walk 앞쪽 통로	**5.** chimney 굴뚝	**8.** driveway 차 통행로
3. steps 계단	**6.** satellite dish 위성방송 안테나	**9.** gate 문

Front Porch 앞쪽 현관

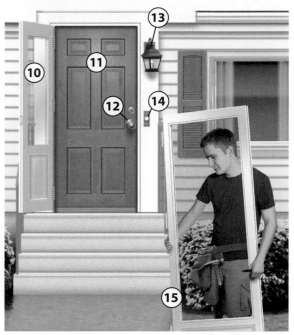

10. storm door 덧문	**13.** porch light 현관등
11. front door 앞문	**14.** doorbell 초인종
12. doorknob 문 손잡이	**15.** screen door 방충문

Backyard 뒷마당

16. patio 파티오	**19.** patio furniture 파티오 가구	**22.** sprinkler 스프링클러	**25.** compost pile 퇴비 더미	**A.** **take** a nap 낮잠을 **자다**
17. grill 그릴	**20.** flower bed 꽃밭	**23.** hammock 해먹	**26.** lawn 잔디	**B.** **garden** 정원
18. sliding glass door 미닫이 유리문	**21.** hose 호스	**24.** garbage can 쓰레기통	**27.** vegetable garden 채소밭	

1. cabinet 찬장	**8.** dishwasher 식기세척기	**15.** toaster oven 오븐 토스터	**22.** counter 카운터
2. shelf 선반	**9.** refrigerator 냉장고	**16.** pot 냄비	**23.** drawer 서랍
3. paper towels 키친 타월	**10.** freezer 냉동고	**17.** teakettle 차 주전자	**24.** pan 팬
4. sink 싱크	**11.** coffeemaker 커피메이커	**18.** stove 스토브	**25.** electric mixer 전기 믹서
5. dish rack 접시 걸이	**12.** blender 블렌더	**19.** burner 버너	**26.** food processor 식품 가공기
6. toaster 토스터	**13.** microwave 전자렌지	**20.** oven 오븐	**27.** cutting board 도마
7. garbage disposal 음식찌거기 처리기	**14.** electric can opener 전기 깡통 따개	**21.** broiler 브로일러	**28.** mixing bowl 믹스용 그릇

Ways to talk about location using *on* and *in*

Use *on* for the counter, shelf, burner, stove, and cutting board. *It's **on** the counter.* Use *in* for the dishwasher, oven, sink, and drawer. *Put it **in** the sink.*

Pair practice. Make new conversations.

A: *Please move <u>the blender</u>.*
B: *Sure. Do you want it <u>in the cabinet</u>?*
A: *No, put it <u>on the counter</u>.*

①

②

③

④

⑤

⑥

⑦

1. dish / plate
접시

2. bowl
사발

3. fork
포크

4. knife
칼

5. spoon
숟가락

6. teacup
찻잔

7. coffee mug
커피잔

8. dining room chair
식탁 의자

9. dining room table
식탁

10. napkin
냅킨

11. placemat
접시 매트

12. tablecloth
식탁보

13. salt and pepper shakers
소금 후추통(식탁용)

14. sugar bowl
설탕 그릇

15. creamer
크림 그릇

16. teapot
차 주전자

17. tray
쟁반

18. light fixture
조명 기구

19. fan
팬

20. platter
큰 접시

21. serving bowl
서빙용 그릇

22. hutch
찬장

23. vase
꽃병

24. buffet
식기 선반

Ways to make requests at the table

May I have the sugar bowl?
Would you pass the creamer, please?
Could I have a coffee mug?

Role play. Request items at the table.

A: *What do you need?*
B: *Could I have a coffee mug?*
A: *Certainly. And would you...*

55

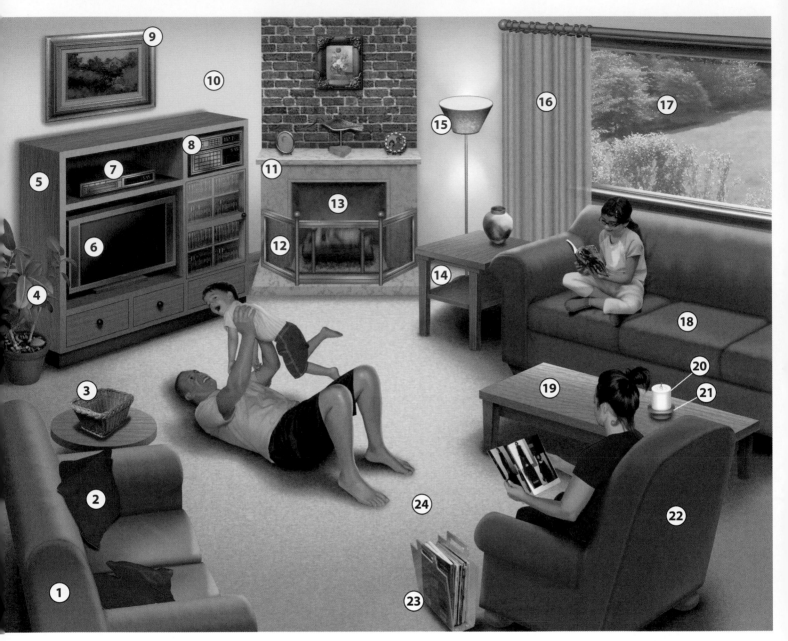

1. love seat 2인용 소파	**7.** DVD player DVD 플레이어	**13.** fireplace 벽난로	**19.** coffee table 커피 탁자
2. throw pillow 장식용 쿠션	**8.** stereo system 스테레오 시스템	**14.** end table 소보조 테이블	**20.** candle 초
3. basket 바구니	**9.** painting 그림	**15.** floor lamp 플로어 램프	**21.** candle holder 촛대
4. houseplant 실내화초	**10.** wall 벽	**16.** drapes 커튼	**22.** armchair / easy chair 안락의자
5. entertainment center 오디오 비디오 장	**11.** mantle 벽난로 선반	**17.** window 창문	**23.** magazine holder 잡지 꽂이대
6. TV (television) 텔레비전	**12.** fire screen 불꽃 가리개	**18.** sofa / couch 소파	**24.** carpet 카페트

Use the new words.
Look at pages 44–45. Name the things in the room.

A: *There's a TV*.
B: *There's a carpet*.

More vocabulary

light bulb: the light inside a lamp
lampshade: the part of the lamp that covers the light bulb
sofa cushions: the pillows that are part of the sofa

1. hamper 빨래 바구니	**8.** faucet 수도꼭지	**15.** towel rack 수건걸이	**22.** medicine cabinet 약품 수납장
2. bathtub 욕조	**9.** hot water 온수	**16.** bath towel 목욕수건	**23.** toothbrush 치솔
3. soap dish 비누 받침대	**10.** cold water 냉수	**17.** hand towel 작은 타월	**24.** toothbrush holder 치솔 꽂이
4. soap 비누	**11.** grab bar 손잡이	**18.** mirror 거울	**25.** sink 싱크
5. rubber mat 고무 매트	**12.** tile 타일	**19.** toilet paper 화장지	**26.** wastebasket 쓰레기통
6. washcloth 세수 수건	**13.** showerhead 샤워헤드	**20.** toilet brush 변기 세척솔	**27.** scale 저울
7. drain 배수구	**14.** shower curtain 샤워 커튼	**21.** toilet 변기	**28.** bath mat 욕실용 매트

More vocabulary

stall shower: a shower without a bathtub
half bath: a bathroom with no shower or tub
linen closet: a closet for towels and sheets

Ask your classmates. Share the answers.

1. Is your toothbrush on the sink or in the medicine cabinet?
2. Do you have a bathtub or a shower?
3. Do you have a shower curtain or a shower door?

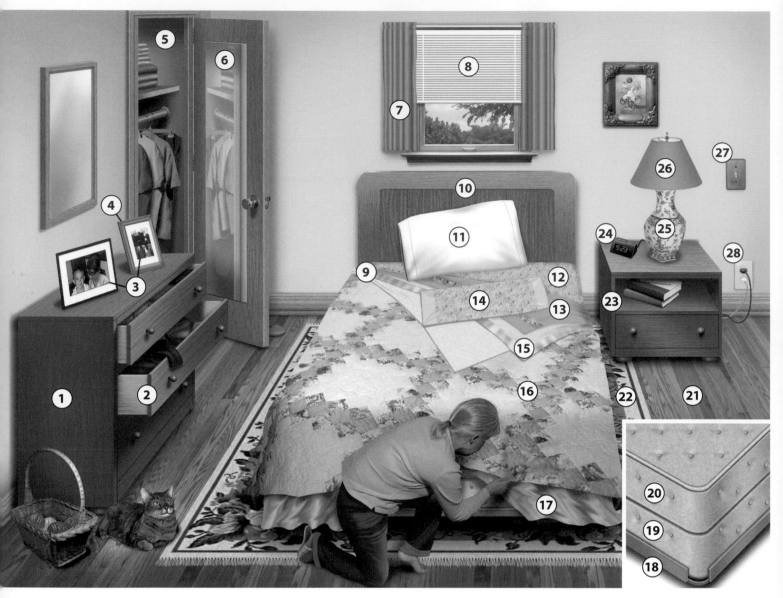

1. dresser / bureau 서랍장	8. mini-blinds 미니 블라인드	15. blanket 담요	22. rug 양탄자
2. drawer 서랍	9. bed 침대	16. quilt 누비 이불	23. night table / nightstand 침실용 탁자
3. photos 사진	10. headboard 침대 머리판	17. dust ruffle 먼지 방지용 프릴	24. alarm clock 알람 시계
4. picture frame 액자	11. pillow 베개	18. bed frame 침대 틀	25. lamp 전등
5. closet 옷장	12. fitted sheet 매트리스 시트	19. box spring 침대 박스 스프링	26. lampshade 전등갓
6. full-length mirror 전신 거울	13. flat sheet 이불 커버	20. mattress 매트리스	27. light switch 전등 스위치
7. curtains 커튼	14. pillowcase 베갯잇	21. wood floor 마루바닥	28. outlet 콘센트

Look at the pictures.
Describe the bedroom.

A: There's _a lamp_ _on_ _the nightstand_.
B: There's _a mirror_ _in_ _the closet_.

Ask your classmates. Share the answers.

1. Do you prefer a hard or a soft mattress?
2. Do you prefer mini-blinds or curtains?
3. How many pillows do you like on your bed?

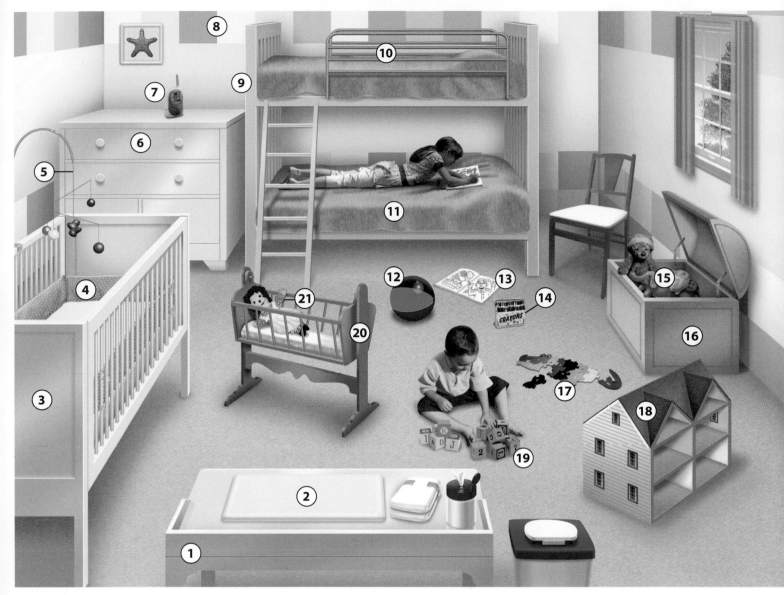

Furniture and Accessories 가구와 기타 살림

1. changing table
   기저귀 갈이용 테이블

2. changing pad
   기저귀 갈이용 패드

3. crib
   유아용 침대

4. bumper pad
   완충 패드

5. mobile
   모빌

6. chest of drawers
   서랍장

7. baby monitor
   아기 모니터

8. wallpaper
   벽지

9. bunk beds
   2층 침대

10. safety rail
    안전 레일

11. bedspread
    침대보

Toys and Games 장난감과 게임

12. ball
    공

13. coloring book
    색칠 공부책

14. crayons
    크레용

15. stuffed animals
    봉제 동물 완구

16. toy chest
    장난감 상자

17. puzzle
    퍼즐

18. dollhouse
    인형집

19. blocks
    블록

20. cradle
    요람

21. doll
    인형

Pair practice. Make conversations.

A: *Where's the changing pad?*
B: *It's on the changing table.*

Think about it. Discuss.

1. Which toys help children learn? How?
2. Which toys are good for older and younger children?
3. What safety features does this room need? Why?

A. dust the furniture
가구의 **먼지를 털다**

B. recycle the newspapers
신문을 **재활용하다**

C. clean the oven
오븐을 **청소하다**

D. mop the floor
마루를 **걸레질하다**

E. polish the furniture
가구에 **광을 내다**

F. make the bed
침대를 **정돈하다**

G. put away the toys
장난감을 **치우다**

H. vacuum the carpet
카페트를 **진공 청소하다**

I. wash the windows
창문을 **닦다**

J. sweep the floor
마루를 **쓸다**

K. scrub the sink
세면대를 **닦다**

L. empty the trash
쓰레기통을 **비우다**

M. wash the dishes
접시를 **닦다**

N. dry the dishes
접시를 **말리다**

O. wipe the counter
카운터를 **닦다**

P. change the sheets
시트를 **갈다**

Q. take out the garbage
쓰레기를 **내다놓다**

Pair practice. Make new conversations.

A: *Let's clean this place. First, I'll* <u>*sweep the floor*</u>.
B: *I'll* <u>*mop the floor*</u> *when you finish.*

Ask your classmates. Share the answers.

1. Who does the housework in your home?
2. How often do you wash the windows?
3. When should kids start to do housework?

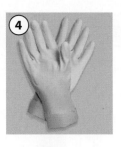

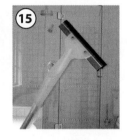

1. feather duster
   깃털 총채

2. recycling bin
   재활용 통

3. oven cleaner
   오븐 클리너

4. rubber gloves
   고무 장갑

5. steel-wool soap pads
   강모 비누 패드

6. sponge mop
   스폰지 대걸레

7. bucket / pail
   양동이 / 들통

8. furniture polish
   가구 광택제

9. rags
   헝겊

10. vacuum cleaner
    진공 청소기

11. vacuum cleaner attachments
    진공 청소기 부품

12. vacuum cleaner bag
    진공 청소기 주머니

13. stepladder
    사다리

14. glass cleaner
    유리 클리너

15. squeegee
    스퀴지

16. broom
    빗자루

17. dustpan
    쓰레받기

18. cleanser
    세제

19. sponge
    스폰지

20. scrub brush
    청소용 솔

21. dishwashing liquid
    식기 세척용 세제

22. dish towel
    접시 닦는 행주

23. disinfectant wipes
    소독용 물티슈

24. trash bags
    쓰레기 봉투

Ways to ask for something

Please hand me <u>the squeegee</u>.
Can you get me <u>the broom</u>?
I need <u>the sponge mop</u>.

Pair practice. Make new conversations.

A: *Please hand me <u>the sponge mop</u>.*
B: *Here you go. Do you need <u>the bucket</u>?*
A: *Yes, please. Can you get me <u>the rubber gloves</u>, too?*

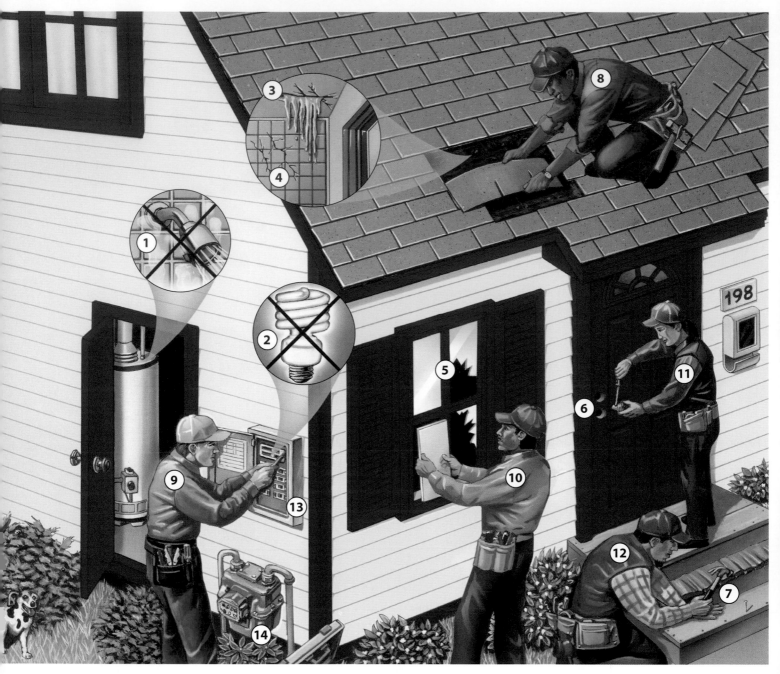

1. The water heater is **not working**.
   온수기가 **고장나다**.

2. The power is **out**.
   전원이 **나가다**.

3. The roof is **leaking**.
   지붕이 **새**다.

4. The tile is **cracked**.
   타일에 **금이 가다**.

5. The window is **broken**.
   유리창이 **깨지다**.

6. The lock is **broken**.
   자물쇠가 **고장나다**.

7. The steps are **broken**.
   계단이 **부서지다**.

8. roofer
   지붕 수리공

9. electrician
   전기공

10. repair person
    수리공

11. locksmith
    자물쇠 수리공

12. carpenter
    목수

13. fuse box
    두꺼비집-퓨즈 상자

14. gas meter
    가스미터 / 가스계량기

More vocabulary

fix: to repair something that is broken
pests: termites, fleas, rats, etc.
exterminate: to kill household pests

Pair practice. Make new conversations.

A: *The faucet is <u>leaking</u>.*
B: *Let's call <u>the plumber</u>. He can fix it.*

15. The furnace is **broken**.
보일러가 **고장나다**.

16. The pipes are **frozen**.
파이프가 **얼다**.

17. The faucet is **dripping**.
수도꼭지가 **새다**.

18. The sink is **overflowing**.
세면대 물이 **넘치다**.

19. The toilet is **stopped up**.
변기가 **막히다**.

20. plumber
배관공

21. exterminator
해충 구제업자

22. termites
흰개미

23. ants
개미

24. bedbugs
빈대

25. fleas
벼룩

26. cockroaches / roaches
바퀴벌레

27. rats
쥐

28. mice*
생쥐

*Note: one mouse, two mice

Ways to ask about repairs

How much will this repair cost?
When can you begin?
How long will the repair take?

Role play. Talk to a repair person.

A: *Can you fix <u>the roof</u>?*
B: *Yes, but it will take <u>two weeks</u>.*
A: *How much will the repair cost?*

THE NEXT DAY...

Meeting Tonight! 7:00 REC ROOM

LATER THAT EVENING...

• Use rec room for large parties
• No loud music on weeknights

Come to Our "We're Sorry!" Party SAT 8pm REC ROOM

1. roommates 룸메이트	**3.** music 음악	**5.** noise 소음	**7.** rules 규칙	**9.** invitation 초대
2. party 파티	**4.** DJ DJ	**6.** irritated 성난	**8.** mess 난장판	**A.** **dance** 댄스

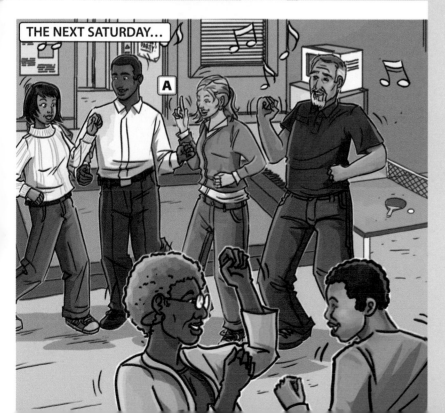

THE NEXT SATURDAY...

Look at the pictures. What do you see?

Answer the questions.

1. What happened in apartment 2B? How many people were there?

2. How did the neighbor feel? Why?

3. What rules did they write at the tenant meeting?

4. What did the roommates do after the tenant meeting?

📖 Read the story.

The Tenant Meeting

Sally Lopez and Tina Green are <u>roommates</u>. They live in apartment 2B. One night they had a big <u>party</u> with <u>music</u> and a <u>DJ</u>. There was a <u>mess</u> in the hallway. Their neighbors were very unhappy. Mr. Clark in 2A was very <u>irritated</u>. He hates <u>noise</u>!

The next day there was a tenant meeting. Everyone wanted <u>rules</u> about parties and loud music. The girls were very embarrassed.

After the meeting, the girls cleaned the mess in the hallway. Then they gave each neighbor an <u>invitation</u> to a new party. Everyone had a good time at the rec room party. Now the tenants have two new rules and a new place to <u>dance</u>.

Think about it.

1. What are the most important rules in an apartment building? Why?

2. Imagine you are the neighbor in 2A. What do you say to Tina and Sally?

65

1. fish
   생선
2. meat
   고기
3. chicken
   닭고기
4. cheese
   치즈
5. milk
   우유
6. butter
   버터
7. eggs
   계란
8. vegetables
   야채

Listen and point. Take turns.

A: *Point to the vegetables.*
B: *Point to the bread.*
A: *Point to the fruit.*

Pair Dictation

A: *Write vegetables.*
B: *Please spell vegetables for me.*
A: *V-e-g-e-t-a-b-l-e-s.*

9. fruit
과일

10. rice
쌀

11. bread
빵

12. pasta
파스타

13. grocery bag
식료품 백

14. shopping list
쇼핑 목록

15. coupons
쿠폰

Ways to talk about food.

Do we need <u>eggs</u>?
Do we have any <u>pasta</u>?
We have some <u>vegetables</u>, but we need <u>fruit</u>.

Role play. Talk about your shopping list.

A: *Do we need eggs?*
B: *No, we have some.*
A: *Do we have any...*

67

1. apples 사과	**9.** tangerines 귤	**17.** blackberries 블랙베리	**25.** raisins 건포도
2. bananas 바나나	**10.** peaches 복숭아	**18.** watermelons 수박	**26.** prunes 말린 자두
3. grapes 포도	**11.** cherries 체리	**19.** melons 멜론	**27.** figs 무화과
4. pears 배	**12.** apricots 살구	**20.** papayas 파파야	**28.** dates 대추
5. oranges 오렌지	**13.** plums 자두	**21.** mangoes 망고	**29.** a bunch of bananas 바나나 한 묶음
6. grapefruit 자몽	**14.** strawberries 딸기	**22.** kiwi 키위	**30.** **ripe** banana **익은** 바나나
7. lemons 레몬	**15.** raspberries 산딸기	**23.** pineapples 파인애플	**31.** **unripe** banana **덜 익은** 바나나
8. limes 라임	**16.** blueberries 블루베리	**24.** coconuts 코코넛	**32.** **rotten** banana **상한** 바나나

Pair practice. Make new conversations.

A: *What's your favorite fruit?*
B: *I like <u>apples</u>. Do you?*
A: *I prefer <u>bananas</u>.*

Ask your classmates. Share the answers.

1. Which fruit do you put in a fruit salad?
2. What kinds of fruit are common in your native country?
3. What kinds of fruit are in your kitchen right now?

1. lettuce
상추

2. cabbage
양배추

3. carrots
당근

4. radishes
무

5. beets
사탕무

6. tomatoes
토마토

7. bell peppers
피망

8. string beans
깍지콩

9. celery
셀러리

10. cucumbers
오이

11. spinach
시금치

12. corn
옥수수

13. broccoli
브로콜리

14. cauliflower
꽃양배추

15. bok choy
중국 배추

16. turnips
순무

17. potatoes
감자

18. sweet potatoes
고구마

19. onions
양파

20. green onions / scallions
파

21. peas
콩

22. artichokes
아티초크

23. eggplants
가지

24. squash
호박

25. zucchini
양호박

26. asparagus
아스파라거스

27. mushrooms
버섯

28. parsley
파슬리

29. chili peppers
매운 고추

30. garlic
마늘

31. a **bag of** lettuce
상추 한 **봉지**

32. a **head of** lettuce
상추 한 **단**

Pair practice. Make new conversations.

A: *Do you eat <u>broccoli</u>?*
B: *Yes. I like most vegetables, but not <u>peppers</u>.*
A: *Really? Well, I don't like <u>cauliflower</u>.*

Ask your classmates. Share the answers.

1. Which vegetables do you eat raw? cooked?
2. Which vegetables do you put in a green salad?
3. Which vegetables are in your refrigerator right now?

69

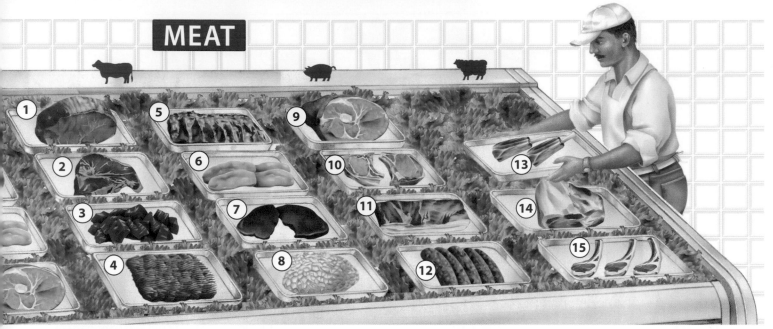

MEAT

POULTRY

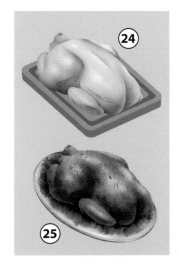

Beef 쇠고기

1. roast
   로스트
2. steak
   스테이크
3. stewing beef
   스튜용 쇠고기
4. ground beef
   다진 쇠고기

5. beef ribs
   쇠갈비
6. veal cutlets
   송아지 고기 커틀렛
7. liver
   간
8. tripe
   위

Pork 돼지고기

9. ham
   햄
10. pork chops
    폭찹
11. bacon
    베이컨
12. sausage
    소시지

Lamb 양고기

13. lamb shanks
    양 정강이 살
14. leg of lamb
    양 다리
15. lamb chops
    양고기 찹

Poultry 가금류

16. chicken
    닭고기
17. turkey
    칠면조

18. duck
    오리
19. breasts
    가슴살

20. wings
    날개
21. legs
    다리

22. thighs
    넓적다리
23. drumsticks
    닭·오리 다리

24. **raw** chicken
    생 닭고기
25. **cooked** chicken
    조리한 닭고기

More vocabulary

vegetarian: a person who doesn't eat meat
boneless: meat and poultry without bones
skinless: poultry without skin

Ask your classmates. Share the answers.

1. What kind of meat do you eat most often?
2. What kind of meat do you use in soups?
3. What part of the chicken do you like the most?

SEAFOOD

Fish 생선

1. trout
   송어

2. catfish
   메기

3. whole salmon
   연어 한 마리

4. salmon steak
   스테이크용 연어

5. swordfish
   황새치

6. halibut steak
   스테이크용 넙치

7. tuna
   참치

8. cod
   대구

Shellfish 갑각류

9. crab
   게

10. lobster
    가재

11. shrimp
    새우

12. scallops
    가리비

13. mussels
    홍합

14. oysters
    굴

15. clams
    대합 조개

16. **fresh** fish
    생물 생선

17. **frozen** fish
    냉동 생선

DELI

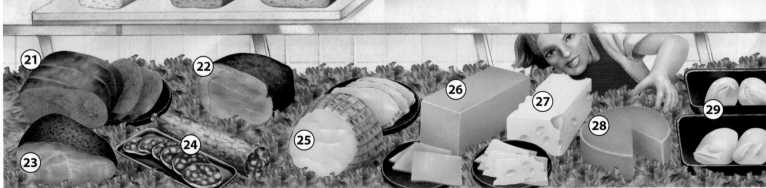

18. white bread
    흰 빵

19. wheat bread
    밀 빵

20. rye bread
    호밀 빵

21. roast beef
    로스트 비프

22. corned beef
    콘드 비프

23. pastrami
    훈제 쇠고기

24. salami
    살라미

25. smoked turkey
    훈제 칠면조

26. American cheese
    아메리칸 치즈

27. Swiss cheese
    스위스 치즈

28. cheddar cheese
    체다 치즈

29. mozzarella cheese
    모짜렐라 치즈

Ways to order at the counter

I'd like some <u>roast beef</u>.
I'll have <u>a halibut steak</u> and some <u>shrimp</u>.
Could I get some <u>Swiss cheese</u>?

Pair practice. Make new conversations.

A: *What can I get for you?*
B: *<u>I'd like some roast beef</u>. How about a pound?*
A: *A pound of <u>roast beef</u> coming up!*

71

SEAFOOD

POULTRY

MEAT

DAIRY

2A 2B

FROZEN FOODS

1. customer 손님	**3.** scale 저울	**5.** pet food 애완동물 식품	**7.** cart 카트
2. produce section 농산물 코너	**4.** grocery clerk 식료품점 직원	**6.** aisle 복도	**8.** manager 매니저

Canned Foods
캔류

Dairy
유제품

Grocery Products
식료품 관련 제품

Frozen Foods
냉동 식품

17. beans 콩	**20.** margarine 마가린	**23.** aluminum foil 알루미늄 포일	**26.** ice cream 아이스크림
18. soup 스프	**21.** sour cream 사워크림	**24.** plastic wrap 플라스틱 랩	**27.** frozen vegetables 냉동 야채
19. tuna 참치	**22.** yogurt 요거트	**25.** plastic storage bags 플라스틱 저장백	**28.** frozen dinner 냉동 식사

Ways to ask for information in a grocery store

Excuse me, where are the carrots?

Can you please tell me where to find the dog food?

Do you have any lamb chops today?

Pair practice. Make conversations.

A: *Can you please tell me where to find the dog food?*

B: *Sure. It's in aisle 1B. Do you need anything else?*

A: *Yes, where are the carrots?*

BAKERY

Best Baked Goods

15 items or less

Cash for Bottles | Cash for Bottle

IN | OUT

3A | 3B

SNACKS

9.	shopping basket	11.	line	13.	cashier	15.	cash register
	쇼핑 바구니		줄		계산원		금전 등록기
10.	self-checkout	12.	checkstand	14.	bagger	16.	bottle return
	셀프 계산대		계산대		물건 담아주는 사람		병 회수

J&G

WHOLE WHEAT

Franco's

Tasty Cola

Italian Roast

Baked not Fried!

YUM! CHOCOLATE

Baking Products
제빵 관련 제품

Beverages
음료수

Snack Foods
스낵류

Baked Goods
제과류

29.	flour	32.	apple juice	35.	potato chips	38.	cookies
	밀가루		사과 쥬스		감자 칩		쿠키
30.	sugar	33.	coffee	36.	nuts	39.	cake
	설탕		커피		견과류		케이크
31.	oil	34.	soda / pop	37.	candy bar	40.	bagels
	오일		탄산음료수		초코렛 바		베이글

Ask your classmates. Share the answers.

1. What is your favorite grocery store?
2. Do you prefer to shop alone or with friends?
3. Which foods from your country are hard to find?

Think about it. Discuss.

1. Is it better to shop every day or once a week? Why?
2. Why do grocery stores put snacks near the checkstands?
3. What's good and what's bad about small grocery stores?

1. bottles
병

2. jars
아가리가
넓은 병

3. cans
캔

4. cartons
카톤

5. containers
용기

6. boxes
상자

7. bags
봉지

8. packages
포장

9. six-packs
6개 들이 팩

10. loaves
덩어리

11. rolls
롤

12. tubes
튜브

13. a bottle of water
물 한 병

14. a jar of jam
잼 한 병

15. a can of beans
콩 한 캔

16. a carton of eggs
달걀 한 카톤

17. a container of cottage cheese
카티지치즈 한 통

18. a box of cereal
시리얼 한 상자

19. a bag of flour
밀가루 한 봉지

20. a package of cookies
쿠키 한 봉지

21. a six-pack of soda (pop)
6개팩 탄산음료수

22. a loaf of bread
빵 한 덩어리

23. a roll of paper towels
종이 타월 한 두루말이

24. a tube of toothpaste
치약 튜브 하나

Grammar Point: count and non-count

Some foods can be counted: *an apple, two apples.*

Some foods can't be counted: *some rice, some water.*

For non-count foods, count containers: *two bags of rice.*

Pair practice. Make conversations.

A: *How many boxes of cereal do we need?*

B: *We need two boxes.*

A. **Measure** the ingredients.
재료를 **측량하다**.

B. **Weigh** the food.
음식 **무게를 달다**.

C. **Convert** the measurements.
측량치를 **환산하다**.

> 1 cup = 237 milliliters

Liquid Measures 액체류 측정

| ① | ② | ③ | ④ | ⑤ |
| 1 fl. oz. | 1 c. | 1 pt. | 1 qt. | 1 gal. |

Dry Measures 분말류 측정

| ⑥ | ⑦ | ⑧ | ⑨ | ⑩ |
| 1 tsp. | 1 TBS. | 1/4 c. | 1/2 c. | 1 c. |

Weight 중량

1. a fluid ounce of milk
우유 1 온스

2. a cup of oil
기름 한 컵

3. a pint of frozen yogurt
냉동 요거트 1 파인트

4. a quart of milk
우유 1 쿼트

5. a gallon of water
생수 1 갤론

6. a teaspoon of salt
소금 한 티스푼

7. a tablespoon of sugar
설탕 한 테이블 스푼

8. a quarter cup of brown sugar
흑설탕 1/4 컵

9. a half cup of raisins
건포도 1/2 컵

10. a cup of flour
밀가루 1컵

11. an ounce of cheese
치즈 1 온스

12. a pound of roast beef
로스트 비프 1 파운드

Equivalencies	
3 tsp. = 1 TBS.	2 c. = 1 pt.
2 TBS. = 1 fl. oz.	2 pt. = 1 qt.
8 fl. oz. = 1 c.	4 qt. = 1 gal.

Volume
1 fl. oz. = 30 ml
1 c. = 237 ml
1 pt. = .47 L
1 qt. = .95 L
1 gal. = 3.79 L

Weight
1 oz. = 28.35 grams (g)
1 lb. = 453.6 g
2.205 lbs. = 1 kilogram (kg)
1 lb. = 16 oz.

75

Food Safety 식품 안전

A. **clean**
   씻다

B. **separate**
   분리하다

C. **cook**
   요리하다

D. **chill**
   냉장하다

A Clean counters! 20 SECONDS Wash your hands!

B Use separate cutting boards for vegetables and meat!

C Cook to the right temperature!

D Refrigerate leftovers quickly!

Ways to Serve Meat and Poultry 육류 조리법

1. fried chicken
닭 튀김

2. barbecued / grilled ribs
바베큐 / 그릴 립

3. broiled steak
연어 구이

4. roasted turkey
칠면조 구이

5. boiled ham
삶은 햄

6. stir-fried beef
소고기 볶음

Ways to Serve Eggs 계란 조리법

7. scrambled eggs
에그 스크램블

8. hardboiled eggs
삶은 계란

9. poached eggs
살짝 삶은 계란

10. eggs sunny-side up
노른자를 터트리지 않은 계란 후라이

11. eggs over easy
한 번만 뒤집어 살짝 익힌 계란 후라이

12. omelet
오믈렛

Role play. Make new conversations.

A: *How do you like your eggs?*
B: *I like them <u>scrambled</u>. And you?*
A: *I like them <u>hardboiled</u>.*

Ask your classmates. Share the answers.

1. Do you use separate cutting boards?
2. What is your favorite way to serve meat? poultry?
3. What are healthy ways of preparing meat? poultry?

Cheesy Tofu Vegetable Casserole 치즈 두부 야채 케서롤

A. Preheat the oven.
오븐을 **예열한다**.

B. Grease a baking pan.
베이킹 팬에 **기름칠을 한다**.

C. Slice the tofu.
두부를 **얇게 썬다**.

D. Steam the broccoli.
브로콜리를 **찐다**.

E. Saute the mushrooms.
버섯을 **살짝 튀긴다**.

F. Spoon sauce on top.
위에 소스를 **숟가락으로 끼얹는다**.

G. Grate the cheese.
치즈를 **간다**.

H. Bake.
굽는다.

Easy Chicken Soup 만들기 쉬운 닭고기 스프

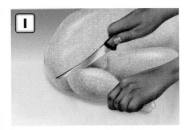

I. Cut up the chicken.
닭고기를 **자른다**.

J. Dice the celery.
셀러리를 **다진다**.

K. Peel the carrots.
당근 껍질을 **벗긴다**.

L. Chop the onions.
양파를 **잘게 썬다**.

M. Boil the chicken.
닭고기를 **삶는다**.

N. Add the vegetables.
야채를 **첨가한다**.

O. Stir.
젓는다.

P. Simmer.
천천히 **끓인다**.

Quick and Easy Cake 간편한 케이크 만들기

Q. Break 2 eggs into a microwave-safe bowl.
전자레인지용 볼에 계란 2개를 **깨뜨린다**.

R. Mix the ingredients.
재료를 **섞는다**.

S. Beat the mixture.
섞은 재료를 **휘젓는다**.

T. Microwave for 5 minutes.
5분간 **전자레인지에 돌린다**.

1. can opener
   깡통 따개

2. grater
   강판

3. steamer
   찜통

4. plastic storage container
   플라스틱 저장 용기

5. frying pan
   후라이팬

6. pot
   냄비

7. ladle
   국자

8. double boiler
   이중 냄비

9. wooden spoon
   나무 숟가락

10. casserole dish
    캐서롤 접시

11. garlic press
    마늘 압착기

12. carving knife
    고기 썰기용 칼

13. roasting pan
    굽기용 팬

14. roasting rack
    굽기용 쇠선반

15. vegetable peeler
    야채 껍질 제거기

16. paring knife
    껍질 벗기는 칼

17. colander
    여과기

18. kitchen timer
    부엌용 타이머

19. spatula
    주걱

20. eggbeater
    계란 교반기

21. whisk
    거품기

22. strainer
    체

23. tongs
    집게

24. lid
    뚜껑

25. saucepan
    소스 냄비

26. cake pan
    케이크팬

27. cookie sheet
    쿠키 판

28. pie pan
    파이 팬

29. pot holders
    냄비 집게

30. rolling pin
    밀방망이

31. mixing bowl
    믹스용 그릇

Pair practice. Make new conversations.

A: *Please hand me the whisk.*
B: *Here's the whisk. Do you need anything else?*
A: *Yes, pass me the casserole dish.*

Use the new words.
Look at page 77. Name the kitchen utensils you see.

A: *Here's a grater.*
B: *This is a mixing bowl.*

1. hamburger
   햄버거

2. french fries
   감자 튀김

3. cheeseburger
   치즈버거

4. onion rings
   양파링

5. chicken sandwich
   닭고기 샌드위치

6. hot dog
   핫도그

7. nachos
   나초

8. taco
   타코

9. burrito
   부리토

10. pizza
    피자

11. soda
    탄산음료수

12. iced tea
    아이스티

13. ice-cream cone
    아이스크림 콘

14. milkshake
    밀크쉐이크

15. donut
    도넛

16. muffin
    머핀

17. counterperson
    계산원

18. straw
    빨대

19. plastic utensils
    일회용 식도구

20. sugar substitute
    설탕 대체품

21. ketchup
    케찹

22. mustard
    머스타드

23. mayonnaise
    마요네즈

24. salad bar
    샐러드 바

Grammar Point: yes/no questions *(do)*

Do you like hamburgers? Yes, I do.
Do you like nachos? No, I don't.

Think about it. Discuss.

1. Do you think that fast food is bad for people? Why or why not?
2. What fast foods do you have in your country?
3. Do you have a favorite fast food restaurant? Which one?

1. bacon
   베이컨
2. sausage
   소시지
3. hash browns
   해쉬 브라운
4. toast
   토스트
5. English muffin
   잉글리쉬 머핀
6. biscuits
   비스킷
7. pancakes
   팬케이크
8. waffles
   와플
9. hot cereal
   핫 씨리얼

10. grilled cheese sandwich
    그릴 치즈 샌드위치
11. pickle
    피클
12. club sandwich
    클럽 샌드위치
13. spinach salad
    시금치 샐러드
14. chef's salad
    셰프 샐러드
15. dinner salad
    디너 샐러드
16. soup
    스프
17. rolls
    롤
18. coleslaw
    코울슬로우
19. potato salad
    감자 샐러드
20. pasta salad
    파스타 샐러드
21. fruit salad
    과일 샐러드

BREAKFAST SPECIAL
Served 6 a.m. to 11 a.m.

Two egg omelet with one side

LUNCH
Served 11 a.m. to 2 p.m.
All sandwiches come with soup or salad

SIDE SALADS

SALAD DRESSINGS

Thousand Island   Ranch

Italian   Blue Cheese

Ways to order from a menu

I'd like a grilled cheese sandwich.
I'll have a bowl of tomato soup.
Could I get the chef's salad with ranch dressing?

Pair practice. Make conversations.

A: *I'd like a grilled cheese sandwich, please.*
B: *Anything else for you?*
A: *Yes, I'll have a bowl of tomato soup with that.*

DINNER

DESSERTS

BEVERAGES

22. roast chicken
구운 닭고기

23. mashed potatoes
매시포테이토

24. steak
스테이크

25. baked potato
구운 감자

26. spaghetti
스파게티

27. meatballs
미트볼

28. garlic bread
마늘빵

29. grilled fish
구운 생선

30. rice
밥

31. meatloaf
미트로프

32. steamed vegetables
삶은 야채

33. layer cake
케이크

34. cheesecake
치즈 케이크

35. pie
파이

36. mixed berries
베리 칵테일

37. coffee
커피

38. decaf coffee
무카페인 커피

39. tea
차

40. herbal tea
허브차

41. cream
크림

42. low-fat milk
저지방 우유

Ask your classmates. Share the answers.

1. Do you prefer vegetable soup or chicken soup?
2. Do you prefer tea or coffee?
3. Which desserts on the menu do you like?

Role play. Order a dinner from the menu.

A: *Are you ready to order?*
B: *I think so. I'll have <u>the roast chicken</u>.*
A: *Would you also like…?*

81

1. **dining room**
   식당

2. **hostess**
   식당 여직원

3. **high chair**
   어린이용 의자

4. **booth**
   칸막이한 좌석

5. **to-go box**
   포장 용기

6. **patron / diner**
   식당 손님

7. **menu**
   메뉴

8. **server / waiter**
   종업원 / 웨이터

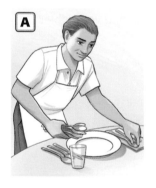

A. **set** the table
   식탁을 **차리다**

B. **seat** the customer
   손님을 **앉히다**

C. **pour** the water
   물을 **따르다**

D. **order** from the menu
   메뉴를 보고 **주문하다**

E. **take** the order
   주문을 **받다**

F. **serve** the meal
   음식을 **서빙하다**

G. **clear / bus** the dishes
   그릇을 **치우다**

H. **carry** the tray
   쟁반을 **나르다**

I. **pay** the check
   계산**하다**

J. **leave** a tip
   팁을 **놓다**

More vocabulary

eat out: to go to a restaurant to eat

take out: to buy food at a restaurant and take it home to eat

Look at the pictures.
Describe what is happening.

A: *She's seating the customer*.
B: *He's taking the order*.

9. server / waitress 종업원 / 웨이트리스	**11.** bread basket 빵바구니
10. dessert tray 디저트 쟁반	**12.** busser 버서(서빙 보조)

13. dish room 설거지하는 곳	**15.** kitchen 주방
14. dishwasher 식기세척기	**16.** chef 주방장

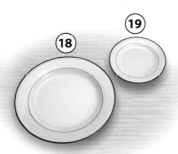
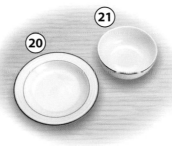

17. place setting 식도구 세팅	**21.** soup bowl 스프용 그릇	**25.** saucer 받침 접시	**29.** steak knife 스테이크용 칼
18. dinner plate 디너 접시	**22.** water glass 물잔	**26.** napkin 냅킨	**30.** knife 칼
19. bread-and-butter plate 빵- 버터용 접시	**23.** wine glass 포도주 잔	**27.** salad fork 샐러드 포크	**31.** teaspoon 차 스푼
20. salad plate 샐러드 접시	**24.** cup 컵	**28.** dinner fork 디너 포크	**32.** soupspoon 스프 스푼

Pair practice. Make new conversations.

A: *Excuse me, this <u>spoon</u> is dirty.*
B: *I'm so sorry. I'll get you a clean <u>spoon</u> right away.*
A: *Thanks.*

Role play. Talk to a new busser.

A: *Do the <u>salad forks</u> go on <u>the left</u>?*
B: *Yes. They go <u>next to the dinner forks</u>.*
A: *What about the…?*

83

1. live music
생음악

2. organic
유기농

3. lemonade
레모네이드

4. sour
신맛

5. samples
시식용

6. avocados
아보카도

7. vendors
상인

8. sweets
단 식품류

9. herbs
허브

A. **count**
세다

**Look at the pictures.
What do you see?**

Answer the questions.

1. How many vendors are at the market today?

2. Which vegetables are organic?

3. What are the children eating?

4. What is the woman counting? Why?

 Read the story.

The Farmers' Market

On Saturdays, the Novaks go to the farmers' market. They like to visit the vendors. Alex Novak always goes to the hot food stand for lunch. His children love to eat the fruit samples. Alex's father usually buys some sweets and lemonade. The lemonade is very sour.

Nina Novak likes to buy organic herbs and vegetables. Today, she is buying avocados. The market worker counts eight avocados. She gives Nina one more for free.

There are other things to do at the market. The Novaks like to listen to the live music. Sometimes they meet friends there. The farmers' market is a great place for families on a Saturday afternoon.

Think about it.

1. What's good or bad about shopping at a farmers' market?

2. Imagine you are at the farmers' market. What will you buy?

Everyday Clothes 평상복

1. shirt
   셔츠
2. jeans
   청바지
3. dress
   원피스
4. T-shirt
   티셔츠
5. baseball cap
   야구 모자
6. socks
   양말
7. athletic shoes
   운동화
A. **tie**
   끈을 묶다

BEST OF JAZZ CONCERT

TICKETS

BEST OF JAZZ

Listen and point. Take turns.

A: *Point to the dress.*
B: *Point to the T-shirt.*
A: *Point to the baseball cap.*

Dictate to your partner. Take turns.

A: *Write dress.*
B: *Is that spelled d-r-e-s-s?*
A: *Yes. That's right.*

86

ONE NIGHT ONLY

DOORS OPEN AT 8:00

8. blouse
블라우스

9. handbag
핸드백

10. skirt
치마

11. suit
정장

12. slacks / pants
바지

13. shoes
신발

14. sweater
스웨터

B. **put on**
입다

Ways to compliment clothes

That's a pretty <u>dress</u>!
Those are great <u>shoes</u>!
I really like your <u>baseball cap</u>!

Role play. Compliment a friend.

A: *<u>That's a pretty dress</u>! <u>Green</u> is a great color on you.*
B: *Thanks! I really like your…*

Casual Clothes 캐주얼 복장

1. cap
   모자

2. cardigan sweater
   카디건 스웨터

3. pullover sweater
   풀오버 스웨터

4. sports shirt
   스포츠 셔츠

5. maternity dress
   임산부용 원피스

6. overalls
   멜빵 바지

7. knit top
   니트 상의

8. capris
   7부 바지

9. sandals
   샌들

Work Clothes 근무복

10. uniform
    유니폼

11. business suit
    정장

12. tie
    넥타이

13. briefcase
    서류 가방

More vocabulary

three piece suit: matching jacket, vest, and slacks
outfit: clothes that look nice together
in fashion / in style: clothes that are popular now

Describe the people. Take turns.

A: *She's wearing a maternity dress.*
B: *He's wearing a uniform.*

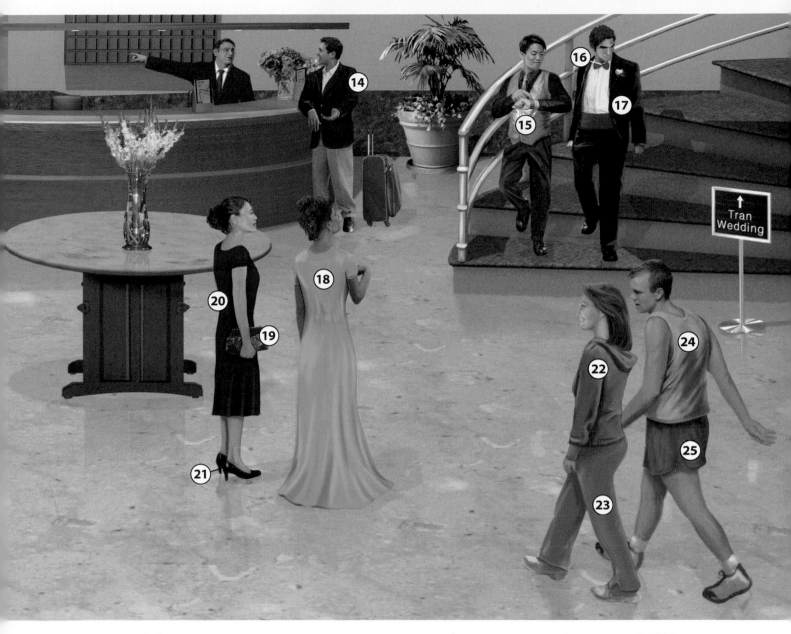

Formal Clothes 정장

14. sports jacket / sports coat
스포츠 자켓 / 코트

15. vest
조끼

16. bow tie
나비 넥타이

17. tuxedo
턱시도

18. evening gown
이브닝 가운

19. clutch bag
소형 핸드백

20. cocktail dress
칵테일 드레스

21. high heels
하이힐

Exercise Wear 운동복

22. sweatshirt / hoodie
트레이닝 윗도리

23. sweatpants
트레이닝 바지

24. tank top
소매없는 짧은 상의

25. shorts
반바지

Ask your classmates. Share the answers.

1. What's your favorite outfit?
2. Do you like to wear formal clothes? Why or why not?
3. Do you prefer to exercise in shorts or sweatpants?

Think about it. Discuss.

1. What jobs require formal clothes? Uniforms?
2. What's good and bad about wearing school uniforms?
3. What is your opinion of today's popular clothing?

89

1. hat 모자	**5.** winter scarf 겨울용 스카프
2. (over)coat (오버)코트	**6.** gloves 장갑
3. headband 머리띠	**7.** headwrap 머리감싸개
4. leather jacket 가죽 자켓	**8.** jacket 자켓

9. parka 파카	**13.** earmuffs 귀가리개
10. mittens 벙어리 장갑	**14.** down vest 오리털 조끼
11. ski hat 스키 모자	**15.** ski mask 스키 마스크
12. leggings 레깅스	**16.** down jacket 오리털 자켓

17. umbrella 우산	**20.** rain boots 장화
18. raincoat 레인코트	**21.** trench coat 트렌치 코트
19. poncho 판초	

22. swimming trunks 수영 팬츠	**25.** cover-up 비치 가운
23. straw hat 밀짚모자	**26.** swimsuit / bathing suit 수영복
24. windbreaker 스포츠용 잠바	**27.** sunglasses 선글라스

Grammar Point: should

*It's raining. You **should** take an umbrella.*
*It's snowing. You **should** wear a scarf.*
*It's sunny. You **should** wear a straw hat.*

Pair practice. Make new conversations.

A: *It's <u>snowing</u>. You should wear <u>a scarf</u>.*
B: *Don't worry. I'm wearing my <u>parka</u>.*
A: *Good, and don't forget your <u>mittens</u>.*

Unisex Underwear
남녀 공용 속옷

1. undershirt
   남녀 공용
2. thermal undershirt
   내복
3. long underwear
   긴 내의

Men's Underwear
남성용 속옷

4. boxer shorts
   사각 팬티
5. briefs
   삼각 팬티
6. athletic supporter / jockstrap
   운동경기용 서포터

Unisex Socks
남녀 공용 양말

7. ankle socks
   발목까지 오는 양말
8. crew socks
   긴 양말
9. dress socks
   정장용 양말

Women's Socks
여성용 양말

10. low-cut socks
    목없는 양말
11. anklets
    발목까지 오는 양말
12. knee highs
    무릎 높이까지 오는 양말

Women's Underwear 여성용 속옷

13. (bikini) panties
    (비키니) 팬티
14. briefs / underpants
    팬티
15. body shaper / girdle
    거들
16. garter belt
    가터 벨트
17. stockings
    스타킹
18. panty hose
    팬티 스타킹
19. tights
    타이츠
20. bra
    브라
21. camisole
    캐미솔
22. full slip
    전신용 슬립
23. half slip
    하의용 슬립

Sleepwear 잠옷

24. pajamas
    파자마
25. nightgown
    나이트가운
26. slippers
    슬리퍼
27. blanket sleeper
    전신 잠옷
28. nightshirt
    나이트셔츠
29. robe
    가운

More vocabulary

lingerie: underwear or sleepwear for women
loungewear: very casual clothing for relaxing around the home

Ask your classmates. Share the answers.

1. What kind of socks are you wearing today?
2. What kind of sleepwear do you prefer?
3. Do you wear slippers at home?

Construction Worker

Road Worker

Automotive Painter

Food Processor

1. hard hat
   안전모

2. work shirt
   작업 셔츠

3. tool belt
   공구 벨트

4. Hi-Visibility safety vest
   형광색 안전 조끼

5. work pants
   작업용 바지

6. steel toe boots
   작업용 부츠

7. ventilation mask
   공기 여과 마스크

8. coveralls
   상하가 붙은 작업복

9. bump cap
   충격 완충 모자

10. safety glasses
    보호 안경

11. apron
    앞치마

Manager **Salesperson**

Farmworker

Ranch Hand

12. blazer
    블레이저

13. tie
    넥타이

14. polo shirt
    폴로 셔츠

15. name tag
    이름표

16. bandana
    대형 손수건

17. work gloves
    작업용 장갑

18. cowboy hat
    카우보이 모자

19. jeans
    청바지

Pair practice. Make new conversations.

A: *What do <u>construction workers</u> wear to work?*
B: *They wear <u>hard hats</u> and <u>tool belts</u>.*
A: *What do <u>road workers</u> wear to work?*

Use the new words.

Look at pages 166–169. Name the workplace clothing you see.

A: *He's wearing <u>a hard hat</u>.*
B: *She's wearing <u>scrubs</u>.*

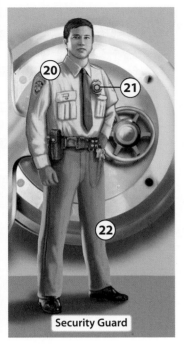

Security Guard

Emergency Worker

Counterperson

Chef

Line Cook

20. security shirt
방범용 셔츠

21. badge
배지

22. security pants
빙빔용 바지

23. helmet
헬멧

24. jumpsuit
점프수트

25. hairnet
위생모

26. smock
작업복

27. disposable gloves
일회용 장갑

28. chef's hat
주방장 모자

29. chef's jacket
주방장 가운

30. waist apron
(허리에 매는) 앞치마

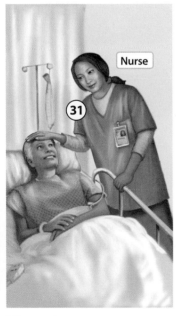

Nurse

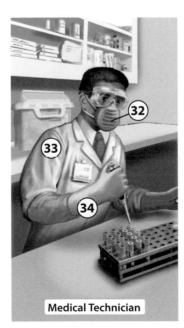

Medical Technician

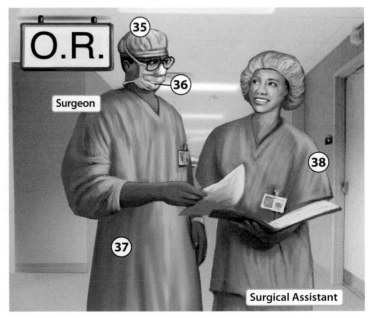

O.R.

Surgeon

Surgical Assistant

31. scrubs
간호복

32. face mask
안면 마스크

33. lab coat
실험복

34. latex gloves
라텍스 장갑

35. surgical scrub cap
수술용 모자

36. surgical mask
수술용 마스크

37. surgical gown
의사의 수술복

38. surgical scrubs
간호사 수술복

Ask your classmates. Share the answers.

1. Which of these outfits would you like to wear?
2. Which of these items are in your closet?
3. Do you wear safety clothing at work? What kinds?

Think about it. Discuss.

1. What other jobs require helmets? disposable gloves?
2. Is it better to have a uniform or wear your own clothes at work? Why?

A. purchase
구입하다

B. wait in line
줄을 서서 **기다리다**

1. suspenders
멜빵

2. purses / handbags
핸드백

3. salesclerk
점원

4. customer
손님

5. display case
진열장

6. belts
벨트

13. wallet
남자용 지갑

14. change purse / coin purse
동전 지갑

15. cell phone holder
휴대 전화 홀더

16. (wrist)watch
(손목)시계

17. shoulder bag
숄더 백

18. backpack
배낭

19. tote bag
토트 백

20. belt buckle
벨트 버클

21. sole
신발 밑창

22. heel
구두굽

23. toe
구두 앞 편자

24. shoelaces
구두끈

More vocabulary

gift: something you give or receive from friends or family for a special occasion

present: a gift

Grammar Point: object pronouns

*My **sister** loves jewelry. I'll buy **her** a necklace.*
*My **dad** likes belts. I'll buy **him** a belt buckle.*
*My **friends** love scarves. I'll buy **them** scarves.*

7. shoe department
신발 코너

8. jewelry department
보석 코너

9. bracelets
팔찌

10. necklaces
목걸이

11. hats
모자

12. scarves
스카프

C. **try on** shoes
신발을 **신어보다**

D. **assist** a customer
손님을 **도와주다**

25. high heels
하이힐

26. pumps
끈없는 가벼운 구두

27. flats
낮은 신발

28. boots
부츠

29. oxfords
발등을 끈으로 매는 신사화

30. loafers
간편화

31. hiking boots
등산화

32. tennis shoes
테니스화

33. chain
체인 목걸이

34. beads
구슬 목걸이

35. locket
로켓 목걸이

36. pierced earrings
뚫은 귀용 귀고리

37. clip-on earrings
클립형 귀고리

38. pin
핀

39. string of pearls
진주 목걸이

40. ring
반지

Ways to talk about accessories

I need <u>a hat</u> to wear with <u>this scarf</u>.
I'd like <u>earrings</u> to go with <u>the necklace</u>.
Do you have <u>a belt</u> that would go with my <u>shoes</u>?

Role play. Talk to a salesperson.

A: *Do you have <u>boots</u> that would go with <u>this skirt</u>?*
B: *Let me see. How about <u>these brown ones</u>?*
A: *Perfect. I also need…*

95

Describing Clothes

Sizes 사이즈

1. extra small
   특소
2. small
   소
3. medium
   중
4. large
   대
5. extra large
   특대
6. one-size-fits-all
   프리 사이즈

Styles 스타일

Sweaters 50% off

7. **crewneck** sweater
   크루넥 스웨터
8. **V-neck** sweater
   브이넥 스웨터
9. **turtleneck** sweater
   터틀넥 스웨터
10. **scoop neck** sweater
    스쿱넥 스웨터

11. **sleeveless** shirt
    민소매 셔츠
12. **short-sleeved** shirt
    반소매 셔츠
13. **3/4-sleeved** shirt
    7부 소매 셔츠
14. **long-sleeved** shirt
    긴소매 셔츠

15. **mini**-skirt
    미니 스커트
16. **short** skirt
    짧은 치마
17. **mid-length** / **calf-length** skirt
    무릎 길이 / 발목 길이 치마
18. **long** skirt
    긴 치마

Patterns 패턴

19. solid
    단색
20. striped
    줄무늬
21. polka-dotted
    물방울 무늬
22. plaid
    격자 무늬
23. print
    프린트 무늬
24. checked
    체크 무늬
25. floral
    꽃무늬
26. paisley
    페이즐리 무늬

Ask your classmates. Share the answers.

1. Do you prefer crewneck or V-neck sweaters?
2. Do you prefer checked or striped shirts?
3. Do you prefer short-sleeved or sleeveless shirts?

Role play. Talk to a salesperson.

A: *Excuse me. I'm looking for this <u>V-neck sweater</u> in <u>large</u>.*
B: *Here's a <u>large</u>. It's on sale for $<u>19.99</u>.*
A: *Wonderful! I'll take it. I'm also looking for…*

96

Comparing Clothing 의복 비교

27. heavy jacket 두꺼운 재킷	**29. tight** pants 꼭끼는 바지	**31. low** heels 낮은 굽	**33. plain** blouse 단순한 블라우스	**35. narrow** tie 좁은 넥타이
28. light jacket 얇은 재킷	**30. loose / baggy** pants 헐거운 바지 / 헐렁한 바지	**32. high** heels 하이힐	**34. fancy** blouse 화려한 블라우스	**36. wide** tie 넓은 넥타이

Clothing Problems 의복 문제

37. It's **too small**.
너무 작다.

38. It's **too big**.
너무 크다.

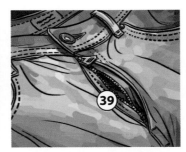

39. The zipper is **broken**.
지퍼가 **고장나다**.

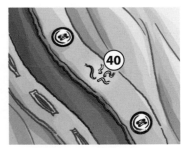

40. A button is **missing**.
단추가 **떨어지다**.

41. It's **ripped / torn**.
찢어지다.

42. It's **stained**.
얼룩지다.

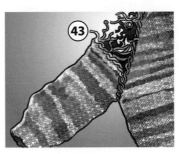

43. It's **unraveling**.
올이 **풀리다**.

44. It's **too expensive**.
너무 비싸다.

More vocabulary

refund: money you get back when you return an item to the store
complaint: a statement that something is not right
customer service: the place customers go with their complaints

Role play. Return an item to a salesperson.

A: *Welcome to Shopmart. How may I help you?*
B: *This sweater is new, but it's unraveling.*
A: *I'm sorry. Would you like a refund?*

Making Clothes

옷 만들기

Types of Material 천 종류

1. cotton
   면

2. linen
   마

3. wool
   모

4. cashmere
   캐시미어

5. silk
   실크

6. leather
   가죽

A Garment Factory 의류 공장

Parts of a Sewing Machine
재봉틀 부품

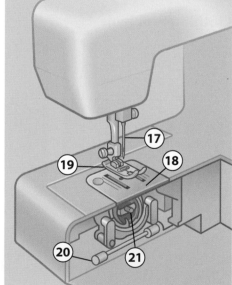

A. **sew** by machine
   재봉틀로 **바느질하다**

B. **sew** by hand
   손으로 **바느질하다**

13. sewing machine
    재봉틀

14. sewing machine operator
    재봉틀 사용자

15. bolt of fabric
    천 한 필

16. rack
    옷걸이

17. needle
    바늘

18. needle plate
    미끄럼판

19. presser foot
    노루발

20. feed dog / feed bar
    피드 독/피드 바

21. bobbin
    실패

More vocabulary

fashion designer: a person who makes original clothes
natural materials: cloth made from things that grow in nature
synthetic materials: cloth made by people, such as nylon

Use the new words.
Look at pages 86–87. Name the materials you see.

A: *That's <u>denim</u>.*
B: *That's <u>leather</u>.*

Types of Material 천 종류

7. denim
데님

8. suede
스웨이드

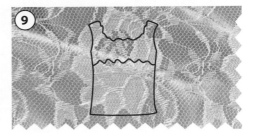

9. lace
레이스

10. velvet
벨벳

11. corduroy
코듀로이

12. nylon
나일론

A Fabric Store 직물점

Closures 잠금용

Trim 밑단용

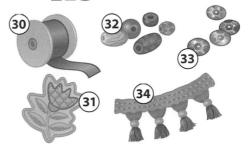

22. pattern 패턴	**25.** zipper 지퍼	**28.** buckle 버클
23. thread 실	**26.** snap 스냅	**29.** hook and loop fastener 벨크로 테이프
24. button 단추	**27.** hook and eye 훅단추	**30.** ribbon 리본

31. appliqué 애플리케	**33.** sequins 시퀸
32. beads 비드	**34.** fringe 술장식

Ask your classmates. Share the answers.

1. Can you sew?
2. What's your favorite type of material?
3. How many types of material are you wearing today?

Think about it. Discuss.

1. Do most people make or buy clothes in your country?
2. Is it better to make or buy clothes? Why?
3. Which materials are best for formal clothes?

Making Alterations

옷 수선

An Alterations Shop 옷 수선점

1. dressmaker
   양재사
2. dressmaker's dummy
   양재용 마네킹
3. tailor
   재봉사
4. collar
   칼라
5. waistband
   허리띠
6. sleeve
   소매
7. pocket
   주머니
8. hem
   밑단
9. cuff
   아랫단

Sewing Supplies 바느질 용품

10. needle
    바늘
11. thread
    실
12. (straight) pin
    시침핀
13. pin cushion
    바늘꽂이
14. safety pin
    옷핀
15. thimble
    골무
16. pair of scissors
    가위
17. tape measure
    줄자
18. seam ripper
    솔기 트는 기구

Alterations 수선

 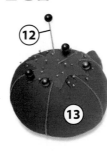  

A. **Lengthen** the pants.
바지 **길이를 늘리다**.

B. **Shorten** the pants.
바지 **길이를 줄이다**.

C. **Let out** the pants.
바지 **품을 늘리다**.

D. **Take in** the pants.
바지 **품을 줄이다**.

Pair practice. Make new conversations.

A: *Would you hand me the thread?*
B: *OK. What are you going to do?*
A: *I'm going to take in these pants.*

Ask your classmates. Share the answers.

1. Is there an alterations shop near your home?
2. Do you ever go to a tailor or a dressmaker?
3. What sewing supplies do you have at home?

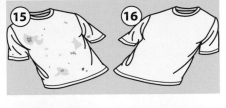

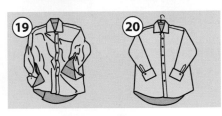

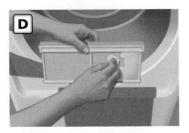

1. **laundry**
빨래

2. **laundry basket**
빨래통

3. **washer**
세탁기

4. **dryer**
건조기

5. **dryer sheets**
건조기용 섬유 유연제

6. **fabric softener**
섬유 유연제

7. **bleach**
표백제

8. **laundry detergent**
세탁 세제

9. **clothesline**
빨랫 줄

10. **clothespin**
빨래집게

11. **hanger**
옷걸이

12. **spray starch**
스프레이 풀

13. **iron**
다리미

14. **ironing board**
다리미판

15. **dirty** T-shirt
더러운 티셔츠

16. **clean** T-shirt
깨끗한 티셔츠

17. **wet** shirt
젖은 셔츠

18. **dry** shirt
마른 셔츠

19. **wrinkled** shirt
구겨진 셔츠

20. **ironed** shirt
다린 셔츠

A. **Sort** the laundry.
빨래**를** **분류하다**.

B. **Add** the detergent.
세제**를** **넣다**.

C. **Load** the washer.
세탁기에 빨래**를** **넣다**.

D. **Clean** the lint trap.
보풀 트랩을 **제거하다**.

E. **Unload** the dryer.
건조기에서 빨래**를** **꺼내다**.

F. **Fold** the laundry.
빨래**를** **개다**.

G. **Iron** the clothes.
옷을 **다림질하다**.

H. **Hang up** the clothes.
옷을 **걸다**.

 wash in cold water

 no bleach

 line dry

 dry clean only, do not wash

Pair practice. Make new conversations.

A: *I have to <u>sort the laundry</u>. Can you help?*
B: *Sure. Here's <u>the laundry basket</u>.*
A: *Thanks a lot!*

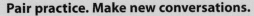

1. flyer
   광고지

2. used clothing
   중고 의복

3. sticker
   스티커

4. folding card table
   접이식 테이블

5. folding chair
   접이식 의자

6. clock radio
   시계겸용 라디오

7. VCR
   VCR

A. **bargain**
   흥정하다

B. **browse**
   찾아보다

102

Answer the questions.

1. What kind of used clothing do you see?
2. What information is on the flyer?
3. Why are the stickers different colors?
4. How much is the clock radio? the VCR?

 Read the story.

A Garage Sale

Last Sunday, I had a garage sale. At 5:00 a.m., I put up <u>flyers</u> in my neighborhood. Next, I put price <u>stickers</u> on my <u>used clothing</u>, my <u>VCR</u>, and some other old things. At 7:00 a.m., I opened my <u>folding card table</u> and <u>folding chair</u>. Then I waited.

At 7:05 a.m., my first customer arrived. She asked, "How much is the sweatshirt?"

"Two dollars," I said.

She said, "It's stained. I can give you seventy-five cents." We <u>bargained</u> for a minute and she paid $1.00.

All day people came to <u>browse</u>, bargain, and buy. At 7:00 p.m., I had $85.00.

Now I know two things: Garage sales are hard work and nobody wants to buy an old <u>clock radio</u>!

Think about it.

1. Do you like to buy things at garage sales? Why or why not?
2. Imagine you want the VCR. How will you bargain for it?

1. head
   머리
2. hair
   머리카락
3. neck
   목
4. chest
   가슴
5. back
   등
6. nose
   코
7. mouth
   입
8. foot
   발

Listen and point. Take turns.

A: *Point to the chest.*

B: *Point to the neck.*

A: *Point to the mouth.*

Dictate to your partner. Take turns.

A: *Write hair.*

B: *Did you say hair?*

A: *That's right, h-a-i-r.*

9. leg
다리

10. toe
발가락

11. eye
눈

12. ear
귀

13. shoulder
어깨

14. arm
팔

15. hand
손

16. finger
손가락

Grammar Point: imperatives

*Please **touch** your right foot.*
***Put** your hands on your feet.*
***Don't** put your hands on your shoulders.*

Pair practice. Take turns giving commands.

A: *Raise your arms.*
B: *Touch your feet.*
A: *Put your hand on your shoulder.*

105

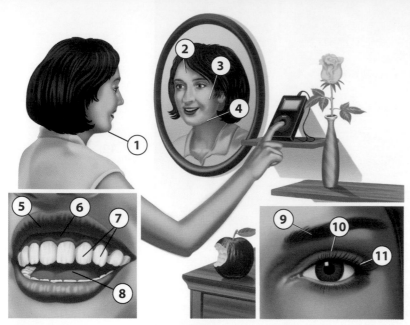

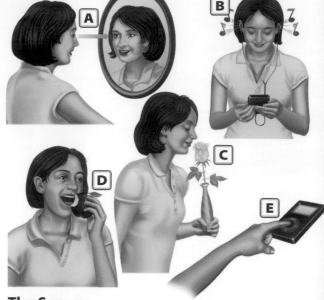

The Face
얼굴

1. chin
   아래턱
2. forehead
   이마
3. cheek
   볼
4. jaw
   턱

The Mouth
입

5. lip
   입술
6. gums
   잇몸
7. teeth
   치아
8. tongue
   혀

The Eye
눈

9. eyebrow
   눈썹
10. eyelid
    눈꺼풀
11. eyelashes
    속눈썹

The Senses
감각

A. see
   보다
B. hear
   듣다
C. smell
   냄새를 맡다

D. taste
   맛보다
E. touch
   만지다

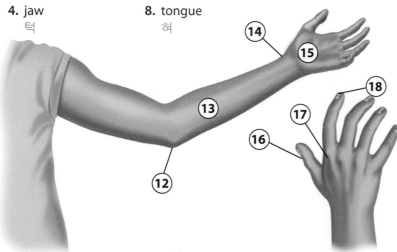

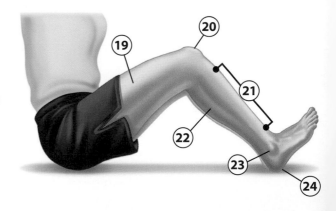

The Arm, Hand, and Fingers 팔, 손 및 손가락

12. elbow
    팔꿈치
13. forearm
    팔뚝
14. wrist
    손목

15. palm
    손바닥
16. thumb
    엄지

17. knuckle
    손가락 마디
18. fingernail
    손톱

The Leg and Foot 다리 및 발

19. thigh
    허벅지
20. knee
    무릎
21. shin
    정강이

22. calf
    종아리
23. ankle
    발목
24. heel
    발꿈치

More vocabulary

torso: the part of the body from the shoulders to the pelvis
limbs: arms and legs
toenail: the nail on your toe

Pair practice. Make new conversations.

A: Is your <u>arm</u> OK?
B: Yes, but now my <u>elbow</u> hurts.
A: I'm sorry to hear that.

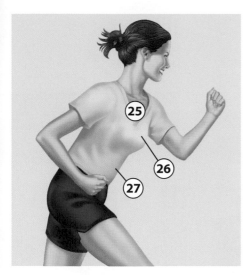

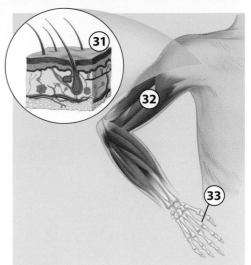

25. chest
가슴

26. breast
유방

27. abdomen
복부

28. shoulder blade
어깨뼈

29. lower back
등

30. buttocks
둔부

31. skin
피부

32. muscle
근육

33. bone
뼈

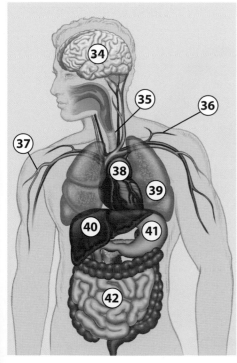

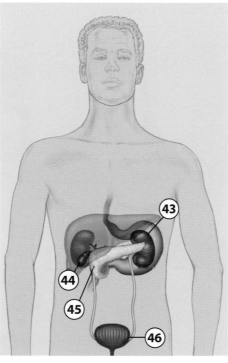

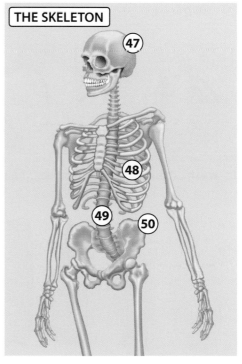

THE SKELETON

34. brain
뇌

35. throat
목

36. artery
동맥

37. vein
정맥

38. heart
심장

39. lung
폐

40. liver
간

41. stomach
위

42. intestines
장

43. kidney
신장

44. gallbladder
담낭

45. pancreas
췌장

46. bladder
방광

47. skull
두개골

48. rib cage
흉곽

49. spinal column
척추

50. pelvis
골반

A. take a shower
샤워하다

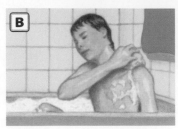

B. take a bath / **bathe**
목욕하다

C. use deodorant
방취제를 **사용하다**

D. put on sunscreen
자외선 차단제를 **바르다**

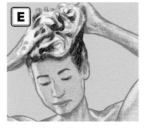

1. shower cap
   샤워캡

2. shower gel
   샤워젤

3. soap
   비누

4. bath powder
   목욕 파우더

5. deodorant / antiperspirant
   방취제 / 발한 억제제

6. perfume / cologne
   향수 / 콜롱

7. sunscreen
   자외선 차단제

8. sunblock
   선블락

9. body lotion / moisturizer
   바디 로숀 / 보습제

E. wash…hair
머리를 **감다**

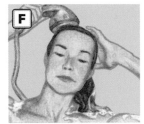

F. rinse…hair
머리를 **헹구다**

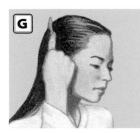

G. comb…hair
머리를 **빗다**

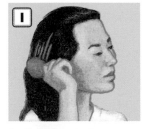

H. dry…hair
머리를 **말리다**

I. brush…hair
머리를 **브러쉬로 빗다**

10. shampoo
    샴푸

11. conditioner
    컨디셔너

12. hair spray
    헤어 스프레이

13. comb
    빗

14. brush
    브러쉬

15. pick
    피크

16. hair gel
    헤어젤

17. curling iron
    고대기

18. blow dryer
    헤어 드라이기

19. hair clip
    헤어 클립

20. barrette
    머리핀

21. bobby pins
    실핀

More vocabulary

unscented: a product without perfume or scent
hypoallergenic: a product that is better for people with allergies

Think about it. Discuss.

1. Which personal hygiene products should someone use before a job interview?
2. What is the right age to start wearing makeup? Why?

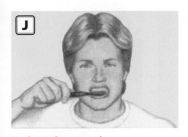

J. brush…teeth
양치하다

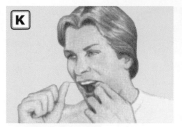

K. floss…teeth
치실을 사용하다

L. gargle
가글하다

M. shave
면도하다

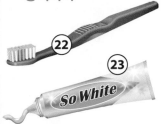

22. toothbrush
치솔

23. toothpaste
치약

24. dental floss
치실

25. mouthwash
구강 청정제

26. electric shaver
전기 면도기

27. razor
면도기

28. razorblade
면도날

29. shaving cream
면도용 크림

30. aftershave
면도 후 바르는 로션

N. cut…nails
손톱을 **깎다**

O. polish…nails
손톱에 **매니큐어를 칠하다**

P. put on / apply
바르다

Q. take off / remove
지우다

Makeup 화장

31. nail clipper
손톱 깎기

32. emery board
손톱줄

33. nail polish
손톱 광택제(매니큐어)

34. eyebrow pencil
눈썹 연필

35. eye shadow
아이섀도우

36. eyeliner
아이라이너

37. blush
볼터치

38. lipstick
립스틱

39. mascara
마스카라

40. foundation
화운데이션

41. face powder
파우더

42. makeup remover
메이컵 리무버

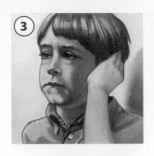

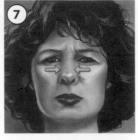
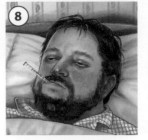

1. headache
두통

2. toothache
치통

3. earache
이통

4. stomachache
복통

5. backache
요통

6. sore throat
인후통

7. nasal congestion
코막힘

8. fever / temperature
열

9. chills
오한

10. rash
발진

A. **cough**
기침하다

B. **sneeze**
재채기하다

C. **feel** dizzy
어지러움을 **느끼다**

D. **feel** nauseous
메스꺼움을 **느끼다**

E. **throw up / vomit**
구토하다 / 토하다

11. insect bite
벌레에게 물린 상처

12. bruise
멍

13. cut
벤 상처 (자상)

14. sunburn
햇볕에 타다

15. blister
물집

16. swollen finger
부어오른 손가락

17. bloody nose
코피가 나다

18. sprained ankle
발목을 삐다

Look at the pictures.
Describe the symptoms and injuries.

A: *He has a backache*.
B: *She has a toothache*.

Think about it. Discuss.

1. What are some common cold symptoms?
2. What do you recommend for a stomachache?
3. What is the best way to stop a bloody nose?

Common Illnesses and Childhood Diseases 흔한 병 및 어린이 질병

1. cold
감기

2. flu
독감

3. ear infection
중이염

4. strep throat
후두염

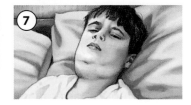

5. measles
홍역

6. chicken pox
수두

7. mumps
볼거리

8. allergies
알레르기

Serious Medical Conditions and Diseases 심각한 증상 및 질병

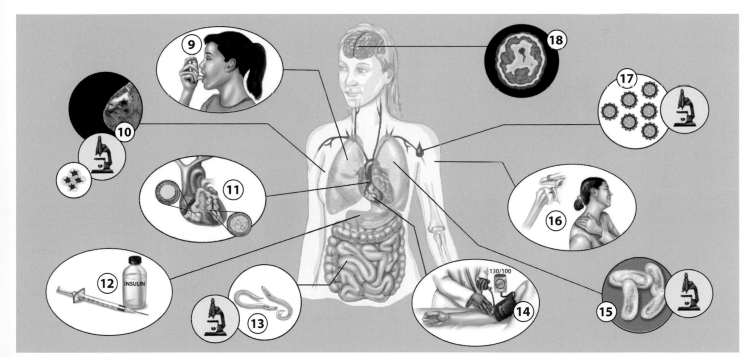

9. asthma
천식

10. cancer
암

11. heart disease
심장병

12. diabetes
당뇨병

13. intestinal parasites
장내 기생충

14. high blood pressure / hypertension
고혈압

15. TB (tuberculosis)
결핵

16. arthritis
관절염

17. HIV (human immunodeficiency virus)
HIV (인체 면역 결핍 바이러스)

18. dementia
치매

More vocabulary

AIDS (acquired immune deficiency syndrome): a medical condition that results from contracting the HIV virus

Alzheimer's disease: a disease that causes dementia

coronary disease: heart disease

infectious disease: a disease that is spread through air or water

influenza: flu

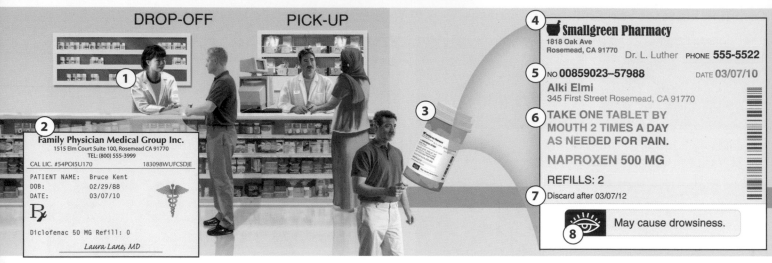

DROP-OFF   PICK-UP

① Smallgreen Pharmacy
1818 Oak Ave
Rosemead, CA 91770
Dr. L. Luther PHONE **555-5522**

⑤ NO **00859023–57988**   DATE **03/07/10**
Alki Elmi
345 First Street Rosemead, CA 91770

⑥ TAKE ONE TABLET BY MOUTH 2 TIMES A DAY AS NEEDED FOR PAIN.

NAPROXEN 500 MG

REFILLS: 2

⑦ Discard after 03/07/12

⑧ [eye icon] May cause drowsiness.

Family Physician Medical Group Inc.
1515 Elm Court Suite 100, Rosemead CA 91770
TEL: (800) 555-3999
CAL LIC. #54POI5U170   183098WUFCSDJE

PATIENT NAME: Bruce Kent
DOB: 02/29/88
DATE: 03/07/10

℞

Diclofenac 50 MG Refill: 0

Laura Lane, MD

1. pharmacist 약사	**3. prescription medication** 처방약
2. prescription 처방전	**4. prescription label** 처방약 정보 라벨

5. prescription number 처방 번호	**7. expiration date** 유효기한
6. dosage 복용량	**8. warning label** 경고문

Medical Warnings 경고문

A. Take with food or milk.
음식 또는 우유와 함께 **복용하십시오**.

B. Take one hour before eating.
식사하기 1시간 전에 **복용하십시오**.

C. Finish all medication.
약을 모두 **복용하십시오**.

D. Do not take with dairy products.
유제품과 함께 **복용하지 마십시오**.

E. Do not drive or operate heavy machinery.
차 또는 중장비를 **운전하지 마십시오**.

F. Do not drink alcohol.
술을 **마시지 마십시오**.

More vocabulary

prescribe medication: to write a prescription
fill prescriptions: to prepare medication for patients
pick up a prescription: to get prescription medication

Role play. Talk to the pharmacist.

A: *Hi. I need to pick up a prescription for* <u>Jones</u>.
B: *Here's your medication,* <u>Mr. Jones</u>. *Take these* <u>once a day with milk or food</u>.

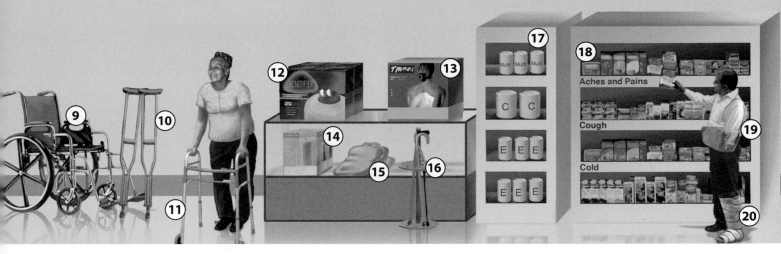

9. wheelchair 휠체어	**13.** heating pad 보온 패드	**17.** vitamins 비타민
10. crutches 목발	**14.** air purifier 공기 정화기	**18.** over-the-counter medication 비처방약
11. walker 성인용 보행 보조기	**15.** hot water bottle 핫팩	**19.** sling 삼각건
12. humidifier 가습기	**16.** cane 지팡이	**20.** cast 깁스

Types of Medication 약의 종류

21. pill 알약	**22.** tablet 정제	**23.** capsule 캡슐	**24.** ointment 연고	**25.** cream 크림

Over-the-Counter Medication 비처방약

26. pain reliever 진통제	**28.** antacid 제산제	**30.** throat lozenges 목알약	**32.** nasal spray 코 스프레이
27. cold tablets 감기용 정제약	**29.** cough syrup 기침시럽	**31.** eye drops 안약	**33.** inhaler 흡입기

Ways to talk about medication

Use *take* for pills, tablets, capsules, and cough syrup.
Use *apply* for ointments and creams.
Use *use* for drops, nasal sprays, and inhalers.

Ask your classmates. Share the answers.

1. What pharmacy do you go to?
2. Do you ever ask the pharmacist for advice?
3. Do you take any vitamins? Which ones?

Ways to Get Well 건강을 회복하는 방법

A. Seek medical attention.
진료소를 **방문한다**.

B. Get bed rest.
침상에서 휴식을 **취한다**.

C. Drink fluids.
수분을 **섭취한다**.

D. Take medicine.
약을 **복용한다**.

Ways to Stay Well 건강을 유지하는 방법

E. Stay fit.
운동을 한다.

F. Eat a healthy diet.
건강에 좋은 음식을 **먹는다**.

G. Don't smoke.
금연한다.

Ms. Jones, you must stop smoking!

H. Have regular checkups.
정기 검사를 **받는다**.

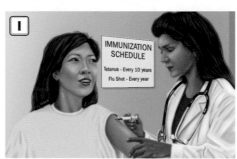

IMMUNIZATION SCHEDULE
Tetanus - Every 10 years
Flu Shot - Every year

I. Get immunized.
예방주사를 **맞는다**.

J. Follow medical advice.
의사의 지시를 **따른다**.

More vocabulary

injection: medicine in a syringe that is put into the body
immunization / vaccination: an injection that stops serious diseases

Ask your classmates. Share the answers.

1. How do you stay fit?
2. What do you do when you're sick?
3. Which two foods are a part of your healthy diet?

Types of Health Problems 건강 문제의 유형

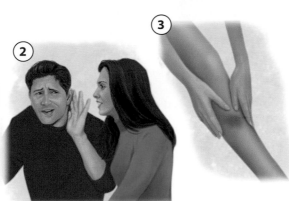

1. vision problems
시력 문제

2. hearing loss
청력 손실

3. pain
통증

4. stress
스트레스

5. depression
우울증

Help with Health Problems 건강 보조 용품

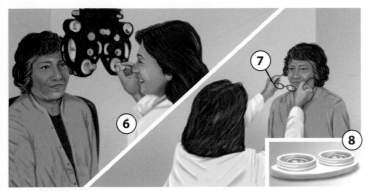

6. optometrist
검안사

7. glasses
안경

8. contact lenses
콘택트 렌즈

9. audiologist
청력 전문의

10. hearing aid
보청기

11. physical therapy
물리치료

12. physical therapist
물리치료사

13. talk therapy
대화요법

14. therapist
치료사

15. support group
지원 모임

Ways to ask about health problems

Are you <u>in pain</u>?
Are you having <u>vision problems</u>?
Are you experiencing <u>depression</u>?

Pair practice. Make new conversations.

A: *Do you know a good <u>optometrist</u>?*
B: *Why? <u>Are you having vision problems</u>?*
A: *Yes, I might need <u>glasses</u>.*

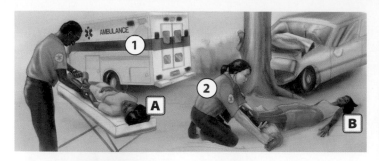

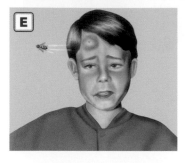

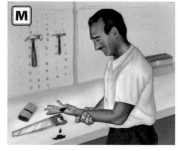

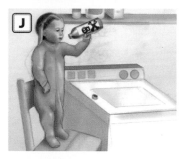

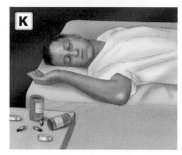

1. ambulance
구급차

2. paramedic
의료 보조자

A. **be** unconscious
의식을 **잃다**

B. **be** in shock
쇼크 상태에 **있다**

C. **be** injured / **be** hurt
다치다

D. **have** a heart attack
심장마비를 **일으키다**

E. **have** an allergic reaction
알레르기 반응을 **보이다**

F. **get** an electric shock
전기 충격을 **받다**

G. **get** frostbite
동상에 **걸리다**

H. **burn** (your)self
화상을 **입다**

I. **drown**
물에 **빠지다**

J. **swallow** poison
독성분을 **삼키다**

K. **overdose** on drugs
약을 **과다 복용하다**

L. **choke**
질식하다

M. **bleed**
출혈하다

N. **can't breathe**
숨을 **못쉬다**

O. **fall**
낙상하다

P. **break** a bone
뼈가 **부러지다**

Grammar Point: past tense

For past tense add –ed:
burned, drowned, swallowed,
overdosed, choked

These verbs are different (irregular):

be – was, were	bleed – bled	fall – fell
have – had	can't – couldn't	
get – got	break – broke	

First Aid 응급 치료

1. first aid kit
응급 치료 상자

2. first aid manual
응급 치료 지침서

3. medical emergency bracelet
응급환자 식별 팔찌

Inside the Kit 상자 내용물

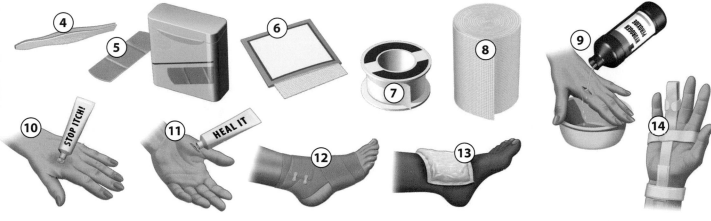

4. tweezers
핀셋

5. adhesive bandage
반창고

6. sterile pad
무균 패드

7. sterile tape
무균 테이프

8. gauze
가제

9. hydrogen peroxide
과산화수소

10. antihistamine cream
항히스타민 크림

11. antibacterial ointment
항생연고제

12. elastic bandage
탄력 붕대

13. ice pack
얼음 찜질팩

14. splint
부목

First Aid Procedures 응급치료 절차

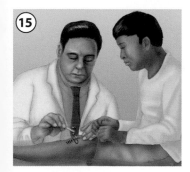
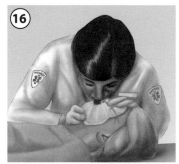
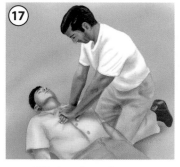
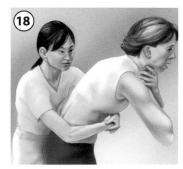

15. stitches
봉합

16. rescue breathing
응급 호흡법

17. CPR (cardiopulmonary resuscitation)
CPR (심폐기능 소생법)

18. Heimlich maneuver
하임리크 처치법

Pair practice. Make new conversations.

A: *What do we need in the first aid kit?*
B: *We need <u>tweezers</u> and <u>gauze</u>.*
A: *I think we need <u>sterile tape</u>, too.*

Think about it. Discuss.

1. What are the three most important first aid items? Why?
2. Which first aid procedures should everyone know? Why?
3. What are some good places to keep a first aid kit?

Medical Care 진료

In the Waiting Room 대기실에서

HEALTH FIRST

Name: Andre Zolmar
Group Number: 98765
Membership Number: 60756789

Health Form

Name: *Andre Zolmar*
Date of birth: *July 8, 1973*
Current symptoms: *stomachache*

Health History:

Childhood Diseases:
☑ chicken pox
☑ diphtheria
☑ rubella
☑ measles
☐ mumps
☐ other

Description of
symptoms:

1. appointment
   약속
2. receptionist
   접수원
3. health insurance card
   의료 보험 카드
4. health history form
   병력 기록 양식

In the Examining Room 검사실에서

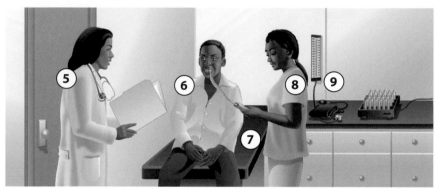

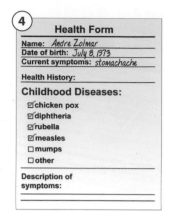

5. doctor
   의사
6. patient
   환자
7. examination table
   진료대
8. nurse
   간호사
9. blood pressure gauge
   혈압계
10. stethoscope
    청진기
11. thermometer
    체온계
12. syringe
    주사

Medical Procedures 진료 절차

A. **check**…blood pressure
   혈압을 **재다**

B. **take**…temperature
   체온을 **재다**

C. **listen** to…heart
   심장 박동을 **듣다**

D. **examine**…eyes
   눈을 **검사하다**

E. **examine**…throat
   목을 **검사하다**

F. **draw**…blood
   피를 **뽑다**

Grammar Point: future tense with *will* + verb

To show a future action, use *will* + verb.
The subject pronoun contraction of *will* is *-'ll*.
She *will draw* your blood. = She*'ll draw* your blood.

Role play. Talk to a medical receptionist.

A: *Will the nurse* <u>examine my eyes</u>?
B: *No, but she'll* <u>draw your blood</u>.
A: *What will the doctor do?*

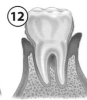
Dentistry 치과

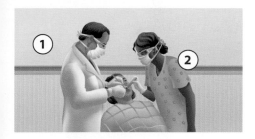

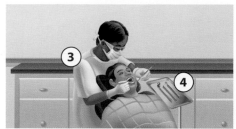

1. dentist
치과의사

2. dental assistant
치과 보조원

3. dental hygienist
구강 위생사

4. dental instruments
치과 장비

Orthodontics 교정과

 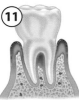

5. orthodontist
교정치과의

6. braces
교정기

Dental Problems 치과 질환

7. cavity / decay
충치

8. filling
충전재

9. crown
인공 치관

10. dentures
틀니

11. gum disease
잇몸질환

12. plaque
치석

An Office Visit 진료실에서

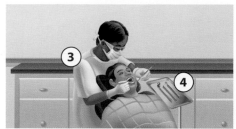

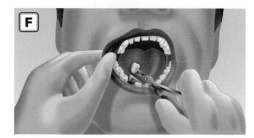

A. clean…teeth
치아를 **닦다**

B. take x-rays
x선 촬영을 **하다**

C. numb the mouth
구강을 **마취하다**

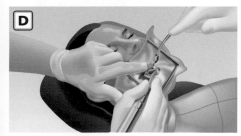

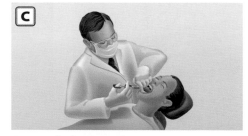

D. drill a tooth
이를 **드릴하다**

E. fill a cavity
충치를 **메우다**

F. pull a tooth
이를 **뽑다**

Ask your classmates. Share the answers.

1. Do you know someone with braces? Who?
2. Do dentists make you nervous? Why or why not?
3. How often do you go to the dentist?

Role play. Talk to a dentist.

A: *I think I have a cavity.*
B: *Let me take a look.*
A: *Will I need a filling?*

Medical Specialists 전문의

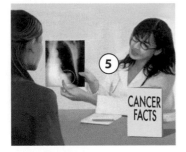

1. internist
내과 의사

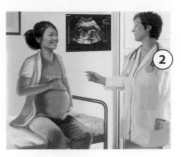

2. obstetrician
산과 의사

3. cardiologist
심장 전문의

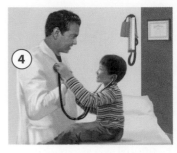

4. pediatrician
소아과 의사

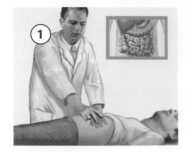

5. oncologist
종양학 전문의

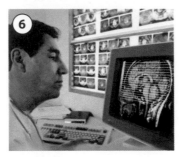

6. radiologist
방사선과 의사

7. ophthalmologist
안과 의사

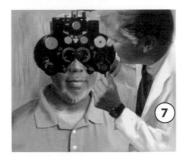

8. psychiatrist
정신과 의사

Nursing Staff 간호사

9. surgical nurse
수술실 간호원

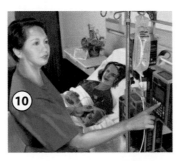

10. registered nurse (RN)
공인 간호사

11. licensed practical nurse (LPN)
간호 조무사

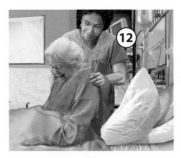

12. certified nursing assistant (CNA)
유자격 간호 보조원

Hospital Staff 병원 직원

13. administrator
행정 직원

14. admissions clerk
입원과 직원

15. dietician
영양사

16. orderly
보조원

More vocabulary

Gynecologists examine and treat women.
Nurse practitioners can give medical exams.
Nurse midwives deliver babies.

Chiropractors move the spine to improve health.
Orthopedists treat bone and joint problems.

A Hospital Room 병실

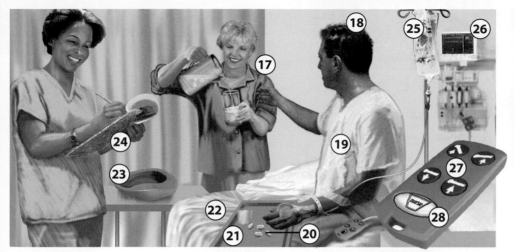

Lab 검사실

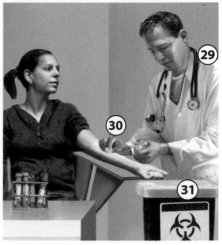

17. volunteer 자원 봉사자	**21.** bed table 침대 옆 작은 탁자	**25.** IV (intravenous drip) 정맥 주사
18. patient 환자	**22.** hospital bed 병원 침대	**26.** vital signs monitor 생명 징후 모니터
19. hospital gown 환자복	**23.** bed pan 실내용 변기	**27.** bed control 침대 조절기
20. medication 약	**24.** medical chart 병원 차트	**28.** call button 호출 단추

29. phlebotomist
채혈 전문의

30. blood work / blood test
혈액 검사

31. medical waste disposal
의료 폐기물 처리기

Emergency Room Entrance
응급실 입구

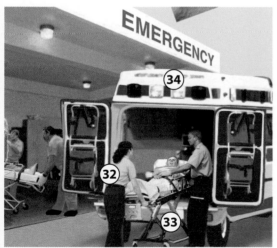

Operating Room
수술실

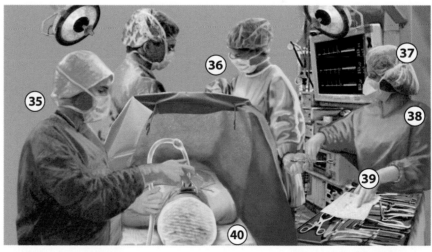

32. emergency medical technician (EMT)
응급 의료 기술자

33. stretcher / gurney
들것 / 바퀴 달린 들것

34. ambulance
구급차

35. anesthesiologist 마취 전문의	**37.** surgical cap 수술용 캡	**39.** surgical gloves 수술용 장갑
36. surgeon 외과 의사	**38.** surgical gown 의사의 수술복	**40.** operating table 수술대

Dictate to your partner. Take turns.

A: *Write this sentence. She's a volunteer.*
B: *She's a what?*
A: *Volunteer. That's v-o-l-u-n-t-e-e-r.*

Role play. Ask about a doctor.

A: *I need to find a good surgeon.*
B: *Dr. Jones is a great surgeon. You should call him.*
A: *I will! Please give me his number.*

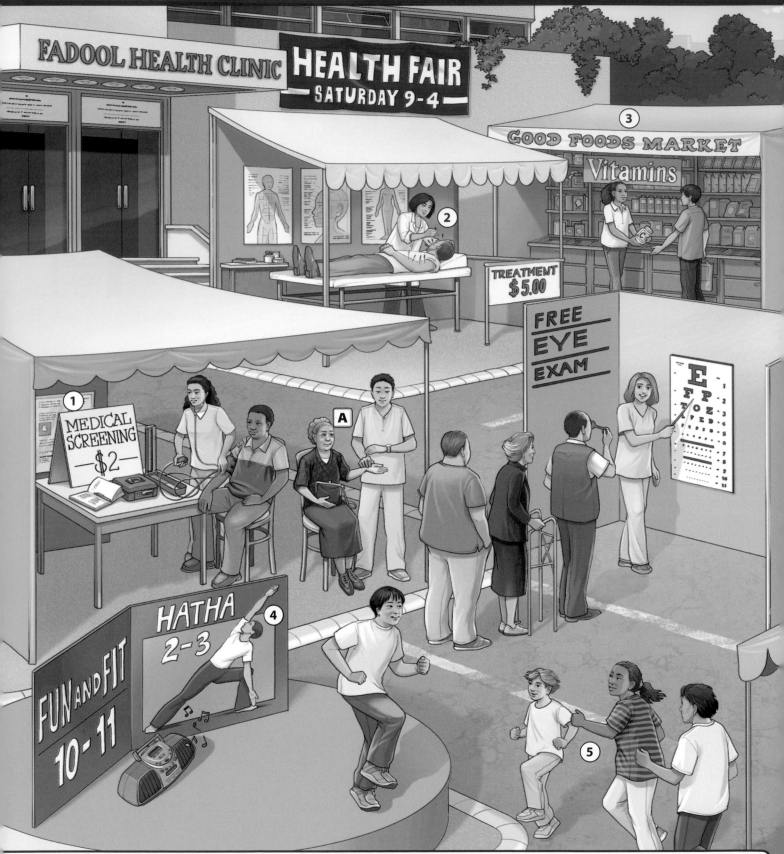

1. low-cost exam
   저가 검사

2. acupuncture
   침

3. booth
   부스

4. yoga
   요가

5. aerobic exercise
   에어로빅

6. demonstration
   시연

7. sugar-free
   무설탕

8. nutrition label
   영양 성분 표시 라벨

A. **check** ... pulse
   맥박을 **검사하다**

B. **give** a lecture
   강의를 **하다**

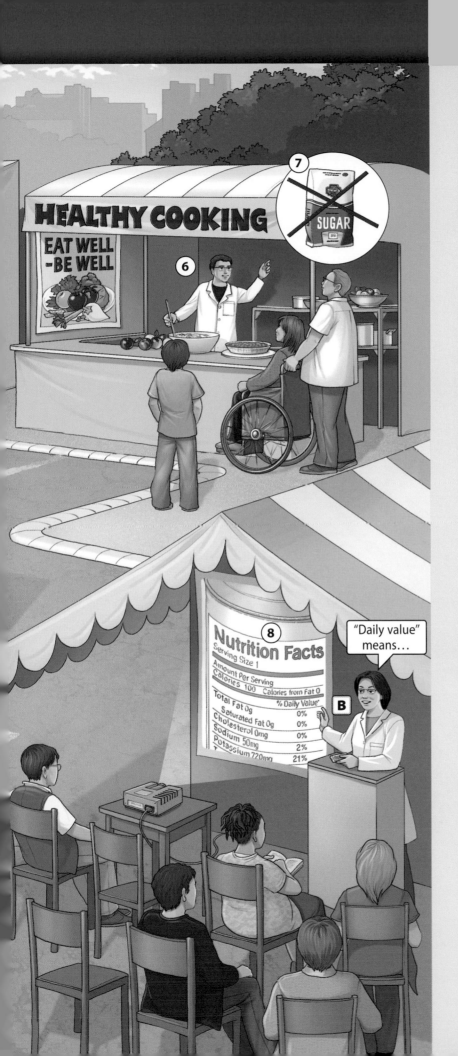

Look at the picture.
What do you see?

Answer the questions.

1. How many different booths are there at the health fair?

2. What kinds of exams and treatments can you get at the fair?

3. What kinds of lectures and demonstrations are there?

4. How much is an acupuncture treatment? a medical screening?

📖 **Read the story.**

A Health Fair

Once a month the Fadool Health Clinic has a health fair. You can get a <u>low-cost</u> medical <u>exam</u> at one <u>booth</u>. The nurses check your blood pressure and <u>check</u> your <u>pulse</u>. At another booth you can get a free eye exam. And an <u>acupuncture</u> treatment is only $5.00.

You can learn a lot at the fair. This month a doctor <u>is giving a lecture</u> on <u>nutrition labels</u>. There is also a <u>demonstration</u> on <u>sugar-free</u> cooking. You can learn to do <u>aerobic exercise</u> and <u>yoga</u>, too.

Do you want to get healthy and stay healthy? Then come to the Fadool Clinic Health Fair!

Think about it.

1. Which booths at this fair look interesting to you? Why?

2. Do you read nutrition labels? Why or why not?

1. parking garage
   주차장 (옥내)
2. office building
   사무실 빌딩
3. hotel
   호텔
4. Department of
   Motor Vehicles
   운전 면허국
5. bank
   은행
6. police station
   경찰서
7. bus station
   버스 정류장
8. city hall
   시청

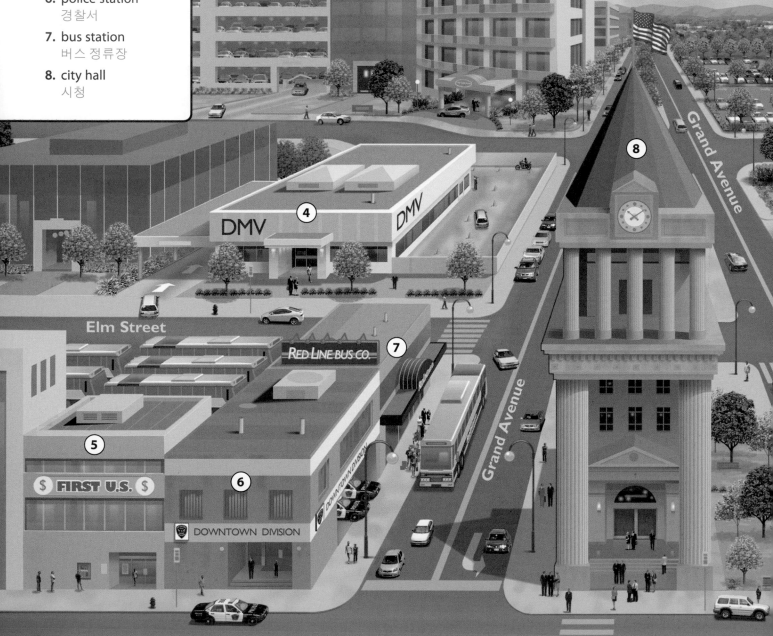

THE SHELTON

DMV   DMV

Elm Street

RED LINE BUS CO.

$ FIRST U.S. $

DOWNTOWN DIVISION

Grand Avenue

Grand Avenue

Listen and point. Take turns.

A: *Point to the bank.*
B: *Point to the hotel.*
A: *Point to the restaurant.*

Dictate to your partner. Take turns.

A: *Write bank.*
B: *Is that spelled b-a-n-k?*
A: *Yes, that's right.*

124

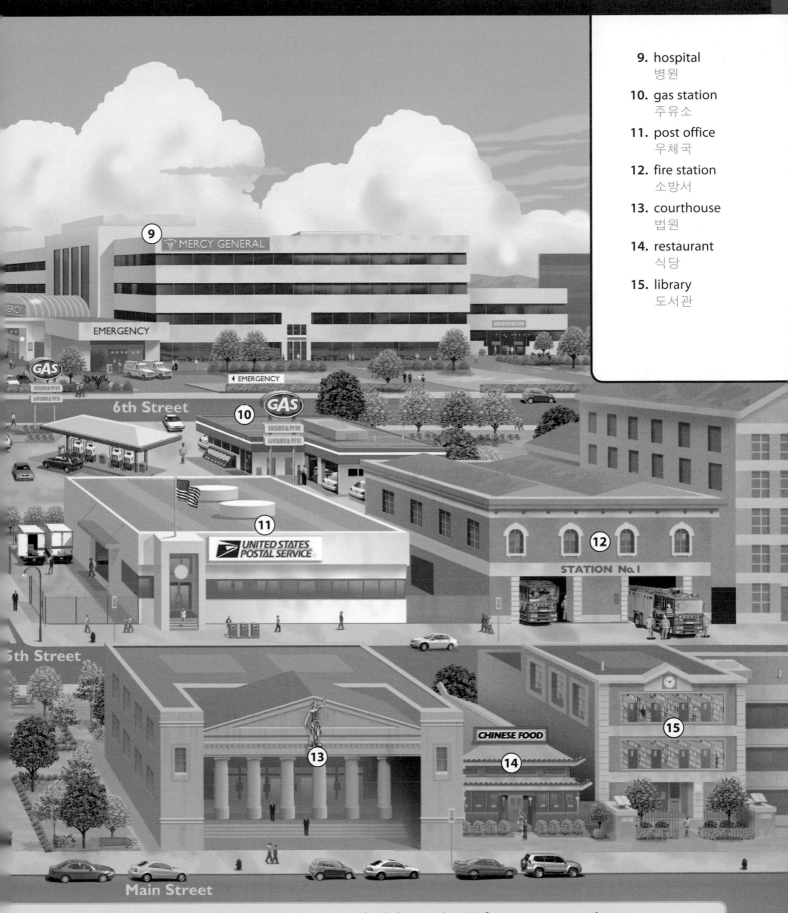

9. hospital
병원

10. gas station
주유소

11. post office
우체국

12. fire station
소방서

13. courthouse
법원

14. restaurant
식당

15. library
도서관

Grammar Point: *in* and *at* with locations

Use ***in*** when you are inside the building. *I am **in**
(inside) the bank.* Use ***at*** to describe your general
location. *I am **at** the bank.*

Pair practice. Make new conversations.

A: *I'm in the <u>bank</u>. Where are you?*
B: *I'm at the <u>bank</u>, too, but I'm outside.*
A: *OK. I'll meet you there.*

125

1. stadium
경기장

2. construction site
공사 현장

3. factory
공장

4. car dealership
자동차 딜러

5. mosque
회교사원

6. movie theater
극장

7. shopping mall
쇼핑 센터

8. furniture store
가구점

9. school
학교

10. gym
체육관

11. coffee shop
커피 숍

12. motel
모텔

Ways to state your destination using *to* and *to the*

Use ***to*** for schools, churches, and synagogues.
*I'm going **to** <u>school</u>.*
Use ***to the*** for all other locations. *I have to go **to the** <u>bakery</u>.*

Pair practice. Make new conversations.

A: *Where are you going today?*
B: *I'm going to <u>school</u>. How about you?*
A: *I have to go to the <u>bakery</u>.*

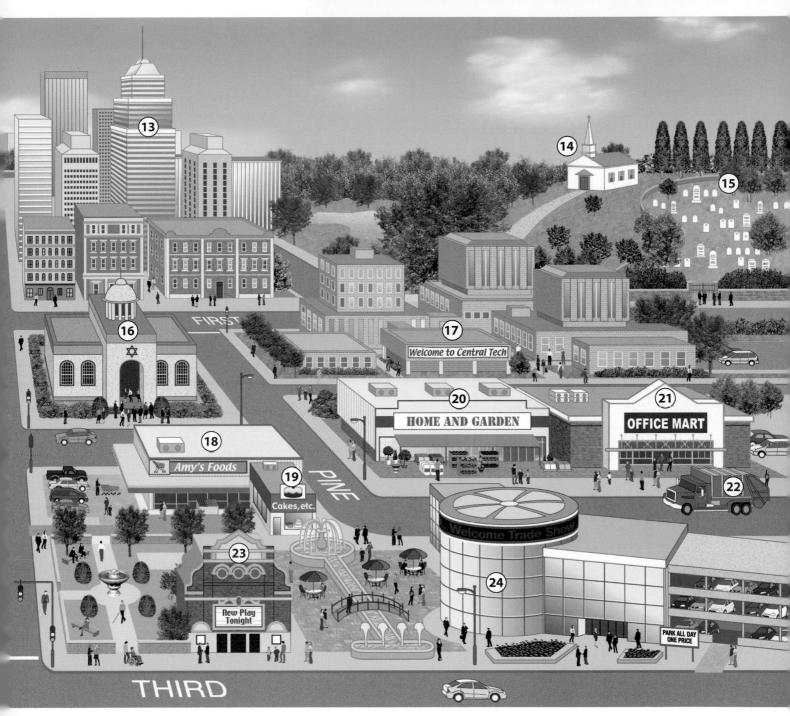

FIRST

PINE

Welcome to Central Tech

HOME AND GARDEN

OFFICE MART

Amy's Foods

Cakes, etc.

Welcome Trade Show

New Play Tonight

PARK ALL DAY ONE PRICE

THIRD

13. skyscraper / high-rise
고층 건물

14. church
교회

15. cemetery
묘지

16. synagogue
유대 교회

17. community college
지역 대학

18. supermarket
수퍼마켓

19. bakery
제과점

20. home improvement store
건축 자재 판매점

21. office supply store
사무실 용품 판매점

22. garbage truck
쓰레기차

23. theater
극장

24. convention center
컨벤션 센터

Ways to give locations

The mall is on 2nd Street.
The mall is on the corner of 2nd and Elm.
The mall is next to the movie theater.

Ask your classmates. Share the answers.

1. Where's your favorite coffee shop?
2. Where's your favorite supermarket?
3. Where's your favorite movie theater?

127

1. **laundromat**
   빨래방

2. **dry cleaners**
   세탁소

3. **convenience store**
   편의점

4. **pharmacy**
   약국

5. **parking space**
   주차 공간

6. **handicapped parking**
   장애인 주차장

7. **corner**
   모퉁이

8. **traffic light**
   신호등

9. **bus**
   버스

10. **fast food restaurant**
    패스트 푸드 식당

11. **drive-thru window**
    차에 탄 채 주문하고 음식을
    받아가는 (식의) 식당

12. **newsstand**
    신문 가판대

13. **mailbox**
    우체통

14. **pedestrian**
    보행자

15. **crosswalk**
    횡단보도

A. **cross** the street
   길을 **건너다**

B. **wait for** the light
   신호등을 **기다리다**

C. **jaywalk**
   무단 횡단하다

Pair practice. Make new conversations.

A: *I have a lot of errands to do today.*
B: *Me, too. First, I'm going to the laundromat.*
A: *I'll see you there after I stop at the copy center.*

Think about it. Discuss.

1. Which businesses are good to have in a neighborhood? Why?
2. Would you like to own a small business? If yes, what kind? If no, why not?

16. bus stop 버스 정류장	**22. bike** 자전거	**28. cart** 카트
17. donut shop 도넛 가게	**23. pay phone** 공중 전화	**29. street vendor** 행상인
18. copy center 복사 센터	**24. sidewalk** 보도	**30. childcare center** 보육 시설
19. barbershop 이발소	**25. parking meter** 주차 미터	**D. ride a bike** 자전거를 **타다**
20. video store 비디오 가게	**26. street sign** 도로 표지판	**E. park the car** 자동차를 **주차하다**
21. curb 연석	**27. fire hydrant** 소화전	**F. walk a dog** 강아지를 **산책시키다**

More vocabulary

neighborhood: the area close to your home
do errands: to make a short trip from your home to buy or pick up things

Ask your classmates. Share the answers.

1. What errands do you do every week?
2. What stores do you go to in your neighborhood?
3. What things can you buy from a street vendor?

1. music store
   음반 판매점

2. jewelry store
   보석상

3. nail salon
   네일 살롱

4. bookstore
   서점

5. toy store
   장난감 가게

6. pet store
   애완동물 가게

7. card store
   카드 가게

8. florist
   꽃집

9. optician
   안경점

10. shoe store
    신발 가게

11. play area
    놀이공간

12. guest services
    고객 서비스 센터

More vocabulary

beauty shop: hair salon

men's store: men's clothing store

gift shop: a store that sells t-shirts, mugs, and other small gifts

Pair practice. Make new conversations.

A: *Where is the florist?*

B: *It's on the first floor, next to the optician.*

13. department store
백화점

14. travel agency
여행사

15. food court
식당 구역

16. ice cream shop
아이스크림 가게

17. candy store
캔디 가게

18. hair salon
미장원

19. maternity store
임부복 상점

20. electronics store
전자제품 가게

21. elevator
엘리베이터

22. cell phone kiosk
휴대 전화 판매소

23. escalator
에스컬레이터

24. directory
안내판

Ways to talk about plans

Let's go to the <u>card store</u>.
I have to go to the <u>card store</u>.
I want to go to the <u>card store</u>.

Role play. Talk to a friend at the mall.

A: *Let's go to the <u>card store</u>. I need to buy <u>a card</u> for <u>Maggie's birthday</u>.*
B: *OK, but can we go to the <u>shoe store</u> next?*

131

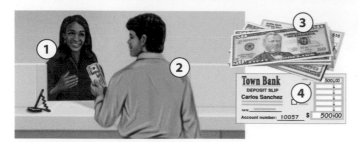
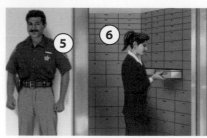

1. teller 금전 출납 계원	3. deposit 입금	5. security guard 경비원	7. safety deposit box 귀중품 보관함
2. customer 손님	4. deposit slip 입금 용지	6. vault 금고	8. valuables 귀중품

Opening an Account 계좌 열기

9. account manager 계좌 담당 매니저	12. check book 수표책	15. ATM card 현금 자동 출납기 카드
10. passbook 통장	13. check 수표	16. bank statement 은행 명세서
11. savings account number 예금 계좌번호	14. checking account number 당좌 계좌번호	17. balance 잔고

A. **Cash** a check. 수표를 **현금화하다**.	B. **Make** a deposit. **입금하다**.	C. **Bank** online. 온라인으로 **은행 업무를 보다**.

The ATM (Automated Teller Machine) ATM (자동 현금 인출기)

D. **Insert** your ATM card. ATM 카드를 **넣다**.	E. **Enter** your PIN.* PIN 번호를 **입력하다**.	F. **Withdraw** cash. 현금을 **인출하다**.	G. **Remove** your card. 카드를 **빼다**.

*PIN = personal identification number

A. get a library card
도서관 카드를 **수령하다**

B. look for a book
책을 **찾아보다**

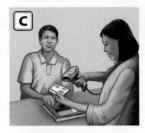

C. check out a book
책을 **빌리다**

D. return a book
책을 **반납하다**

E. pay a late fine
벌금을 **내다**

1. library clerk
도서관 서기

2. circulation desk
대출 카운터

3. library patron
도서관 이용자

4. periodicals
정기 간행물

5. magazine
잡지

6. newspaper
신문

7. headline
헤드라인

8. atlas
지도책

9. reference librarian
참고도서 사서

10. self-checkout
자동 대출/반납 처리기

11. online catalog
온라인 카탈로그

12. picture book
그림책

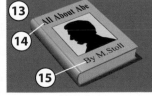

13. biography
전기물

14. title
제목

15. author
저자

16. novel
소설

17. audiobook
오디오북

18. videocassette
비디오 카세트

19. DVD
DVD

1. Priority Mail®
빠른 우편

2. Express Mail®
특급 우편

3. media mail
미디어 우편

4. Certified Mail™
등기 우편

5. airmail
국제 우편

6. ground post / parcel post
육상 우편 / 소포 우편

13. letter
편지

14. envelope
봉투

15. greeting card
카드

16. post card
우편 엽서

17. package
소포

18. book of stamps
우표 1권

19. postal forms
우편물 기입 양식

20. letter carrier
우체부

21. return address
반송 주소

22. mailing address
우편 주소

23. stamp
우표

24. postmark
우체국 소인

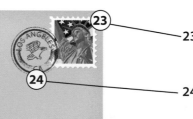

Sonya Enriquez
258 Quentin Avenue
Los Angeles, CA 90068-141

Cindy Lin
807 Glenn Drive
Charlotte, NC 28201

Ways to talk about sending mail

This letter has to <u>get there tomorrow</u>. (Express Mail®)
This letter has to <u>arrive in two days</u>. (Priority Mail®)
This letter can go in <u>regular mail</u>. (First Class)

Pair practice. Make new conversations.

A: *Hi. <u>This letter has to get there tomorrow</u>.*
B: *You can send it by <u>Express Mail</u>®.*
A: *OK. I need <u>a book of stamps</u>, too.*

7. postal clerk
우체국 직원

8. scale
저울

9. post office box (PO box)
사서함

10. automated postal center (APC)
자동 우편 센터

11. stamp machine
우표 판매기

12. mailbox
우체통

Sending a Card 카드 보내기

A. Write a note in a card.
카드에 글을 **쓴다**.

B. Address the envelope.
봉투에 주소를 **쓴다**.

C. Put on a stamp.
우표를 **붙인다**.

D. Mail the card.
카드를 **보낸다**.

E. Deliver the card.
카드를 **배달한다**.

F. Receive the card.
카드를 **받는다**.

G. Read the card.
카드를 **읽는다**.

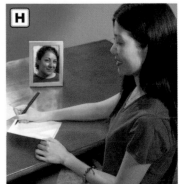

H. Write back.
답장을 **쓴다**.

More vocabulary

overnight / next day mail: Express Mail®
postage: the cost to send mail
junk mail: mail you don't want

Think about it. Discuss.

1. What kind of mail do you send overnight?
2. Do you want to be a letter carrier? Why or why not?
3. Do you get junk mail? What do you do with it?

135

1. **DMV handbook**
   DMV 핸드북

2. **testing area**
   시험 장소

3. **DMV clerk**
   DMV 직원

4. **photo**
   사진

5. **fingerprint**
   지문

6. **vision exam**
   시력 검사

7. **window**
   창구

8. **proof of insurance**
   보험 가입 확인 증서

9. **driver's license**
   운전 면허증

10. **expiration date**
    유효 기한

11. **driver's license number**
    운전 면허 번호

12. **license plate**
    번호판

13. **registration sticker / tag**
    등록 스티커 / 표

More vocabulary

expire: a license is no good, or **expires**, after the expiration date
renew a license: to apply to keep a license before it expires
vanity plate: a more expensive, personal license plate

Ask your classmates. Share the answers.

1. How far is the DMV from your home?
2. Do you have a driver's license? If yes, when does it expire? If not, do you want one?

Getting Your First License 처음 면허 따기

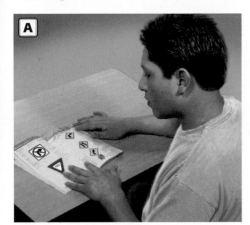

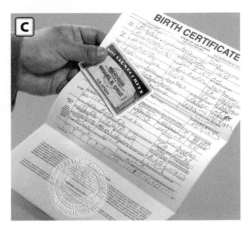

A. Study the handbook.
핸드북을 **공부한다**.

B. Take a driver education course.*
운전자 교육 코스를 **듣는다**.

C. Show your identification.
신분증을 **제시한다**.

D. Pay the application fee.
신청료를 **지불한다**.

E. Take a written test.
필기 시험을 **본다**.

F. Get a learner's permit.
임시 연습 허가증을 **받는다**.

G. Take a driver's training course.*
운전자 훈련 코스를 **듣는다**.

H. Pass a driving test.
주행 시험을 **통과한다**.

I. Get your license.
면허증을 **발급받는다**.

*Note: This is not required for drivers 18 and older.

Ways to request more information

What do I do next?
What's the next step?
Where do I go from here?

Role play. Talk to a DMV clerk.

A: *I want to apply for a driver's license.*
B: *Did you study the handbook?*
A: *Yes, I did. What do I do next?*

Government and Military Service 정부 및 군 복무

Federal Government 연방 정부

Legislative Branch
입법 부서

1. U.S. Capitol
미국회의사당

2. Congress
의회

3. House of Representatives
하원

4. congressperson
하원 의원

5. Senate
상원

6. senator
상원 의원

Executive Branch
행정 부서

7. White House
백악관

8. president
대통령

9. vice president
부통령

10. Cabinet
내각

Judicial Branch
사법부서

11. Supreme Court
대법원

12. justices
대법관

13. chief justice
대법원장

The Military 군

14. Army
육군

15. Navy
해군

16. Air Force
공군

17. Marines
해병

18. Coast Guard
해안 경비대

19. National Guard
방위군

State Government 주 정부

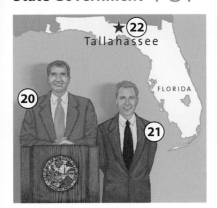

City Government 시 정부

20. governor
주지사

21. lieutenant governor
부지사

22. state capital
주도

23. Legislature
주의회

24. assemblyperson
의원

25. state senator
주 상원의원

26. mayor
시장

27. city council
시 의회

28. councilperson
시의원

An Election 선거

A. run for office
선거에 **출마하다**

29. political campaign
정치 캠페인

B. debate
토론하다

30. opponent
상대방

C. get elected
당선되다

31. election results
선거 결과

D. serve
재직하다

32. elected official
당선된 공무원

More vocabulary

term: the period of time an elected official serves
political party: a group of people with the same political goals

Think about it. Discuss.

1. Should everyone have to serve in the military? Why or why not?
2. Would you prefer to run for city council or mayor? Why?

Responsibilities 의무

A. vote
투표하다

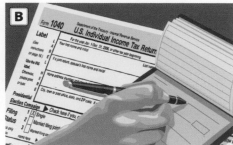

B. pay taxes
세금을 **납부하다**

C. obey the law
법을 **준수하다**

D. register with Selective Service*
선발 징병제에 **등록하다**

E. serve on a jury
배심원 임무 **수행하다**

F. be informed
소식에 정통하다

Citizenship Requirements 시민권 요건

G. be 18 or older
18세 이상일 **것**

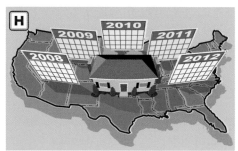

H. live in the U.S. for 5 years
미국에서 5년 동안 **거주**

I. take a citizenship test
시민권 시험 **통과**

Rights 권리

1. peaceful assembly
평화적인 집회

2. free speech
표현의 자유

3. freedom of religion
종교의 자유

4. freedom of the press
언론의 자유

5. fair trial
공정한 재판의 권리

*Note: All males 18 to 26 who live in the U.S. are required to register with Selective Service.

A. **arrest** a suspect
용의자를 **체포하다**

1. police officer
경찰관

2. handcuffs
수갑

B. **hire** a lawyer / **hire** an attorney
변호사를 **고용하다**

3. guard
경비원

4. defense attorney
피고측 변호사

Bail is set at $20,000.

C. **appear** in court
법정에 **출두하다**

5. defendant
피고

6. judge
재판관

D. **stand** trial
재판을 **받다**

7. courtroom
법정

8. jury
배심원

9. evidence
증거

10. prosecuting attorney
검사

11. witness
증인

12. court reporter
법원 속기사

13. bailiff
법정 간수

Guilty.

E. **convict** the defendant
피고에게 **유죄를 선고하다**

14. verdict*
평결

7 years

F. **sentence** the defendant
피고에게 **판결을 내리다**

G. **go** to jail / **go** to prison
감옥에 들어 **가다**

15. convict / prisoner
죄인 / 죄수

H. **be** released
석방**되다**

*Note: There are two possible verdicts, "guilty" and "not guilty."

Look at the pictures.
Describe what happened.

A: *The police officer arrested a suspect.*
B: *He put handcuffs on him.*

Think about it. Discuss.

1. Would you want to serve on a jury? Why or why not?
2. Look at the crimes on page 142. What sentence would you give for each crime? Why?

1. **vandalism**
   파괴 행위
2. **burglary**
   강도

3. **assault**
   폭행
4. **gang violence**
   폭력단 폭력

5. **drunk driving**
   음주 운전
6. **illegal drugs**
   불법 마약

7. **arson**
   방화
8. **shoplifting**
   가게 좀도둑질

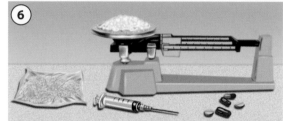

9. **identity theft**
   신분 도용
10. **victim**
    피해자

11. **mugging**
    폭력 강도
12. **murder**
    살인
13. **gun**
    총

More vocabulary

steal: to take money or things from someone illegally
commit a crime: to do something illegal
criminal: someone who does something illegal

Think about it. Discuss.

1. Is there too much crime on TV or in the movies? Explain.
2. How can communities help stop crime?

142

A. Walk with a friend.
친구와 같이 **걷는다**.

B. Stay on well-lit streets.
환한 길로 **간다**.

C. Conceal your PIN number.
PIN 번호를 **노출시키지 않는다**.

D. Protect your purse or wallet.
지갑을 **지킨다**.

E. Lock your doors.
문을 **잠근다**.

F. Don't **open** your door to strangers.
모르는 사람에게 문을 **열어** 주지 않는다.

G. Don't **drink** and **drive**.
음주 운전을 하지 않는다.

H. Shop on secure websites.
안전한 웹사이트에서 **쇼핑한다**.

I. Be aware of your surroundings.
주위를 **살펴본다**.

J. Report suspicious packages.
수상한 물건은 **신고한다**.

K. Report crimes to the police.
범죄를 보면 경찰에 **신고한다**.

L. Join a Neighborhood Watch.
이웃 감시 프로그램에 **참가한다**.

More vocabulary

sober: not drunk
designated drivers: sober drivers who drive drunk people home safely

Ask your classmates. Share the answers.

1. Do you feel safe in your neighborhood?
2. Look at the pictures. Which of these things do you do?
3. What other things do you do to stay safe?

143

1. lost child
   미아

2. car accident
   자동차 사고

3. airplane crash
   비행기 추락

4. explosion
   폭발

5. earthquake
   지진

6. mudslide
   진흙 사태

7. forest fire
   산불

8. fire
   불

9. firefighter
   소방수

10. fire truck
    소방차

Ways to report an emergency

First, give your name. *My name is <u>Tim Johnson</u>.*
Then, state the emergency and give the address.
There was <u>a car accident</u> at <u>219 Elm Street</u>.

Role play. Call 911.

A: *911 Emergency Operator.*
B: *My name is <u>Lisa Diaz</u>. There is <u>a fire</u> at <u>323 Oak Street</u>.*
Please hurry!

11. drought
가뭄

12. famine
기근

13. blizzard
눈보라

14. hurricane
허리케인

15. tornado
토네이도

16. volcanic eruption
화산 폭발

17. tidal wave / tsunami
해일

18. avalanche
눈사태

19. flood
홍수

20. search and rescue team
수색구조팀

Ask your classmates. Share the answers.

1. Which natural disaster worries you the most?
2. Which natural disaster worries you the least?
3. Which disasters are common in your local area?

Think about it. Discuss.

1. What organizations can help you in an emergency?
2. What are some ways to prepare for natural disasters?
3. Where would you go in an emergency?

Before an Emergency 대비책

A. **Plan** for an emergency.
응급 상황에 대비한 **계획을 세운다**.

1. meeting place
만날 장소

2. out-of-state contact
타주 연락책

3. escape route
탈출 경로

4. gas shut-off valve
가스 잠금 밸브

5. evacuation route
피난 경로

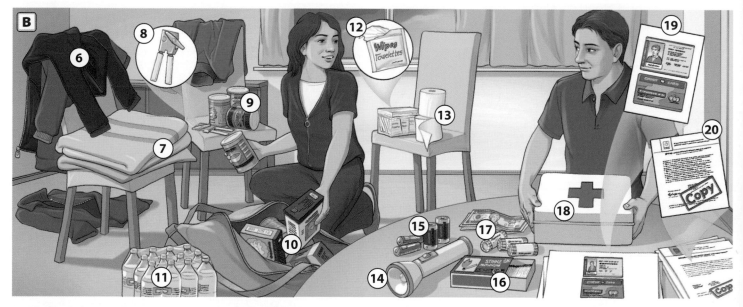

B. **Make** a disaster kit.
재해 대책 키트를 **만든다**.

6. warm clothes
따뜻한 옷

7. blankets
담요

8. can opener
깡통 따개

9. canned food
캔 식품

10. packaged food
포장된 식품

11. bottled water
생수

12. moist towelettes
물티슈

13. toilet paper
화장지

14. flashlight
손전등

15. batteries
건전지

16. matches
성냥

17. cash and coins
현금과 동전

18. first aid kit
응급 치료 상자

19. copies of ID and credit cards
신분증과 신용 카드 사본

20. copies of important papers
주요 서류 사본

Pair practice. Make new conversations.

A: *What do we need for our disaster kit?*
B: *We need blankets and matches.*
A: *I think we also need batteries.*

Ask your classmates. Share the answers.

1. Who would you call first after an emergency?
2. Do you have escape and evacuation routes planned?
3. Are you a calm person in case of an emergency?

During an Emergency 응급 상황 중에

C. Watch the weather.
날씨를 **지켜본다**.

D. Pay attention to warnings.
경고에 주의를 **기울인다**.

E. Remain calm.
침착함을 **유지한다**.

F. Follow directions.
지시를 **따른다**.

G. Help people with disabilities.
장애인을 **도와준다**.

H. Seek shelter.
보호소를 **찾는다**.

I. Stay away from windows.
창문에서 **떨어져 있는다**.

J. Take cover.
몸을 **숨긴다**.

K. Evacuate the area.
해당 지역을 **빠져 나간다**.

After an Emergency 응급 상황 종료 후

L. Call out-of-state contacts.
타주 연락책에 **전화한다**.

M. Clean up debris.
잔해 를 **청소한다**.

N. Inspect utilities.
가정 내 가스, 보일러, 수도 등을 **점검한다**.

Ways to say you're OK

I'm fine.
We're OK here.
Everything's under control.

Ways to say you need help

We need help.
Someone is hurt.
I'm injured. Please get help.

Role play. Prepare for an emergency.

A: *They just issued <u>a hurricane</u> warning.*
B: *OK. We need to stay calm and follow directions.*
A: *What do we need to do first?*

147

1. **graffiti**
   낙서
2. **litter**
   쓰레기
3. **streetlight**
   가로등
4. **hardware store**
   철물점
5. **petition**
   청원서
A. **give** a speech
   연설을 **하다**
B. **applaud**
   박수치다
C. **change**
   변화하다

Look at the pictures. What do you see?

Answer the questions.

1. What were the problems on Main Street?

2. What was the petition for?

3. Why did the city council applaud?

4. How did the people change the street?

📖 Read the story.

Community Cleanup

Marta Lopez has a donut shop on Main Street. One day she looked at her street and was very upset. She saw graffiti on her donut shop and the other stores. Litter was everywhere. All the streetlights were broken. Marta wanted to fix the lights and clean up the street.

Marta started a petition about the streetlights. Five hundred people signed it. Then she gave a speech to the city council. The council members voted to repair the streetlights. Everyone applauded. Marta was happy, but her work wasn't finished.

Next, Marta asked for volunteers to clean up Main Street. The hardware store manager gave the volunteers free paint. Marta gave them free donuts and coffee. The volunteers painted and cleaned. They changed Main Street. Now Main Street is beautiful and Marta is proud.

Think about it.

1. What are some problems in your community? How can people help?

2. Imagine you are Marta. What do you say in your speech to the city council?

1. car
   자동차

2. passenger
   승객

3. taxi
   택시

4. motorcycle
   오토바이

5. street
   거리

6. truck
   트럭

7. train
   기차

8. (air)plane
   비행기

Listen and point. Take turns.

A: *Point to <u>the motorcycle</u>.*
B: *Point to <u>the truck</u>.*
A: *Point to <u>the train</u>.*

Dictate to your partner. Take turns.

A: *Write <u>motorcycle</u>.*
B: *Could you repeat that for me?*
A: *<u>Motorcycle</u>. <u>M-o-t-o-r-c-y-c-l-e</u>.*

9. helicopter
   헬리콥터
10. airport
    공항
11. subway station
    지하철 역
12. subway
    지하철
13. bus stop
    버스 정류장
14. bus
    버스
15. bicycle
    자전거

Ways to talk about using transportation

Use **take** for buses, trains, subways, taxis, planes, and helicopters. Use **drive** for cars and trucks. Use **ride** for bicycles and motorcycles.

Pair practice. Make new conversations.

A: *How do you get to school?*
B: *I take the bus. How about you?*
A: *I ride a bicycle to school.*

151

A Bus Stop 버스 정류장

BUS 10 Northbound		
Main	Elm	Oak
6:00	6:10	6:13
6:30	6:40	6:43
7:00	7:10	7:13
7:30	7:40	7:43

New York City Transit
MTA Transfer
○ Going your way

A Subway Station 지하철 역

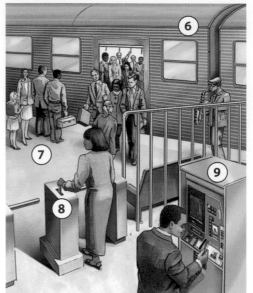

MTA RED LINE
1 FARE
NORTH HOLLYWOOD

MTA MetroCard
◄◄◄ Insert this way/This side facing you

1. bus route
   버스 노선
2. fare
   요금
3. rider
   승객
4. schedule
   일정표
5. transfer
   환승

6. subway car
   지하철 전동차
7. platform
   플랫폼
8. turnstile
   개찰구
9. vending machine
   자동 판매기
10. token
    토큰
11. fare card
    요금 카드

A Train Station 전철역

15.
HART DAVIS/DAMON
From DOVER, NH
To BOSTON NRTH STA,MA
Carrier 2V Train 684 Date 17FEB03
Accm 2V BUSINESS CL
Form of Payment AP XXXX0456791 Ax

16.
Fresno
Los Angeles

17.
Fresno
Los Angeles

Airport Transportation 공항 교통 수단

TAXIS
J&J Hotel
TAXI

1036081
22.00

12. ticket window
    매표소
13. conductor
    차장
14. track
    트랙
15. ticket
    승차권
16. one-way trip
    편도 여행
17. round trip
    왕복 여행

18. taxi stand
    택시 승차장
19. shuttle
    셔틀
20. town car
    타운카
21. taxi driver
    택시 운전사
22. taxi license
    택시 면허
23. meter
    미터기

More vocabulary

hail a taxi: to raise your hand to get a taxi
miss the bus: to get to the bus stop after the bus leaves

Ask your classmates. Share the answers.

1. Is there a subway system in your city?
2. Do you ever take taxis? When?
3. Do you ever take the bus? Where?

A. go under the bridge
다리 **아래로 가다**

B. go over the bridge
다리 **위로 가다**

C. walk up the steps
계단을 **오르다**

D. walk down the steps
계단을 **내려오다**

E. get into the taxi
택시를 **타다**

F. get out of the taxi
택시에서 **내리다**

G. run across the street
길을 **뛰어 건너다**

H. run around the corner
모퉁이를 **돌아 뛰다**

I. get on the highway
고속도로**로 진입하다**

J. get off the highway
고속도로에서 **빠져나오다**

K. drive through the tunnel
차가 터널 **밑을 지나가다**

Grammar Point: *into, out of, on, off*

Use ***get into*** for taxis and cars.
Use ***get on*** for buses, trains, planes, and highways.

Use ***get out of*** for taxis and cars.
Use ***get off*** for buses, trains, planes, and highways.

1. stop
정지

2. do not enter / wrong way
진입 금지

3. one way
일방 통행

4. speed limit
제한 속도

5. U-turn OK
U 턴 허용

6. no outlet / dead end
출구 없음 / 막다른 길

7. right turn only
우회전만 허용

8. no left turn
좌회전 금지

9. yield
양보

10. merge
합류 차선

11. no parking
주차 금지

12. handicapped parking
장애인 주차장

13. pedestrian crossing
횡단보도

15. school crossing
학교 횡단보도

17. U.S. route / highway marker
국도/ 하이웨이 표지판

14. railroad crossing
철도 건널목

16. road work
도로 공사

18. hospital
병원

Pair practice. Make new conversations.

A: *Watch out! The sign says <u>no left turn</u>.*
B: *Sorry, I was looking at the <u>stop</u> sign.*
A: *That's OK. Just be careful!*

Ask your classmates. Share the answers.

1. How many traffic signs are on your street?
2. What's the speed limit on your street?
3. What traffic signs are the same in your native country?

Directions 방향

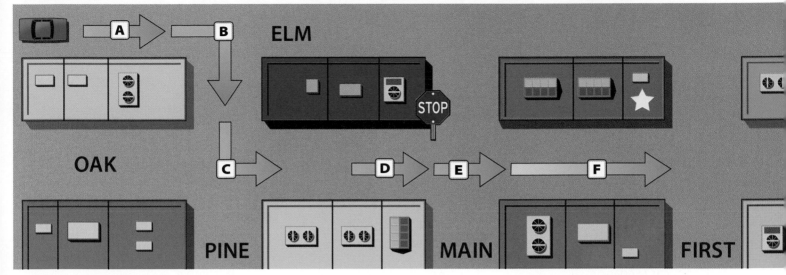

A. Go straight on Elm Street.
Elm St.에서 **직진하다**.

B. Turn right on Pine Street.
Pine St.에서 **우회전하다**.

C. Turn left on Oak Street.
Oak St.에서 **좌회전하다**.

D. Stop at the corner.
모퉁이에서 **정지하다**.

E. Go past Main Street.
Main St.를 **지나다**.

F. Go one block to First Street.
First St.으로 한 블록 **가다**.

Maps 지도

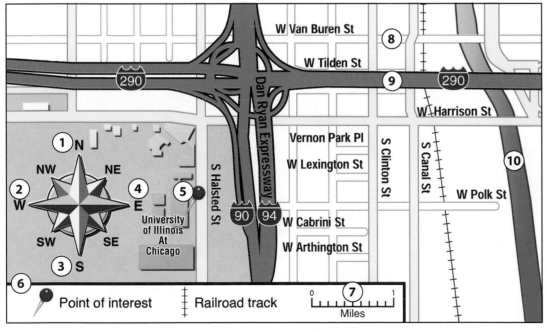

1. north
북

2. west
서

3. south
남

4. east
동

5. symbol
기호

6. key
범례

7. scale
축척

8. street
거리

9. highway
고속도로

10. river
강

11. GPS (global positioning system)
글로벌 위치 확인 시스템

12. Internet map
인터넷 지도

Role play. Ask for directions.

A: *I'm lost. I need to get to <u>Elm and Pine</u>.*
B: *Go <u>straight on Oak</u> and <u>make a right on Pine</u>.*
A: *Thanks so much.*

Ask your classmates. Share the answers.

1. How often do you use Internet maps? GPS? paper maps?
2. What was the last map you used? Why?

155

1. 4-door car / sedan
   4 도어 자동차/세단

2. 2-door car / coupe
   2도어 자동차/쿠페

3. hybrid
   하이브리드

4. sports car
   스포츠 카

5. convertible
   컨버터블

6. station wagon
   스테이션 웨곤

7. SUV (sport–utility vehicle)
   SUV (스포츠 유틸리티 카)

8. minivan
   미니밴

9. camper
   캠핑카

10. RV (recreational vehicle)
    RV

11. limousine / limo
    리무진

12. pickup truck
    픽업 트럭

13. cargo van
    화물 밴

14. tow truck
    견인차

15. tractor trailer /
    semi
    트랙터 트레일러 /
    세미

16. cab
    운전석

17. trailer
    트레일러

18. moving van
    이삿짐 트럭

19. dump truck
    덤프 트럭

20. tank truck
    탱크 트럭

21. school bus
    스쿨 버스

Pair practice. Make new conversations.

A: *I have a new car!*
B: *Did you get a hybrid?*
A: *Yes, but I really wanted a sports car.*

More vocabulary

make: the name of the company that makes the car
model: the style of the car

Buying a Used Car 중고차 사기

'04 Compact.
Only $3,000.

'05 Sedan.
Must sell.
Great deal!

A. Look at car ads.
자동차 광고를 **본다**.

How many miles does it have?

B. Ask the seller about the car.
판매자에게 자동차에 대해 **물어본다**.

It's in good condition.

C. Take the car to a mechanic.
자동차를 정비공에게 **가지고 간다**.

It's $2,500.

I can give you $2,000.

D. Negotiate a price.
가격을 **협상한다**.

E. Get the title from the seller.
판매자로부터 소유권 증서를 **받는다**.

F. Register the car.
자동차를 **등록한다**.

Taking Care of Your Car 자동차 관리

G. Fill the tank with gas.
기름을 **채운다**.

H. Check the oil.
오일을 **점검한다**.

I. Put in coolant.
냉각수를 **넣는다**.

J. Go for a smog check.*
스모그 검사를 받으러 **간다**.

K. Replace the windshield wipers.
앞유리 와이퍼를 **교체한다**.

L. Fill the tires with air.
타이어에 공기를 **넣는다**.

*smog check = emissions test

Ways to request service

Please check the oil.
Could you fill the tank?
Put in coolant, please.

Think about it. Discuss.

1. What's good and bad about a used car?
2. Do you like to negotiate car prices? Why?
3. Do you know any good mechanics? Why are they good?

At the Dealer
자동차 판매점에서

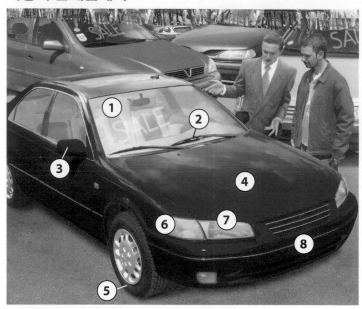

1. windshield 앞유리	5. tire 타이어
2. windshield wipers 앞유리 와이퍼	6. turn signal 방향 지시등
3. sideview mirror 사이드 미러	7. headlight 전조등
4. hood 후드(보닛)	8. bumper 범퍼

At the Mechanic
정비소에서

9. hubcap / wheel cover 휠 커버	13. tail light 후미등
10. gas tank 연료 탱크	14. brake light 제동등
11. trunk 트렁크	15. tail pipe 배기관
12. license plate 번호판	16. muffler 머플러

Under the Hood
보닛 하부

17. fuel injection system 연료분사 장치	19. radiator 라디에이터
18. engine 엔진	20. battery 배터리

Inside the Trunk
트렁크 내부

21. jumper cables 점퍼 케이블	23. spare tire 예비 타이어
22. lug wrench 러그렌치	24. jack 잭

The Dashboard and Instrument Panel
계기판 및 장치 패널

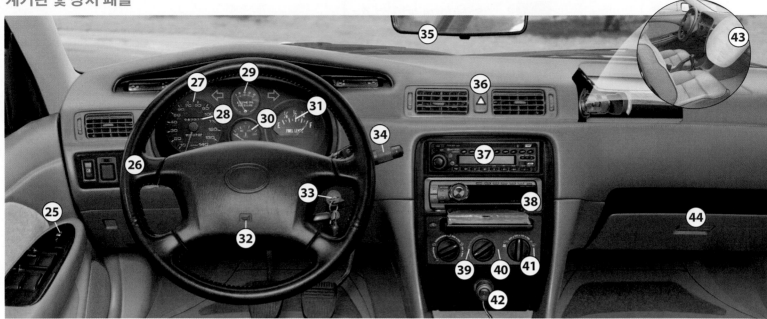

25. door lock 차문 잠금 장치	**30.** temperature gauge 온도 계기	**35.** rearview mirror 백미러	**40.** heater 히터
26. steering wheel 핸들	**31.** gas gauge 연료 계기	**36.** hazard lights 비상등	**41.** defroster 성에 제거 장치
27. speedometer 속도계	**32.** horn 경적	**37.** radio 라디오	**42.** power outlet 콘센트
28. odometer 주행 기록계	**33.** ignition 점화 장치	**38.** CD player CD 플레이어	**43.** air bag 에어백
29. oil gauge 유량계	**34.** turn signal 방향 지시등	**39.** air conditioner 에어컨	**44.** glove compartment 사물함

An Automatic Transmission
자동 변속

A Manual Transmission
수동 변속

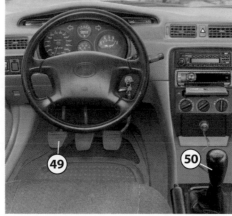

Inside the Car
자동차 내부

45. brake pedal 브레이크 페달	**49.** clutch 클러치	**53.** child safety seat 어린이 안전 시트
46. gas pedal / accelerator 가스 페달 / 액셀러레이터	**50.** stick shift 수동 변속 레버	**54.** backseat 뒷좌석
47. gear shift 기어 변속기	**51.** front seat 앞좌석	
48. hand brake 핸드 브레이크	**52.** seat belt 안전 벨트	

An Airport 공항

In the Airline Terminal 항공사 터미널에서

At the Security Checkpoint 보안 검사 구역에서

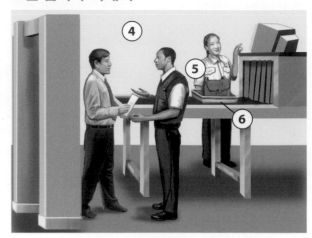

1. **skycap**
   수화물 운반인
2. **check-in kiosk**
   체크인 데스크

3. **ticket agent**
   발권 담당 직원
4. **screening area**
   심사 구역

5. **TSA* agent / security screener**
   TSA 직원 / 보안 검사원
6. **bin**
   용기

Taking a Flight 비행기 타기

A. **Check in** electronically.
컴퓨터로 **체크인한다**.

B. **Check** your bags.
가방을 **검사한다**.

C. **Show** your boarding pass and ID.
탑승권과 신분증을 **제시한다**.

D. **Go through** security.
보안검사를 **통과한다**.

E. **Board** the plane.
비행기에 **탑승한다**.

F. **Find** your seat.
좌석을 **찾는다**.

G. **Stow** your carry-on bag.
기내 휴대물을 보관함에 **넣는다**.

H. **Fasten** your seat belt.
안전 벨트를 **맨다**.

I. **Turn off** your cell phone.
휴대 전화를 **끈다**.

J. **Take off**. / **Leave**.
이륙하다. / **출발하다**.

K. **Land**. / **Arrive**.
착륙하다. / **도착하다**.

L. **Claim** your baggage.
수화물을 **찾는다**.

* Transportation Security Administration

At the Gate 게이트에서

On the Airplane 기내에서

At Customs 세관에서

7. arrival and departure monitors
이착륙 모니터

8. gate
게이트

9. boarding area
탑승 구역

10. cockpit
조종실

11. pilot
조종사

12. flight attendant
승무원

13. overhead compartment
머리 위 짐칸

14. emergency exit
비상구

15. passenger
승객

16. declaration form
신고서

17. customs officer
세관 직원

18. luggage / bag
수하물 / 가방

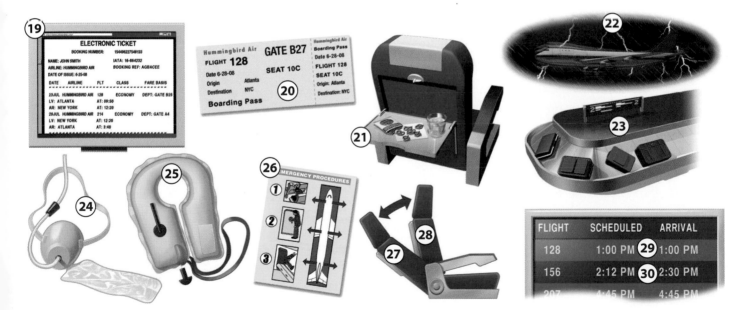

19. e-ticket
전자 티켓

20. boarding pass
탑승권

21. tray table
트레이 테이블

22. turbulence
난류

23. baggage carousel
수하물 컨베이어

24. oxygen mask
산소 마스크

25. life vest
구명 조끼

26. emergency card
비상구 안내 카드

27. reclined seat
뒤로 젖힌 좌석

28. upright seat
바로 세운 좌석

29. on-time
정시에

30. delayed flight
비행 지연

More vocabulary

departure time: the time the plane takes off
arrival time: the time the plane lands
direct flight: a trip with no stops

Pair practice. Make new conversations.

A: *Excuse me. Where do I check in?*
B: *At the check-in kiosk.*
A: *Thanks.*

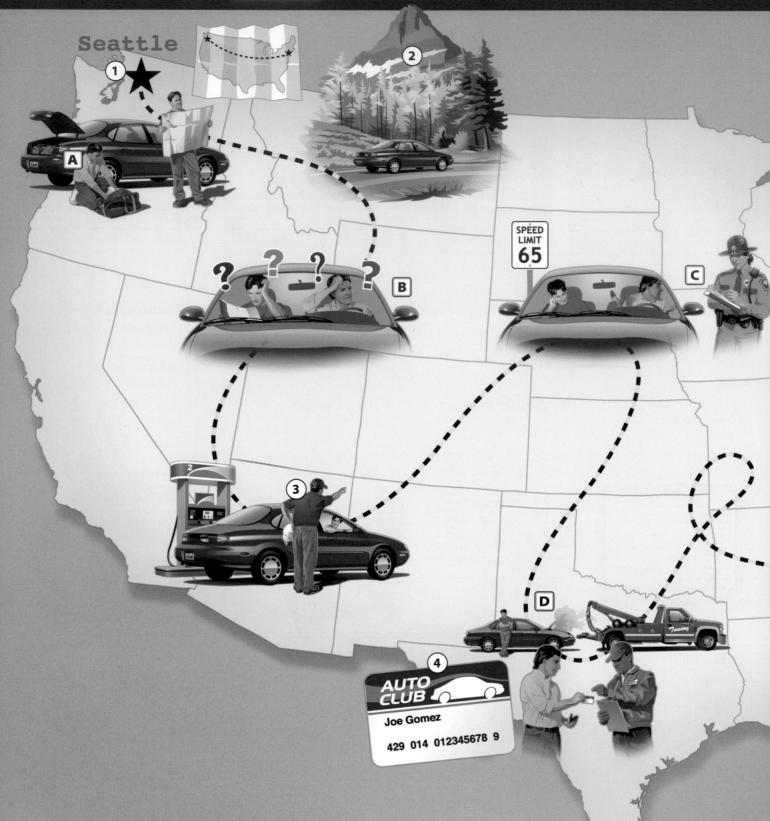

Seattle

SPEED LIMIT 65

AUTO CLUB
Joe Gomez
429 014 012345678 9

1. starting point
   출발점

2. scenery
   경관

3. gas station attendant
   주유소 직원

4. auto club card
   자동차 클럽 카드

5. destination
   도착지

A. **pack**
   짐을 싸다

B. **get** lost
   길을 잃다

C. **get** a speeding ticket
   속도 위반 딱지를 **떼다**

D. **break down**
   고장나다

E. **run out** of gas
   기름이 **떨어지다**

F. **have** a flat tire
   타이어 펑크가 **나다**

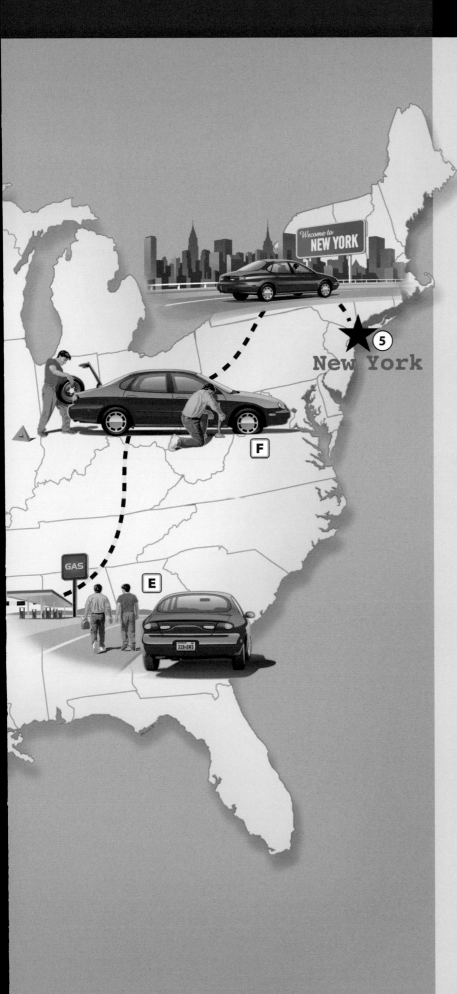

Look at the pictures.
What do you see?

Answer the questions.

1. What are the young men's starting point and destination?

2. What do they see on their trip?

3. What kinds of problems do they have?

Read the story.

A Road Trip

On July 7th Joe and Rob <u>packed</u> their bags for a road trip. Their <u>starting point</u> was Seattle. Their <u>destination</u> was New York City.

The young men saw beautiful <u>scenery</u> on their trip. But there were also problems. They <u>got lost</u>. Then, a <u>gas station attendant</u> gave them bad directions. Next, they <u>got a speeding ticket</u>. Joe was very upset. After that, their car <u>broke down</u>. Joe called a tow truck and used his <u>auto club card</u>.

The end of their trip was difficult, too. They <u>ran out of gas</u> and then they had a <u>flat tire</u>.

After 7,000 miles of problems, Joe and Rob arrived in New York City. They were happy, but tired. Next time, they're going to take the train.

Think about it.

1. What is the best way to travel across the U.S.? by car? by plane? by train? Why?

2. Imagine your car breaks down on the road. Who can you call?
What can you do?

The Workplace 직장

1. **entrance**
   입구
2. **customer**
   손님
3. **office**
   사무실
4. **employer / boss**
   고용주 / 사장
5. **receptionist**
   접수원
6. **safety regulations**
   안전 규정

IRINA'S COMPUTER SERVICE

6 **OSHA**
HAZARDS
SPILLS
CALL 911
SAFETY FIRST

COMPUTER NEWS

Irina Sarkov Owner

Listen and point. Take turns.

A: Point to <u>the front entrance</u>.
B: Point to <u>the receptionist</u>.
A: Point to <u>the time clock</u>.

Dictate to your partner. Take turns.

A: *Can you spell <u>employer</u>?*
B: *I'm not sure. Is it <u>e-m-p-l-o-y-e-r</u>?*
A: *Yes, that's right.*

7. time clock
타임 클록

8. supervisor
감독자

9. employee
직원

10. payroll clerk
급여 담당 직원

11. pay stub
급여 명세서

12. wages
임금

13. deductions
공제

14. paycheck
급여 수표

PLEASE CLOCK IN AND OUT

EMPLOYEES ONLY

9:15

Fix this first.

OK.

10/20

10/23

IRINA'S COMPUTER SERVICE

7000 Main Street
Houston, TX 77031

10/17/11 to 10/23/11

Kate Babic

000-23-4567

Salary — $ 800.00

Deductions
Federal — 88.00
State — 22.40
Social Security — 51.00
Medicare — 12.00
SDI — 7.50

Net — $ 619.10

IRINA'S COMPUTER SERVICE

7000 Main Street
Houston, TX 77031

Check number:
123456789 999999999 123

Pay to the order of _____ Kate Babic _____ $ 619.10

Six hundred nineteen and 10/100 dollars

Town Bank

Irina Jankov

Ways to talk about wages

I **earn** $250 a week.
He **makes** $7 an hour.
I'm **paid** $1,000 a month.

Role play. Talk to an employer.

A: *Is everything correct on your paycheck?*
B: *No, it isn't. I make $250 a week, not $200.*
A: *Let's talk to the payroll clerk. Where is she?*

1. accountant
회계사

2. actor
배우

3. administrative assistant
사무원

4. appliance repair person
가전 제품 수리공

5. architect
건축가

6. artist
예술가

7. assembler
조립공

8. auto mechanic
자동차 기술자

9. babysitter
아기 봐주는 사람

10. baker
제빵사

11. business owner
사업 경영자

12. businessperson
비즈니스맨

13. butcher
푸주한

14. carpenter
목수

15. cashier
계산원

16. childcare worker
탁아소 직원

Ways to ask about someone's job

What's her job?
What does he do?
What kind of work do they do?

Pair practice. Make new conversations.

A: *What kind of work does she do?*
B: *She's an accountant. What do they do?*
A: *They're actors.*

17. commercial fisher
어부

18. computer software engineer
컴퓨터 소프트웨어 엔지니어

19. computer technician
컴퓨터 기술자

We have that shirt in red.

20. customer service representative
고객 서비스 담당 직원

21. delivery person
배달원

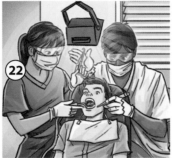

22. dental assistant
치과 보조원

23. dockworker
부두 근로자

24. electronics repair person
전자제품 수리공

25. engineer
엔지니어

26. firefighter
소방수

27. florist
플로리스트

28. gardener
정원사

29. garment worker
재봉사

30. graphic designer
그래픽 디자이너

31. hairdresser / hair stylist
미용사 / 헤어 디자이너

32. home health care aide
재택 간병인

Ways to talk about jobs and occupations

*Sue's a <u>garment worker</u>. She works **in** a factory.*
*Tom's <u>an engineer</u>. He works **for** <u>a large company</u>.*
*Ann's a <u>dental assistant</u>. She works **with** <u>a dentist</u>.*

Role play. Talk about a friend's new job.

A: *Does your friend like <u>his</u> new job?*
B: *Yes, <u>he</u> does. <u>He's a graphic designer</u>.*
A: *Does <u>he</u> work <u>in an office</u>?*

33. homemaker
주부

34. housekeeper
가정부

你好 He says, "Hi."

35. interpreter / translator
통역사 / 번역사

36. lawyer
변호사

37. machine operator
기계 작동자

38. manicurist
매니큐어 미용사

39. medical records technician
병원 기록 관리직

Carlos

40. messenger / courier
택배원

41. model
모델

42. mover
이사짐 배달원

43. musician
음악가

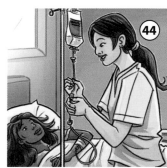

44. nurse
간호사

45. occupational therapist
직업 치료사

46. (house) painter
(주택) 페인트공

47. physician assistant
의사 보조원

48. police officer
경찰관

Grammar Point: past tense of *be*

*I **was** a machine operator for 5 years.*
*She **was** a nurse for a year.*
*They **were** movers from 2003–2007.*

Pair practice. Make new conversations.

A: *What was your first job?*
B: *I was <u>a musician</u>. How about you?*
A: *I was <u>a messenger for a small company</u>.*

49. postal worker
우체국 직원

50. printer
인쇄 기술자

51. receptionist
접수원

52. reporter
기자

53. retail clerk
소매점 직원

54. sanitation worker
환경미화원

55. security guard
경비원

56. server
종업원

57. social worker
사회사업 담당 직원

Here are some programs that will help you.

58. soldier
군인

59. stock clerk
창고원

60. telemarketer
텔레마케팅을 하는 사람

Hello. I'm calling with a very special offer.

61. truck driver
트럭 기사

62. veterinarian
수의사

63. welder
용접공

64. writer / author
작가

Ask your classmates. Share the answers.

1. Which of these jobs could you do now?
2. What is one job you don't want to have?
3. Which jobs do you want to have?

Think about it. Discuss.

1. Which jobs need special training?
2. What kind of person makes a good interpreter? A good nurse? A good reporter? Why?

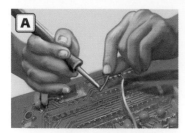
A. **assemble** components
부품을 **조립하다**

B. **assist** medical patients
환자를 **보조하다**

C. **cook**
요리하다

D. **do** manual labor
육체 노동을 **하다**

E. **drive** a truck
트럭을 **운전하다**

F. **fly** a plane
비행기를 **조종하다**

G. **make** furniture
가구를 **만들다**

H. **operate** heavy machinery
중장비를 **운전하다**

I. **program** computers
컴퓨터를 **프로그램하다**

J. **repair** appliances
가전제품을 **수리하다**

K. **sell** cars
자동차를 **팔다**

L. **sew** clothes
옷을 **바느질하다**

M. **solve** math problems
수학 문제를 **풀다**

4% interest of 5K = x

N. **speak** another language
외국어를 **말하다**

ПРИВЕТ

O. **supervise** people
사람을 **관리하다**

P. **take** care of children
어린이를 **돌보다**

Q. **teach**
가르치다

R. **type**
타자를 **치다**

S. **use** a cash register
금전 등록기를 **사용하다**

T. **wait on** customers
손님 **접대하다**

Grammar Point: *can, can't*

I am a chef. I **can** cook.
I'm not a pilot. I **can't** fly a plane.
I **can't** speak French, but I **can** speak Spanish.

Role play. Talk to a job counselor.

A: *Tell me about your skills. Can you <u>type</u>?*
B: <u>*No, I can't*</u>, *but I <u>can use a cash register</u>.*
A: *OK. What other skills do you have?*

Customers need better service…

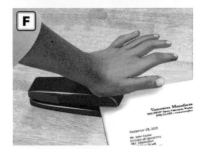

Scan Complete

Let's meet at 2:00.

Sure.

Dear Mr. Smith…

Hello. ABC Company. How may I help you?

Please hold.

Mr. Perez, I'm transferring you.

Hello. This is Sue Jones. Please call me.

This is Lee Tran. Please call me back.

Message Pad
Call From: Ana Puerta
Tel. 555-1234
Message: Please Call

Office Skills
사무실에서 필요한
기술들

A. **type** a letter
편지를 **타이프하다**

B. **enter** data
데이터를 **입력하다**

C. **transcribe** notes
메시지를 **기록하다**

D. **make** copies
복사**하다**

E. **collate** papers
용지 순서를 **맞추다**

F. **staple**
스테이플러로 찍다

G. **fax** a document
문서를 **팩스로 보내다**

H. **scan** a document
문서를 **스캔하다**

I. **print** a document
문서를 **인쇄하다**

J. **schedule** a meeting
회의 **일정을 잡다**

K. **take** dictation
받아 적다

L. **organize** materials
자료를 **정리하다**

Telephone Skills
전화 관련 기능

M. **greet** the caller
전화를 건 사람에게
인사하다

N. **put** the caller on hold
전화를 건 사람을 **기다**
리게 하다

O. **transfer** the call
전화를 **돌리다**

P. **leave** a message
메시지를 **남기다**

Q. **take** a message
메시지를 **받아 적다**

R. **check** messages
메시지를 **확인하다**

Career Path 진로 경로

1. entry-level job
초보적인 직업

2. training
교육

3. new job
새로운 직업

4. promotion
승진

Types of Job Training 직업 교육의 종류

5. vocational training
직업 훈련

6. internship
인턴쉽

Enter the number here.

7. on-the-job training
현장 교육

8. online course
온라인 코스

Planning a Career 진로 계획하기

9. resource center
직업 정보 센터

10. career counselor
진로 상담원

11. interest inventory
관심 분야

12. skill inventory
기술 분야

13. job fair
직업 박람회

14. recruiter
직원 선발자

Ways to talk about job training

I'm looking into an online course.
I'm interested in on-the-job training.
I want to sign up for an internship.

Ask your classmates. Share the answers.

1. What kind of job training are you interested in?
2. Would your rather learn English in an online course or in a classroom?

A. talk to friends / **network**
친구들과 **얘기한다** / **정보를 교환한다**

B. look in the classifieds
광고란을 **본다**

C. look for help wanted signs
구인 광고 게시물을 **찾아본다**

D. check Internet job sites
인터넷 구직 사이트를 **확인한다**

E. go to an employment agency
직업 소개소에 **간다**

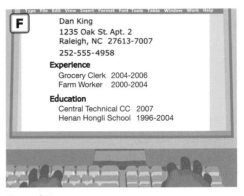

F. write a resume
이력서를 **쓴다**

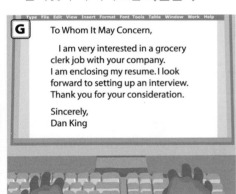

G. write a cover letter
자기 소개서를 **쓴다**

H. send in your resume and cover letter
이력서와 자기 소개서를 **제출하다**

I. set up an interview
면접 일정을 **잡는다**

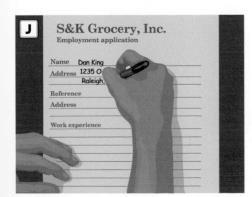

J. fill out an application
신청서를 **작성한다**

K. go on an interview
면접을 **본다**

L. get hired
고용**된다**

A. **Prepare** for the interview.
면접을 **준비한다**.

B. **Dress** appropriately.
적절한 **옷차림을 한다**.

C. **Be** neat.
단정하게 **한다**.

D. **Bring** your resume and ID.
이력서와 신분증을 **가져간다**.

E. **Don't be** late.
지각을 **하지 않는다**.

F. **Be** on time.
정시에 **도착한다**.

G. **Turn off** your cell phone.
휴대 전화를 **끈다**.

H. **Greet** the interviewer.
면접관에게 **인사한다**.

I. **Shake** hands.
악수한다.

Hello, I'm Elias Ortiz.

Hello, Mr. Ortiz. I'm Mrs. Perez.

J. **Make** eye contact.
눈을 **마주친다**.

K. **Listen** carefully.
주의하여 **경청한다**.

L. **Talk** about your experience.
자신의 경력에 대해 **말한다**.

Computer skills are important.

I have those skills.

I worked with computers on my last job.

M. **Ask** questions.
질문**한다**.

N. **Thank** the interviewer.
면접관에게
감사의 뜻을 전한다.

O. **Write** a thank-you note.
면접관에게 감사 노트를 **쓴다**.

Do you offer training?

Thank you for your time.

Dear Mrs. Perez,
Thank you for the opportunity to meet with you.

More vocabulary

benefits: health insurance, vacation pay, or other things the employer can offer an employee

inquire about benefits: ask about benefits

Think about it. Discuss.

1. How can you prepare for an interview?
2. Why is it important to make eye contact?
3. What kinds of questions should you ask?

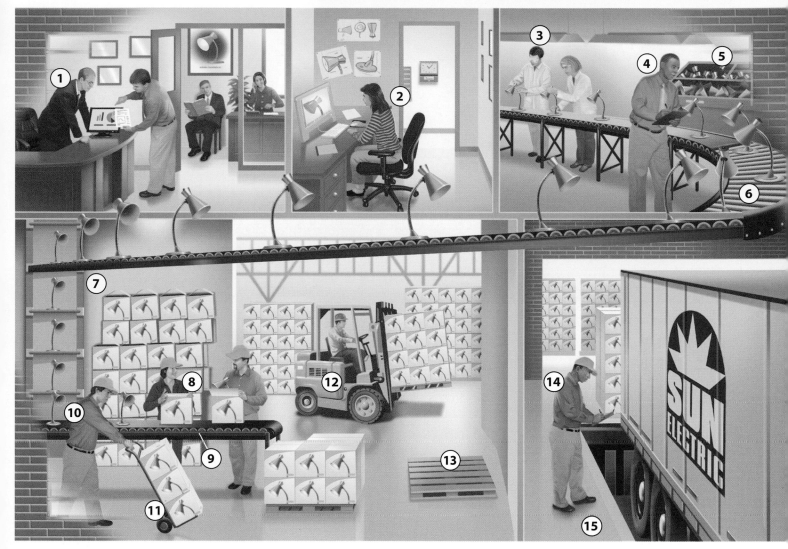

1. factory owner
공장 주인

2. designer
디자이너

3. factory worker
공장 근로자

4. line supervisor
라인 감독자

5. parts
부품

6. assembly line
조립 라인

7. warehouse
창고

8. packer
포장하는 사람(기계)

9. conveyer belt
컨베이어 벨트

10. order puller
주문 담당자

11. hand truck
핸드 트럭

12. forklift
지게차

13. pallet
화물 운반대

14. shipping clerk
출하담당 계원

15. loading dock
적재 도크

A. **design**
디자인

B. **manufacture**
제조

C. **assemble**
조립

D. **ship**
수송

Bloom Nursery

1. **gardening crew**
   정원사

2. **leaf blower**
   낙엽 송풍기

3. **wheelbarrow**
   일륜 수레

4. **gardening crew leader**
   정원 관리 책임자

5. **landscape designer**
   조경 디자이너

6. **lawn mower**
   잔디 깎는 기계

7. **shovel**
   삽

8. **rake**
   갈퀴

9. **pruning shears**
   전정 가위

10. **trowel**
    모종삽

11. **hedge clippers**
    양손 전정 가위

12. **weed whacker / weed eater**
    잡초 제거기

A. **mow** the lawn
   잔디를 **깎다**

B. **trim** the hedges
   나무 울타리를 **다듬다**

C. **rake** the leaves
   낙엽을 **긁어 모으다**

D. **fertilize / feed** the plants
   식물에 **비료 / 물을 주다**

E. **plant** a tree
   나무를 **심다**

F. **water** the plants
   나무에 **물을 주다**

G. **weed** the flower beds
   화단의 **잡초를 뽑다**

H. **install** a sprinkler system
   스프링클러를 **설치하다**

Use the new words.
Look at page 53. Name what you can do in the yard.

A: I can <u>mow the lawn</u>.
B: I can <u>weed the flower bed</u>.

Ask your classmates. Share the answers.
1. Do you know someone who does landscaping? Who?
2. Do you enjoy gardening? Why or why not?
3. Which gardening activity is the hardest to do? Why?

Crops 농작물

1. rice
쌀

2. wheat
밀

3. soybeans
콩

4. corn
옥수수

5. alfalfa
자주개자리

6. cotton
면

7. field
밭

8. farmworker
농장 노동자

9. tractor
트랙터

10. orchard
과수원

11. barn
헛간

12. farm equipment
농기구

13. farmer / grower
농부 / 농산물 재배자

14. vegetable garden
채소밭

15. livestock
가축

16. vineyard
포도원

17. corral
가축 우리

18. hay
건초

19. fence
울타리

20. hired hand
일꾼

21. cattle
숫송아지

22. rancher
목동

A. plant
심다

B. harvest
수확하다

C. milk
젖을 짜다

D. feed
먹이다

1. construction worker
건설 작업자

2. ladder
사다리

3. I beam/girder
들보 / 대들보

4. scaffolding
발판

5. cherry picker
이동식 크레인

6. bulldozer
불도저

7. crane
기중기

8. backhoe
굴착기

9. jackhammer / pneumatic drill
잭해머 / 압축공기 드릴

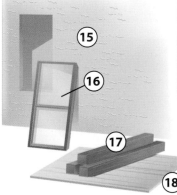

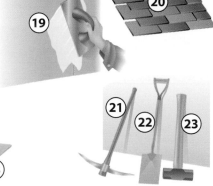

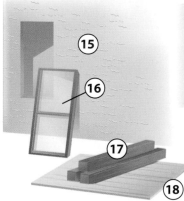

10. concrete
콘크리트

11. tile
타일

12. bricks
벽돌

13. trowel
흙손

14. insulation
단열재

15. stucco
치장 벽토

16. window pane
창유리

17. wood / lumber
목재

18. plywood
합판

19. drywall
건식벽

20. shingles
지붕널

21. pickax
곡괭이

22. shovel
삽

23. sledgehammer
큰 쇠망치

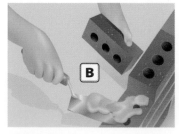

A. paint
페인트칠하다

B. lay bricks
벽돌을 **쌓다**

C. install tile
타일을 **설치하다**

D. hammer
망치질하다

Safety Hazards and Hazardous Materials 위험 및 위험 물질

1. careless worker
   부주의한 작업자
2. careful worker
   주의 깊은 작업자
3. poisonous fumes
   독성 연기
4. broken equipment
   고장난 장비
5. frayed cord
   피복이 벗겨진 코드
6. slippery floor
   미끄러운 마루바닥
7. radioactive materials
   방사능 물질
8. flammable liquids
   가연성 액체

Safety Equipment 안전 장비

9. hard hat
   안전모
10. safety glasses
    보호 안경
11. safety goggles
    작업용 고글
12. safety visor
    안전 마스크
13. respirator
    호흡 마스크
14. particle mask
    공기 여과 마스크 /
    방독 마스크
15. ear plugs
    귀마개
16. earmuffs
    귀가리개
17. work gloves
    작업용 장갑
18. back support belt
    허리 보호 벨트
19. knee pads
    무릎 보호대
20. safety boots
    안전 장화
21. fire extinguisher
    소화기
22. two-way radio
    무전기

HAND TOOLS

HARDWARE

POWER TOOLS

1. hammer
망치

2. mallet
나무메

3. ax
도끼

4. handsaw
톱

5. hacksaw
금속판 절단 톱

6. C-clamp
C-클램프

7. pliers
펜치

8. electric drill
전동 드릴

9. circular saw
원형 톱

10. jigsaw
실톱

11. power sander
전동 샌더

12. router
라우터

26. vise
바이스

27. blade
톱날

28. drill bit
드릴 비트

29. level
수평기

30. screwdriver
드라이버

31. Phillips screwdriver
필립스 드라이버

32. machine screw
기계 나사

33. wood screw
나무용 나사

34. nail
못

35. bolt
볼트

36. nut
너트

37. washer
와셔

38. toggle bolt
토글 볼트

39. hook
훅

40. eye hook
고리 나사

41. chain
체인

Use the new words.
Look at pages 62–63. Name the tools you see.

A: *There's a hammer.*
B: *There's a pipe wrench.*

Ask your classmates. Share the answers.

1. Are you good with tools?
2. Which tools do you have at home?
3. Where can you shop for building supplies?

ELECTRICAL | **PLUMBING** | **LUMBER** | **PAINT**

13. wire 전선	**16.** yardstick 야드 자	**19.** 2 x 4 (two by four) 2 x 4	**22.** paintbrush 페인트 브러쉬	**25.** paint 페인트
14. extension cord 연결 코드	**17.** pipe 파이프	**20.** particle board 건축용 합판	**23.** paint roller 페인트 롤러	
15. bungee cord 번지 코드	**18.** fittings 피팅	**21.** spray gun 스프레이 총	**24.** wood stain 목재용 염료	

42. wire stripper 와이어 스트리퍼	**46.** outlet cover 콘센트 커버	**50.** plunger 플런저	**54.** drop cloth 헝겊
43. electrical tape 전기 테이프	**47.** pipe wrench 파이프 렌치	**51.** paint pan 페인트 팬	**55.** chisel 끌
44. work light 작업등	**48.** adjustable wrench 조정 가능한 렌치	**52.** scraper 스크레이퍼	**56.** sandpaper 사포
45. tape measure 줄자	**49.** duct tape 덕 테이프	**53.** masking tape 마스킹 테이프	**57.** plane 대패

Role play. Find an item in a building supply store.

A: *Where can I find particle board?*
B: *It's on the back wall, in the lumber section.*
A: *Great. And where are the nails?*

Think about it. Discuss.

1. Which tools are the most important to have? Why?
2. Which tools can be dangerous? Why?
3. Do you borrow tools from friends? Why or why not?

181

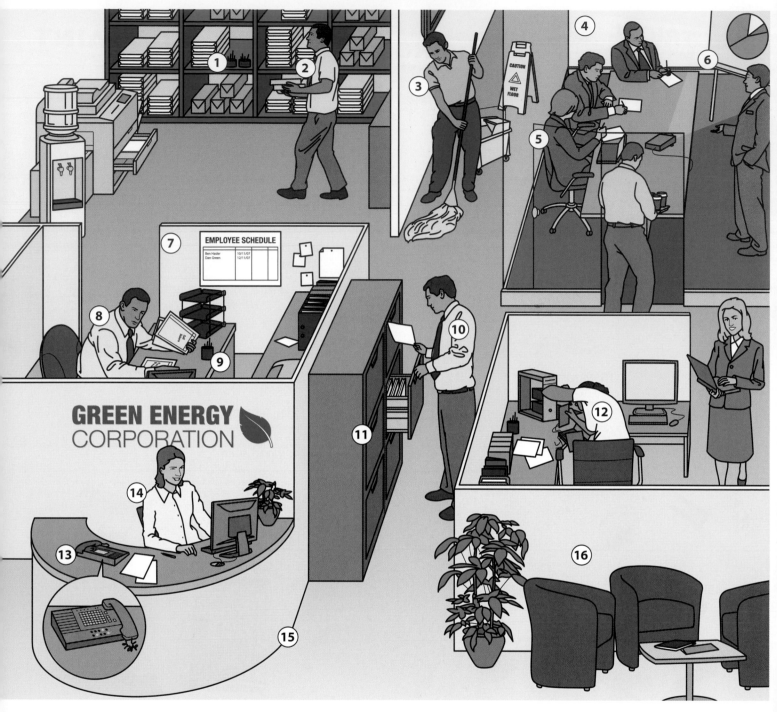

1. supply cabinet
   비품 보관함

2. clerk
   사무원

3. janitor
   청소부

4. conference room
   회의실

5. executive
   경영진

6. presentation
   프레젠테이션

7. cubicle
   칸막이

8. office manager
   사무실 매니저

9. desk
   책상

10. file clerk
    사무 보조원

11. file cabinet
    서류함

12. computer technician
    컴퓨터 기술자

13. PBX
    전화 교환기

14. receptionist
    안내

15. reception area
    접수 안내 구역

16. waiting area
    대기 공간

Ways to greet a receptionist

I'm here for a <u>job interview</u>.
I have a <u>9:00 a.m.</u> appointment with <u>Mr. Lee</u>.
I'd like to leave a message <u>for Mr. Lee</u>.

Role play. Talk to a receptionist.

A: *Hello. How can I help you?*
B: *<u>I'm here for a job interview with Mr. Lee.</u>*
A: *OK. What is your name?*

Office Equipment 사무실 장비

17. computer
컴퓨터

18. inkjet printer
잉크젯 프린터

19. laser printer
레이저 프린터

20. scanner
스캐너

21. fax machine
팩스기

22. paper cutter
종이 재단기

23. photocopier
복사기

24. paper shredder
분쇄기

25. calculator
계산기

26. electric pencil sharpener
전동 연필깎이

27. postal scale
우편물 저울

Office Supplies 사무용품

28. stapler
스테이플러

29. staples
스테이플

30. clear tape
투명 테이프

31. paper clip
페이퍼 클립

32. packing tape
포장 테이프

33. glue
풀

34. rubber band
고무 밴드

35. pushpin
압정

36. correction fluid
수정액

37. correction tape
수정 테이프

38. legal pad
황색 괘선지철

39. sticky notes
포스트잇

40. mailer
메일러

41. mailing label
우편물 라벨

42. letterhead / stationery
회사 로그 인쇄 용지 / 물품

43. envelope
봉투

44. rotary card file
회전 카드 파일

45. ink cartridge
잉크 카트리지

46. ink pad
잉크 패드

47. stamp
스탬프

48. appointment book
일정 관리 수첩

49. organizer
오거나이저

50. file folder
파일 폴더

1. doorman
   도어맨

2. revolving door
   회전문

3. parking attendant
   주차 직원

4. concierge
   접객원

5. gift shop
   선물 가게

6. bell captain
   벨 캡틴

7. bellhop
   벨보이

8. luggage cart
   가방 카트

9. elevator
   엘리베이터

10. guest
    손님

11. desk clerk
    데스크 직원

12. front desk
    프런트 데스크

13. guest room
    객실

14. double bed
    더블 베드

15. king-size bed
    킹 사이즈 베드

16. suite
    스위트룸

17. room service
    룸 서비스

18. hallway
    복도

19. housekeeping cart
    청소 카트

20. housekeeper
    호텔 객실 청소부

21. pool service
    수영장 서비스

22. pool
    수영장

23. maintenance
    시설 관리

24. gym
    체육관

25. meeting room
    회의실

26. ballroom
    연회장

A Restaurant Kitchen 식당 주방

1. short-order cook
   간단한 메뉴 담당 요리사
2. dishwasher
   접시닦는 사람
3. walk-in freezer
   초대형 냉동고
4. food preparation worker
   재료 준비 담당
5. storeroom
   저장소
6. sous chef
   부주방장
7. head chef / executive chef
   수석 주방장

Restaurant Dining 식당에서 식사

8. server
   종업원 / 웨이터
9. diner
   식당 손님
10. buffet
    뷔페
11. maitre d'
    지배인
12. headwaiter
    수석 웨이터
13. bus person
    서빙 보조
14. banquet room
    연회장
15. runner
    주문원
16. caterer
    연회 요리 담당

More vocabulary

line cook: short-order cook
wait staff: servers, headwaiters, and runners

Ask your classmates. Share the answers.

1. Have you ever worked in a hotel? What did you do?
2. What is the hardest job in a hotel?
3. Would you prefer to stay at a hotel in the city or in the country?

1. dangerous
위험한

2. clinic
치료소 / 진료소

3. budget
예산

4. floor plan
평면도

5. contractor
계약자

6. electrical hazard
전기 위험

7. wiring
배선

8. bricklayer
벽돌공

A. **call in** sick
전화로 병결을 **알리다**

Look at the picture. What do you see?

Answer the questions.

1. How many workers are there? How many are working?

2. Why did two workers call in sick?

3. What is dangerous at the construction site?

📖 Read the story.

A Bad Day at Work

Sam Lopez is the <u>contractor</u> for a new building. He makes the schedule and supervises the <u>budget</u>. He also solves problems. Today there are a lot of problems.

Two <u>bricklayers</u> <u>called in sick</u> this morning. Now Sam has only one bricklayer at work. One hour later, a construction worker fell. Now he has to go to the <u>clinic</u>. Sam always tells his workers to be careful. Construction work is <u>dangerous</u>. Sam's also worried because the new <u>wiring</u> is an <u>electrical hazard</u>.

Right now, the building owner is in Sam's office. Her new <u>floor plan</u> has 25 more offices. Sam has a headache. Maybe he needs to call in sick tomorrow.

Think about it.

1. What do you say when you can't come in to work? to school?

2. Imagine you are Sam. What do you tell the building owner? Why?

187

1. preschool /
   nursery school
   유치원 / 보육원

2. elementary school
   초등학교

3. middle school /
   junior high school
   중학교

4. high school
   고등학교

5. vocational school /
   technical school
   직업학교 / 기술학교

6. community college
   지역 대학

7. college / university
   대학교

8. adult school
   성인학교

Reasons for the Civil War

Listen and point. Take turns.

A: Point to _the preschool_.
B: Point to _the high school_.
A: Point to _the adult school_.

Dictate to your partner. Take turns.

A: Write _preschool_.
B: Is that p-r-e-s-c-h-o-o-l?
A: Yes. That's right.

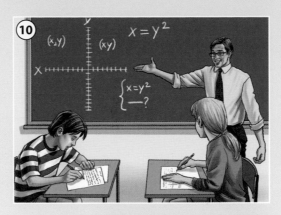

9. language arts
언어

10. math
수학

11. science
과학

12. history
역사

13. world languages
외국어

14. ESL / ESOL
ESL / ESOL

15. arts
미술

16. music
음악

17. physical education
체육

More vocabulary

core course: a subject students have to take. Math is a core course.

elective: a subject students choose to take. Art is an elective.

Pair practice. Make new conversations.

A: *I go to* <u>community college</u>.

B: *What subjects are you taking?*

A: *I'm taking* <u>history</u> *and* <u>science</u>.

1 factory

2 I worked in a factory.

3 Little by little, work and success came to me. My first job wasn't good. I worked in a small factory. Now, I help manage two factories.

4

1. word
   단어
2. sentence
   문장
3. paragraph
   단락
4. essay
   에세이

Parts of an Essay
에세이 구성

5. title
   제목
6. introduction
   서론
7. body
   본론
8. conclusion
   결론
9. quotation
   인용
10. footnote
    각주

Carlos Lopez
Eng. Comp.
10/21/10

5 Success in the U.S.

6 I came to Los Angeles from Mexico in 2006. I had no job, no friends, and no family here. I was homesick and scared, but I did not go home. I took English classes (always at night) and I studied hard. I believed in my future success!

7 More than 400,000 new immigrants come to the U.S every year.[1] Most of us need to find work. During my first year here, my routine was the same: get up; look for work; go to class; go to bed. I had to take jobs with long hours and low pay. Often I had two or three jobs.

Little by little, work and success came to me. My first job wasn't good. I worked in a small factory. Now, I help manage two factories.

8 Hard work makes success possible. Henry David Thoreau said, "Men are born to succeed, not fail." My story **9** shows that he was right.

10 [1] U.S. Census

Punctuation
부호

11. period
    마침표
12. question mark
    물음표
13. exclamation mark
    느낌표
14. comma
    쉼표
15. quotation marks
    따옴표
16. apostrophe
    아포스트로피
17. colon
    콜론
18. semicolon
    세미콜론
19. parentheses
    괄호
20. hyphen
    하이픈

Writing Rules 쓰기 규칙

A

Carlos

Mexico

Los Angeles

A. **Capitalize** names.
이름의 첫 글자는 **대문자로 표기한다**.

B

Hard work makes success possible.

B. **Capitalize** the first letter in a sentence.
문장의 첫자는 **대문자로 표기한다**.

C

I was homesick and scared, but I did not go home.

C. **Use** punctuation.
부호를 **사용하다**.

D

I came to Los Angeles from Mexico in 2006. I had no job, no friends, and no family here. I was homesick and scared, but I did not go home. I took English classes (always at night) and I studied hard. I believed in my future success!

D. **Indent** the first sentence in a paragraph.
단락의 첫 문장은 **들여쓴다**.

190

The Writing Process 쓰기 순서

PREWRITING

E. Think about the assignment.
주어진 과제에 대해 **생각해본다**.

F. Brainstorm ideas.
다양한 아이디어를 **생각해 본다**.

G. Organize your ideas.
아이디어를 **정리한다**.

WRITING AND REVISING

H. Write a first draft.
초안을 **쓴다**.

I. Edit. / Proofread.
편집한다. / 검토한다.

J. Revise. / Rewrite.
수정한다. / 다시 쓴다.

SHARING AND RESPONDING

K. Get feedback.
의견을 **들어본다**.

L. Write a final draft.
최종안을 **쓴다**.

M. Turn in your paper.
작문을 **제출한다**.

Ask your classmates. Share the answers.

1. Do you like to write essays?
2. Which part of the writing process do you like best? least?

Think about it. Discuss.

1. In which jobs are writing skills important?
2. What tools can help you edit your writing?
3. What are some good subjects for essays?

191

Mathematics 수학

Integers 정수

...−4 −3 −2 −1 0 1 2 3 4 ...

① ②

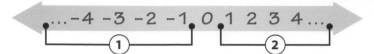

③ 1, 3, 5, 7, 9, 11...

④ 2, 4, 6, 8, 10 ...

Fractions 분수

$\dfrac{3}{8}$ ⑤ ⑥ $\dfrac{3}{8}$

1. negative integers
음수

2. positive integers
양수

3. odd numbers
홀수

4. even numbers
짝수

5. numerator
분자

6. denominator
분모

Math Operations 수학 연산

A. **add**
더하기

B. **subtract**
빼기

C. **multiply**
곱하기

D. **divide**
나누기

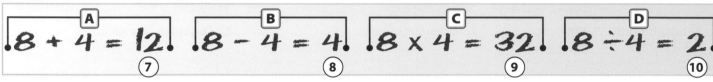

A 8 + 4 = 12 ⑦   B 8 − 4 = 4 ⑧   C 8 × 4 = 32 ⑨   D 8 ÷ 4 = 2 ⑩

7. sum
합계

8. difference
차

9. product
곱

10. quotient
몫

A Math Problem 수학 문제

⑪
Tom is 10 years older than Kim. Next year he will be twice as old as Kim. How old is Tom this year?

⑫ —— x = Kim's age now
$x + 10$ = Tom's age now
$x + 1$ = Kim's age next year
$2(x + 1)$ = Tom's age next year
$x + 10 + 1 = 2(x + 1)$
$x + 11 = 2x + 2$ ⑬
$11 − 2 = 2x − x$

$x = 9$, Kim is 9, Tom is 19 ⑭

⑮
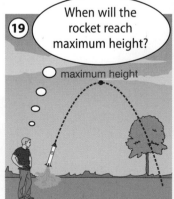
horizontal axis

vertical axis

11. word problem
단어식 문제

12. variable
변수

13. equation
방정식

14. solution
답

15. graph
그래프

Types of Math 수학의 종류

⑯ How much are they?

x = the sale price
$x = 79.00 - .40 (79.00)$
$x = \$47.40$

16. algebra
대수

⑰ How many do I need?

area of path = 24 square ft.
area of brick = 2 square ft.
$24 / 2 = 12$ bricks

17. geometry
기하

⑱ How tall is it?

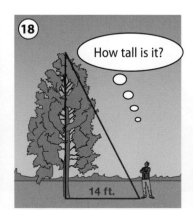

14 ft.

$\tan 63° = \text{height} / 14 \text{ feet}$
$\text{height} = 14 \text{ feet } (\tan 63°)$
$\text{height} \simeq 27.48 \text{ feet}$

18. trigonometry
삼각법

⑲ When will the rocket reach maximum height?

maximum height

$s(t) = -\frac{1}{2} g t^2 + V_0 t + h$
$s^{\mathrm{I}}(t) = -gt + V_0 = 0$
$t = V_0 / g$

19. calculus
미적분

192

Lines 선

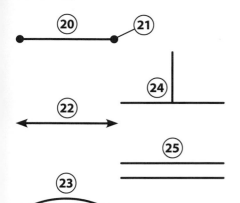

Angles 각도

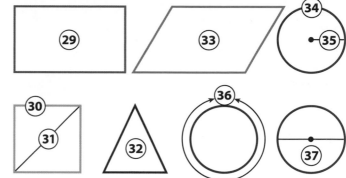

Shapes 도형

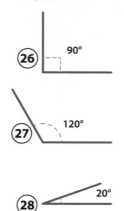

20. line segment
선분

21. endpoint
끝점

22. straight line
직선

23. curved line
곡선

24. perpendicular lines
수직선

25. parallel lines
평행선

26. right angle / 90° angle
직각 / 90°

27. obtuse angle
둔각

28. acute angle
예각

29. rectangle
직사각형

30. square
정사각형

31. diagonal
대각선

32. triangle
삼각형

33. parallelogram
평행사변형

34. circle
원

35. radius
반지름

36. circumference
원주

37. diameter
지름

Geometric Solids
기하학적 입체

38. cube
육면체

39. pyramid
각뿔

40. cone
원뿔

41. cylinder
원기둥

42. sphere
구

Measuring Area and Volume
면적 및 부피 측정

$\ell \times w = \text{area}$

$6 \times f = \text{surface area}$

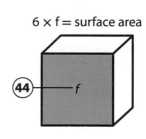

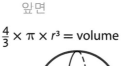

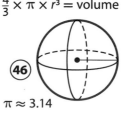

$\pi \times r^2 \times h = \text{volume}$

$\frac{4}{3} \times \pi \times r^3 = \text{volume}$

$\pi \approx 3.14$

43. perimeter
둘레

44. face
앞면

45. base
밑면

46. pi
파이

Ask your classmates. Share the answers.

1. Are you good at math?
2. Which types of math are easy for you?
3. Which types of math are difficult for you?

Think about it. Discuss.

1. What's the best way to learn mathematics?
2. How can you find the area of your classroom?
3. Which jobs use math? Which don't?

193

Biology 생물

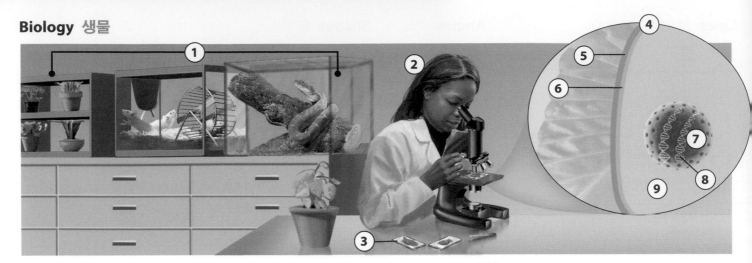

1. organisms 유기체	3. slide 슬라이드	5. cell wall 세포벽	7. nucleus 핵	9. cytoplasm 세포질
2. biologist 생물학자	4. cell 세포	6. cell membrane 세포막	8. chromosome 염색체	

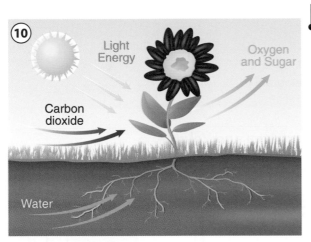

10. photosynthesis
광합성

11. habitat
서식지

12. vertebrates
척추동물

13. invertebrates
무척추동물

A Microscope 현미경

14. eyepiece
접안 렌즈

15. revolving nosepiece
회전식 대물렌즈대

16. objective
대물 렌즈

17. stage
재물대

18. diaphragm
조리개

19. light source
광원

20. base
받침대

21. stage clips
재물대 고정 클립

22. fine adjustment knob
미세 조정 다이얼

23. arm
손잡이

24. coarse adjustment knob
조동 나사

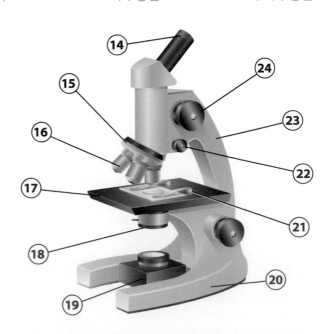

Chemistry 화학

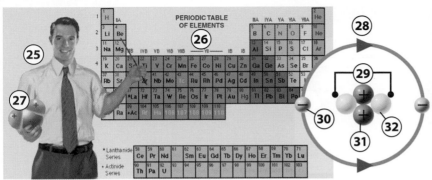

25. chemist
화학자

26. periodic table
주기율표

27. molecule
분자

28. atom
원자

29. nucleus
핵

30. electron
전자

31. proton
양성자

32. neutron
중성자

33. physicist
물리학자

34. formula
공식

35. prism
프리즘

36. magnet
자석

Physics 물리

$$c = f\lambda$$

f = frequency

λ = wavelength

A Science Lab 과학실

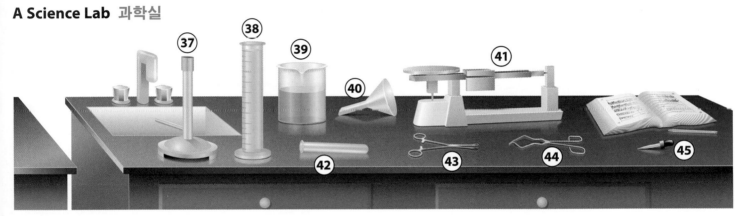

37. Bunsen burner
분젠 가스 버너

38. graduated cylinder
눈금실린더

39. beaker
비커

40. funnel
깔때기

41. balance / scale
저울

42. test tube
시험관

43. forceps
핀셋

44. crucible tongs
도가니 집게

45. dropper
점적기

An Experiment 실험

Salt and sugar crystals will grow the same way.

Salt crystals grow faster than sugar crystals.

A. State a hypothesis.
가설을 **설명한다**.

B. Do an experiment.
실험을 **실시한다**.

C. Observe.
관찰한다.

D. Record the results.
결과를 **기록한다**.

E. Draw a conclusion.
결론을 **도출한다**.

Desktop Computer 데스크탑 컴퓨터

1. surge protector 이상 전압 보호기	**6.** hard drive 하드 드라이브	**11.** monitor / screen 모니터 / 화면	**16.** laptop 랩톱
2. power cord 전원 코드	**7.** USB port USB 포트	**12.** webcam 웹캠	**17.** printer 프린터
3. tower 타워	**8.** flash drive 플래시 드라이브	**13.** cable 케이블	
4. microprocessor / CPU 마이크로프로세서 / CPU	**9.** DVD and CD-ROM drive DVD 및 CD-ROM 드라이브	**14.** keyboard 키보드	
5. motherboard 마더보드	**10.** software 소프트웨어	**15.** mouse 마우스	

Keyboarding 키보드

A. type
타자를 치다

B. select
선택하다

C. delete
삭제하다

D. go to the next line
다음 줄로 **이동하다**

Navigating a Webpage 웹 페이지 검색

1. **menu bar**
   메뉴 표시줄

2. **back button**
   뒤로 단추

3. **forward button**
   앞으로 단추

4. **URL / website address**
   URL / 웹 사이트 주소

5. **search box**
   검색 상자

6. **search engine**
   검색 엔진

7. **tab**
   탭

8. **drop-down menu**
   드롭다운 메뉴

9. **pop-up ad**
   팝업 광고물

10. **links**
    링크

11. **video player**
    비디오 플레이어

12. **pointer**
    포인터

13. **text box**
    텍스트 상자

14. **cursor**
    커서

15. **scroll bar**
    스크롤 바

Logging on and Sending Email 이메일 로그온 및 발송

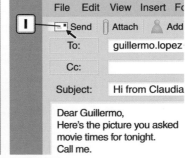

A. **type** your password
   비밀번호를 **입력한다**

B. **click** "sign in"
   "로그인" 을 **클릭한다**

C. **address** the email
   이메일 **주소를 쓴다**

D. **type** the subject
   제목을 **쓴다**

E. **type** the message
   메시지를 **입력한다**

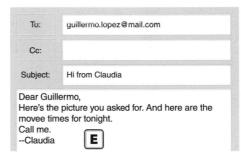

F. **check** your spelling
   맞춤법을 **검사한다**

G. **attach** a picture
   사진을 **첨부한다**

H. **attach** a file
   파일을 **첨부한다**

I. **send** the email
   이메일을 **전송한다**

Colonial Period 식민지 시대

1. thirteen colonies
   13개 식민지
2. colonists
   식민지 주민
3. Native Americans
   원주민
4. slave
   노예
5. Declaration of Independence
   독립선언문
6. First Continental Congress
   최초의 의회
7. founders
   설립자
8. Revolutionary War
   독립전쟁
9. redcoat
   영국 군인
10. minuteman
    긴급소집병
11. first president
    초대 대통령
12. Constitution
    헌법
13. Bill of Rights
    권리장전

Western Expansion
1803 – 1893

Civil War
1861 – 1865

World War I
1914 – 1918

Jazz Age
1920 – 1929

World War II
1941 – 1945

Civil Rights Movement
1954 – 1972

Information Age
1959 – now

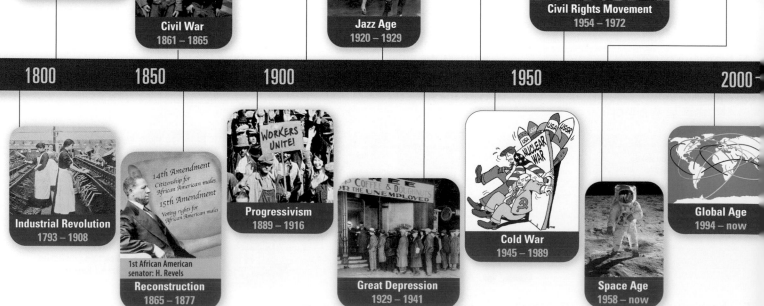

1800   1850   1900   1950   2000

Industrial Revolution
1793 – 1908

14th Amendment
Citizenship for African American males

15th Amendment
Voting rights for African American males

1st African American senator: H. Revels
Reconstruction
1865 – 1877

Progressivism
1889 – 1916

Great Depression
1929 – 1941

Cold War
1945 – 1989

Space Age
1958 – now

Global Age
1994 – now

Civilizations 문명

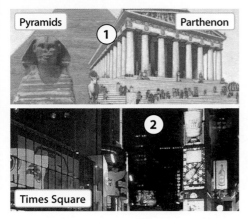
Pyramids
Parthenon
1

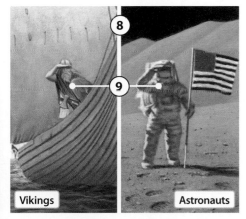
2
Times Square

Caesar
3

Qin Shi Huang

King Henry VIII
4

Queen Elizabeth I

5
Juarez

6
Mussolini

7
Churchill

1. ancient
고대

2. modern
현대

3. emperor
황제

4. monarch
군주

5. president
대통령

6. dictator
독재자

7. prime minister
수상

Historical Terms 역사적 용어

8
9
Vikings
Astronauts

10
11

12
13

8. exploration
탐험

9. explorer
탐험가

10. war
전쟁

11. army
군대

12. immigration
이민

13. immigrant
이민자

14
15
Mozart
Duke Ellington

16
17
Susan B. Anthony
César Chávez

18
19
Edison
Camarena

14. composer
작곡가

15. composition
작곡

16. political movement
정치 운동

17. activist
운동가

18. inventor
발명가

19. invention
발명

ATLANTIC OCEAN

BERMUDA ISLANDS (UK)

GREENLAND

Labrador Sea

Newfoundland and Labrador

Prince Edward Island

Nova Scotia

New Brunswick

Maine

Vermont
New Hampshire
Massachusetts
Rhode Island
Connecticut

New Jersey
Delaware
Maryland
WASHINGTON, D.C.

New York

Pennsylvania

West Virginia

Virginia

North Carolina

South Carolina

Georgia

Florida

Gulf

Baffin Bay

Devon Island

Baffin Island

Québec

OTTAWA

Ohio

Kentucky

Tennessee

Alabama

Mississippi

Louisiana

Hudson Bay

Ontario

Michigan

Wisconsin

Illinois Indiana

Missouri

Arkansas

Ellesmere Island

Nunavut

Minnesota

Iowa

ARCTIC OCEAN

Beaufort Sea

Banks Island

Victoria Island

Northwest Territories

Manitoba

Saskatchewan

CANADA

North Dakota

South Dakota

Nebraska

Kansas

Oklahoma

Texas

New Mexico

Colorado

Utah

Arizona

Coahuila

Chihuahua

Sonora

Gulf of

Yukon

British Columbia

Montana

Wyoming

Idaho

Nevada

Washington

Oregon

California

Baja California Norte

Baja

Alaska (US)

Gulf of Alaska

Bering Sea

Aleutian Islands

PACIFIC OCEAN

Hawaii (US)

200

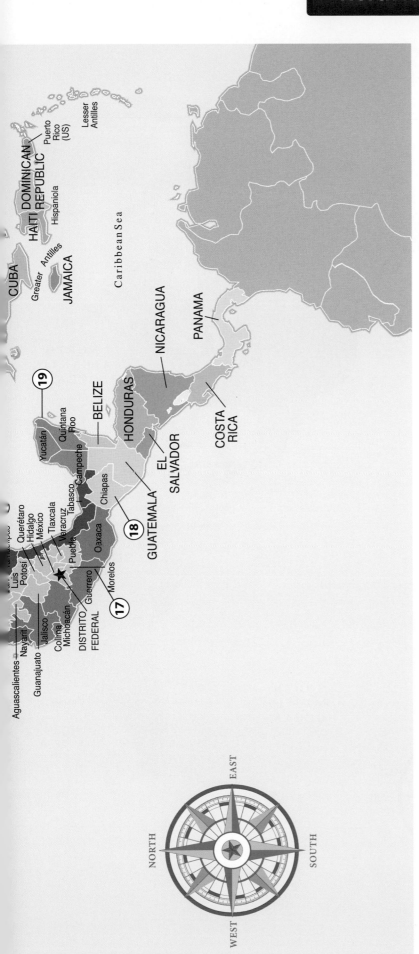

CUBA

HAITI

DOMINICAN REPUBLIC

Puerto Rico (US)

Lesser Antilles

Hispaniola

Greater Antilles

JAMAICA

Caribbean Sea

유카탄반도

NICARAGUA

PANAMA

BELIZE

HONDURAS

COSTA RICA

GUATEMALA

EL SALVADOR

Quintana Roo

Yucatán

Campeche

Chiapas

Tabasco

Veracruz

Tlaxcala

Oaxaca

Querétaro

Hidalgo

México

Puebla

Morelos

Guerrero

Michoacán

DISTRITO FEDERAL

Colima

Jalisco

Guanajuato

Nayarit

Aguascalientes

Luis Potosí

EAST

NORTH

SOUTH

WEST

Regions of Canada
캐나다 지역

1. Northern Canada
   북 캐나다

2. British Columbia
   브리티시 콜롬비아

3. The Prairie Provinces
   프레리 프로빈스

4. Ontario
   온타리오

5. Québec
   퀘벡

6. The Maritime Provinces
   마리타임 프로빈스

Regions of the United States
미국 지역

7. The Pacific States / the West Coast
   태평양 연안주 / 서해안

8. The Rocky Mountain States
   록키 산주

9. The Midwest
   중서부

10. The Mid-Atlantic States
    미드 애틀란틱 주

11. New England
    뉴잉글랜드

12. The Southwest
    남서부

13. The Southeast / the South
    남동부 / 남부

Regions of Mexico
멕시코 지역

14. The Pacific Northwest
    태평양 북서부

15. The Plateau of Mexico
    멕시코 고원

16. The Gulf Coastal Plain
    걸프 해안 평원

17. The Southern Uplands
    남부 고원

18. The Chiapas Highlands
    치아파스 고지

19. The Yucatan Peninsula
    유카탄 반도

Continents
대륙

1. **North America**
   북아메리카
2. **South America**
   남 아메리카
3. **Europe**
   유럽
4. **Asia**
   아시아
5. **Africa**
   아프리카
6. **Australia**
   호주
7. **Antarctica**
   남극대륙

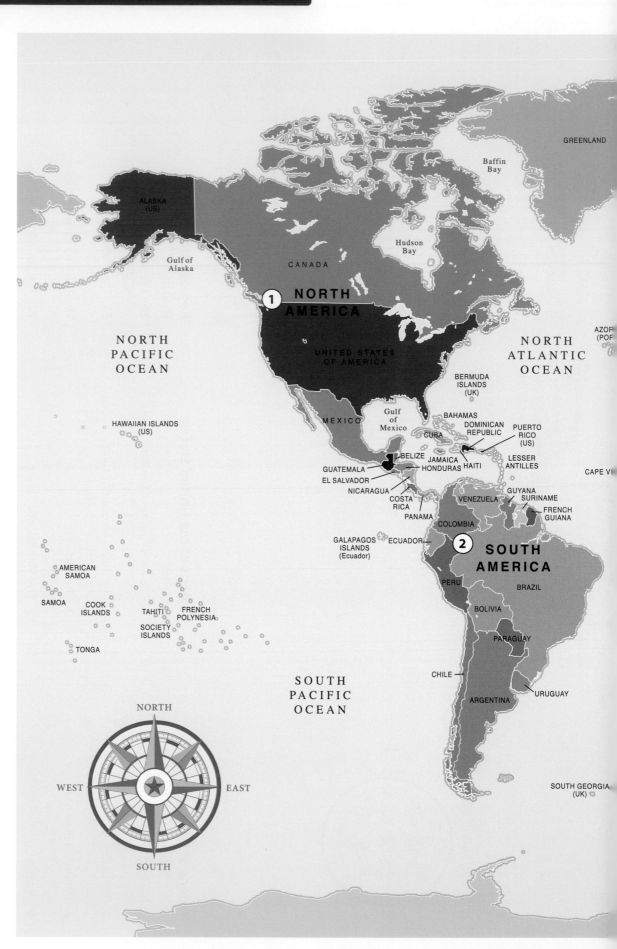

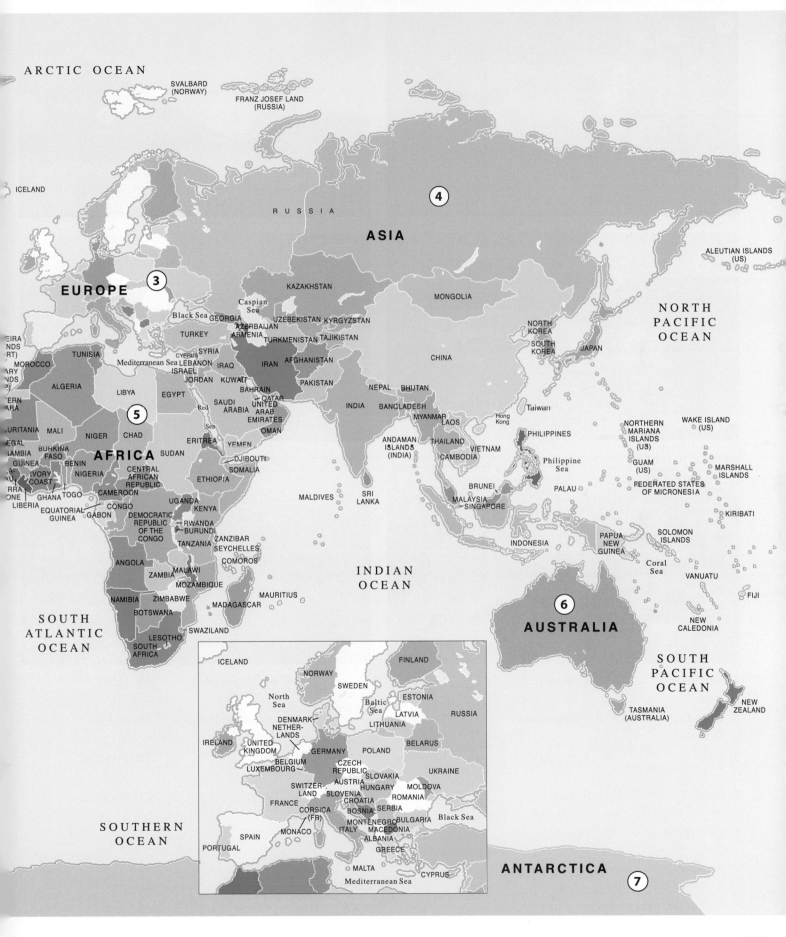

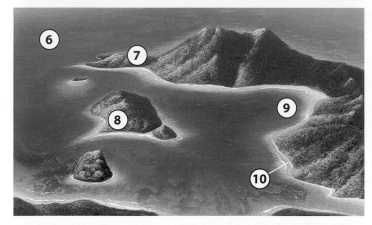

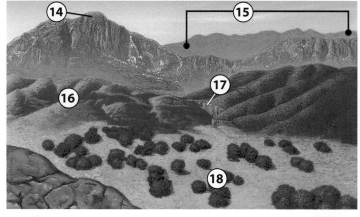

1. rain forest
우림

2. waterfall
폭포

3. river
강

4. desert
사막

5. sand dune
모래 언덕

6. ocean
대양

7. peninsula
반도

8. island
섬

9. bay
만

10. beach
해변

11. forest
숲

12. shore
해안

13. lake
호수

14. mountain peak
산봉우리

15. mountain range
산맥

16. hills
언덕

17. canyon
협곡

18. valley
계곡

19. plains
평원

20. meadow
초원

21. pond
연못

More vocabulary

a body of water: a river, lake, or ocean
stream / creek: a very small river

Ask your classmates. Share the answers.

1. Would you rather live near a river or a lake?
2. Would you rather travel through a forest or a desert?
3. How often do you go to the beach or the shore?

The Solar System and the Planets 태양계 및 행성

Sun   ① ② ③ ④ ⑤ ⑥ ⑦ ⑧

Asteroid Belt

Orbit

1. Mercury 수성	**3.** Earth 지구	**5.** Jupiter 목성	**7.** Uranus 천왕성
2. Venus 금성	**4.** Mars 화성	**6.** Saturn 토성	**8.** Neptune 해왕성

PHASES OF THE MOON

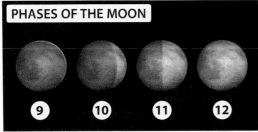

⑨ ⑩ ⑪ ⑫

SPACE

⑬ ⑭ ⑮

⑯

9. new moon 신월	**11.** quarter moon 하현달	**13.** star 별	**15.** galaxy 은하계
10. crescent moon 초승달	**12.** full moon 만월 / 보름달	**14.** constellation 별자리	**16.** solar eclipse 일식

SPACE EXPLORATION

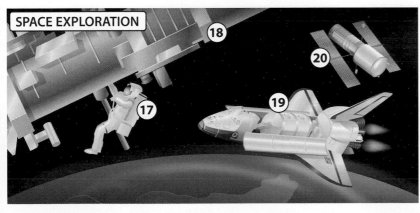

⑰ ⑱ ⑲ ⑳

ASTRONOMY

㉑ ㉒ ㉓ ㉔

17. astronaut 우주비행사	**19.** space shuttle 우주선	**21.** observatory 관측소	**23.** telescope 망원경
18. space station 우주 정류장	**20.** satellite 위성	**22.** astronomer 천문학자	**24.** comet 혜성

More vocabulary

solar eclipse: when the moon is between the earth and the sun
Big Dipper: a famous part of the constellation Ursa Major
Sirius: the brightest star in the night sky

Ask your classmates. Share the answers.

1. How do you feel when you look at the night sky?
2. Can you name one or more constellations?
3. Do you want to travel in space?

A Graduation 졸업

All Adelia's photos

I loved Art History.

My last economics lesson

Marching Band is great!

The photographer was upset.

We look good!

I get my diploma.

Dad and his digital camera

1. photographer
   사진사
2. funny photo
   장난스러운 사진
3. serious photo
   진지한 표정의
   사진
4. guest speaker
   초빙 연사
5. podium
   연단
6. ceremony
   식
7. cap
   졸업 모자
8. gown
   졸업 가운

A. **take** a picture
   사진을 **찍다**
B. **cry**
   울다
C. **celebrate**
   축하하다

206

People	Comments	
Sara	June 29th 8:19 p.m.	
	Great pictures! What a day!	Delete
Zannie baby	June 30th 10 a.m.	
	Love the funny photo.	Delete

I'm behind the mayor.

We're all very happy.

Look at the pictures. What do you see?

Answer the questions.

1. How many people are wearing caps and gowns?

2. How many people are being funny? How many are being serious?

3. Who is standing at the podium?

4. Why are the graduates throwing their caps in the air?

Read the story.

A Graduation

Look at these great photos on my web page! The first three are from my favorite classes, but the other pictures are from graduation day.

There are two pictures of my classmates in <u>caps</u> and <u>gowns</u>. In the first picture, we're laughing and the <u>photographer</u> is upset. In the second photo, we're serious. I like the <u>serious photo</u>, but I love the <u>funny photo</u>!

There's also a picture of our <u>guest speaker</u>, the mayor. She is standing at the <u>podium</u>. Next, you can see me at the graduation <u>ceremony</u>. My dad wanted to <u>take a picture</u> of me with my diploma. That's my mom next to him. She <u>cries</u> when she's happy.

After the ceremony, everyone was happy, but no one cried. We wanted to <u>celebrate</u> and we did!

Think about it.

1. What kinds of ceremonies are important for children? for teens? for adults?

2. Imagine you are the guest speaker at a graduation. What will you say to the graduates?

207

1. trees
   니무
2. soil
   흙
3. path
   길
4. bird
   새
5. plants
   식물
6. rock
   돌
7. flowers
   꽃

OAK

WILLOW

ELM

PLANT SALE 50% OFF

$7.

Listen and point. Take turns.

A: *Point to the trees.*
B: *Point to a bird.*
A: *Point to the flowers.*

Dictate to your partner. Take turns.

A: *Write it's a tree.*
B: *Let me check that. I-t-'s -a- t-r-e-e?*
A: *Yes, that's right.*

LOOK FOR ME!

8. sun
태양

9. sky
하늘

10. mammals
포유동물

11. insects
곤충

12. nest
둥지

13. water
물

14. fish
물고기

GLASS
PLASTIC
ONLY

PLEASE DON'T FEED

OPEN DAILY 9-5

❀LILLO❀
Nature Center

Ways to talk about nature

Look at <u>the sky</u>! Isn't it beautiful?
Did you see <u>the fish</u> / <u>insects</u>?
It's / They're so interesting.

Pair practice. Make new conversations.

A: *Do you know the name of that <u>yellow flower</u>?*
B: *I think it's <u>a sunflower</u>.*
A: *Oh, and what about that <u>blue bird</u>?*

209

Trees and Plants / 나무와 식물

PARTS OF A TREE

1. twig
   잔가지
2. branch
   가지
3. limb
   큰 가지
4. trunk
   줄기
5. root
   뿌리
6. leaf
   잎

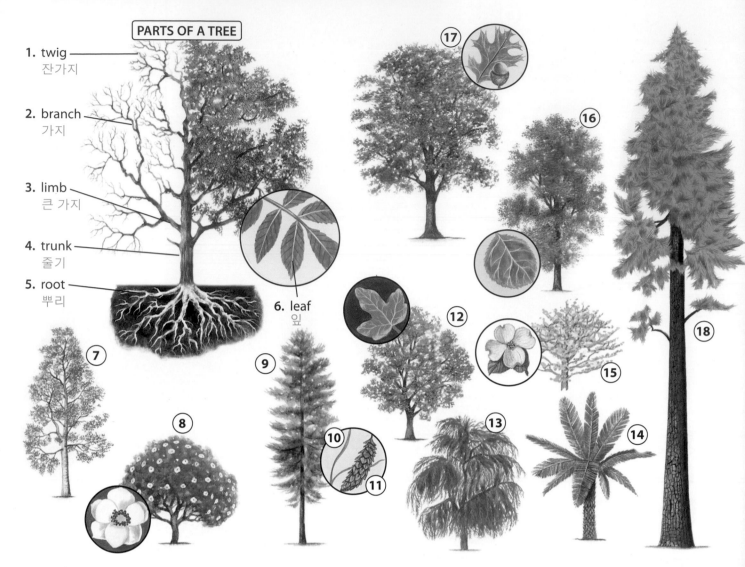

7. birch
   자작나무
8. magnolia
   태산목
9. pine
   소나무

10. needle
    침상엽
11. pinecone
    솔방울
12. maple
    단풍나무

13. willow
    버드나무
14. palm
    야자나무
15. dogwood
    층층나무

16. elm
    느릅나무
17. oak
    오크
18. redwood
    아메리카삼나무

Plants 식물

19. holly
    서양호랑가시나무
20. berries
    베리

21. cactus
    선인장
22. vine
    덩굴

23. poison sumac
    독있는 옻나무
24. poison oak
    독있는 오크

25. poison ivy
    덩굴옻나무

210

Parts of a Flower 꽃의 각 부위 명칭

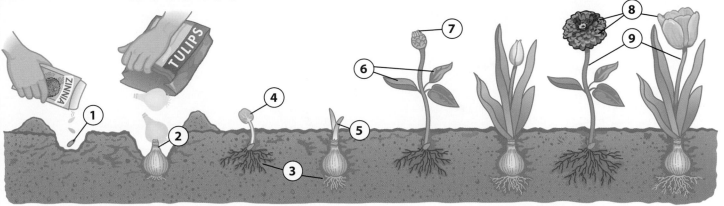

1. seed
씨

2. bulb
구근

3. roots
뿌리

4. seedling
묘목

5. shoot
싹

6. leaves
잎

7. bud
봉우리

8. petals
꽃잎

9. stems
줄기

10. sunflower
해바라기

11. tulip
튤립

12. hibiscus
하이비스커스

13. marigold
금잔화

14. daisy
데이지

15. rose
장미

16. iris
아이리스

17. crocus
크로커스

18. gardenia
가디니아

19. orchid
난초

20. carnation
카네이션

21. chrysanthemum
국화

22. jasmine
재스민

23. violet
제비꽃

24. poinsettia
포인세티아

25. daffodil
수선화

26. lily
백합

27. houseplant
실내화초

28. bouquet
꽃다발

29. thorn
가시

Sea Animals 바다 동물

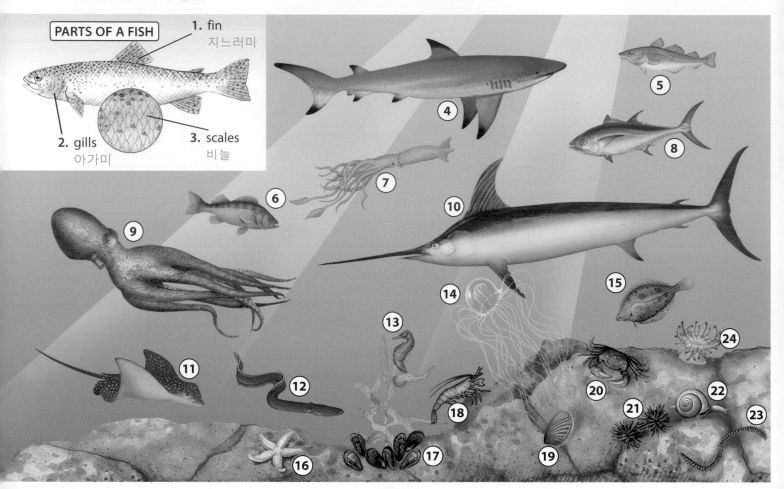

PARTS OF A FISH

1. fin
지느러미

2. gills
아가미

3. scales
비늘

4. shark 상어	**9.** octopus 문어	**14.** jellyfish 해파리	**19.** scallop 가리비	**24.** sea anemone 말미잘
5. cod 대구	**10.** swordfish 황새치	**15.** flounder 가자미	**20.** crab 게	
6. bass 배스	**11.** ray 가오리	**16.** starfish 불가사리	**21.** sea urchin 성게	
7. squid 오징어	**12.** eel 장어	**17.** mussel 홍합	**22.** snail 달팽이	
8. tuna 참치	**13.** seahorse 해마	**18.** shrimp 새우	**23.** worm 벌레	

Amphibians 양서류

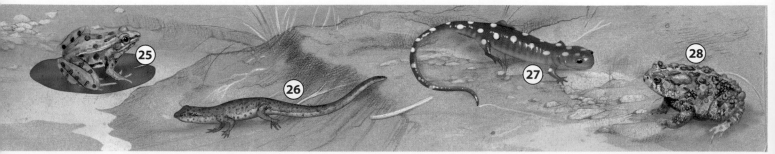

25. frog 개구리	**26.** newt 영원	**27.** salamander 도롱뇽	**28.** toad 두꺼비

Sea Mammals 바다에 사는 포유동물

29. whale 고래	**31.** dolphin 돌고래	**33.** sea lion 바다 사자	**35.** sea otter 수달
30. porpoise 돌고래 무리	**32.** walrus 바다코끼리	**34.** seal 물개	

Reptiles 파충류

36. alligator 악어	**38.** rattlesnake 방울뱀	**40.** lizard 도마뱀	**42.** tortoise 거북
37. crocodile 크로코다일	**39.** garter snake 누룩뱀	**41.** cobra 코브라	**43.** turtle 거북이

213

PARTS OF A BIRD

1. wing
   날개
2. claw
   발톱
3. beak / bill
   부리
4. feather
   깃털

5. owl 올빼미	**8.** woodpecker 딱따구리	**11.** penguin 펭귄	**14.** peacock 공작
6. blue jay 큰어치	**9.** eagle 독수리	**12.** duck 오리	**15.** pigeon 비둘기
7. sparrow 참새	**10.** hummingbird 벌새	**13.** goose 거위	**16.** robin 로빈

Insects and Arachnids 곤충 그리고 거미류

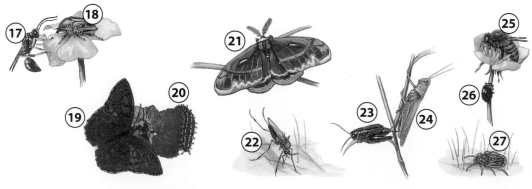

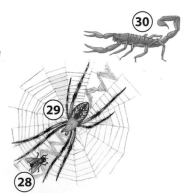

17. wasp 말벌	**21.** moth 나방	**25.** honeybee 꿀벌	**29.** spider 거미
18. beetle 딱정벌레	**22.** mosquito 모기	**26.** ladybug 무당 벌레	**30.** scorpion 전갈
19. butterfly 나비	**23.** cricket 귀뚜라미	**27.** tick 진드기	
20. caterpillar 애벌레	**24.** grasshopper 메뚜기	**28.** fly 파리	

가축과 설치류 동물　　　**Domestic Animals and Rodents**

Farm Animals 농장 동물

1. cow
소
2. pig
돼지
3. donkey
당나귀
4. horse
말
5. goat
염소
6. sheep
양
7. rooster
수탉
8. hen
암탉

Pets 애완동물

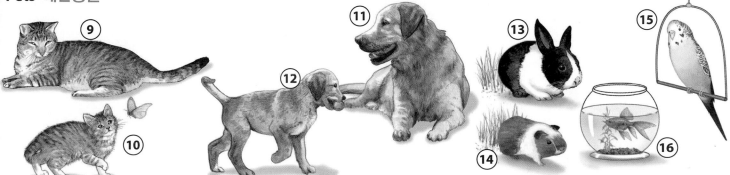

9. cat
고양이
10. kitten
새끼 고양이
11. dog
개
12. puppy
강아지
13. rabbit
토끼
14. guinea pig
기니피그
15. parakeet
잉꼬
16. goldfish
금붕어

Rodents 설치류

17. rat
쥐
18. mouse
생쥐
19. gopher
들쥐
20. chipmunk
얼룩 다람쥐
21. squirrel
다람쥐
22. prairie dog
프레리 도그

More vocabulary

domesticated: animals that work for and / or live with people
wild: animals that live away from people

Ask your classmates. Share the answers.

1. Have you worked with farm animals? Which ones?
2. Are you afraid of rodents? Which ones?
3. Do you have a pet? What kind?

215

1. moose
   무스

2. mountain lion
   쿠거

3. coyote
   코요테

4. opossum
   주머니쥐

5. wolf
   늑대

6. buffalo / bison
   들소

7. bat
   박쥐

8. armadillo
   아르마딜로

9. beaver
   비버

10. porcupine
    고슴도치

11. bear
    곰

12. skunk
    스컹크

13. raccoon
    너구리

14. deer
    사슴

15. fox
    여우

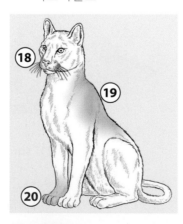

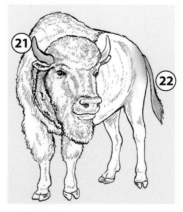

16. antlers
    (사슴의)가지진 뿔

17. hooves
    발굽

18. whiskers
    수염

19. coat / fur
    털 / 가죽

20. paw
    발

21. horn
    뿔

22. tail
    꼬리

23. quill
    깃대

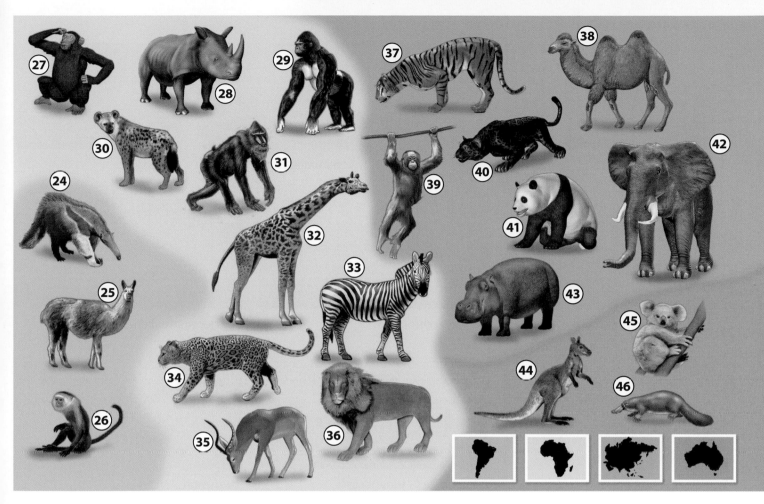

24. anteater 개미핥기	**29.** gorilla 고릴라	**34.** leopard 표범	**39.** orangutan 오랑우탄	**44.** kangaroo 캥거루
25. llama 아메리카 낙타	**30.** hyena 하이에나	**35.** antelope 영양	**40.** panther 표범	**45.** koala 코알라
26. monkey 원숭이	**31.** baboon 개코원숭이	**36.** lion 사자	**41.** panda 판다	**46.** platypus 오리구리
27. chimpanzee 침팬지	**32.** giraffe 기린	**37.** tiger 호랑이	**42.** elephant 코끼리	
28. rhinoceros 코뿔소	**33.** zebra 얼룩말	**38.** camel 낙타	**43.** hippopotamus 하마	

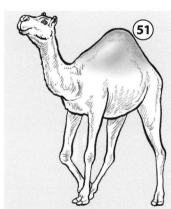

47. trunk 코끼리 코	**48.** tusk 상아	**49.** mane 갈기	**50.** pouch 주머니	**51.** hump 혹

Energy Sources 에너지 자원

1. solar energy
태양 에너지

2. wind power
풍력

3. natural gas
천연 가스

4. coal
석탄

5. hydroelectric power
수력 발전

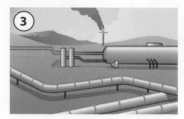

6. oil / petroleum
오일 / 석유

7. geothermal energy
지열 에너지

8. nuclear energy
원자력 에너지

9. biomass / bioenergy
생물 자원 / 생물 에너지

10. fusion
융합

Pollution 공해

11. air pollution / smog
대기 오염 / 스모그

12. hazardous waste
위험 폐기물

13. acid rain
산성 비

14. water pollution
수질 오염

15. radiation
방사능

16. pesticide poisoning
살충제 중독

17. oil spill
기름 유출

Ask your classmates. Share the answers.

1. What types of things do you recycle?
2. What types of energy sources are in your area?
3. What types of pollution do you worry about?

Think about it. Discuss.

1. How can you save energy in the summer? winter?
2. What are some other ways that people can conserve energy or prevent pollution?

Ways to Conserve Energy and Resources 에너지와 자원을 보존하는 방법

A. reduce trash
쓰레기를 **줄인다**

B. reuse shopping bags
쇼핑 백을 **재사용한다**

C. recycle
재활용한다

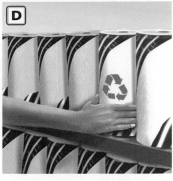

D. buy recycled products
재활용 제품을 **구입한다**

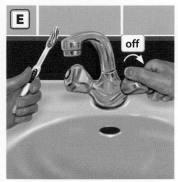

E. save water
물을 **아낀다**

F. fix leaky faucets
물이 새는 수도꼭지를
수리한다

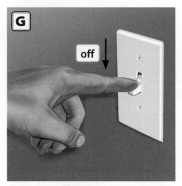

G. turn off lights
불을 **끈다**

H. use energy-efficient bulbs
에너지 효율성이 높은 전구
를 **사용한다**

I. carpool
카풀을 **한다**

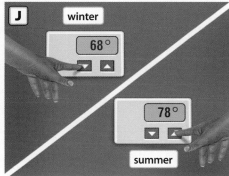

J. adjust the thermostat
온도를 **조정한다**

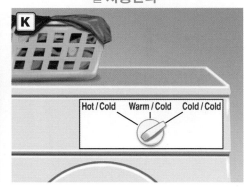

K. wash clothes in cold water
차가운 물로 **세탁한다**

L. don't litter
쓰레기를 버리지 **않는다**

M. compost food scraps
음식물 쓰레기는 **퇴비로 사용한다**

N. plant a tree
나무를 **심는다**

U.S. National Parks 미국 국립 공원

Yosemite
NATIONAL PARK

Half Dome

1

2

3

Dry Tortugas
NATIONAL PARK

1

Fort Jefferson

4

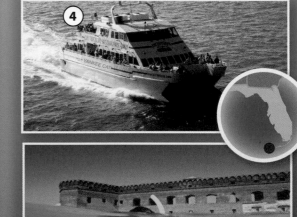

5

---

1. **landmarks**
   지형지물

2. **park ranger**
   공원 관리인

3. **wildlife**
   야생 생물

4. **ferry**
   페리

5. **coral**
   산호

6. **cave**
   동굴

7. **caverns**
   큰 동굴

A. **take** a tour
   여행을 **하다**

Answer the questions.

1. How many U.S. landmarks are in the pictures?

2. What kinds of wildlife do you see?

3. What can you do at Carlsbad Caverns?

 Read the story.

U.S. National Parks

More than 200 million people visit U.S. National Parks every year. These parks protect the <u>wildlife</u> and <u>landmarks</u> of the United States. Each park is different, and each one is beautiful.

At Yosemite, in California, you can take a nature walk with a <u>park ranger</u>. You'll see waterfalls, redwoods, and deer there.

In south Florida, you can take a <u>ferry</u> to Dry Tortugas. It's great to snorkel around the park's <u>coral</u> islands.

There are 113 <u>caves</u> at Carlsbad <u>Caverns</u> in New Mexico. The deepest cave is 830 feet below the desert! You can <u>take a tour</u> of these beautiful caverns.

There are 391 national parks to see. Go online for information about a park near you.

Think about it.

1. Why are national parks important?

2. Imagine you are a park ranger at a national park. Give your classmates a tour of the landmarks and wildlife.

1. zoo
   동물원
2. movies
   영화관
3. botanical garden
   식물원
4. bowling alley
   볼링장
5. rock concert
   록 콘서트
6. swap meet /
   flea market
   중고품 시장 / 벼룩 시장
7. aquarium
   수족관

| File | Edit | View | History | Bookmarks | Tools |

Places to Go in Our City

Listen and point. Take turns.

A: *Point to the zoo.*
B: *Point to the flea market.*
A: *Point to the rock concert.*

Dictate to your partner. Take turns.

A: *Write these words: zoo, movies, aquarium.*
B: *Zoo, movies, and what?*
A: *Aquarium.*

Search

8. play
연극

9. art museum
미술관

10. amusement park
유원지

11. opera
오페라

12. nightclub
나이트클럽

13. county fair
카운티 페어

14. classical concert
클래식 콘서트

BACH FESTIVAL

Ways to make plans using *Let's go*

Let's go to <u>the amusement park</u> tomorrow.
Let's go to <u>the opera</u> on Saturday.
Let's go to <u>the movies</u> tonight.

Pair practice. Make new conversations.

A: <u>*Let's go to the zoo this afternoon*</u>.
B: *OK. And let's go to <u>the movies tonight</u>*.
A: *That sounds like a good plan.*

1. ball field
   구장

2. cyclist
   자전거 타는 사람

3. bike path
   자전거 길

4. jump rope
   줄넘기

5. fountain
   분수대

6. tennis court
   테니스 코트

7. skateboard
   스케이트보드

8. picnic table
   피크닉 테이블

9. water fountain
   음료대

10. bench
    벤치

11. swings
    그네

12. tricycle
    세발 자전거

13. slide
    미끄럼틀

14. climbing apparatus
    기어오르는 놀이 기구

15. sandbox
    모래상자

16. seesaw
    시소

A. pull the wagon
수레를 **잡아당기다**

B. push the swing
그네를 **밀다**

C. climb the bars
놀이 틀 위를 **기어오르다**

D. picnic / have a picnic
소풍 / 소풍 가다

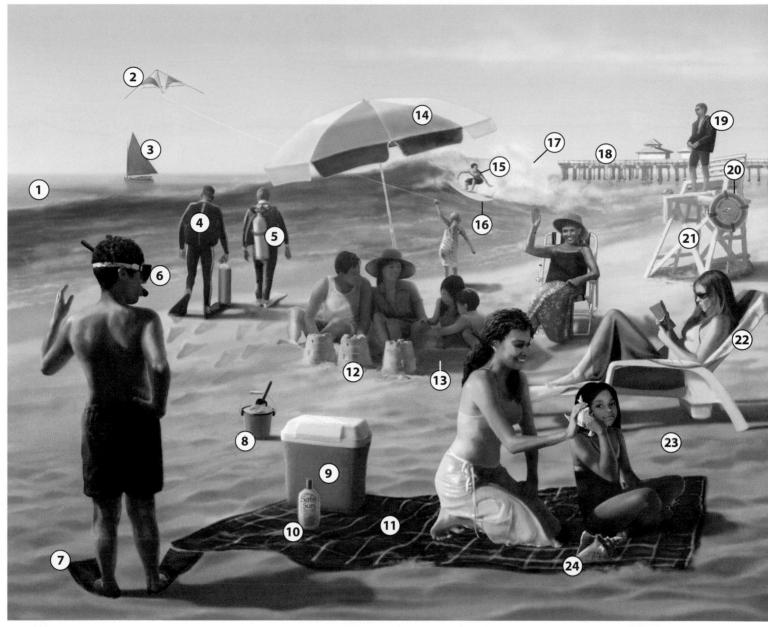

1. ocean / water	7. fins	13. shade	19. lifeguard
대양 / 물	오리발	그늘	구조대원
2. kite	8. pail / bucket	14. beach umbrella	20. lifesaving device
연	양동이 / 들통	비치 파라솔	인명구조 기구
3. sailboat	9. cooler	15. surfer	21. lifeguard station
요트	아이스박스	서퍼	구조대원실
4. wet suit	10. sunscreen / sunblock	16. surfboard	22. beach chair
잠수복	자외선 차단제	서프보드	해변용 의자
5. scuba tank	11. blanket	17. wave	23. sand
스쿠버 탱크	담요	파도	모래
6. diving mask	12. sand castle	18. pier	24. seashell
다이빙 마스크	모래성	부두	조개

More vocabulary

seaweed: a plant that grows in the ocean
tide: the level of the ocean. The tide goes in and out every 12 hours.

Ask your classmates. Share the answers.

1. Do you like to go to the beach?
2. Are there famous beaches in your native country?
3. Do you prefer to be on the sand or in the water?

225

1. boating
   보트타기

2. rafting
   래프팅

3. canoeing
   카누 타기

4. fishing
   낚시

5. camping
   캠핑

6. backpacking
   배낭여행

7. hiking
   하이킹

8. mountain biking
   산악 자전거 타기

9. horseback riding
   말타기

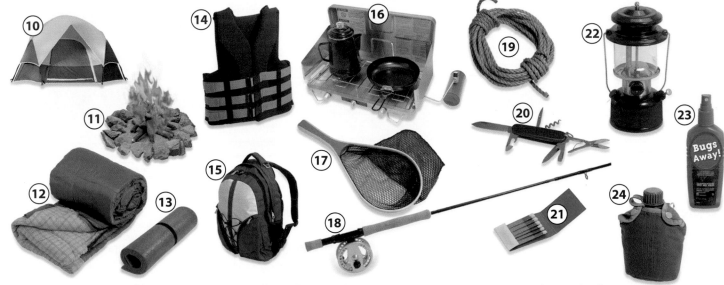

10. tent
    텐트

11. campfire
    캠프파이어

12. sleeping bag
    슬리핑백

13. foam pad
    폼 패드

14. life vest
    구명 조끼

15. backpack
    배낭

16. camping stove
    캠핑 스토브

17. fishing net
    고기잡이 그물

18. fishing pole
    낚싯대

19. rope
    줄

20. multi-use knife
    다용도 칼

21. matches
    성냥

22. lantern
    랜턴

23. insect repellent
    방충제

24. canteen
    수통

1. downhill skiing
활강 스키

2. snowboarding
스노보딩

3. cross-country skiing
크로스 컨트리 스키

4. ice skating
아이스 스케이팅

5. figure skating
피겨 스케이팅

6. sledding
썰매타기

7. waterskiing
수상스키

8. sailing
요트

9. surfing
서핑

10. windsurfing
윈드서핑

11. snorkeling
스노클링

12. scuba diving
스쿠버 다이빙

More vocabulary

speed skating: racing while ice skating
windsurfing: sailboarding

Ask your classmates. Share the answers.

1. Which of these sports do you like?
2. Which of these sports would you like to learn?
3. Which of these sports is the most fun to watch?

1. archery
양궁

2. billiards / pool
당구 / 포켓볼

3. bowling
볼링

4. boxing
권투

5. cycling / biking
사이클링

6. badminton
배드민턴

7. fencing
펜싱

8. golf
골프

9. gymnastics
체조

10. inline skating
인라인 스케이팅

11. martial arts
무술

12. racquetball
라켓볼

13. skateboarding
스케이트보드

14. table tennis
탁구

15. tennis
테니스

16. weightlifting
역도

17. wrestling
레슬링

18. track and field
육상 경기

19. horse racing
경마

Pair practice. Make new conversations.

A: *What sports do you like?*
B: *I like* <u>bowling</u>. *What do you like?*
A: *I like* <u>gymnastics</u>.

Think about it. Discuss.

1. Why do people like to watch sports?
2. Which sports can be dangerous?
3. Why do people do dangerous sports?

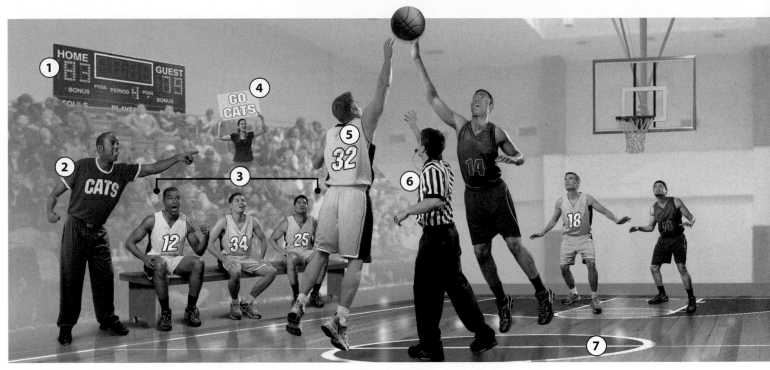

1. score
점수

2. coach
코치

3. team
팀

4. fan
팬

5. player
선수

6. official / referee
심판 / 레프리

7. basketball court
농구 코트

8. basketball
농구

9. baseball
야구

10. softball
소프트볼

11. football
풋볼/미식축구

12. soccer
축구

13. ice hockey
아이스 하키

14. volleyball
배구

15. water polo
수구

More Vocabulary

win: to have the best score
lose: the opposite of win
tie: to have the same score

captain: the team leader
umpire: the name of the referee in baseball
Little League: a baseball and softball program for children

A. **pitch**
던지다

B. **hit**
치다

C. **throw**
던지다

D. **catch**
잡다

E. **kick**
차다

F. **tackle**
태클하다

G. **pass**
패스하다

H. **shoot**
슛하다

I. **jump**
점프하다

J. **dribble**
드리블하다

K. **dive**
다이빙하다

L. **swim**
수영하다

M. **stretch**
스트레칭하다

N. **exercise / work out**
운동하다

O. **bend**
구부리다

P. **serve**
서브하다

Q. **swing**
스윙하다

R. **start**
출발하다

S. **race**
경주하다

T. **finish**
결승점에 닿다

U. **skate**
스케이트를 타다

V. **ski**
스키를 타다

Use the new words.
Look on page 229. Name the actions you see.

A: *He's throwing.*

B: *She's jumping.*

Ways to talk about your sports skills

I can throw, but I can't catch.
I swim well, but I don't dive well.
I'm good at skating, but I'm terrible at skiing.

230

1. golf club
골프 채

2. tennis racket
테니스 라켓

3. volleyball
배구공

4. basketball
농구공

5. bowling ball
볼링 볼

6. bow
활

7. target
과녁

8. arrow
화살

9. ice skates
아이스 스케이트

10. inline skates
인라인 스케이트

11. hockey stick
하키 스틱

12. soccer ball
축구공

13. shin guards
무릎 보호대

14. baseball bat
야구 방망이

15. catcher's mask
캐처 마스크

16. uniform
유니폼

17. glove
장갑

18. baseball
야구공

19. football helmet
풋볼 헬멧

20. shoulder pads
어깨 패드

21. football
풋볼공

22. weights
아령

23. snowboard
스노보드

24. skis
스키

25. ski poles
스키 폴

26. ski boots
스키화

27. flying disc*
프리즈비

*Note: one brand is Frisbee®, of Wham-O, Inc.

Use the new words.
Look at pages 228–229. Name the sports equipment you see.

A: *Those are ice skates.*
B: *That's a football.*

Ask your classmates. Share the answers.

1. Do you own any sports equipment? What kind?
2. What do you want to buy at this store?
3. Where is the best place to buy sports equipment?

231

A. collect things
물건을 **수집하다**

B. play games
게임을 **하다**

C. quilt
퀼트를 하다

D. do crafts
공예를 **하다**

1. figurine (금속•도기등의)작은 상	**5.** board game 보드게임	**9.** model kit 모형 키트	**13.** doll making kit 인형 만드는 키트
2. baseball cards 야구 카드	**6.** dice 주사위	**10.** acrylic paint 아크릴 페인트	**14.** woodworking kit 목공 키트
3. video game console 비디오 게임기	**7.** checkers 서양 장기	**11.** glue stick 딱풀	**15.** quilt block 퀼트 조각
4. video game control 비디오 게임 조종기	**8.** chess 체스	**12.** construction paper 색종이	**16.** rotary cutter 원형 재단기

Grammar Point: *How often do you play cards?*

*I play **all the time**. (every day)*
*I play **sometimes**. (once a month)*
*I **never** play. (0 times)*

Pair practice. Make new conversations.

A: *How often do you do your hobbies?*
B: *I play games all the time. I love chess.*
A: *Really? I never play chess.*

E. paint
그리다

F. knit
짜다

G. pretend
흉내를 내다

H. play cards
카드놀이를 **하다**

17. canvas
캔버스

18. easel
이젤

19. oil paint
유화

20. paintbrush
페인트 브러쉬

21. watercolor
수채화 물감

22. yarn
뜨개실

23. knitting needles
뜨개 바늘

24. embroidery
자수

25. crocheting
코바늘뜨기

26. action figure
액션 인물

27. model trains
모델 기차

28. paper dolls
종이 인형

29. diamonds
다이아몬드

30. spades
스페이드

31. hearts
하트

32. clubs
클럽

Ways to talk about hobbies and games

This <u>board game</u> is **interesting**. It makes me think.
That <u>video game</u> is **boring**. Nothing happens.
I love to <u>play cards</u>. It's **fun** to play with my friends.

Ask your classmates. Share the answers.

1. Do you collect anything? What?
2. Which games do you like to play?
3. What hobbies did you have as a child?

233

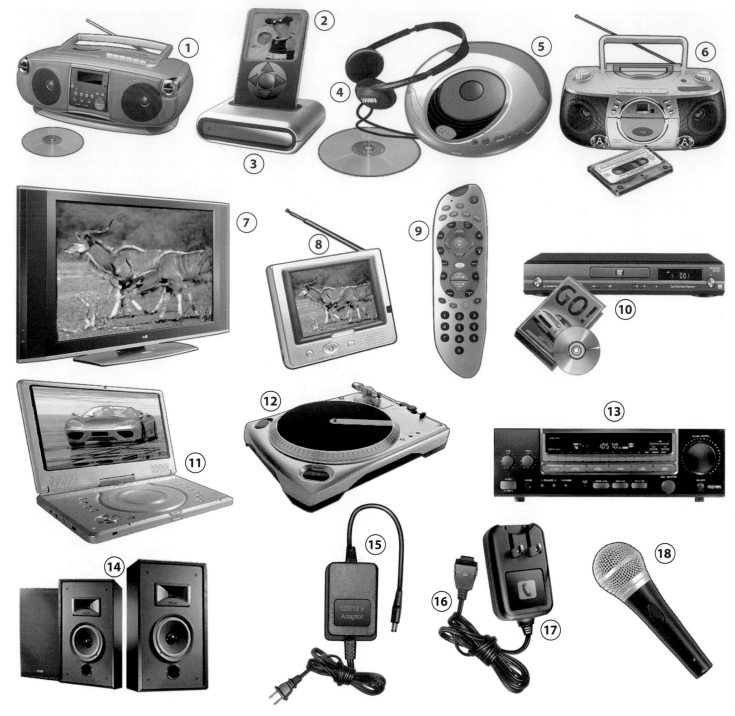

1. **CD boombox**
   CD 플레이어

2. **MP3 player**
   MP3 플레이어

3. **dock**
   도크

4. **headphones**
   헤드폰

5. **personal CD player**
   개인 CD 플레이어

6. **portable cassette player**
   휴대용 카세트 플레이어

7. **flat screen TV / flat panel TV**
   평면 TV

8. **portable TV**
   휴대용 TV

9. **universal remote**
   범용 리모콘

10. **DVD player**
    DVD 플레이어

11. **portable DVD player**
    휴대용 DVD 플레이어

12. **turntable**
    전축

13. **tuner**
    튜너

14. **speakers**
    스피커

15. **adapter**
    어댑터

16. **plug**
    플러그

17. **charger**
    충전기

18. **microphone**
    마이크

19. digital camera
디지털 카메라

20. memory card
메모리 카드

21. film camera / 35 mm camera
필름 카메라 / 35 mm 카메라

22. film
필름

23. zoom lens
줌 렌즈

24. camcorder
캠코더

25. tripod
삼각대

26. battery pack
배터리 팩

27. battery charger
배터리 충전기

28. camera case
카메라 케이스

29. LCD projector
LCD 프로젝터

30. screen
스크린

31. photo album
사진 앨범

32. digital photo album
디지털 사진 앨범

33. out of focus
촛점이 안맞다

34. overexposed
노출 과다

35. underexposed
노출 부족

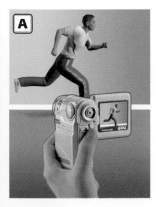

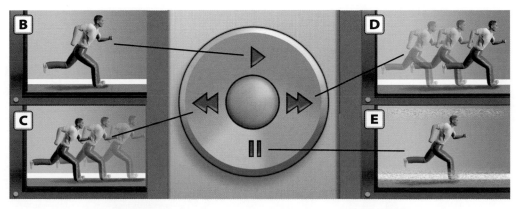

A. record
촬영하다

B. play
재생하다

C. rewind
되감다

D. fast forward
고속 앞으로

E. pause
일시 정지

Types of TV Programs　TV 프로그램 종류

1. news program
뉴스

2. sitcom (situation comedy)
시트콤

3. cartoon
만화

4. talk show
토크 쇼

5. soap opera
멜로 드라마

6. reality show
리얼리티 쇼

7. nature program
자연 프로그램

8. game show
게임 쇼

9. children's program
어린이 프로그램

10. shopping program
쇼핑 프로그램

11. sports program
스포츠 프로그램

12. drama
드라마

Types of Movies 영화의 종류

13. comedy
코미디

14. tragedy
비극

15. western
서부영화

16. romance
로맨스

17. horror story
공포물

18. science fiction story
공상과학

19. action story / adventure
story
액션 / 모험

20. mystery / suspense
미스터리 / 서스펜스

Types of Music 음악의 종류

21. classical
클래식

22. blues
블루스

23. rock
록

24. jazz
재즈

25. pop
팝

26. hip hop
힙합

27. country
컨츄리

28. R&B / soul
R&B / 소울

29. folk
포크

30. gospel
가스펠

31. reggae
레게

32. world music
세계 음악

A. play an instrument
악기를 **연주하다**

B. sing a song
노래를 **부르다**

C. conduct an orchestra
오케스트라를 **지휘하다**

D. be in a rock band
록 밴드 **활동을 하다**

Woodwinds 목관악기

1. flute
   플루트

2. clarinet
   클라리넷

3. oboe
   오보에

4. bassoon
   바순

5. saxophone
   색소폰

Strings 현악기

6. violin
   바이올린

7. cello
   첼로

8. bass
   베이스

9. guitar
   기타

Brass 금관악기

10. trombone
    트롬본

11. trumpet /
    horn
    트럼펫 / 혼

12. tuba
    튜바

13. French horn
    프렌치 혼

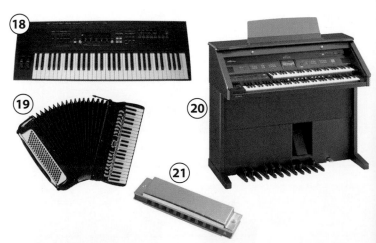

Percussion 타악기

14. piano
    피아노

15. xylophone
    실로폰

16. drums
    드럼

17. tambourine
    탬버린

Other Instruments 기타 악기

18. electric keyboard
    전자 키보드

19. accordion
    아코디언

20. organ
    오르간

21. harmonica
    하모니카

1. parade
   퍼레이드

2. float
   이동식 무대차

3. confetti
   색종이 조각

4. couple
   커플

5. card
   카드

6. heart
   하트

7. fireworks
   악기를 연주하다

8. flag
   국기

9. mask
   가면

10. jack-o'-lantern
    잭-오-랜턴

11. costume
    복장

12. candy
    캔디

13. feast
    축제

14. turkey
    칠면조

15. ornament
    장식

16. Christmas tree
    크리스마스 트리

17. candy cane
    지팡이 모양 캔디

18. string lights
    장식용 전구

*Thanksgiving is on the fourth Thursday in November.

1. decorations
   장식
2. deck
   덱
3. present / gift
   선물

A. **videotape**
   비디오 촬영을 하다
B. **make** a wish
   소원을 말하다
C. **blow out**
   촛불을 불다
D. **hide**
   숨다
E. **bring**
   가져오다
F. **wrap**
   포장하다

Happy Birthday!

Look at the picture. What do you see?

Answer the questions.

1. What kinds of decorations do you see?
2. What are people doing at this birthday party?
3. What wish did the teenager make?
4. How many presents did people bring?

 Read the story.

A Birthday Party

Today is Lou and Gani Bombata's birthday barbecue. There are <u>decorations</u> around the backyard, and food and drinks on the <u>deck</u>. There are also <u>presents</u>. Everyone in the Bombata family likes to <u>bring</u> presents.

Right now, it's time for cake. Gani <u>is blowing out</u> the candles, and Lou <u>is making a wish</u>. Lou's mom wants to <u>videotape</u> everyone, but she can't find Lou's brother, Todd. Todd hates to sing, so he always <u>hides</u> for the birthday song.

Lou's sister, Amaka, has to <u>wrap</u> some <u>gifts</u>. She doesn't want Lou to see. Amaka isn't worried. She knows her family loves to sing. She can put her gifts on the present table before they finish the first song.

Think about it.

1. What wish do you think Gani made?
2. What kinds of presents do you give to relatives? What kinds of presents can you give to friends or co-workers?

Verb Guide

Verbs in English are either regular or irregular in the past tense and past participle forms.

Regular Verbs

The regular verbs below are marked 1, 2, 3, or 4 according to four different spelling patterns.
(See page 244 for the irregular verbs which do not follow any of these patterns.)

Spelling Patterns for the Past and the Past Participle	Example	
1. Add -ed to the end of the verb.	**ASK**	**ASKED**
2. Add -d to the end of the verb.	**LIVE**	**LIVED**
3. Double the final consonant and add -ed to the end of the verb.	**DROP**	**DROPPED**
4. Drop the final y and add -ied to the end of the verb.	**CRY**	**CRIED**

The Oxford Picture Dictionary List of Regular Verbs

accept (1)
add (1)
address (1)
adjust (1)
agree (2)
answer (1)
apologize (2)
appear (1)
applaud (1)
apply (4)
arrange (2)
arrest (1)
arrive (2)
ask (1)
assemble (2)
assist (1)
attach (1)
bake (2)
bank (1)
bargain (1)
bathe (2)
board (1)
boil (1)
borrow (1)
bow (1)
brainstorm (1)
breathe (2)
browse (2)
brush (1)
bubble (2)
buckle (2)
burn (1)
bus (1)
calculate (2)
call (1)
capitalize (2)
carpool (1)

carry (4)
cash (1)
celebrate (2)
change (2)
check (1)
chill (1)
choke (2)
chop (3)
circle (2)
claim (1)
clean (1)
clear (1)
click (1)
climb (1)
close (2)
collate (2)
collect (1)
color (1)
comb (1)
comfort (1)
commit (3)
compliment (1)
compost (1)
conceal (1)
conduct (1)
convert (1)
convict (1)
cook (1)
copy (4)
correct (1)
cough (1)
count (1)
cross (1)
cry (4)
dance (2)
debate (2)
decline (2)

delete (2)
deliver (1)
design (1)
dial (1)
dice (2)
dictate (2)
die (2)
disagree (2)
discipline (2)
discuss (1)
dive (2)
divide (2)
dress (1)
dribble (2)
drill (1)
drop (3)
drown (1)
dry (4)
dust (1)
dye (2)
edit (1)
empty (4)
enter (1)
erase (2)
evacuate (2)
examine (2)
exchange (2)
exercise (2)
expire (2)
explain (1)
exterminate (2)
fasten (1)
fast forward (1)
fax (1)
fertilize (2)
fill (1)
finish (1)

fix (1)
floss (1)
fold (1)
follow (1)
garden (1)
gargle (2)
graduate (2)
grate (2)
grease (2)
greet (1)
hail (1)
hammer (1)
hand (1)
harvest (1)
help (1)
hire (2)
hug (3)
immigrate (2)
indent (1)
inquire (2)
insert (1)
inspect (1)
install (1)
introduce (2)
invite (2)
iron (1)
jaywalk (1)
join (1)
jump (1)
kick (1)
kiss (1)
knit (3)
label (1)
land (1)
laugh (1)
learn (1)
lengthen (1)

lift (1)	pitch (1)	rock (1)	supervise (2)
listen (1)	plan (3)	sauté (1)	swallow (1)
litter (1)	plant (1)	save (2)	tackle (2)
live (2)	play (1)	scan (3)	talk (1)
load (1)	polish (1)	schedule (2)	taste (2)
lock (1)	pour (1)	scrub (3)	thank (1)
look (1)	praise (2)	seat (1)	tie (2)
mail (1)	preheat (1)	select (1)	touch (1)
manufacture (2)	prepare (2)	sentence (2)	transcribe (2)
match (1)	prescribe (2)	separate (2)	transfer (3)
measure (2)	press (1)	serve (2)	translate (2)
microwave (2)	pretend (1)	share (2)	travel (1)
milk (1)	print (1)	shave (2)	trim (3)
misbehave (2)	program (3)	ship (3)	try (4)
miss (1)	protect (1)	shop (3)	turn (1)
mix (1)	pull (1)	shorten (1)	type (2)
mop (3)	purchase (2)	sign (1)	underline (2)
move (2)	push (1)	simmer (1)	undress (1)
mow (1)	quilt (1)	skate (2)	unload (1)
multiply (4)	race (2)	ski (1)	unpack (1)
negotiate (2)	raise (2)	slice (2)	unscramble (2)
network (1)	rake (2)	smell (1)	use (2)
numb (1)	receive (2)	smile (2)	vacuum (1)
nurse (2)	record (1)	smoke (2)	videotape (2)
obey (1)	recycle (2)	sneeze (2)	volunteer (1)
observe (2)	redecorate (2)	solve (2)	vomit (1)
offer (1)	reduce (2)	sort (1)	vote (2)
open (1)	register (1)	spell (1)	wait (1)
operate (2)	relax (1)	spoon (1)	walk (1)
order (1)	remain (1)	staple (2)	wash (1)
organize (2)	remove (2)	start (1)	watch (1)
overdose (2)	renew (1)	state (2)	water (1)
pack (1)	repair (1)	stay (1)	wave (2)
paint (1)	replace (2)	steam (1)	weed (1)
park (1)	report (1)	stir (3)	weigh (1)
participate (2)	request (1)	stop (3)	wipe (2)
pass (1)	retire (2)	stow (1)	work (1)
pause (2)	return (1)	stretch (1)	wrap (3)
peel (1)	reuse (2)	study (4)	
perm (1)	revise (2)	submit (3)	
pick (1)	rinse (2)	subtract (1)	

Verb Guide

Irregular Verbs

These verbs have irregular endings in the past and/or the past participle.

The Oxford Picture Dictionary List of Irregular Verbs

simple	past	past participle	simple	past	past participle
be	was	been	make	made	made
beat	beat	beaten	meet	met	met
become	became	become	pay	paid	paid
bend	bent	bent	picnic	picnicked	picnicked
bleed	bled	bled	proofread	proofread	proofread
blow	blew	blown	put	put	put
break	broke	broken	read	read	read
bring	brought	brought	rewind	rewound	rewound
buy	bought	bought	rewrite	rewrote	rewritten
catch	caught	caught	ride	rode	ridden
choose	chose	chosen	run	ran	run
come	came	come	say	said	said
cut	cut	cut	see	saw	seen
do	did	done	seek	sought	sought
draw	drew	drawn	sell	sold	sold
drink	drank	drunk	send	sent	sent
drive	drove	driven	set	set	set
eat	ate	eaten	sew	sewed	sewn
fall	fell	fallen	shake	shook	shaken
feed	fed	fed	shoot	shot	shot
feel	felt	felt	show	showed	shown
find	found	found	sing	sang	sung
fly	flew	flown	sit	sat	sat
get	got	gotten	speak	spoke	spoken
give	gave	given	stand	stood	stood
go	went	gone	steal	stole	stolen
hang	hung	hung	sweep	swept	swept
have	had	had	swim	swam	swum
hear	heard	heard	swing	swung	swung
hide	hid	hidden	take	took	taken
hit	hit	hit	teach	taught	taught
hold	held	held	think	thought	thought
keep	kept	kept	throw	threw	thrown
lay	laid	laid	wake	woke	woken
leave	left	left	withdraw	withdrew	withdrawn
lend	lent	lent	write	wrote	written
let	let	let			

Index

Index Key

Font
bold type = verbs or verb phrases (example: **catch**)
ordinary type = all other parts of speech (example: baseball)
ALL CAPS = unit titles (example: MATHEMATICS)
Initial caps = subunit titles (example: Equivalencies)

Symbols
✦ = word found in exercise band at bottom of page

Numbers/Letters
first number in **bold** type = page on which word appears
second number, or letter, following number in **bold** type = item number on page
(examples: cool [ko͞ol] **13**-5 means that the word *cool* is item number 5 on page 13;
across [ə krös/] **153**–G means that the word *across* is item G on page 153).

Pronunciation Guide

The index includes a pronunciation guide for all the words and phrases illustrated in the book. This guide uses symbols commonly found in dictionaries for native speakers. These symbols, unlike those used in pronunciation systems such as the International Phonetic Alphabet, tend to use English spelling patterns and so should help you to become more aware of the connections between written English and spoken English.

Consonants

[b] as in back [băk]
[ch] as in cheek [chēk]
[d] as in date [dāt]
[dh] as in this [dhĭs]
[f] as in face [fās]
[g] as in gas [găs]
[h] as in half [hăf]
[j] as in jam [jăm]

[k] as in key [kē]
[l] as in leaf [lēf]
[m] as in match [măch]
[n] as in neck [něk]
[ng] as in ring [rĭng]
[p] as in park [pärk]
[r] as in rice [rīs]
[s] as in sand [sănd]

[sh] as in shoe [sho͞o]
[t] as in tape [tāp]
[th] as in three [thrē]
[v] as in vine [vīn]
[w] as in wait [wāt]
[y] as in yams [yămz]
[z] as in zoo [zo͞o]
[zh] as in measure [mĕzhər]

Vowels

[ā] as in bake [bāk]
[ă] as in back [băk]
[ä] as in car [kär] or box [bäks]
[ē] as in beat [bēt]
[ĕ] as in bed [bĕd]
[ë] as in bear [bër]

[ī] as in line [līn]
[ĭ] as in lip [lĭp]
[ï] as in near [nïr]
[ō] as in cold [kōld]
[ö] as in short [shört] or claw [klö]
[o͞o] as in cool [ko͞ol]

[o͝o] as in cook [ko͝ok]
[ow] as in cow [kow]
[oy] as in boy [boy]
[ŭ] as in cut [kŭt]
[ü] as in curb [kürb]
[ə] as in above [ə bŭv/]

All the pronunciation symbols used are alphabetical except for the schwa [ə]. The schwa is the most frequent vowel sound in English. If you use the schwa appropriately in unstressed syllables, your pronunciation will sound more natural.

Vowels before [r] are shown with the symbol [ ] to call attention to the special quality that vowels have before [r]. (Note that the symbols [ä] and [ö] are also used for vowels not followed by [r], as in *box* or *claw*.) You should listen carefully to native speakers to discover how these vowels actually sound.

Stress
This index follows the system for marking stress used in many dictionaries for native speakers.
1. Stress is not marked if a word consisting of a single syllable occurs by itself.
2. Where stress is marked, two levels are distinguished:
a bold accent [/] is placed after each syllable with primary (or strong) stress, a light accent [/] is placed after each syllable with secondary (or weaker) stress. In phrases and other combinations of words, stress is indicated for each word as it would be pronounced within the whole phrase.

Syllable Boundaries
Syllable boundaries are indicated by a single space or by a stress mark.

Note: The pronunciations shown in this index are based on patterns of American English. There has been no attempt to represent all of the varieties of American English. Students should listen to native speakers to hear how the language actually sounds in a particular region.

Index

Abbreviations [ə brē/vē ā/shənz] **48**
abdomen [ăb/də mən] **107**–27
about [ə bowt/] **48**–B, **174**–L, **191**–E
above [ə bŭv/] **25**–4
accelerator [ĭk sĕl/ə rā/tər] **159**–46
accept [ĭk sĕpt/] **12**–G, **12**–I, **12** ✦
access number [ăk/sĕs/ nŭm/bər] **14**–16
Accessories [ĭk sĕs/ə rēz] **59, 94–95**
accident [ăk/sə dənt] **144**–2
accordion [ə kör/dē ən] **238**–19
account [ə kownt/] **132**–11, **132**–14
    account manager [ə kownt/ măn/ə jər] **132**–9
Account [ə kownt/] **132**
accountant [ə kown/tənt] **166**–1
ache [āk]
    backache [băk/āk/] **110**–5
    earache [ïr/āk/] **110**–3
    headache [hĕd/āk/] **110**–1
    stomachache [stŭm/ək/ āk] **110**–4
    toothache [tōōth/āk/] **110**–2
acid rain [ăs/əd rān/] **218**–13
across [ə krös] **153**–G
acrylic paint [ə krĭl/ĭk pānt] **232**–10
action [ăk/shən]
    action figure [ăk/shən fĭg/yər] **233**–26
    action story [ăk/shən stör/ē] **237**–19
activist [ăk/tə vĭst] **199**–17
actor [ăk/tər] **166**–2
acupuncture [ăk/yə pŭngk/chər] **122**–2
acute angle [ə kyōōt/ ăng/gəl] **193**–28
ad [ăd] **48**–2, **197**–9
adapter [ə dăp/tər] **234**–15
add [ăd] **77**–N, **101**–B, **192**–A
address [ə drĕs/, ă/drĕs] **4**–5
    mailing address [mā/lĭng ə drĕs/, –ă/drĕs] **134**–22
    return address [rĭ türn/ ə drĕs/, –ă/drĕs] **134**–21
    website address [wĕb/sīt ə drĕs/, –ă/drĕs] **197**–4
address [ə drĕs/] **135**–B, **197**–C
adhesive bandage [əd hē/sĭv băn/dĭj] **117**–5
adjust [ə jŭst/] **219**–J
    adjustable wrench [ə jŭs/tə bəl rĕnch/] **181**–48
    adjustment [ə jŭst/mənt] **194**–23, **194**–24
administrative assistant
    [əd mĭn/ə strā/tĭv ə sĭs/tənt] **166**–3
administrator [əd mĭn/ə strā/tər] **120**–13
Administrators [əd mĭn/ə strā/tərz] **5**
admissions clerk [əd mĭ/shənz klürk/] **120**–14
ADULTS AND CHILDREN [ə dŭlts/ en chĭl/ drən] **30**–31
adult school [ə dŭlt/ skōōl/, ăd/ŭlt–] **188**–8
adventure story [əd vĕn/chər stör/ē] **237**–19
aerobic exercise [ə rō/bĭk ĕk/sər sīz/] **122**–5
afraid [ə frād/] **43**–23
after [ăf/tər]
    afternoon [ăf/tər nōōn/] **18**–17
    aftershave [ăf/tər shāv/] **109**–30
    five after one [fïv/ ăf/tər wŭn/] **18**–7
    quarter after one [kwör/tər ăf/tər wŭn/] **18**–9
    ten after one [tĕn/ ăf/tər wŭn/] **18**–8
    twenty after one [twĕn/tē ăf/tər wŭn/] **18**–10
After an Emergency [ăf/tər ən ĭ mür/jən sē] **147**
Age [āj] **32**
agency [ā/jən sē] **131**–14

agent [ā/jənt] **160**–3, **160**–5
agree [ə grē/] **12**–K
agreement [ə grē/mənt] **51**–28
aid [ād]
    first aid kit [fürst/ ād/ kĭt/] **117**–1, **146**–18
    first aid manual [fürst/ ād/ măn/yōō əl] **117**–2
    hearing aid [hïr/ĭng ād/] **115**–10
aide [ād] **167**–32
AIDS (acquired immune deficiency syndrome) [ādz] /
    [ə kwī/rd ĭ myōōn/ də fĭ/shən sē sĭn/drōm] **111** ✦
air [ër]
    air bag [ër/ băg/] **159**–43
    air conditioner [ër/ kən dĭsh/ə nər] **159**–39
    Air Force [ër/ förs/] **138**–16
    airmail [ër/māl/] **134**–5
    airplane [ër/plān/] **150**–8
    airplane crash [ër/plān/ krăsh/] **144**–3
    air pollution [ër/ pə lōō/shən] **218**–11
    airport [ër/pört/] **151**–10
    air purifier [ër/ pyōōr/ə fī ər] **113**–14
Airline Terminal [ër/līn/ tür/mə nəl] **160**
Airplane [ër/plān/] **161**
AIRPORT [ër/pört/] **160–161**
Airport Transportation
    [ër/pört/ trăns/pər tā/shən] **152**
aisle [īl] **72**–6
alarm clock [ə lärm/ kläk/] **58**–24
Alaska time [ə lăs/kə tīm/] **19**–28
album [ăl/bəm] **235**–31, **235**–32
alfalfa [ăl făl/fə] **177**–5
algebra [al/jə brə] **192**–16
allergic reaction [ə lür/jĭk rē ăk/shən] **116**–E
allergies [ăl/ər jēz] **111**–8
alley [ăl/ē] **51**–24, **222**–4
alligator [ăl/ə gā/tər] **213**–36
alphabet [ăl/fə bĕt/] **7**–13
Alterations [öl/tə rā/shənz] **100**
ALTERATIONS [öl/tə rā/shənz] **100**
Alteration Shop [öl/tə rā/shən shăp/] **100**
aluminum foil [ə lōō/mə nəm foyl/] **72**–23
Alzheimer's disease [älts/hī mərz dĭ zēz/, älts–] **111** ✦
a.m. [ā/ĕm/] **18**–4
ambulance [ăm/byə ləns] **116**–1, **121**–34
AMERICA [ə mĕr/ə kə] **200–201**
American cheese [ə mĕr/ə kən chēz/] **71**–26
Americans [ə mĕr/ə kənz] **198**–3
Amphibians [ăm fĭb/ē ənz] **212**
AMPHIBIANS [ăm fĭb/ē ənz] **212–213**
amusement park [ə myōōz/mənt pärk/] **223**–10
ancient [ān/shənt] **199**–1
anemone [ə nĕ/mə nē] **212**–24
anesthesiologist [ă/nəs thē/zē ä/lə jĭst] **121**–35
angle [ăng/gəl] **193**–26, **193**–27, **193**–28
Angles [ăng/gəlz] **193**
angry [ăng/grē] **43**–29
animals [ăn/ə məlz] **59**–15
Animals [ăn/ə məlz] **212, 215**
ANIMALS [ăn/ə məlz] **215**
ankle [ăng/kəl] **106**–23, **110**–18
    ankle socks [ăng/kəl säks/] **91**–7
anklets [ăngk/ləts/] **91**–11
anniversary [ăn/ə vür/sə rē] **22**–3

answer [ăn/sər] **8**–L
answering machine [ăn/sə rĭng mə shēn/] **14**–17
answer sheet [ăn/sər shēt/] **10**–2
antacid [ănt ăs/əd] **113**–28
anteater [ănt/ē/tər] **217**–24
antelope [ăn/tə lōp/] **217**–35
antenna [ăn tĕ/nə] **14**–9
antibacterial ointment
    [ăn/tē băk tĭr/ē əl oynt/mənt] **117**–10
antihistamine cream [ăn/tī hĭs/tə mēn krēm/] **117**–11
antiperspirant [ăn/tē pürs/pə rənt] **108**–5
antlers [ănt/lərz] **216**–16
ants [ăntz] **63**–23
apartment [ə pärt/mənt] **48**–3, **48**–4
    apartment building [ə pärt/mənt bĭl/dĭng] **50**–1
    apartment number [ə pärt/mənt nüm/bər] **4**–6
Apartment [ə pärt/mənt] **48**
Apartment Complex [ə pärt/mənt käm/plĕx] **51**
Apartment Entryway [ə pärt/mənt ĕn/trē wā/] **51**
APARTMENTS [ə pärt/məntz] **50–51**
APC (automated postal center) [ā/pē/sē/] /
    [ö/tə māt ĭd pōs/təl–sĕn/tər] **135**–10
apologize [ə päl/ə jīz/] **12**–F
apostrophe [ə päs/trə fē] **190**–16
apparatus [ăp/ə rā/təs] **224**–14
appear [ə pïr/] **141**–C
Appearance [ə pïr/əns] **32**
applaud [ə plöd/] **148**–B
apples [ăp/əlz] **68**–1
    apple juice [ăp/əl jōōs/] **73**–32
appliance repair person
    [ə pli/əns rĭ përr/ pür/sən] **166**–4
appliqué [ăp/lə kā/] **99**–31
apply [ə plī/] **109**–P
appointment [ə poynt/mənt] **22**–4, **118**–1
    appointment book [ə poynt/mənt bōōk/] **183**–48
apricots [ăp/rə käts/] **68**–12
April [ā/prəl] **21**–28
apron [ā/prən] **92**–11, **93**–30
aquarium [ə kwĕr/ē əm] **222**–7
Arachnids [ə răk/nĭdz/] **214**
ARACHNIDS [ə răk/nĭdz/] **214**
archery [är/chə rē] **228**–1
architect [är/kə tĕkt/] **166**–5
area [ër/ē ə]
    area code [ër/ē ə kōd/] **4**–10, **15**–29
    boarding area [bör/dĭng ër/ē ə] **161**–9
    dining area [dī/nĭng ër/ē ə] **46**–7
    play area [plā/ ër/ē ə] **130**–11
    reception area [rĭ sĕp/shən ër/ē ə] **182**–5
    rural area [rŏŏr/əl ër/ē ə] **52**–4
    screening area [skrē/nĭng ër/ē ə] **160**–4
    testing area [tĕs/tĭng ër/ē ə] **136**–2
    urban area [ür/bən ër/ē ə] **52**–1
AREA [ër/ē ə] **55**
Area and Volume [ër/ē ə ən văl/yəm, –yōōm] **193**
arm [ärm] **105**–14, **194**–15
    armchair [ärm/chër/] **56**–22
armadillo [är/mə dïl/ō] **216**–8
Arm, Hand, and Fingers [ärm/ hănd/ ən fĭng/gərz] **106**
Army [är/mē] **138**–14, **199**–11
around [ə rownd/] **153**–H

Around Campus [ə rownd/ kăm/pəs] **5**
arrange [ə rănj/] **49**–Q
arrest [ə rĕst/] **141**–A
arrival [ə rī/vəl] **161**–7, **161** ✚
arrive [ə rīv/] **160**–K
arrow [ăr/ō] **231**–8
arson [är/sən] **142**–7
artery [är/tə rē] **107**–36
arthritis [är thrī/təs] **111**–16
artichokes [är/tə chōks/] **69**–22
artist [är/tĭst] **166**–6
arts [ärts] **189**–9, **189**–15, **228**–11
    art museum [ärt/ myōō zē/əm] **223**–9
ask [ăsk] **2**–B
    ask about [ăsk/ ə bowt/] **48**–B, **157**–B
    ask for [ăsk/ för/] **10**–F
    ask questions [ăsk/ kwĕs/chənz] **8**–K, **174**–M
asparagus [ə spër/ə gəs] **69**–26
assault [ə sölt/] **142**–3
assemble [ə sĕm/bəl] **170**–A, **175**–C
assembler [ə sĕm/blər] **166**–7
assembly [ə sĕm/blē/] **140**–1
    assembly line [ə sĕm/blē lĭn/] **175**–6
    assemblyperson [ə sĕm/blē pür/sən] **139**–24
assist [ə sĭst/] **95**–D, **170**–B
assistance [ə sĭs/təns] **14**–22
assistant [ə sĭs/tənt]
    administrative assistant
        [əd mĭn/ ə strā/ tĭv ə sĭs/tənt] **166**–3
    assistant principal [ə sĭs/tənt prĭn/sə pəl] **5**–5
    certified nursing assistant (CNA) [sür/tə fĭd/
        nür/sĭng ə sĭs/tənt] / [sē/ĕn/ā/] **120**–12
    dental assistant [dĕn/təl ə sĭs/tənt] **119**–2, **167**–22
    physician assistant [fə zĭ/shən ə sĭs/tənt] **168**–47
Assistant [ə sĭs/tənt] **93**
asthma [ăz/mə] **111**–9
astronaut [ăs/trə nöt/] **205**–17
astronomer [ə strä/nə mər] **205**–22
Astronomy [ə strä/nə mē] **205**
At Customs [ăt/ kŭs/təmz] **161**
athletic [ăth lĕt/ĭk]
    athletic shoes [ăth lĕt/ĭk shōōz/] **86**–7
    athletic supporter [ăth lĕt/ĭk sə pör/tər] **91**–6
Atlantic time [ət lăn/tĭk tīm/] **19**–33
atlas [ăt/ləs] **133**–8
ATM (Automated Teller Machine) [ā/tē/ĕm/] /
    [ö/tə mat ĭd te/lər mə shēn/] **132**
ATM card [ā/tē/ĕm/ kärd/] **132**–15
atom [ăt/əm] **195**–28
attach [ə tăch/] **197**–G, **197**–H
attachments [ə tăch/mənts] **61**–11
attack [ə tăk/] **116**–D
attendant [ə tĕn/dənt] **161**–12, **162**–3, **184**–3
At the Dealer [ăt/ dhə dē/lər] **158**
At the Gate [ăt/ dhə gāt/] **161**
At the Mechanic [ăt/ dhə mə kăn/ĭk] **158**
At the Security Checkpoint
    [ăt/ dhə sə kyōō/ rə tē/ chĕk/ poynt/] **160**
attic [ăt/ək] **47**–7
attorney [ə tür/nē] **141**–4, **141**–10
attractive [ə trăk/tĭv] **32**–13
audiobook [ö/dē ō bŏŏk/] **133**–17

audiologist [ö dē ä/lə jĭst] **115**–9
auditorium [ö/də tör/ē əm] **5**–18
August [ö/gəst] **21**–32
aunt [ănt] **34**–7
author [ö/thər] **133**–15, **169**–64
auto [ö/tō]
    auto club card [ö/tō klŭb/ kärd/] **162**–4
    auto mechanic [ö/tō mə kăn/ĭk] **166**–8
automated [ö/tə māt ĭd]
    automated phone system
        [ö/tə māt ĭd fōn/ sĭs/təm] **14**–23
    automated postal center (APC)
        [ö/tə māt ĭd pōs/təl sĕn/tər] / [ā/pē/sē/] **135**–10
Automated Teller Machine
    [ö/tə māt ĭd tĕl/ər mə shĕn/] **132**
Automatic Transmission
    [ö tə măt/ĭk trănz mĭ/shən] **159**
Automotive Painter [ö tə mōt/ĭv pān/tər] **92**
autumn [ö/təm] **21**–39
avalanche [ăv/ə lănch/] **145**–18
average [ăv/rĭj]
    average height [ăv/rĭj hīt/] **32**–5
    average weight [ăv/rĭj wāt/] **32**–8
avocados [ä/və kä/dōz, ăv/ə–] **84**–6
ax [ăks] **180**–3
baboon [bă bōōn/] **217**–31
baby [bā/bē] **31**–7
    baby bag [bā/bē băg/] **37**–16
    baby carrier [bā/bē kă/rē/ər] **37**–17
    baby food [bā/bē fōōd/] **37**–4
    baby lotion [bā/bē lō/shən] **37**–13
    baby monitor [bā/bē măn/ə tər] **59**–7
    baby powder [bā/bē pow/dər] **37**–14
    babysitter [bā/bē sĭt/ər] **166**–9
    baby's room [bā/bēz/ rōōm/] **47**–10
back [băk] **104**–5
    backache [băk/āk/] **110**–5
    back button [băk/ bŭt/n] **197**–2
    backhoe [băk/hō/] **178**–8
    backpack [băk/păk/] **94**–18, **226**–15
    backpacking [băk/păk/ĭng] **226**–6
    backseat [băk/sēt/] **159**–54
    back support belt [băk/ sə pört/ bĕlt/] **179**–18
    go back [gō/ băk/] **11**–M
    horseback riding [hörs/băk/ rī/dĭng] **226**–9
    lower back [lō/ər băk/] **107**–29
    pay back [pā/ băk/] **26**–D
Backyard [băk/yärd/] **53**
BACK FROM THE MARKET
    [băk/ frəm dhə mär/kət] **66**–67
bacon [bā/kən] **70**–11, **80**–1
bad [băd] **23**–18
BAD DAY AT WORK [băd/ dā/ ăt würk/] **186**–187
badge [băj] **93**–21
badminton [băd/mĭn tən] **228**–6
bag [băg] **69**–31, **74**–7, **74**–19, **161**–18
    air bag [ër/ băg/] **159**–43
    baby bag [bā/bē băg/] **37**–16
    clutch bag [klŭch/ băg/] **89**–19
    grocery bag [grōs/rē băg/] **67**–13
    handbag [hănd/ băg/] **87**–9, **94**–2
    plastic storage bags [plăs/tĭk stör/ĭj băgz/] **72**–25

    shoulder bag [shōl/dər băg/] **94**–17
    sleeping bag [slē/pĭng băg/] **226**–12
    totebag [tōt/ băg/] **94**–19
    trash bags [trăsh/ băgz/] **61**–24
    vacuum cleaner bag
        [văk/yōōm klē/nər băg/] **61**–12
bagels [bā/gəlz] **73**–40
baggage [băg/ĭj]
    baggage carousel [băg/ĭj kăr/ə sĕl/] **161**–23
bagger [băg/ər] **73**–14
baggy [băg/ē] **97**–30
bailiff [bā/lĭf] **141**–13
bake [bāk] **77**–H
Baked Goods [băkt/ gŏŏdz/] **73**
baked potato [băkt/ pə tā/tō] **81**–25
baker [bā/kər] **166**–10
bakery [bā/kə rē] **127**–19
Baking Products [bā/kĭng präd/ŭkts] **73**
balance [băl/əns] **132**–17, **195**–41
balcony [băl/kə nē] **51**–20
bald [böld] **33**–12
ball [böl] **59**–12, **231**–5, **231**–12
    ball field [böl/ fēld/] **224**–1
    ballroom [böl/rōōm/] **184**–26
    baseball [bās/böl/] **231**–18, **231**–14
    basketball [băs/kət böl/] **229**–8, **231**–4
    basketball court [băs/kət böl/ kört/] **229**–7
    football [fŏŏt/böl/] **229**–11, **231**–21
    meatballs [mēt/bölz/] **81**–27
    racquetball [răk/ət böl/] **228**–12
    softball [söft/böl/] **229**–10
    volleyball [väl/ē böl/] **229**–14, **231**–3
balloons [bə lōōnz/] **44**–4
bananas [bə năn/əz] **68**–2
band [bănd] **183**–34
    headband [hĕd/bănd/] **90**–3
    waistband [wāst/bănd/] **100**–5
bandage [băn/dĭj] **117**–5, **117**–12
bandana [băn dă/nə] **92**–16
bangs [băngz] **33**–8
bank [băngk] **124**–5
    bank statement [băngk/ stāt/mənt] **132**–16
bank online [băngk/ än līn/] **132**–C
BANK [băngk] **132**
banner [băn/ər] **44**–1
banquet room [băng/kwət rōōm/] **185**–14
bar [bär]
    bar code [bär/ kōd/] **27**–4
    candy bar [kăn/dē bär/] **73**–37
    grab bar [grăb/ bär/] **57**–9
    menu bar [mĕn/yōō bär/] **197**–1
    salad bar [săl/əd bär/] **79**–24
    scroll bar [skröl/ bär/] **197**–15
barbecued ribs [bär/bĭ kyōō/d rĭbz/] **76**–2
barbershop [bär/bər shäp/] **129**–19
bargain [bär/gən] **102**–A
barn [bärn] **177**–11
barrette [bə rĕt/] **108**–20
base [bās] **193**–45, **194**–20
baseball [bās/böl/] **229**–9, **231**–18
    baseball bat [bās/böl/ băt/] **231**–14
    baseball cap [bās/böl/ kăp/] **86**–5

Index

baseball cards [bās/böl/ kärds/] **232**–2
baseball game [bās/böl/ gām/] **44**–2
basement [bās/mənt] **47**–13
Basement [bās/mənt] **50**
Basic Colors [bā/sĭk kŭ/lərz] **24**
BASIC TRANSPORTATION
  [bā/sĭk tränz/pər tā/shən] **150**–**151**
basket [bās/kət] **56**–3
  basketball [bās/kət böl/] **229**–8, **231**–4
  basketball court [bās/kət böl kört/] **229**–7
  bread basket [brĕd/ bās/kət] **83**–11
  laundry basket [lön/drē bās/kət] **101**–2
  shopping basket [shäp/ĭng bās/kət] **73**–9
  wastebasket [wāst/bās/kət] **57**–26
bass [bās] **212**–6, [bās] **238**–8
bassoon [bə sōōn/] **238**–4
bat [băt] **216**–7, **231**–14
bath [băth]
  bath mat [băth/ măt/] **57**–28
  bath powder [băth/ pow/dər] **108**–4
  bathroom [băth/rōōm/] **46**–4
  bath towel [băth/ tow/əl] **57**–13
  bathtub [băth/tŭb/] **57**–2
  half bath [hăf/ băth/] **57** ✦
bathe [bādh] **36**–F, **108**–B
bathing suit [bā/dhĭng sōōt/] **90**–26
BATHROOM [băth/rōōm/] **57**
battery / batteries [băt/ə rē] / [băt/ə rēz]
  146–15, **158**–20
  battery charger [băt/ə rē chär/jər] **235**–27
  battery pack [băt/ə rē păk/] **235**–26
bay [bā] **204**–9
be [bē]
  be aware [bē ə wër/] **143**–I
  be born [bē börn/] **40**–A
  be 18 or older [bē ā/tēn/ ör ōld/ər] **140**–G
  be hurt [bē hürt/] **116**–C
  be in a rock band [bē ĭn ə räk/ bănd/] **238**–D
  be informed [bē ĭn förmd/] **140**–F
  be injured [bē ĭn/jərd] **116**–C
  be in shock [bē ĭn shäk/] **116**–B
  be neat [bē nēt/] **174**–C
  be on time [bē ön tīm/] **174**–F
  be released [bē rĭ lēst/] **141**–H
  be unconscious [bē ŭn kän/shəs] **116**–A
  don't be late [dōnt/ bē lāt/] **174**–D
beach [bēch] **204**–10
  beach chair [bēch/ chër/] **225**–22
  beach umbrella [bēch/ ŭm brĕl/ə] **225**–14
BEACH [bēch] **225**
beads [bēdz] **95**–34, **99**–32
beak [bēk] **214**–3
beaker [bē/kər] **195**–39
beam [bēm] **178**–3
beans [bēnz] **69**–8, **72**–17
  soybeans [soy/bēnz/] **177**–3
bear [bër] **37**–23, **216**–11
beard [bërd] **33**–6
beat [bēt] **77**–S
beater [bē/tər]
  eggbeater [ĕg/bē/tər] **78**–20
beautiful [byōō/tə fəl] **23**–21

beauty shop [byōō/tē shäp/] **130** ✦
beaver [bē/vər] **216**–9
become [bē kŭm/] **40**–G, **41**–N
bed [bĕd] **58**–9
  bedbugs [bĕd/bŭgz/] **63**–24
  bed control [bĕd/ kən trōl/] **121**–27
  bed frame [bĕd/ frām/] **58**–18
  bed pan [bĕd/ păn/] **121**–23
  bedroom [bĕd/rōōm/] **46**–2
  bedspread [bĕd/sprĕd/] **59**–11
  bed table [bĕd/ tā/bəl] **121**–21
  bunk beds [bŭnk/ bĕdz/] **59**–9
  double bed [dŭb/əl bĕd/] **184**–14
  flower bed [flow/ər bĕd/] **53**–20
  hospital bed [häs/pĭ tl bĕd/] **121**–22
  kids' bedroom [kĭdz/ bĕd/rōōm/] **47**–9
  king-size bed [kĭng/sīz/ bĕd/] **184**–15
BEDROOM [bĕd/rōōm/] **58, 59**
bee [bē]
  honeybee [hŭn/ē bē/] **214**–25
beef [bēf]
  beef ribs [bēf/ rĭbz/] **70**–5
  corned beef [körnd/ bēf/] **71**–22
  ground beef [grownd/ bēf/] **70**–4
  roast beef [rōst/ bēf/] **71**–21
  stewing beef [stōō/ĭng bēf/] **70**–3
  stir-fried beef [stür/frīd/ bēf/] **76**–6
Beef [bēf] **70**
beetle [bēt/l] **214**–18
beets [bēts] **69**–5
Before an Emergency [bĭ för/ ən ĭ mür/ jən sē] **146**
behind [bĭ hīnd/] **25**–8
beige [bāzh] **24**–18
bell [bĕl]
  bell captain [bĕl/ kăp/tən] **184**–6
  bellhop [bĕl/häp/] **184**–7
  bell peppers [bĕl/ pĕp/ərz] **69**–7
  doorbell [dör/bĕl/] **53**–14
below [bĭ lō/] **25**–5
belts [bĕlts] **94**–6
  back support belt [băk/ sə pört/ bĕlt/] **179**–18
  belt buckle [bĕlt/ bŭk/əl] **94**–20
  conveyor belt [kən vā/ər bĕlt/] **175**–9
  garter belt [gär/tər bĕlt/] **91**–16
  seat belt [sēt/ bĕlt/] **159**–52
  tool belt [tōōl/ bĕlt/] **92**–3
bench [bĕnch] **224**–10
bend [bĕnd] **230**–O
benefits [bĕn/ə fĭts] **174** ✦
berries [bĕr/ēz] **210**–20
  blackberries [blăk/bĕr/ēz] **68**–17
  blueberries [blōō/bĕr/ēz] **68**–16
  mixed berries [mĭkst/ bĕr/ēz] **81**–36
  raspberries [răz/bĕr/ēz] **68**–15
  strawberries [strö/bĕr/ēz] **68**–14
between [bĭ twēn/] **25**–12
Beverages [bĕv/rə jəz] **73, 81**
bib [bĭb] **37**–5
bicycle / bike [bī/sĭ kəl] / [bīk] **129**–22, **151**–15
big [bĭg] **23**–2, **97**–38
  Big Dipper [bĭg/ dĭ/pər] **205** ✦
  big-screen TV [bĭg/skrēn/ tē/vē/] **50**–15

bike / bicycle [bīk] / [bī/sĭ kəl] **129**–22, **151**–15
  bike path [bīk/ păth/] **224**–3
biking [bī/kĭng] **226**–8, **228**–5
bikini panties [bə kē/nē păn/tēz] **91**–13
bill [bĭl] **214**–3
Bill [bĭl] **15**
billiards [bĭl/yərdz] **228**–2
Bill of Rights [bĭl/ əv rīts/] **198**–10
Bills [bĭlz] **26**
bin [bĭn] **51**–23, **61**–2, **160**–6
bioenergy [bī/ō ĕn/ər jē] **218**–9
biography [bī ä/grə fē] **133**–15
biologist [bī ä/lə jĭst] **194**–2
Biology [bī ä/lə jē] **194**
biomass [bī/ō măs/] **218**–9
birch [bürch] **210**–7
bird [bürd] **208**–4
Bird [bürd] **214**
BIRDS, INSECTS, AND ARACHNIDS
  [bürdz/ ĭn/sĕkts ən ə răk/nĭdz] **214**
birth [bürth]
  birth certificate [bürth/ sər tĭf/ə kət] **40**–1
  birthday [bürth/dā/] **22**–1
BIRTHDAY PARTY [bürth/dā/ pär/tē] **240**–**241**
biscuits [bĭs/kəts] **80**–6
bison [bī/sən] **216**–6
bit [bĭt] **180**–28
bite [bīt] **110**–11
black [blăk] **24**–13
  blackberries [blăk/bĕr/ēz] **68**–17
  black hair [blăk/ hër/] **33**–16
bladder [blăd/ər] **107**–46
blade [blād] **107**–28, **109**–28, **180**–27
blankets [blăng/kəts] **58**–15, **146**–7, **225**–11
  blanket sleeper [blăng/kət slē/pər] **91**–27
blazer [blā/zər] **92**–12
bleach [blēch] **101**–7
bleachers [blē/chərz] **5**–3
bleed [blēd] **116**–M
blender [blĕn/dər] **54**–12
blind [blīnd] **32**–11
blister [blĭs/tər] **110**–15
blizzard [blĭz/ərd] **13**–23, **145**–13
blocks [bläks] **59**–19
  quilt block [kwĭlt/ bläk/] **232**–15
  sunblock [sŭn/bläk/] **108**–8, **225**–10
blond hair [bländ/ hër/] **33**–17
blood [blŭd] **111**–14
  blood pressure gauge [blŭd/ prĕsh/ər gāj/] **118**–9
  blood test [blŭd/ tĕst/] **121**–30
  blood work [blŭd/ würk/] **121**–30
  bloody nose [blŭd/ē nōz/] **110**–17
blouse [blows] **87**–8
blow dryer [blō/ drī/ər] **33**–23, **108**–18
blower [blō/ər] **176**–2
blow out [blō/ owt/] **240**–C
blue [blōō] **24**–3
  blueberries [blōō/bĕr/ēz] **68**–16
  blue jay [blōō/ jā/] **214**–6
  bright blue [brīt/ blōō/] **24**–12
  dark blue [därk/ blōō/] **24**–10
  light blue [līt/ blōō/] **24**–11
  navy blue [nā/vē blōō/] **28**–5

blues [blōōz] **237**–22
blush [blŭsh] **109**–37
board [börd]
   board game [börd/ gām/] **232**–5
   bulletin board [bŏŏl/ə tn börd/] **7**–14
   chalkboard [chök/börd/] **6**–1
   cutting board [kŭt/ĭng börd/] **54**–27
   emery board [ĕm/ə rē börd/, ĕm/rē–] **109**–32
   headboard [hĕd/börd/] **58**–10
   ironing board [ī/ər nĭng börd/] **101**–14
   motherboard [mŭdh/ər börd/] **196**–5
   particle board [pär/tə kəl börd/] **181**–20
   skateboard [skāt/börd/] **224**–7
   snowboard [snō/börd/] **231**–23
   surfboard [sürf/börd/] **225**–16
   whiteboard [wīt/börd/] **6**–3
board [börd] **160**–E
boarding [bör/dĭng]
   boarding area [bör/dĭng ër/ē ə] **161**–9
   boarding pass [bör/dĭng păs/] **161**–20
   sailboarding [sāl/bör/dĭng] **227** ✦
   skateboarding [skāt/bör/dĭng] **228**–13
   snowboarding [snō/bör/dĭng] **227**–2
boat [bōt]
   sailboat [sāl/bōt/] **225**–3
boating [bō/tĭng] **226**–1
bobbin [bä/bĭn] **98**–21
bobby pins [bäb/ē pĭnz/] **108**–21
body [bäd/ē] **190**–7
   body lotion [bäd/ē lō/shən] **108**–9
   body of water [bäd/ē əv wö/tər] **204** ✦
   body shaper [bäd/ē shā/pər] **91**–15
BODY [bäd/ē] **104**–**105**, **106**–**107**
boil [boyl] **77**–M
boiled ham [boyld/ hăm/] **76**–5
boiler [boy/lər] **78**–8
bok choy [bäk/ choy/] **69**–15
bolt [bōlt] **51**–34, **180**–35, **180**–38
   bolt of fabric [bōlt/ əv făb/rĭk] **98**–15
bone [bōn] **107**–33, **116**–P
   boneless [bōn/ləs] **70** ✦
book [bŏŏk]
   appointment book [ə poynt/mənt bŏŏk/] **183**–48
   audiobook [ö/dē ō bŏŏk/] **133**–17
   bookkeeper [bŏŏk/ kē/pər] **175**–2
   book of stamps [bŏŏk/ əv stămps/] **134**–18
   bookcase [bŏŏk/ kās/] **7**–10
   bookstore [bŏŏk/ stör/] **130**–4
   check book [chĕk/ bŏŏk/] **132**–12
   coloring book [kŭl/ə rĭng bŏŏk/] **59**–13
   DMV handbook [dē/ĕm/vē/ hănd/bŏŏk/] **136**–1
   notebook [nōt/bŏŏk/] **7**–27
   passbook [păs/bŏŏk/] **132**–10
   picture book [pĭk/chər bŏŏk/] **133**–12
   spiral notebook [spī/rəl nōt/bŏŏk/] **7**–29
   test booklet [tĕst/ bŏŏk/lət] **10**–1
   textbook [tĕkst/bŏŏk/, tĕks/–] **7**–25
   workbook [würk/bŏŏk/] **7**–26
boombox [bōōm/bäks/] **234**–1
booth [bōōth] **82**–4, **122**–3

boots [bōōts] **95**–28
   hiking boots [hī/kĭng bōōts/] **95**–31
   rain boots [rān/ bōōts/] **90**–20
   safety boots [sāf/tē bōōts/] **179**–20
   ski boots [skē/ bōōts/] **231**–26
   steel toe boots [stēl/ tō/ bōōts/] **92**–6
bored [börd] **43**–25
borrow [bär/ō, bör/ō] **26**–B
boss [bäs] **164**–4
botanical garden [bə tăn/ĭ kəl gär/dn] **222**–3
bottle [bät/l] **37**–1, **74**–1, **74**–13
   bottle return [bät/l rĭ türn/] **73**–16
   hot water bottle [hät/ wö/tər bät/l] **113**–15
bottled water [bät/ld wö/tər] **146**–11
bouquet [bō kā/, bōō–] **211**–28
bow [bō] **231**–6
   bow tie [bō/ tī/] **89**–16
bow [bow] **3**–H
bowl [bōl] **55**–2
   mixing bowl [mĭks/ĭng bōl/] **54**–28, **78**–31
   serving bowl [sürv/ĭng bōl/] **55**–21
   soup bowl [sōōp/ bōl/] **83**–21
   sugar bowl [shŏŏg/ər bōl/] **55**–14
bowling [bō/lĭng] **228**–3
   bowling alley [bō/lĭng ăl/ē] **222**–4
   bowling ball [bō/lĭng bōl/] **231**–5
box / boxes [bäks/, bäks/ĭz] **74**–6, **74**–18
   box spring [bäks/ sprĭng/] **58**–19
   CD boombox [sē/dē/ bōōm/bäks/] **234**–1
   fuse box [fyōōz/ bäks/] **62**–13
   mailboxes [māl/bäk/səz] **50**–11, **128**–13
   post office box (PO box)
     [pōst/ ö/fəs bäks/] / [pē/ō bäks/] **135**–9
   safety deposit box [sāf/tē dĭ päz/ət bäks/] **132**–7
   sandbox [sănd/bäks/] **224**–15
   search box [sürch/ bäks/] **197**–5
   text box [tĕkst/ bäks/] **197**–13
   to-go box [tə gō/ bäks/] **82**–5
boxer shorts [bäk/sər shörts/] **91**–4
boxing [bäks/ĭng] **228**–4
boy [boy] **31**–9
bra [brä] **91**–20
bracelets [brās/ləts] **95**–9, **117**–3
braces [brā/səz] **119**–6
brain [brān] **107**–34
brainstorm [brān/störm/] **8**–H, **191**–F
brake [brāk] **159**–48
   brake light [brāk/ līt/] **158**–14
   brake pedal [brāk/ pĕd/l] **159**–45
branch [brănch] **210**–2
Branch [brănch] **138**
Brass [brăs] **238**
bread [brĕd] **67**–11
   bread-and-butter plate [brĕd/ n bŭt/ər plāt/] **83**–19
   bread basket [brĕd/ băs/kət] **83**–11
   garlic bread [gär/lĭk brĕd/] **81**–28
   rye bread [rī/ brĕd/] **71**–20
   wheat bread [wēt/ brĕd/] **71**–19
   white bread [wīt/ brĕd/] **71**–18
break [brāk] **77**–Q, **116**–P
   break down [brāk/ down/] **162**–D

Breakfast Special [brĕk/fəst spē/shəl] **80**
breasts [brĕsts] **70**–19, **107**–26
breathe [brēdh] **116**–N
breathing [brē/dhĭng] **117**–16
bricklayer [brĭk/lā/ər] **186**–8
bricks [brĭks] **178**–12, **178**–B
briefcase [brēf/kās/] **88**–13
briefs [brēfs] **91**–5, **91**–14
bright blue [brīt/ blōō/] **24**–12
bring [brĭng] **174**–D, **240**–E
broccoli [bräk/ə lē] **69**–13
broiled steak [broyld/ stāk/] **76**–3
broiler [broy/lər] **54**–21
broken [brō/kən] **62**–5, **62**–6, **62**–7, **63**–15, **97**–39
   broken equipment [brō/kən ĭ kwĭp/mənt] **179**–4
broom [brōōm] **61**–16
brother [brŭdh/ər] **34**–6, **35**–28
   brother-in-law [brŭdh/ər ĭn lö/] **34**–17
   stepbrother [stĕp/brŭdh/ər] **35**–30
brown [brown] **24**–17
   brown hair [brown/ hër/] **33**–18
   hash browns [hăsh/ brownz/] **80**–3
browse [browz] **102**–B
bruise [brōōz] **110**–12
brush [brŭsh] **33**–22, **108**–14
   paintbrush [pānt/brŭsh/] **181**–22, **233**–20
   scrub brush [skrŭb/ brŭsh/] **61**–20
   toilet brush [toy/lət brŭsh/] **57**–18
   toothbrush [tōōth/brŭsh/] **109**–22
brush [brŭsh] **108**–I, **109**–J
bubble in [bŭ/bəl ĭn/] **10**–K
bucket [bŭk/ət] **61**–7, **225**–8
buckle [bŭk/əl] **94**–20, **99**–28
buckle up [bŭk/əl ŭp/] **36**–L
bud [bŭd] **211**–7
budget [bŭ jĭt/] **186**–3
buffalo [bŭf/ə lō] **216**–6
buffet [bə fā/] **55**–24, **185**–10
bugs [bŭgz]
   bedbugs [bĕd/bŭgz/] **63**–24
building [bĭl/dĭng] **50**–1, **124**–2
BUILDING SUPPLIES [bĭl/dĭng sə plīz/] **180**–**181**
bulb [bŭlb] **56** ✦, **211**–2
bulldozer [bŏŏl/dō/zər] **178**–6
bulletin board [bŏŏl/ə tn börd/] **7**–14
bump cap [bŭmp/ kăp/] **92**–9
bumper [bŭm/pər] **158**–8
   bumper pad [bŭm/pər păd/] **59**–4
bunch [bŭnch] **68**–29
bunk beds [bŭngk/ bĕdz/] **59**–9
Bunsen burner [bŭn/sən bür/nər] **195**–37
bureau [byŏŏr/ō] **58**–1
burger [bür/gər]
   cheeseburger [chēz/bür/gər] **79**–3
   hamburger [hăm/bür/gər] **79**–1
burglary [bür/glə rē] **142**–2
burn [bürn]
   sunburn [sŭn/bürn/] **110**–14
burn [bürn] **116**–H
burner [bür/nər] **54**–19, **195**–37
burrito [bə rē/tō] **79**–9

bus [bŭs] **128**–9, **151**–14
    bus person [bŭs/ pür/sən] **185**–13
    bus route [bŭs/ rōōt/, –rowt/] **152**–1
    bus station [bŭs/ stā/shən] **124**–7
    bus stop [bŭs/ stäp/] **129**–16, **151**–13
    miss the bus [mïs/ dhə bŭs/] **152** ✦
bus [bŭs] **82**–G
business [bïz/nəs]
    business owner [bïz/nəs ō/nər] **166**–11
    businessperson [bïz/nəs pür/sən] **166**–12
    business suit [bïz/nəs sōōt/] **88**–11
busser [bŭ/sər] **83**–12
Bus Stop [bŭs/ stäp/] **152**
butcher [bŏŏch/ər] **166**–13
butter [bŭt/ər] **66**–6, **83**–19
butterfly [bŭt/ər flï/] **214**–19
buttocks [bŭt/əks] **107**–30
button [bŭt/n] **99**–24
    back button [băk/ bŭt/n] **197**–2
    call button [köl/ bŭt/n] **121**–28
    forward button [för/wərd bŭt/n] **197**–3
buy [bï] **27**–G
    buy a home [bï/ ə hōm/] **41**–M
    buy a snack [bï/ ə snăk/] **11**–K
    buy recycled products
        [bï/ rē sï/kəld präd/ŭkts] **219**–D
Buying a House [bï/ïng ə hows/] **49**
BUYING AND MAINTAINING A CAR
    [bï/ïng ən mān tā/nïng ə kär/] **157**
Buying a Used Car [bï/ïng ə yōōzd/ kär/] **157**
buzzer [bŭz/ər] **51**–31
cab [kăb] **156**–16
cabbage [kăb/ïj] **69**–2
Cabinet [kăb/ə nət] **138**–10
cabinet [kăb/ə nət] **54**–1
    file cabinet [fïl/ kăb/ə nət] **182**–11
    medicine cabinet [mĕd/ə sən kăb/ə nət] **57**–20
    supply cabinet [sə plï/ kăb/ə nət] **182**–1
cables [kā/bəlz] **158**–21, **196**–13
cactus [kăk/təs] **210**–21
cafeteria [kăf/ə tïr/ē ə] **5**–14
cage [kāj] **107**–48
cake [kāk] **73**–39, **81**–33
    cake pan [kāk/ păn/] **78**–26
    cheesecake [chēz/kāk/] **81**–34
    pancakes [păn/kāks/] **80**–7
Cake [kāk] **77**
calculate [kăl/kyə lāt/] **17**–B
calculator [kăl/kyə lā/tər] **17**–6, **183**–25
calculus [kăl/kyə ləs] **192**–19
CALENDAR [kăl/ən dər] **20**–21
CALENDAR EVENTS [kăl/ən dər ï vĕnts/] **22**
calf [kăf] **106**–22
    calf-length [kăf/ lĕnth/] **96**–17
call [köl]
    call button [köl/ bŭt/n] **121**–28
    international call [ïn/tər năsh/ə nəl köl/] **15**–35
    Internet phone call [ïn/tər nĕt/ fōn/ köl/] **14**–20
    local call [lō/kəl köl/] **15**–31
    long distance call [löng/ dïs/təns köl/] **15**–32
call [köl] **48**–A, **147**–L
    call in [köl/ ïn/] **186**–A

calling card [kö/lïng kärd/] **14**–15
calm [köm] **42**–8
camcorder [kăm/kör dər] **235**–24
camel [kăm/əl] **217**–38
camera [kăm/rə]
    camera case [kăm/rə kās/] **235**–28
    digital camera [dï/jə təl kăm/rə] **235**–19
    film camera [fïlm/ kăm/rə] **235**–21
    security camera [sï kyŏŏr/ə tē kăm/rə] **50**–19
    35 mm camera
        [thür/tē fïv/ mïl/ə mē/tər kăm/rə] **235**–21
camisole [kăm/ə sōl/] **91**–21
campaign [kăm pān/] **139**–29
camper [kăm/pər] **156**–9
campfire [kămp/fïr/] **226**–11
camping [kăm/pïng] **226**–5
    camping stove [kăm/pïng stōv/] **226**–16
Campus [kăm/pəs] **5**
can [kăn] **74**–3, **74**–15
    can opener [kăn/ ō/pə nər] **78**–1, **146**–8
    electric can opener [ï lĕk/trïk/ kăn/ ō/pə nər] **54**–14
    garbage can [gär/bïj kăn/] **53**–24
cancer [kăn/sər] **111**–10
candle [kăn/dl] **56**–20
    candle holder [kăn/dl hōl/dər] **56**–21
candy [kăn/dē] **239**–12
    candy bar [kăn/dē bär/] **73**–37
    candy cane [kăn/dē kăn/] **239**–17
    candy store [kăn/dē stör/] **131**–17
cane [kăn] **113**–16, **239**–17
canned food [kănd/ fōōd/] **146**–9
Canned Foods [kănd/ fōōdz/] **72**
canoeing [kə nōō/ïng] **226**–3
can't breathe [kănt/ brēdh/] **116**–N
canteen [kăn tēn/] **226**–24
canvas [kăn/vəs] **233**–17
canyon [kăn/yən] **204**–17
cap [kăp] **88**–1, **206**–7
    baseball cap [bās/böl/ kăp/] **86**–5
    bump cap [bŭmp/ kăp/] **92**–9
    shower cap [show/ər kăp/] **108**–1
    surgical cap [sür/jï kəl kăp/] **121**–37
    surgical scrub cap [sür/jï kəl skrŭb/ kăp/] **93**–35
capital [kă/pət əl] **139**–22
capitalize [kă/pət əl īz/] **190**–A, **190**–B
Capitol [kă/pət əl] **138**–1
capris [kə prēz/] **88**–8
capsule [kăp/səl] **113**–23
car [kär] **150**–1
    car accident [kär/ ăk/sə dənt] **144**–2
    car dealership [kär/ dē/lər shïp/] **126**–4
    car safety seat [kär/ sāf/tē sēt/] **37**–19
    4-door car [för/dör/ kär/] **156**–1
    sports car [spörts/kär/] **156**–4
    subway car [sŭb/wā/ kär/] **152**–6
    town car [town/ kär/] **152**–20
    2-door car [tōō/dör/ kär/] **156**–2
Car [kär] **157**, **159**
CAR [kär] **156**, **157**, **158**–159
card [kärd] **239**–5
    ATM card [ā/tē/ĕm/ kärd/] **132**–15
    auto club card [ö tō/ klŭb/ kärd/] **162**–4

baseball cards [bās/böl/ kärdz/] **232**–2
card store [kärd/ stör/] **130**–7
copies of ID and credit cards
    [käp/ēz əv ī/dē/ ən krĕd/ət/ kärdz/] **146**–19
emergency card [ï mür/jən sē/ kärd/] **161**–23
fare card [fër/ kärd/] **152**–11
folding card table [fōl/dïng/ kärd/ tā/bəl] **102**–4
green card [grēn/ kärd/] **40**–2
greeting card [grē/tïng kärd/] **134**–15
health insurance card
    [hĕlth/ ïn shŏŏr/əns kärd/] **118**–3
memory card [mĕm/ə rē kärd/] **235**–20
post card [pōst/ kärd/] **134**–16
Resident Alien card [rĕz/ə dənt ā/lē ən kärd/] **40**–2
rotary card file [rō/tə rē kärd/ fïl/] **183**–44
Social Security card
    [sō/shəl sï kyŏŏr/ə tē kärd/] **40**–5
Card [kärd] **135**
cardigan sweater [kär/də gən swĕt/ər] **88**–2
Cardinal Numbers [kärd/nəl nŭm/bərz] **16**
cardiologist [kär/dē äl/ə jïst] **120**–3
cardiopulmonary resuscitation (CPR)
    [kär/dē ō pŏŏl mə nër/ē rï sŭs/ə tā/shən] /
    [sē/pē/är/] **117**–17
care [kër] **167**–32
careful worker [kër/fəl wür/kər] **179**–2
careless worker [kër/ləs wür/kər] **179**–1
childcare worker [chïld/kër wür/kər] **166**–16
CARE [kër] **114**–**115**, **118**, **119**
Care of Your Car [kër/ əv yər kär/] **157**
career counselor [kə rēr/ kown/slər] **172**–10
Career Path [kə rēr/ păth/] **172**
CAREER PLANNING [kə rēr/ plăn/ïng] **172**
cargo van [kär/gō văn/] **156**–13
carnation [kär nā/shən] **211**–20
carousel [kär/ə sĕl/] **161**–23
carpenter [kär/pən tər] **62**–12, **166**–14
carpet [kär/pət] **56**–24
carpool [kär/pōōl/] **219**–I
carriage [kär/ïj] **37**–20
carrier [kär/ē ər] **37**–17, **134**–20
carrots [kär/əts] **69**–3
carry [kär/ē] **11**–F, **82**–H
CARS AND TRUCKS [kärz/ ən trŭks/] **156**
cart [kärt] **72**–7, **129**–28
    housekeeping cart [hows/kē/pïng kärt/] **184**–19
    luggage cart [lŭg/ïj/ kärt/] **184**–8
carton [kär/tn] **74**–4, **74**–16
cartoon [kär/tōōn] **236**–3
cartridge [kär/trïj] **183**–45
carving knife [kär/vïng nïf/] **78**–12
case [kās] **94**–5, **235**–28
cash [kăsh]
    cash and coins [kăsh/ ən koynz/] **146**–17
    cash register [kăsh/ rĕj/ə stər] **27**–10, **73**–15
cash [kăsh] **27**–F, **132**–A
cashier [kă shïr/] **73**–13, **166**–15
cashmere [kăzh/mïr/] **98**–4
Casserole [kăs/ə rōl] **77**
    casserole dish [kăs/ə rōl dïsh/] **78**–10
cassette [kə sĕt/] **234**–6
    videocassette [vï/dē ō kə sĕt/] **133**–18

cast [kăst] **113**–20
castle [kă**/**səl] **225**–12
Casual Clothes [kăzh**/**ōō əl klōz**/**] **88**
CASUAL, WORK, AND FORMAL CLOTHES
[kăzh**/**ōō əl würk**/** ən för**/**məl klōz**/**] **88**–**89**
cat [kăt] **215**–9
catfish [kăt**/**fĭsh**/**] **71**–2
catalog [kăt ə **/**lög] **133**–11
catch [kăch] **230**–D
catcher's mask [kăch**/**ərz măsk**/**] **231**–15
caterer [kā**/**tər ər] **185**–16
caterpillar [kăt**/**ə pĭl**/**ər, kăt**/**ər–] **214**–20
cattle [kăt**/**l] **177**–21
cauliflower [kö**/**lĭ flow**/**ər, kä**/**–] **69**–14
cave [kāv] **220**–6
caverns [kă**/**vərnz] **220**–7
cavity [kăv**/**ə tē] **119**–7
C-clamp [sē**/**klămp**/**] **180**–6
CD [sē**/**dē**/**] **196**–9, **234**–5
CD boombox [sē**/**dē**/** bōōm**/**băks**/**] **234**–1
CD player [sē**/**dē**/** plā**/**ər] **159**–38
celebrate [sĕl**/**ə brāt] **206**–C
celery [sĕl**/**ə rē] **69**–9
cell [sĕl] **194**–4
cell membrane [sĕl**/** mĕm**/**brān] **194**–6
cell phone holder [sĕl**/** fōn**/** hōl**/**dər] **94**–15
cell phone kiosk [sĕl**/** fōn**/** kē**/**ösk] **131**–22
cell phone number [sĕl**/** fōn**/** nŭm**/**bər] **4**–12
cell wall [sĕl**/** wäl**/**] **194**–5
cello [chĕl**/**ō] **238**–7
cellular phone [sĕl**/**yə lər fōn**/**] **14**–8
Celsius [sĕl**/**sē əs] **13**–2
cemetery [sĕ**/**mə tĕr**/**ē] **127**–15
cent [sĕnt] **26**–1, **26**–2, **26**–3, **26**–4
center [sĕn**/**tər]
automated postal center (APC)
[ö**/**tə măt ĭd pōs**/**təl sĕn**/**tər] / [ā**/**pē**/**sē**/**] **135**–10
childcare center [chīld**/**kër**/** sĕn**/**tər] **129**–30
convention center [kən vĕn**/**shən sĕn**/**tər] **127**–24
copy center [käp**/**ē sĕn**/**tər] **129**–18
entertainment center
[ĕn**/**tər tān**/**mənt sĕn**/**tər] **56**–5
resource center [rē**/**sörs sĕn**/**tər] **172**–9
CENTER [sĕn**/**tər] **208**–**209**
centimeter [cm] [sĕn**/**tə mē**/**tər] **17**–14
CENTRAL AMERICA [sĕn**/**trəl ə mĕr**/**ə kə] **200**–**201**
Central time [sĕn**/**trəl tīm**/**] **19**–31
cereal [sïr**/**ē əl] **80**–9
ceremony [sĕr**/**ə mō**/**nē] **206**–6
certificate [sər tĭf**/**ə kət] **40**–1, **41**–11
Certificate of Naturalization
[sər tĭf**/**ə kət əv năch**/**rə lə zā**/**shən] **40**–6
certified [sür**/**tə fīd**/**]
Certified Mail® [sür**/**tə fīd**/** māl**/**] **134**–4
certified nursing assistant (CNA)
[sür**/**tə fīd**/** nür**/**sĭng ə sĭs**/**tənt] / [sē**/**ĕn**/**ā**/**] **120**–12
chain [chān] **51**–33, **95**–33, **180**–41
chair [chër] **7**–11
armchair [ärm**/**chër] **56**–22
beach chair [bēch**/** chër**/**] **225**–22
dining room chair [dī**/**nĭng rōōm**/**chër**/**] **55**–8

easy chair [ē**/**zē**/** chër] **56**–22
folding chair [fōld**/**ĭng chër**/**] **102**–5
high chair [hī**/** chër**/**] **37**–6, **82**–3
rocking chair [räk**/**ĭng chër**/**] **37**–21
wheelchair [wēl**/**chër**/**] **113**–9
chalk [chök] **7**–18
chalkboard [chök**/**börd**/**] **6**–1
challenged [chăl**/**əngd] **32**–10
change [chānj] **36**–G, **60**–P, **148**–C
change purse [chānj**/** pürs**/**] **94**–14
changing [chān**/**jĭng]
changing pad [chān**/**jĭng păd**/**] **59**–2
changing table [chān**/**jĭng tā**/**bəl] **59**–1
charger [chär**/**jər] **14**–10, **234**–17, **235**–27
chart [chärt] **121**–24
cheap [chēp] **23**–20
check [chĕk] **132**–13
check book [chĕk**/** bŏŏk**/**] **132**–12
check-in kiosk [chĕk**/**ĭn**/** kē**/**ösk] **160**–2
checkstand [chĕk**/**stănd**/**] **73**–12
paycheck [pā**/**chĕk**/**] **165**–14
check [chĕk]
check blood pressure [chĕk**/** blŭd**/** prĕsh**/**ər] **118**–A
check email [chĕk**/** ē**/** māl**/**] **39**–W
check in [chĕk**/** ĭn**/**] **160**–A
check Internet job sites
[chĕk**/** ĭn**/**tər nĕt**/** jäb**/** sīts**/**] **173**–D
check messages [chĕk**/** mĕs**/**ə jĭz] **171**–R
check out [chĕk**/** owt**/**] **133**–C
check the correct boxes
[chĕk**/** dhə kə rĕkt**/** bäk**/**səz] **9**–U
check the oil [chĕk**/** dhə oyl**/**] **157**–H
check the pronunciation
[chĕk**/** dhe prə nən sē ā**/** shən] **8**–D
check your bags [chĕk**/** yər băgz**/**] **160**–B
check pulse [chĕk**/** pŭls**/**] **122**–A
check your spelling [chĕk**/** yər spĕl**/**ĭng] **197**–F
check your understanding
[chĕk**/** yər ŭn**/**dər stănd**/**ĭng] **12**–N
check your work [chĕk**/** yər würk**/**] **10**–L
checked [chĕkt] **96**–24
checkers [chĕk**/**ərz] **232**–7
checking account number
[chĕk**/**ĭng ə kownt**/** nŭm**/**bər] **132**–14
checkout [chĕk**/**owt**/**] **133**–10
Checkpoint [chĕk**/**poynt**/**] **160**
cheddar cheese [chĕd**/**ər chēz**/**] **71**–28
cheek [chēk] **106**–3
cheese [chēz] **66**–4
American cheese [ə mĕr**/**ə kən chēz**/**] **71**–26
cheddar cheese [chĕd**/**ər chēz**/**] **71**–28
cheeseburger [chēz**/**bür**/**gər] **79**–3
cheesecake [chēz**/**kāk**/**] **81**–34
grilled cheese sandwich
[grĭld**/** chēz**/** săn**/**wĭch, –sănd/–] **80**–10
Swiss cheese [swĭs**/** chēz**/**] **71**–27
Cheesy Tofu Vegetable Casserole
[chē**/**zē tō**/**fōō vĕj**/**tə bəl kăs**/**ə rōl] **77**
chef [shĕf] **83**–16
chef's hat [shĕfs**/** hăt**/**] **93**–28
chef's jacket [shĕfs**/** jăk**/**ət] **93**–29
chef's salad [shĕfs**/** săl**/** əd] **80**–14

executive chef [ĭg zĕk**/**yə tĭv shĕf**/**] **185**–7
head chef [hĕd**/** shĕf**/**] **185**–7
sous chef [sōō**/** shĕf**/**] **185**–6
Chef [shĕf] **93**
chemist [kĕm**/**ĭst] **195**–25
Chemistry [kĕm**/**ə strē] **195**
cherries [chĕr**/**ēz] **68**–11
cherry picker [chĕr**/**ē pĭk**/**ər] **178**–5
chess [chĕs] **232**–8
chest [chĕst] **59**–16, **104**–4, **107**–25
chest of drawers [chĕst**/** əv drörz**/**] **59**–6
chicken [chĭk**/**ən] **66**–3, **70**–16
chicken pox [chĭk**/**ən päks**/**] **111**–6
chicken sandwich [chĭk**/**ən săn**/**wĭch, –sănd–] **79**–5
fried chicken [frīd**/** chĭk**/**ən] **76**–1
roast chicken [rōst**/** chĭk**/**ən] **81**–22
Chicken [chĭk**/**ən] **77**
chief justice [chēf**/** jŭs**/**təs] **138**–13
CHILDCARE AND PARENTING
[chīld**/**kër ən për**/**ən tĭng] **36**–**37**
child / children [chīld] / [chĭl**/** drən]
childcare center [chīld**/**kër sĕn**/**tər] **129**–30
childcare worker [chīld**/**kër wür**/**kər] **166**–16
children's program [chĭl**/**drənz prō**/**grăm] **236**–9
child safety seat [chīld**/** săf**/**tē sēt**/**] **159**–53
grandchild [grăn**/**chīld**/**, grănd**/**–] **34** ✦
lost child [löst**/** chīld**/**] **144**–1
Childhood Diseases [chīld**/**hŏŏd dĭ zē**/**zəz] **111**
chili peppers [chĭl**/**ē pĕp**/**ərz] **69**–29
chill [chĭl] **76**–D
chills [chĭlz] **110**–9
chimney [chĭm**/**nē] **53**–5
chimpanzee [chĭm**/**păn zē**/**] **217**–27
chin [chĭn] **106**–1
chipmunk [chĭp**/**müngk] **215**–20
chips [chĭps] **73**–35
chiropractors [kī**/**rō präk**/**tərz] **120**
chisel [chĭz**/**əl] **181**–55
choke [chōk] **116**–L
choose [chōōz] **9**–P
chop [chäp] **77**–L
chops [chäps] **70**–10, **70**–15
Christmas [krĭs**/**məs] **22**–18
Christmas tree [krĭs**/**məs trē**/**] **239**–16
chromosome [krō**/**mə zōm**/**] **194**–8
chrysanthemum [krĭ sän**/**thə məm] **211**–21
church [chürch] **127**–14
chute [shōōt] **51**–26
circle [sür**/** kəl] **193**–34
circle [sür**/** kəl] **9**–Q
circular saw [sür**/**kyə lər sö**/**] **180**–9
circulation desk [sür**/**kyə lā**/**shən dĕsk**/**] **133**–2
circumference [sər kŭm**/**frəns] **193**–36
citizen [sĭt**/**ə zən] **30**–5
Citizenship Requirements
[sĭt**/**ə zən shĭp**/** rĭ kwīr**/**mənts] **140**
city [sĭt**/**ē] **4**–7, **52**–1
city code [sĭt**/**ē kōd**/**] **15**–34
city council [sĭt**/**ē kown**/**səl] **139**–27
city hall [sĭt**/**ē häl**/**] **124**–8
City Government [sĭt**/**ē gŭ**/**vərn mənt] **139**
CITY STREETS [sĭt**/**ē strēts**/**] **126**–**127**

Index

CIVIC RIGHTS AND RESPONSIBILITIES
[sĭ/vĭk rīts n rĭ spän/sə bĭl/ə tēz] **140**
Civilizations [sĭ/və lə zā/shenz] **199**
claim [klām] **160**–L
clamp [klămp] **180**–6
clams [klămz] **71**–15
clarinet [klăr/ə nĕt/] **238**–2
classical [kla/sĭ kəl] **237**–21
     classical concert [kla/sĭ kəl kän/sərt] **223**–14
classified ad [klăs/e fid] **48**–2
Classmates [klăs/māts/] **8**
classroom [klăs/rōōm/] **5**–7
CLASSROOM [klăs/rōōm/] **6**–7
claw [klö] **214**–2
clean [klēn] **101**–16
clean [klēn] **76**–A
     clean teeth [klēn/ tēth/] **119**–A
     clean the house [klēn/ dhə hows/] **39**–O
     clean the lint trap [klēn/ dhə lĭnt/ trăp/] **101**–D
     clean the oven [klēn/ dhə ŭv/ən] **60**–C
     clean up [klēn/ ŭp/] **147**–M
cleaner [klēn/ər]
     dry cleaners [drī/ klēn/ərz] **128**–2
     glass cleaner [glăs/ klēn/ər] **61**–14
     oven cleaner [ŭv/ən klēn/ər] **61**–3
     vacuum cleaner [văk/yōōm klēn/ər] **61**–10
     vacuum cleaner attachments
          [văk/yōōm klēn/ər ə tăch/mənts] **61**–11
     vacuum cleaner bag [văk/yəm klēn/ər băg/] **61**–12
CLEANING SUPPLIES [klē/nĭng sə plīz/] **61**
cleanser [klēn/zər] **61**–18
CLEANUP [klēn/ŭp/] **148**–149
clear [klĭr] **13**–9
     clear tape [klĭr/tāp/] **183**–30
clear [klĭr] **82**–G
     clear off [klĭr/ äf/] **10**–I
clerk [klŭrk] **5**–13, **182**–2
     admissions clerk [əd mĭsh/ənz klŭrk/] **120**–14
     desk clerk [dĕsk/ klŭrk/] **184**–11
     DMV clerk [dē/ĕm/vē/ klŭrk/] **136**–3
     file clerk [fīl/ klŭrk/] **182**–10
     grocery clerk [grōs/rē klŭrk/, grōsh/–, grō/sə–] **72**–4
     library clerk [lī/brĕr ē klŭrk/] **133**–1
     payroll clerk [pā/rōl/ klŭrk/] **165**–10
     postal clerk [pō/stəl klŭrk/] **135**–7
     retail clerk [rē/tāl/ klŭrk/] **169**–53
     salesclerk [sālz/klŭrk/] **94**–3
     shipping clerk [shĭp/ĭng klŭrk/] **175**–16
     stock clerk [stäk/ klŭrk/] **169**–59
click [klĭk] **197**–B
climb [klīm] **224**–C
climbing apparatus [klīm/ĭng ă/pə ră/təs] **224**–14
clinic [klĭn/ĭk] **186**–2
clip-on earrings [klĭp/än ĭr/ĭngz, –ön–] **95**–37
clipper [klĭp/ər] **109**–31, **176**–11
clips [klĭps] **108**–19, **183**–31, **194**–24
clock [kläk] **7**–9, **58**–24, **165**–7
     clock radio [kläk/ rā/dē ō] **102**–6
close [klōz] **6**–H
closet [kläz/ət] **57** ♦, **58**–5
Closures [klō/zhərz] **99**

cloth [klöth] **181**–54
     cloth diaper [klöth/ dī/pərz] **37**–8
     tablecloth [tā/bəl klöth/] **55**–12
     washcloth [wäsh/klöth/] **57**–4
clothes [klōz] **146**–6
     clothesline [klōz/līn/] **101**–9
     clothespin [klōz/pĭn/] **101**–10
CLOTHES [klōz] **86**–**87**, **88**–**89**, **96**–**97**, **98**–**99**
clothing [klō/dhĭng] **102**–2
CLOTHING [klō/dhĭng] **90**, **92**–**93**
Clothing Problems [klō/dhĭng präb/ləmz] **97**
cloudy [klow/dē] **13**–10
club [klŭb] **162**–4, **223**–12, **231**–1
     club sandwich [klŭb săn/wĭch/, –sănd–] **80**–12
clubs [klŭbz] **233**–32
clutch [klŭch] **159**–49
     clutch bag [klŭch/ băg/] **89**–19
CNA (certified nursing assistant) [sē/ĕn/ā/] /
     [sür/tə tə fĭd/ nür/sĭng ə sĭs/tənt] **120**–12
coach [kōch] **5**–20, **229**–2
coal [kōl] **218**–4
coarse adjustment knob
     [körs/ ə jŭst/mənt näb/] **194**–22
Coast Guard [kōst/ gärd/] **138**–18
coat [kōt] **90**–2, **216**–19
     lab coat [lăb/ kōt/] **93**–33
     raincoat [rān/ kōt/] **90**–18
     sports coat [spörts/ kōt/] **89**–14
     trench coat [trĕnch/ kōt/] **90**–21
cobra [kō/brə] **213**–41
cockpit [käk/pĭt/] **161**–10
cockroaches [käk/rō/chəz] **63**–26
cocktail dress [käk/tāl/ drĕs/] **89**–20
coconuts [kō/kə nŭts/] **68**–24
cod [käd] **71**–8, **212**–5
code [kōd]
     area code [ër/ē ə kōd/] **15**–29
     bar code [bär/ kōd/] **27**–4
     city code [sĭt/ē kōd/] **15**–34
     country code [kŭn/trē kōd/] **15**–33
coffee [kö/fē] **73**–33, **81**–37, **81**–38
     coffeemaker [kö/fē mā/kər] **54**–11
     coffee mug [kö/fē mŭg/] **55**–7
     coffee shop [kö/fē shäp/] **126**–11
     coffee table [kö/fē tā/bəl] **56**–19
COFFEE SHOP MENU [kö/fē shäp/ mĕn/yōō] **80**–**81**
coins [koynz] **146**–17
     coin purse [koyn/ pürs/] **94**–14
Coins [koynz] **26**
colander [käl/ən dər] **78**–17
cold [kōld] **13**–6, **42**–4, **111**–1
     cold tablets [kōld tăb/ləts] **113**–27
     cold water [kōld wö/tər] **57**–7
coleslaw [kōl/slö/] **80**–18
collar [käl/ər] **100**–4
collate [kō/lāt/, kə lāt/] **171**–E
collect [kə lĕkt/] **232**–A
college [käl/ĭj] **127**–17, **188**–6, **188**–7
     college degree [käl/ĭj də grē/] **41**–7
     college dormitory [käl/ĭj dör/mə tör/ē] **52**–8
cologne [kə lōn/] **108**–6
colon [kō/lən] **190**–17

Colonial Period [kə lō/nē əl pïr/ē əd] **198**
colonies [kä/lə nēz] **198**–1
colonists [kä/lə nĭsts] **198**–2
color [kŭl/ər]
     watercolor [wö/tər kŭl/ər] **233**–21
color [kŭl/ər] **33**–D
coloring book [kŭl/ə rĭng bŏŏk/] **59**–13
Colors [kŭl/ərs] **24**
COLORS [kŭl/ərs] **24**
Columbus Day [kə lŭm/bəs dā/] **22**–15
column [käl/ŭm] **107**–49
comb [kōm] **33**–21, **108**–13
comb [kōm] **108**–G
come [kŭm] **39**–R
comedy [käm/ə dē] **236**–2, **237**–13
comet [käm/ət] **205**–24
comfort [kŭm/fərt] **36**–I
comma [käm/ə] **190**–14
commercial fisher [kə mür/shəl fĭsh/ər] **167**–17
commit a crime [kə mĭt/ ə krīm/] **142** ♦
Common Illnesses and Childhood Diseases
     [käm/ən ĭl/nə səz ən chĭld/hŏŏd-dĭ zē/zəz] **111**
COMMUNITY CLEANUP
     [kə myōō/nə tē klēn/ŭp] **148**–149
community college
     [kə myōō/nə tē käl/ĭj] **127**–17, **188**–6
Comparing Clothing [kəm për/ĭng klō/dhĭng] **97**
compartment [kəm pärt/mənt] **159**–44, **161**–13
complaint [kəm plānt/] **97** ♦
Complex [käm/plĕks/] **51**
compliment [käm/plə mĕnt/] **12** ♦
compliment [käm/plə mĕnt/] **12**–C
composer [kəm pō/zər] **199**–15
composition [käm/pə zĭsh/ən] **199**–14
compost [käm/pōst/] **219**–M
compost pile [käm/pōst pīl/] **53**–25
computer [kəm pyōō/tər] **7**–15, **183**–17
     computer lab [kəm pyōō/tər lăb/] **5**–15
     computer software engineer
          [kəm pyōō/tər söft/wër/ ĕn/jə nïr/] **167**–18
     computer technician [kəm pyōō/tər tĕk nĭsh/ən]
          167–19, **182**–12
Computer [kəm pyōō/tər] **196**
COMPUTERS [kəm pyōō/tərz] **196**
conceal [kən sēl/] **143**–C
concert [kän/sərt] **222**–5, **223**–14
concierge [kän/sē ërzh/, kön/–] **184**–4
conclusion [kən klōō/zhən] **190**–8
concrete [käng/krēt, kän krēt/] **178**–10
conditioner [kən dĭsh/ə nər] **108**–11, **159**–39
Conditions [kən dĭsh/ənz] **13**, **111**
CONDITIONS [kən dĭsh/ənz] **111**
condominium [kän/də mĭn/ē əm] **52**–5
conduct [kən dŭkt/] **238**–C
conductor [kən dŭk/tər] **152**–13
cone [kōn] **79**–13, **193**–40
     pinecone [pīn/kōn] **210**–11
conference room [kän/frəns rōōm/] **182**–4
confetti [kən fĕt/ē] **239**–3
confused [kən fyōōzd/] **43**–26
congestion [kən jĕs/chən] **110**–7
Congress [käng/grəs] **138**–2, **198**–6

congressperson [kän/grəs pür/sən] 138–4
CONSERVATION [kän/sər vā/shən] 218–219
Conserve Energy and Resources
  [kən sürv/ ĕn/ər jē ən rē/sörs/əz] 219
console [kän/sōl] 232–3
constellation [kän/stə lā/shən] 205–14
Constitution [kän/stə tōō/shən] 198–19
construction [kən strŭk/shən]
  construction paper [kən strŭk/shən pā/pər] 232–12
  construction site [kən strŭk/shən sīt/] 126–2
  construction worker
    [kən strŭk/shən wür/kər] 178–1
CONSTRUCTION [kən strŭk/shən] 178
Construction Worker [kən strŭk/shən wür/kər] 92
contact [kän/tăkt] 146–2
  contact lenses [kän/tăkt lĕn/zəz] 115–8
container [kən tā/nər] 74–5, 74–17, 78–4
CONTAINERS AND PACKAGING
  [kən tā/nərz ən păk/ĭ jĭng] 74
continental [kän/tə nĕnt/əl] 198–6
contractor [kän/trăk tər] 186–5
control [kən trōl/] 121–27, 232–4
convenience store [kən vēn/yəns stör/] 128–3
convention center [kən vĕn/shən sĕn/tər] 127–24
convert [kən vürt/] 17–D, 75–C
convertible [kən vür/tə bəl] 156–5
conveyer belt [kən vā/ər bĕlt/] 175–16
convict [kän/vĭkt] 141–15
convict [kən vĭkt/] 141–E
cook [kōōk] 185–1, 185 ✦
cook [kōōk] 39–Q, 76–C, 170–C
cooked [kōōkt] 70–25
cookies [kōōk/ēz] 73–38
  cookie sheet [kōōk/ē shēt/] 78–27
cool [kōōl] 13–5
cooler [kōō/lər] 225–19
co-op [kō/äp/] 52 ✦
copier [kä/pē ər]
  photocopier [fō/tō kä/pē ər] 183–23
copies / copy [kä/pēz] / [kä/pē]
  copies of ID and credit cards
    [käp/ēz əv ī/dē ən krĕd/ət kärdz/] 146–19
  copies of important papers
    [käp/ēz əv ĭm pört/ənt pā/pərz] 146–20
  copy center [käp/ē sĕn/tər] 129–18
copy [käp/ē] 8–E
coral [kör/əl] 220–5
cord [körd] 14–2
  bungee cord [bŭn/jē körd/] 181–15
  cordless phone [körd/ləs fōn/] 15–24
  extension cord [ĭk stĕn/shən körd/] 181–14
  frayed cord [frād/ körd/] 179–5
  power cord [pow/ər körd/] 196–2
corduroy [kör/də roy/] 99–11
core course [kör/ körs/] 189 ✦
corn [körn] 69–12, 177–4
  corn rows [körn/ rōz/] 33–14
corned beef [körnd/ bēf/] 71–22
corner [kör/nər] 128–7
coronary disease [kör/ə nĕ/rē dĭ zēz/] 111 ✦
corral [kə răl/] 177–17
correct [kə rĕkt/] 10–N

correction [kə rĕk/shən]
  correction fluid [kə rĕk/shən flōō/əd] 183–36
  correction tape [kə rĕk/shən tāp/] 183–37
cost [köst] 27–7, 122–1
costume [käs/tōōm] 239–11
cotton [kät/n] 98–1, 177–6
couch [kowch] 56–18
cough [köf] 110–A
  cough syrup [köf/ sĭr/əp, –sür/–] 113–29
council [kown/səl] 139–27
  councilperson [kown/səl pür/sən] 139–28
counselor [kown/slər] 5–6, 172–10
count [kownt] 84–A
counter [kown/tər] 54–22, 113–18
  counterperson [kown/tər pür/sən] 79–17
Counterperson [kown/tər pür/sən] 93
country [kŭn/trē] 52–4, 227–3, 237–27
  country code [kŭn/trē kōd/] 15–33
county fair [kown/tē fër/] 223–13
coupe [kōōp] 156–2
couple [kŭ/pəl] 35–20, 35–21, 239–4
coupons [kōō/pönz/] 67–15
courier [kür/ē ər, kōōr/–] 168–40
course [körs] 172–8, 189 ✦
court [kört]
  basketball court [băs/kət böl/ kört/] 229–7
  courthouse [kört/hows/] 125–13
  courtroom [kört/rōōm/] 141–7
  court reporter [kört/ rĭ pör/tər] 141–12
  courtyard [kört/yärd/] 51–21
  food court [fōōd/ kört/] 131–15
  Supreme Court [sə prēm/ kört/] 138–11
  tennis court [tĕ/nəs kört/] 224–6
cousin [kŭz/ən] 34–9
cover [kŭv/ər] 158–9, 181–46
  coveralls [kŭv/ər ölz/] 92–8
  cover-up [kŭv/ər ŭp/] 90–25
cow [kow] 215–1
cowboy hat [kow/boy/ hăt/] 92–18
coyote [kī ō/tē, kī/ōt/] 216–3
CPR (cardiopulmonary resuscitation) [sē/pē/är/] /
  [kär/dē ō pōōl/mə nër/ē-rē sŭs/ə tā/shən] 117–17
CPU [sē/pē/yōō/] 196–4
crab [krăb] 71–9, 212–20
cracked [krăkt] 62–4
cradle [krād/l] 59–20
crane [krān] 178–7
crash [krăsh] 144–3
crayons [krā/änz] 59–14
cream [krēm] 24–16, 81–41, 113–25
  antihistamine cream
    [ăn/tĭ hĭs/tə mēn krēm/] 117–11
  ice-cream [īs/ krēm/] 72–26
  ice-cream cone [īs/ krēm kōn/] 79–13
  ice cream shop [īs/ krēm shäp/] 131–16
  shaving cream [shā/vĭng krēm/] 109–29
  sour cream [sow/ər krēm/] 72–21
creamer [krē/mər] 55–15
credit [krĕd/ət] 146–19
creek [krēk, krĭk] 204 ✦
crescent moon [krĕs/ənt mōōn/] 205–10

crew [krōō] 176–1, 176–4
  crewneck [krōō/nĕk] 96–7
  crew socks [krōō/säks/] 91–8
crib [krĭb] 59–3
cricket [krĭk/ət] 214–23
crime [krīm] 142 ✦
CRIME [krīm] 142
criminal [krĭm/ə nəl] 142 ✦
crocheting [krō shā/ĭng] 233–25
crocodile [kräk/ə dīl/] 213–37
crocus [krō/kəs] 211–17
Crops [kräps] 177
cross [krös]
  cross-country skiing [krös/kŭn/trē skē/ĭng] 227–3
  crosswalk [krös/wök/] 128–15
cross [krös] 128–A
  cross out [krös/ owt/] 9–R
crossing [krö/sĭng] 154–13, 154–14, 154–15
crown [krown] 119–9
crucible tongs [krōō/sə bəl tängz/, –töngz/] 195–44
crutches [krŭch/əz] 113–10
cry [krī] 206–B
cube [kyōōb] 193–38
cubicle [kyōōb/ə kəl] 182–7
cucumbers [kyōō/kŭm bərz] 69–10
cuff [kŭf] 100–9
cup [kŭp] 75–2, 75–10, 83–24
  1/2 cup [hăf/ kŭp/] 75–9
  1/4 cup [kwör/tər kŭp/] 75–8
  teacup [tē/kŭp/] 55–6
curb [kürb] 129–21
curling iron [kür/lĭng ī/ərn] 108–17
curly hair [kür/lē hër/] 33–11
cursor [kür/sər] 197–14
curtains [kür/tnz] 57–12, 58–7
curved line [kürvd/ lĭn/] 193–23
cushion [kōō/shən] 56 ✦, 100–13
customer [kŭs/tə mər] 72–1, 94–4, 132–2, 164–2
  customer service [kŭs/tə mər sür/vəs] 97 ✦
  customer service representative
    [kŭs/tə mər-sür/vəs rĕ/prə zĕn/tə tĭv] 167–20
Customs [kŭs/təmz] 161
customs officer [kŭs/təmz ö/fə sər] 161–17
cut [kŭt] 91–10, 110–13
cut [kŭt] 33–A, 109–N
  cut up [kŭt/ ŭp/] 77–I
cute [kyōōt] 32–14
cutlets [kŭt/ləts] 70–6
cutter [kut/ər] 183–22, 232–16
cutting board [kŭt/ĭng börd/] 54–27
cycling [sī/klĭng] 228–5
cyclist [sī/klĭst] 224–2
cylinder [sĭl/ən dər] 193–41, 195–38
cytoplasm [sī/tə plăzm] 194–9
daffodil [dăf/ə dĭl/] 211–25
daily [dā/lē] 20–21
DAILY ROUTINES [dā/lē rōō tēnz/] 38–39
Dairy [dër/ē] 72
daisy [dā/zē] 211–14
dance [dăns] 64–A
dangerous [dān/jər əs] 186–1
dark blue [därk/ blōō/] 24–10

Index

Dashboard and Instrument Panel
[dăsh/börd/ ən ĭn/strə mənt păn/əl] **159**
dates [dāts] **20**–1, **68**–28
  date of birth [dāt əv bürth/] **4**–13
  expiration date
    [ĕk/spə rā/shən dāt/] **112**–7, **136**–10
daughter [dö/tər] **34**–14
  daughter-in-law [dö/tər ĭn lö/] **34** ✦
  granddaughters [grăn/dö/tərz] **34** ✦
  stepdaughter [stĕp/dö/tər] **35** ✦
day [dā] **20**–2
  birthday [bürth/dā/] **22**–1
  Columbus Day [kə lŭm/bəs dā] **22**–15
  daylight saving time [dā/līt/ sā/vĭng tīm/] **19**–25
  every day [ĕv/rē dā/] **20**–21
  Independence Day [ĭn/də pĕn/dəns dā/] **22**–13
  Labor Day [lā/bər dā/] **22**–14
  Martin Luther King Jr. Day
    [mär/tən lōō/thər kĭng/ jōōn/yər-dā/] **22**–10
  Memorial Day [mə mör/ē əl dā/] **22**–12
  New Year's Day [nōō/ yïrz/ dā/] **22**–9
  Presidents' Day [prĕz/ə dənts dā/] **22**–11
  Veterans Day [vĕt/ər ənz dā/] **22**–16
Day [dā] **18**
DAY AT SCHOOL [dā/ ăt skōōl/] **11**
DAY AT WORK [dā/ ăt würk/] **186**–**187**
Days of the Week [dāz/ əv dhə wēk/] **20**
dead [dĕd]
  dead-bolt lock [dĕd/bōlt/ läk/] **51**–34
  dead end [dĕd/ĕnd/] **154**–6
deaf [dĕf] **32**–12
Dealer [dē/lər] **158**
dealership [dē/lər shĭp/] **126**–4
death certificate [dĕth/ sər tĭf/ə kət] **41**–11
debate [də bāt/] **139**–B
decaf coffee [dē/kăf/ kö/fē] **81**–38
decay [də kā/] **119**–7
December [dĭ sĕm/bər] **21**–36
decimal point [dĕ/sə məl poynt/] **17**–7
Decimals [dĕ/sə məlz] **17**
deck [dĕk] **240**–2
declaration [dĕk/lə rā/shən]
  declaration form [dĕk/lə rā/shən förm/] **161**–16
  Declaration of Independence
    [dĕk/lə rā/shən əv ĭn/də pĕn/dəns] **198**–5
decline [də klīn/] **12**–J
decorations [dĕk/ə rā/shənz] **240**–1
deductions [də dŭk/shənz] **165**–13
deed [dĕd] **41**–9
deer [dïr] **216**–14
defendant [dĭ fĕn/dənt] **141**–5
defense attorney [dĭ fĕns/ ə tür/nē] **141**–4
defroster [də frös/tər] **159**–41
degrees [də grēz/] **13**–8, **193**–26
delayed flight [də lād/ flīt/] **161**–30
delete [də lēt/] **196**–C
DELI [dĕl/ē] **71**
deliver [də lĭv/ər] **11**–G, **135**–E
delivery person [də lĭv/ə rē pür/sən] **167**–21
dementia [də mĕn/shə] **111**–18
demonstration [dĕm/mən strā/shən] **122**–6
denim [dĕ/nəm] **99**–7

denominator [də nömə nā/tər] **192**–6
dental [dĕn/təl]
  dental assistant [dĕn/təl ə sĭs/tənt] **119**–2, **167**–22
  dental floss [dĕn/təl flös/, –fläs/] **109**–24
  dental hygienist [dĕn/təl hī jĕ/nĭst, –jē/nĭst] **119**–3
  dental instruments [dĕn/təl ĭn/strə mənts] **119**–4
DENTAL CARE [dĕn/təl kër/] **119**
Dental Problems [dĕn/təl präb/ləmz] **119**
dentist [dĕn/tĭst] **119**–1
Dentistry [dĕn/təs trē/] **119**
dentures [dĕn/chərz] **119**–10
deodorant [dē ō/dər ənt] **108**–5
department [dĭ pärt/mənt] **95**–7, **95**–8
  Department of Motor Vehicles
    [dĭ pärt/mənt əv mō/tər vē/ĭ kəlz] **124**–4
  department store [dĭ pärt/mənt stör/] **131**–13
DEPARTMENT OF MOTOR VEHICLES (DMV)
  [dĭ pärt/mənt əv mō/tər vē/ĭ kəlz] / [dē/ĕm/vē/]
  136–**137**
departure [dĭ pär/chər] **161**–5, **161**–7
deposit [dĭ päz/ət] **132**–3, **132**–7
  deposit slip [dĭ päz/ət slĭp/] **132**–4
depression [də prĕ/shən] **115**–5
depth [dĕpth] **17**–18
DESCRIBING CLOTHES [dĭ skrī/bĭng klōz/] **96**–**97**
DESCRIBING HAIR [dĭ skrī/bĭng hër/] **33**
DESCRIBING PEOPLE [dĭ skrī/bĭng pē/pəl] **32**
DESCRIBING THINGS [dĭ skrī/bĭng thĭngz/] **23**
desert [dĕz/ərt] **204**–4
design [dĭ zīn/] **175**–A
designated drivers [dĕz/ĭg nā/təd drī/vərz] **143** ✦
designer [dĭ zī/nər] **98** ✦, **167**–30, **175**–2, **176**–5
desk [dĕsk] **6**–7, **182**–9
  circulation desk [sür/kyə lā/shən dĕsk/] **133**–2
  desk clerk [dĕsk klürk/] **184**–11
  front desk [frŭnt/ dĕsk/] **184**–12
Desktop Computer [dĕsk/täp/ kəm pyōō/tər] **196**
Desserts [dĭ zürts] **81**
dessert tray [dĭ zürt/ trā/] **83**–10
destination [dĕs/tə nā/shən] **161** ✦
detector [dĭ tĕk/tər] **51**–29
detergent [dĭ tür/jənt] **101**–8
device [də vīs/] **225**–20
diabetes [dī/ə bē/tēz, –təs] **111**–12
diagonal [dī ăg/ə nəl, –ăg/nəl] **193**–31
dial [dī/əl] **15**–A, **15**–E
diameter [dī ăm/ə tər] **193**–37
diamonds [dī/məndz] **233**–29
diaper [dī/pər] **37**–8, **37**–10
  diaper pail [dī/pər pāl/] **37**–7
diaphragm [dī/ə frăm] **194**–19
dice [dīs] **232**–6
dice [dīs] **77**–J
dictate [dĭk/tāt] **8**–N
dictator [dĭk/tā/tər] **199**–6
dictionary [dĭk/shə nër/ē] **7**–30, **7**–31
die [dī] **41**–R
dietician [dī/ə tĭsh/ən] **120**–15
difference [dĭf/rəns] **192**–8
different [dĭf/frənt, dī/fə rənt] **23**–16
DIFFERENT [dĭf/frənt, dī/fə rənt] **28**–**29**

DIFFERENT PLACES TO LIVE
  [dĭf/frənt plā/səz tə lĭv/, dĭ/fə rənt] **52**
difficult [dĭf/ĭ kŭlt/] **23**–24
digital [dĭ/jə təl]
  digital camera [dĭ/jə təl kăm/rə] **235**–19
  digital photo album [dĭ/jə təl fō/tō ăl/bəm] **235**–32
dime [dīm] **26**–3
Dimensions [də mĕn/shənz] **17**
diner [dī/nər] **82**–6, **185**–9
dining [dī/nĭng]
  dining area [dī/nĭng ër/ē ə] **46**–7
  dining room [dī/nĭng rōōm/] **82**–1
  dining room chair [dī/nĭng rōōm/ chër/] **55**–8
  dining room table [dī/nĭng rōōm/tā/bəl] **55**–9
Dining [dī/nĭng] **185**
DINING AREA [dī/nĭng ër/ē ə] **55**
dinner [dĭn/ər] **72**–28
  dinner fork [dĭn/ər förk/] **83**–28
  dinner plate [dĭn/ər plāt/] **83**–18
  dinner salad [dĭn/ər săl/əd] **80**–15
Dinner [dĭn/ər] **81**
diploma [də plō/mə] **40**–3
direct flight [də rĕkt/ flīt/, dī–] **161** ✦
Directions [də rĕk/shənz] **9**, **155**
DIRECTIONS AND MAPS
  [də rĕk/shənz ən măps/, dī–] **155**
directory [də rĕk/tə rē, dī–] **131**–24
  directory assistance
    [də rĕk/tə rē ə sĭs/təns, dī–] **14**–22
dirty [dür/tē] **101**–15
Disabilities [dĭ/sə bĭ/lə tēz] **32**
disagree [dĭ/sə grē/] **12**–L
disappointed [dĭ/sə poyn/təd] **28**–4
DISASTERS [dĭ/zăs tərz] **144**–**145**
disc [dĭsk] **231**–27
discipline [dĭs/ə plən] **36**–K
discuss [dĭ skŭs/] **8**–G
disease [dĭ zēz/] **111**–11, **111** ✦, **119**–11
Diseases [dĭ zē/zəz] **111**
disgusted [dĭ skŭs/təd] **42**–7
dish [dĭsh] **55**–1
  casserole dish [kăs/ə rōl dĭsh/] **78**–10
  dish rack [dĭsh/ răk/] **54**–5
  dish room [dĭsh/ rōōm/] **83**–13
  dish towel [dĭsh/ tow/əl] **61**–22
  dishwasher [dĭsh/wä/shər, –wö/–]
    54–8, **83**–14, **185**–2
  dishwashing liquid [dĭsh/wä/shĭng lĭk/wəd] **61**–21
  satellite dish [să/tə lĭt dĭsh/] **53**–6
  soap dish [sōp/ dĭsh/] **57**–25
disinfectant wipes [dĭs/ən fĕk/tənt wīps/] **61**–23
display case [dĭ splā/ kās/] **94**–5
disposable [dĭ spō/zə bəl]
  disposable diaper [dĭ spō/zə bəl dī/pər] **37**–10
  disposable gloves [dĭ spō/zə bəl glŭvz/] **93**–27
disposal [dĭ spō/zəl] **54**–7, **121**–31
dive [dīv] **230**–K
divide [də vīd/] **17**–A, **192**–D
diving [dī/vĭng] **227**–12
  diving mask [dī/vĭng măsk/] **225**–6
divorced couple [də vörst/ kŭ/pəl] **35**–21
DJ [dē/jā/] **64**–4

DMV [dē/ĕm/vē/]
    DMV clerk [dē/ĕm/vē/ klürk/] **136**–3
    DMV handbook [dē/ĕm/vē/ hănd/bŏok/] **136**–1
do [dōō] **39**–T
    do an experiment [dōō ən ĭk spĕr/ə mənt] **195**–B
    do crafts [dōō krăfts/] **232**–D
    do errands [dōō ĕr/əndz] **128** ✦
    do manual labor [dōō măn/yōō əl lā/bər] **170**–D
    do not drink [dōō năt drĭnk/] **112**–F
    do not enter [dōō năt/ ĕn/tər] **154**–2
    do not operate [dōō năt/ äp/ə rāt/] **112**–E
    do not take [dōō năt/ tāk/] **112**–F
    don't be late [dōnt/ bē/ lāt/] **174**–E
    don't litter [dōnt/ lĭ/tər] **219**–L
    don't smoke [dōnt/smōk/] **114**–G
dock [däk] **175**–15, **234**–3
    dockworker [däk/wür/kər] **167**–23
doctor [däk/tər] **118**–5
DOCUMENTS [dä/kyə mənts] **40**–**41**
dog [dög] **79**–6, **215**–11, **215**–22
dogwood [dög/wŏod/] **210**–15
DOING THE LAUNDRY [dō/ĭng dhə lön/drē] **101**
doll [däl] **59**–21, **233**–28
    dollhouse [däl/hows/] **59**–16
    doll making kit [däl/ mā/kĭng kĭt/] **232**–13
dollar [däl/ər] **26**–7
    dollar coin [däl/ər koyn/] **26**–6
    fifty dollars [fĭf/te dal/ərz] **26**–11
    five dollars [fĭv/ däl/ərz] **26**–8
    half dollar [hăf/ däl/ər] **26**–5
    one hundred dollars
        [wŭn/ hŭn/drəd däl/ərz] **26**–12
    ten dollars [tĕn/ däl/ərz] **26**–9
    twenty dollars [twĕn/tē däl/ərz] **26**–10
dolphin [däl/fən, döl/–] **213**–31
domesticated [də mĕs/tə kā/təd] **215** ✦
DOMESTIC ANIMALS AND RODENTS
    [də mĕs/tĭk ăn/ə məlz ən rōd/nts] **215**
donkey [däng/kē, dŭng/–, döng/–] **215**–3
donut [dō/nŭt] **79**–15
    donut shop [dō/nŭt shäp/] **129**–17
door [dör] **46**–3
    doorbell [dör/bĕl/] **53**–14
    door chain [dör/ chān/] **51**–33
    doorknob [dör/näb/] **53**–12
    door lock [dör/ läk/] **159**–25
    doorman [dör/măn/] **184**–1
    4-door car [för/dör kär/] **156**–1
    front door [frŭnt/ dör/] **53**–11
    garage door [gə räj/ dör/] **53**–7
    revolving door [rĭ väl/vĭng dör/] **184**–2
    screen door [skrēn/ dör/] **53**–15
    sliding glass door [slī/dĭng glăs/dör] **53**–18
    storm door [störm/ dör/] **53**–10
    2-door car [tōō/dör kär/] **156**–2
dorm / dormitory [dörm/] / [dör/mə tör/ē] **52**–8
dosage [dō/sĭj] **112**–6
double [dŭb/əl]
    double bed [dŭb/əl bĕd] **184**–14
    double boiler [dŭb/əl boy/lər] **78**–8

down [down]
    break down [brāk/ down/] **162**–D
    downhill skiing [down/hĭl/ skē/ĭng] **227**–1
    down jacket [down jăk/ət] **90**–16
    down vest [down vĕst/] **90**–14
    drop-down menu [dräp/ down/ mĕn/yōō/] **197**–8
    put down [pŏot/ down/] **6**–J
    sit down [sĭt down/] **6**–F
    walk down [wäk down/] **153**–D
downstairs [down/stērz/] **51** ✦
DOWNTOWN [down/town/] **124**–**125**
drain [drān] **57**–5
drama [drä/mə] **236**–12
drapes [drāps] **56**–16
draw [drö] **8**–F, **118**–F, **195**–E
drawer [drör] **54**–23, **58**–2, **59**–6
dress [drĕs] **86**–3, **88**–5, **89**–20
    dressmaker [drĕs/mā/kər] **100**–1
    dressmaker's dummy [drĕs/mā/kərz dŭ/mē] **100**–2
    dress socks [drĕs/ säks/] **91**–9
dress [drĕs] **36**–H, **174**–B
dressed [drĕst] **38**–D
dresser [drĕs/ər] **58**–1
Dressings [drĕs/ĭngz] **80**
dribble [drĭb/əl] **230**–J
drill [drĭl] **178**–9, **180**–8
    drill bit [drĭl bĭt] **180**–28
drill [drĭl] **119**–D
drink [drĭnk] **11**–J
    do not drink alcohol
        [dōō/ năt/ drĭnk/ ăl/kə höl/] **112**–F
    don't drink and drive [dōnt/ drĭnk ən drĭv/] **143**–G
    drink fluids [drĭnk flōō/ədz] **114**–C
drip [drĭp] **121**–25
dripping [drĭp/ĭng] **63**–17
drive [drĭv] **196**–6, **196**–8, **196**–9
    drive-thru window [drĭv/thrōō/ wĭn/dō] **128**–11
    driveway [drĭv/wā/] **53**–8
drive [drĭv]
    don't drink and drive [dōnt/drĭnk ən drĭv/] **143**–G
    drive a truck [drĭv ə trŭk/] **170**–E
    drive through [drĭv/ thrōō/] **153**–K
    drive to work [drĭv/ tə würk/] **38**–I
driver [drī/vər] **152**–21, **169**–61
    designated drivers [dĕz/ĭg nā/təd drī/vərz] **143** ✦
    driver's license [drī/vərz lī/səns] **40**–4, **136**–9
    driver's license number
        [drī/vərz lī/səns nŭm/bər] **136**–11
    Phillips screwdriver [fĭl/ĭps skrōō/drī/vər] **180**–31
    screwdriver [skrōō/drī/vər] **180**–30
driving [drī/vĭng] **142**–5
drop [dräp]
    drop cloth [dräp/ klöth/] **181**–54
    drop-down menu [dräp/ down/ mĕn/yōō/] **197**–8
drop off [dräp/ öf/] **38**–G
dropper [dräp/ər] **195**–45
drops [dräps] **113**–31
drought [drowt] **145**–11
drown [drown] **116**–I
drugs [drŭgz] **116**–K, **142**–6
drums [drŭmz] **238**–16
drumsticks [drŭm/stĭks/] **70**–23
drunk driving [drŭngk/ drī/vĭng] **142**–5

dry [drī] **101**–18
    dry cleaners [drī/ klē/nərz] **128**–2
    dry erase marker [drī/ ĭ rās/ mär/kər] **7**–17
    drywall [drī/wöl/] **178**–19
dry [drī] **60**–N, **108**–H
dryer [drī/ər] **50**–13, **101**–4
    blow dryer [blō/ drī/ər] **33**–23, **108**–18
    dryer sheets [drī/ər shēts/] **101**–5
Dry Measures [drī/ mĕzh/ərz] **75**
duck [dŭk] **70**–18, **214**–12
duct tape [dŭkt/ tāp/] **181**–49
dummy [dŭ/mē] **100**–2
dump truck [dŭmp/ trŭk/] **156**–19
dune [dōōn] **204**–5
duplex [dōō/plĕks/] **52** ✦
During an Emergency [dōō/rĭng ən ĭ mür/jən sē] **147**
dust [dŭst]
    dustpan [dŭst/păn/] **61**–17
    dust ruffle [dŭst/ rŭf/əl] **58**–17
    dust storm [dŭst/ störm/] **13**–19
dust [dŭst] **60**–A
duster [dŭs/tər] **61**–1
DVD [dē/vē/dē/] **133**–19, **234**–11
    DVD and CD-ROM drive
        [dē/vē/dē/ ən sē/dē/räm/ drīv/] **196**–9
    DVD player [dē/vē/dē/ plā/ ər] **56**–7, **234**–10
dye [dī] **33**–D
eagle [ē/gəl] **214**–9
ear [ĭr] **32**–17, **105**–11
    earache [ĭr/āk/] **110**–3
    ear infection [ĭr/ ĭn fĕk/shən] **111**–3
    earmuffs [ĭr/mŭfs/] **90**–13, **179**–16
    ear plugs [ĭr/ plŭgz/] **179**–15
    pierced earrings [pïrst/ ïr/ĭngz] **95**–36
early [ür/lē] **19**–22
Earth [ürth] **205**–3
earthquake [ürth/kwāk/] **144**–5
easel [ē/zəl] **233**–18
east [ēst] **155**–4
Eastern time [ē/stərn tīm/] **19**–32
easy [ē/zē] **23**–23, **76**–11
    easy chair [ē/zē chër/] **56**–22
Easy Chicken Soup [ē/zē chĭk/ən sōōp/] **77**
eat [ēt] **11**–1
    eat a healthy diet [ēt ə hĕl/thē dī/ət] **114**–F
    eat breakfast [ēt brĕk/fəst] **38**–E
    eat dinner [ēt dĭn/ər] **39**–S
    eat out [ēt/ owt/] **82** ✦
eater [ē/tər] **176**–12
eclipse [ĭ klĭps/] **205**–16, **205** ✦
edit [ĕd/ət] **191**–I
education [ĕ jyōō/ kā/shən] **189**–17
eel [ēl] **212**–12
eggplants [ĕg/plănts/] **69**–23
eggs [ĕgz] **66**–7
    eggbeater [ĕg/bē/tər] **78**–20
    eggs over easy [ĕgz ō/vər ē/zē] **76**–11
    eggs sunny-side up [ĕgz sŭn/ē sīd/ ŭp/] **76**–10
    hardboiled eggs [härd/ boyld/ ĕgz/] **76**–8
    poached eggs [pōcht/ ĕgz/] **76**–9
    scrambled eggs [skrăm/bəld ĕgz/] **76**–7
Eggs [ĕgz] **76**

Index

eight [āt] **16**
eighteen [ā/tēn/] **16**
eighteenth [ā/tēnth/] **16**
eighth [ātth, āth] **16**
eightieth [ā/tē/əth] **16**
eighty [ā/tē] **16**
elastic bandage [ĭ lăs/tĭk băn/dĭj] **117**–12
elbow [ĕl/bō] **106**–12
elderly [ĕl/dər lē] **32**–3
elected [ĭ lĕk/təd] **139**–C
   elected official [ĭ lĕk/təd ə fĭ/shəl] **139**–32
Election [ĭ lĕk/shən] **139**
election results [ĭ lĕk/shən rĭ zŭltz/] **139**–31
elective [ĭ lĕk/tĭv] **189** ✦
electric [ĭ lĕk/trĭk] **116**–F
   electric can opener [ĭ lĕk/trĭk kăn/ ō/pə nər] **54**–14
   electric drill [ĭ lĕk/trĭk drĭl/] **180**–8
   electric keyboard [ĭ lĕk/trĭk kē/bördˌ] **238**–18
   electric mixer [ĭ lĕk/trĭk mĭk/sər] **54**–25
   electric pencil sharpener
     [ĭ lĕk/trĭk pĕn/səl shär/pə nər] **183**–26
   electric shaver [ĭ lĕk/trĭk shā/vər] **109**–26
electrical [ĭ lĕk/trĭ kəl]
   electrical hazard [ĭ lĕk/trĭ kəl hăz/ərd] **186**–6
   electrical tape [ĭ lĕk/trĭ kəl tāp/] **181**–43
electrician [ĭ lĕk trĭsh/ən] **62**–9
electron [ĭ lĕk/trän] **195**–30
electronics [ĭ lĕk trän/ĭks]
   electronics repair person
     [ĭ lĕk trän/ĭks rĭ pĕr/ pür/sən] **167**–24
   electronics store [ĭ lĕk trän/ĭks stör/] **131**–20
ELECTRONICS AND PHOTOGRAPHY
   [ĭ lĕk trän/ĭks ən fə tägˌrə fē] **234**–235
elementary school [ĕl/ə mĕn/trē skōōl/] **188**–2
elephant [ĕl/ə fənt] **217**–42
elevator [ĕl/ə vā/tər] **50**–9, **131**–21, **184**–9
eleven [ĭ lĕv/ən] **16**
eleventh [ĭ lĕv/ənth] **16**
elm [ĕlm] **210**–16
Email [ē/mālˌ] **197**
embarrassed [ĭm băr/əst] **43**–24
embroidery [ĭm broy/də rē] **233**–24
EMERGENCIES [ĭ mür/jən sēz] **116**
EMERGENCIES AND NATURAL DISASTERS
   [ĭ mür/jən sēz ən năch/rəl dĭ zăs/tərz,–năch/ə rəl–]
   144–145
emergency [ĭ mür/jən sē] **117**–3
   emergency card [ĭ mür/jən sē kärd/] **161**–26
   emergency exit
     [ĭ mür/jən sē ĕg/zət,–ĕk/sət] **51**–25, **161**–14
   emergency medical technician (EMT) [ĭ mür/jən sē
     mĕd/ĭ kəl tĕk nĭsh/ən] / [ē/ĕm/tē/] **121**–32
Emergency [ĭ mür/jən sē] **146**–147
Emergency Call [ĭ mür/jən sē köl/] **15**
EMERGENCY PROCEDURES
   [ĭ mür/jən sē prə sē/jərz] **146**–147
Emergency Room Entrance
   [ĭ mür/jən sē rōōm/ ĕn/trəns] **121**
Emergency Worker [ĭ mür/jən sē wür/kər] **93**
emery board [ĕm/ə rē börd/, ĕm/rē–] **109**–32
emperor [ĕm/pər ər] **199**–3
employee [ĕm ploy/ē] **165**–9

employer [ĕm ploy/ər] **164**–4
empty [ĕmp/tē] **23**–10
empty [ĕmp/tē] **60**–L
EMT (emergency medical technician) [ē/ĕm/tē/] /
   [ĭ mür/jən sē mĕd/ĭ kəl tĕk nish/ən] **121**–32
end [ĕnd] **154**–6
   endpoint [ĕnd/poyntˌ] **193**–21
   end table [ĕnd/ tā/bəl] **56**–14
energy [ĕn/ər jē] **218**–1, **218**–7, **218**–8
   bioenergy [bī/ō ĕn/ər jē] **218**–9
ENERGY AND CONSERVATION
   [ĕn/ər jē ən kän/sər vā/shən] **218**–219
Energy and Resources [ĕn/ər jē ən rē/sör/səz] **219**
Energy Sources [ĕn/ər jē sör/səz] **218**
engine [ĕn/jən] **158**–18, **197**–6
engineer [ĕn/jə nïr/] **167**–18, **167**–25
ENGLISH COMPOSITION
   [ĭng/glĭsh kämˌpə zĭsh/ən] **190**–191
English muffin [ĭng/glĭsh mŭf/ən] **80**–5
enter [ĕn/tər]
   do not **enter** [dōō/ nät/ ĕn/tər] **154**–2
   enter data [ĕn/tər dā/tə] **171**–B
   enter the room [ĕn/tər dhe rōōm/] **11**–A
   enter your PIN [ĕn/tər yər pĭn/] **132**–E
ENTERTAINMENT [ĕn/tər tān/mənt] **236**–237
entertainment center [ĕn/tər tān/mənt sĕn/tər] **56**–5
entrance [ĕn/trəns] **164**–1
Entrance [ĕn/trəns] **50**, **121**
entry-level job [ĕn/trē lĕv/əl jäb/] **172**–1
Entryway [ĕn/trē wā/] **51**
envelope [ĕn/və lōp/] **134**–14, **183**–43
equation [ĭ kwā/zhən] **192**–13
equipment [ĭ kwĭp/mənt] **177**–12, **179**–4
Equipment [ĭ kwĭp/mənt] **179**, **183**
EQUIPMENT [ĭ kwĭp/mənt] **231**
Equivalencies [ĭ kwĭ/və lən sēz/] **17**, **75**
erase [ĭ rās/] **10**–M
eraser [ĭ rā/sər] **7**–19, **7**–21
errands [ĕr/əndz] **128** ✦
eruption [ĭ rŭp/shən] **145**–16
escalator [ĕs/kə lā/tər] **131**–23
escape [ĭs kāp/] **50**–2
   escape route [ĭs kāp/ rōōt/, rowt/] **146**–3
ESL [ē/ĕs/ĕl/] **189**–14
ESOL [ē/ĕs/ō/ĕl/] **189**–14
essay [ĕs/ā] **190**–4
Essay [ĕs/ā] **190**
e-ticket [ē/tĭ kət] **161**–19
evacuate [ĭ văk/yōō/ āt] **147**–K
evacuation route [ĭ văk/yōō/ā shən rōōt/, rowt/] **146**–5
evening [ĕv/nĭng] **18**–19
   evening gown [ĕv/nĭng gown/] **89**–18
even numbers [ē/vən nŭm/bərz] **192**–4
EVENTS [ĭ vĕnts/] **22**, **40**–41
every day [ĕv/rē dā/] **20**–21
EVERYDAY CLOTHES [ĕv/rē dā/ klōz] **86**–87
EVERDAY CONVERSATION
   [ĕv/rē dā/ kän/vər sā/shən] **12**
evidence [ĕv/ĭ dəns] **141**–9
exam [ĭg zăm/] **122**–1, **136**–6
examination table [ĭg zămˌə nā/shən tā/bəl] **118**–7
examine [ĭg zăm/ən] **118**–D, **118**–E

Examining Room [ĭg zămˌə nĭng rōōm/] **118**
exchange [ĭks chänj/] **27**–I
excited [ĭk sī/təd] **43**–22
exclamation mark [ĕk/sklə mā/shən märk/] **190**–13
executive [ĭg zĕk/yə tĭv] **182**–5
   executive chef [ĭg zĕk/yə tĭv shĕf/] **185**–7
Executive Branch [ĭg zĕk/yə tĭv bränch/] **138**
exercise [ĕk/sər sĭz/] **122**–4
exercise [ĕk/sər sĭz/] **39**–P, **230**–N
Exercise Wear [ĕk/sər sĭz/wĕr] **89**
exhausted [ĭg zö/stəd] **43** ✦
ex-husband [ĕks/ hŭz/bənd] **35** ✦
exit [eg/zət, ĕk/sət] **51**–25, **51** ✦, **161**–14
expensive [ĭk spĕn/sĭv] **23**–19, **97**–44
Experiment [ĭk spër/ə mənt] **195**
expiration date [ĕk/spə rā/shən dät/] **112**–7, **136**–10
expire [ĕk/spir/] **136** ✦
explain [ĭk splān/] **12**–M
exploration [ĕk/splə rā/shən] **199**–8
explorer [ĭk splôr/ər] **199**–9
explosion [ĭk splō/zhən] **144**–4
exposed [ĭk spōzd/]
   overexposed [ō/vər ĭk spōzd/] **235**–34
   underexposed [ŭn/dər ĭk spōzd/] **235**–35
Express Mail® [ĭk sprĕs/ mālˌ] **134**–2
Extended Family [ĭk stĕn/dəd făm/lē, fämˌə lē] **34**
extension cord [ĭk stĕn/shən körd/] **181**–14
exterminate [ĭk stür/mə nät/] **62** ✦
exterminator [ĭk stür/mə nā/tər] **63**–21
extinguisher [ĭk stĭn/gwə shər] **179**–21
extra [ĕk/strə]
   extra large [ĕk/strə lärj/] **96**–5
   extra small [ĕk/strə smöl/] **96**–1
ex-wife [ĕks/ wĭf/] **35** ✦
eye [ī] **99**–27, **105**–11
   eyebrow [ī/brow/] **106**–9
   eyebrow pencil [ī/brow/ pĕn/səl] **109**–34
   eye drops [ī/dräps/] **113**–31
   eye hook [ī/hŏŏk/] **180**–40
   eyelashes [ī/lăsh/əz] **106**–11
   eyelid [ī/lĭd/] **106**–10
   eyeliner [ī/li/nər] **109**–36
   eyepiece [ī/pēs/] **194**–14
   eye shadow [ī/shă/dō] **109**–35
Eye [ī] **106**
fabric [făb/rĭk] **98**–15
   fabric softener [făb/rĭk sö/fə nər] **101**–6
Fabric Store [făb/rĭk stör/] **99**
face [fās] **193**–44
   face mask [fās măsk/] **93**–32
   face powder [fās/ pow/dər] **109**–41
Face [fās] **106**
factory [făk/tə rē, –trē] **126**–3
   factory owner [făk/tə rē ō/nər] **175**–1
   factory worker [făk/tə rē wür/kər] **175**–3
Factory [făk/tə rē] **98**
FACTORY [făk/tə rē] **175**
Fahrenheit [făr/ən hīt/] **13**–1
fair [fĕr] **172**–13, **223**–13
   fair trial [fĕr/ trī/əl] **140**–5
FAIR [fĕr] **122**–123
fall [föl] **21**–39

fall [fôl] **40**–H, **116**–O
FAMILIES [făm/lēz, făm/ə lēz] **34–35**
Family [făm/lē, făm/ə lē] **34**
FAMILY REUNION
   [făm/lē rē yōōn/yən, făm/ə lē] **44–45**
famine [fă/mĭn] **145**–12
fan [făn] **55**–19, **229**–4
fancy [făn/sē] **97**–34
far from [fär/ frŭm/, –frəm/] **25** ✦
fare [fër] **152**–2
   fare card [fër kärd/] **152**–11
farm [färm] **52**–9
   farm equipment [färm ĭ kwĭp/mənt] **177**–12
   farmworker [färm/ wür/kər] **177**–8
Farm Animals [färm/ ăn/ə məlz] **215**
farmer [fär/mər] **177**–13
FARMERS' MARKET [fär/mərz mär/kət] **84–85**
FARMING AND RANCHING
   [fär/mĭng ən răn/chĭng] **177**
Farmworker [färm/ wür/kər] **92**
fashion [făsh/ən] **88** ✦
   fashion designer [făsh/ən dĭ zī/nər] **98** ✦
fast [făst] **23**–3
   fast food restaurant [făst/ fōōd/ rĕs/tə rənt, –ränt]
   128–10
fasten [făs/ən] **160**–H
fastener [făs/nər] **99**–29
FAST FOOD RESTAURANT
   [făst/ fōōd/ rĕs/tə rənt, –ränt] **79**
fast forward [făst/ för/wərd] **235**–D
fat [făt] **32**–7
father [fä/dhər] **34**–4, **35**–23
   father-in-law [fä/dhər ĭn lö/] **34**–11
   grandfather [grăn/fä/dhər, grănd/–] **34**–2
   stepfather [stĕp/fädhər] **35**–25
faucet [fö/sət] **57**–6
fax [făks] **171**–G
fax machine [făks/ mə shēn/] **183**–21
feast [fēst] **239**–13
feather [fĕdh/ər] **214**–4
   feather duster [fĕdh/ər dŭs/tər] **61**–1
February [fĕb/yōō ër/ē, fĕb/rōō–] **21**–26
Federal Government
   [fĕ/də rəl gŭ/vərn mənt, fĕ/drəl] **138**
feed [fēd] **36**–C, **176**–D, **177**–D
feed dog / feed bar [fēd/dög/ / fēd/ bär/] **98**–20
feel [fēl] **110**–C, **110**–D
FEELINGS [fē/lĭngz] **42–43**
female [fē/māl/] **4**–18
fence [fĕns] **177**–19
fencing [fĕn/sĭng] **228**–7
ferry [fër/ē] **220**–4
fertilize [fürt/ əl īz/] **176**–D
fever [fē/vər] **110**–8
fiction [fĭk/shən] **237**–18
field [fēld] **5**–2, **177**–7
   ball field [böl/ fēld/] **224**–1
   track and field [trăk/ ən fēld/] **228**–18
fifteen [fĭf/tēn/] **16**
fifteenth [fĭf/tēnth/] **16**
fifth [fĭfth] **16**
fiftieth [fĭf/tē əth] **16**

fifty [fĭf/tē] **16**
   fifty dollars [fĭf/tē däl/ərz] **26**–11
   50 percent [fĭf/tē pər sĕnt/] **17**–10
fighter [fī/tər]
   firefighter [fīr/fī/tər] **144**–9, **167**–26
figs [fĭgz] **68**–27
figure [fĭg/yər] **233**–26
   figure skating [fĭg/yər skā/tĭng] **227**–5
figurine [fĭg/yə rēn/] **232**–1
file [fīl] **183**–44
   file cabinet [fīl käb/ə nət] **182**–11
   file clerk [fīl klürk/] **182**–10
   file folder [fīl fōl/dər] **183**–50
fill [fĭl]
   fill a cavity [fĭl/ ə kăv/ə tē] **119**–E
   fill prescriptions [fĭl/ prĭ skrĭp/shənz] **112** ✦
   fill in [fĭl/ ĭn] **9**–O
   fill out [fĭl/ owt/] **173**–J
   fill the tank [fĭl/ dhe tănk/] **157**–G
   fill the tires [fĭl/ dhe tīrz/] **157**–L
filling [fĭl/ĭng] **119**–8
Filling Out a Form [fĭl/ĭng owt ə förm/] **4**
film [fĭlm] **235**–22
   film camera [fĭlm kăm/rə] **235**–21
find [fīnd] **160**–F
FINDING A HOME [fīn/dĭng ə hōm/] **48–49**
fine adjustment knob [fīn/ ə jüst/mənt näb/] **194**–23
fingers [fĭng/gərz] **105**–16, **110**–16
   fingernail [fĭng/gər nāl/] **106**–18
   fingerprint [fĭng/gər prĭnt/] **136**–5
Fingers [fĭng/gərz] **106**
finish [fĭn/ish] **112**–C, **230**–T
fins [fĭnz] **212**–1, **225**–7
fire [fīr] **144**–7, **144**–8
   campfire [kămp/fīr/] **226**–11
   fire escape [fīr ĭ skāp/] **50**–2
   fire exit [fīr/ ĕg/zət, –ĕk/sət] **51** ✦
   fire extinguisher [fīr ĭk stĭng/gwĭ shər] **179**–21
   firefighter [fīr/fī/tər] **144**–9, **167**–26
   fire hydrant [fīr hī/drənt] **129**–27
   fireplace [fīr/plās/] **56**–13
   fire screen [fīr skrēn/] **56**–12
   fire station [fīr stā/shən] **125**–12
   fire truck [fīr trŭk/] **144**–10
   fireworks [fīr/würks/] **239**–7
first [fürst] **16**
   first aid kit [fürst/ ād/ kĭt/] **117**–1, **146**–18
   first aid manual [fürst/ ād/ măn/yōō əl] **117**–2
   First Continental Congress
      [fürst/ kän/tə nĕnt/ əl käng/grəs] **198**–6
   first name [fürst/ nām/] **4**–2
   first president [fürst/ prĕz/ə dənt] **198**–11
First Aid [fürst/ ād/] **117**
FIRST AID [fürst/ ād/] **117**
First Aid Procedures [fürst/ ād/ prə sē/ jərz] **117**
First Floor [fürst/ flör/] **50**
First License [fürst/ lī/səns] **137**
fish [fĭsh] **66**–1, **81**–29, **209**–14
   catfish [kăt/fĭsh/] **71**–2
   goldfish [gōld/fĭsh/] **215**–16
   jellyfish [jĕ/lē fĭsh/] **212**–14
   starfish [stär/fĭsh/] **212**–16
   swordfish [sörd/fĭsh/] **71**–5

Fish [fĭsh] **71, 212**
fisher [fĭsh/ər] **167**–17
fishing [fĭsh/ĭng] **226**–4
   fishing net [fĭsh/ĭng nĕt/] **226**–17
   fishing pole [fĭsh/ĭng pōl/] **226**–18
fitted sheet [fĭt/əd shēt/] **58**–12
fittings [fĭt/ĭngz] **181**–18
five [fīv] **16**
   five after one [fīv ăf/tər wŭn/] **18**–7
   five dollars [fīv däl/ərz] **26**–8
fix [fĭks] **62** ✦, **219**–F
fixture [fĭks/chər] **55**–18
flag [flăg] **239**–8
flammable liquids [flăm/ə bəl lĭk/wədz] **179**–8
flashlight [flăsh/līt/] **146**–14
flat [flăt]
   flat panel TV [flăt/ păn/əl tē/vē/] **234**–7
   flat screen TV [flăt/ skrēn/ tē/vē/] **234**–7
   flat sheet [flăt/ shēt] **58**–13
   have a flat tire [hăv/ ə flăt/ tīr/] **162**–F
flats [flăts] **95**–27
fleas [flēz] **63**–25
   flea market [flē/ mär/kət] **222**–6
flight [flīt] **161**–30, **161** ✦
   flight attendant [flīt/ ə tĕn/dənt] **161**–12
Flight [flīt] **160**
float [flōt/] **239**–2
flood [flŭd] **145**–19
floor [flör] **46**–6, **58**–21, **179**–6
   floor lamp [flör lămp/] **56**–15
   floor plan [flör plăn/] **186**–4
Floor [flör] **50**
floral [flör/əl] **96**–25
florist [flör/ĭst] **130**–8, **167**–27
floss [flös, fläs] **109**–24
floss [flös, fläs] **109**–K
flounder [flown/dər] **212**–15
flour [flow/ər] **73**–29
Flower [flow/ər] **211**
flowers [flow/ərz] **208**–7
   flower bed [flow/ər bĕd/] **53**–20
FLOWERS [flow/ərz] **211**
flu [flōō] **111**–2
fluid [flōō/əd] **183**–36
   fluid ounce [flōō/əd owns/] **75**–1
flute [flōōt] **238**–1
fly [flī] **214**–28
fly [flī] **170**–F
flyer [flī/ər] **102**–1
flying disc [flī/ĭng dĭsk/] **231**–27
foam pad [fōm/ păd/] **226**–13
focus [fō/kəs] **235**–33
foggy [fö/gē, fäg/ē] **13**–20
foil [foyl] **72**–23
fold [fōld] **101**–F
folder [fōl/dər] **183**–50
folding [fōl/dĭng]
   folding card table [fōl/dĭng kärd/ tā/bəl] **102**–4
   folding chair [fōl/dĭng chër/] **102**–5
folk [fōk] **237**–29
follow [fäl/ō] **114**–J, **147**–F
Following Directions [fäl/ō də rek/shənz, –dī–] **9**

food [fōōd]
    baby food [bā/bē fōōd/] **37**–4
    canned food [kănd/ fōōd] **146**–9
    fast food restaurant [făst/ fōōd/ rĕs/tə ränt] **128**–10
    food court [fōōd/kört] **131**–15
    food preparation worker
        [fōōd/ prĕ/pə rā/shən wür/kər] **185**–4
    food processor [fōōd/ prä/sĕ sər] **54**–26
    packaged food [păk/ĭjd fōōd/] **146**–10
    pet food [pĕt/ fōōd/] **72**–5
FOOD [fōōd] **79**
FOOD PREPARATION AND SAFETY
    [fōōd/ prĕ/pə rā/shən ən sāf/tē] **76**–77
Food Processor [fōōd/ prä/sĕ sər] **92**
Foods [fōōdz] **72, 73**
Food Safety [fōōd/ sāf/tē] **76**
FOOD SERVICE [fōōd/sür/vəs] **185**
foot [fōōt] **104**–8
    football [fōōt/böl/] **229**–11, **231**–21
    football helmet [fōōt/böl/ hĕl/mət] **231**–19
    footnote [fōōt/nōt/] **190**–10
Foot [fōōt] **106**
for [för] **128**–B, **173**–C
forceps [för/səps, –sĕps] **195**–43
forearm [för/ärm] **106**–13
forehead [för/əd/, –hĕd/, fär/–] **106**–2
forest [för/əst, fär/–] **204**–1, **204**–11
    forest fire [för/əst fir/] **144**–7
fork [förk] **55**–3, **83**–27, **83**–28
    forklift [förk/lĭft/] **175**–12
Form [förm] **4**
Formal Clothes [förm/əl klōz/] **89**
former husband [för/mər hŭz/bənd] **35** ✦
former wife [för/mər wif/] **35** ✦
forms [förmz] **118**–4, **134**–19, **161**–16
formula [för/myə lə] **37**–3, **195**–34
fortieth [för/tē əth] **16**
forty [för/tē] **16**
forward [för/wərd] **235**–D
    forward button [för/wərd bŭt/n] **197**–3
foundation [fown dā/shən] **109**–40
founders [fown/dərz] **198**–7
fountain [fown/tn] **224**–5, **224**–9
four [för] **16**
    4-door car [för/dör kär/] **156**–1
    2 x 4 (two by four) [tōō/ bī för/] **181**–19
fourteen [för/tēn/] **16**
fourteenth [för/tēnth/] **16**
fourth [förth] **16**
Fourth Floor [förth flör/] **50**
Fourth of July [förth əv jōō lī/] **22**–13
fox [fäks] **216**–15
Fractions [frăk/shənz] **192**
Fractions and Decimals [frăk/shənz ən dĕ/sə məlz] **17**
frame [frām] **58**–4, **58**–18
frayed cord [frād/ körd/] **179**–5
free [frē] **122**–7
    free speech [frē/ spēch/] **140**–2
freedom [frē/dəm]
    freedom of religion [frē/dəm əv rĭ lĭ/jən] **140**–3
    freedom of the press [frē/dəm əv dhə prĕs/] **140**–4
freezer [frē/zər] **54**–10, **185**–3

freezing [frē/zĭng] **13**–7
French [frĕnch]
    french fries [frĕnch/ frīz/] **79**–2
    French horn [frĕnch/ hörn/] **238**–13
Frequency [frē/kwən sē/] **20**
fresh [frĕsh] **71**–16
Friday [frī/dā, –dē] **20**–13
fried [frīd] **76**–6
    fried chicken [frid/ chĭk/ən] **76**–1
fringe [frĭnj] **99**–34
frog [frög, fräg] **212**–25
front [frŭnt] **25**–7
    front desk [frŭnt/ dĕsk/] **184**–12
    front door [frŭnt/ dör/] **53**–11
    front seat [frŭnt/ sēt/] **159**–51
    front walk [frŭnt/ wök/] **53**–2
Front Porch [frŭnt/ pörch/] **53**
frostbite [fräst/bīt/] **116**–G
frozen [frō/zən] **63**–16, **71**–17
    frozen dinner [frō/zən dĭn/ər] **72**–28
    frozen vegetables [frō/zən vĕj/tə bəlz] **72**–27
Frozen Foods [frō/zən fōōdz/] **72**
fruit [frōōt] **67**–9
    fruit salad [frōōt săl/əd] **80**–21
FRUIT [frōōt] **68**
frustrated [frŭs/trā/təd] **43**–27
frying pan [frī/ĭng păn/] **78**–5
fuel injection system
    [fyōō/əl ĭn jĕk/shən sĭs/təm] **158**–17
full [fōōl] **23**–9, **42**–6
    full-length mirror [fōōl/lĕnth/ mĭr/ər] **58**–6
    full moon [fōōl/ mōōn/] **205**–12
    full slip [fōōl/ slĭp/] **91**–22
fumes [fyōōmz] **179**–3
funnel [fŭn/əl] **195**–40
funny photo [fŭn/ē fō/tō] **206**–2
fur [für] **216**–19
furious [fyŏōr/ē əs] **43** ✦
furnished apartment [für/nĭsht ə pärt/mənt] **48**–3
furniture [für/nĭ chər] **53**–19
    furniture polish [für/nĭ chər päl/ĭsh] **61**–8
    furniture store [für/nĭ chər stör/] **126**–8
Furniture and Accessories
    [für/nĭ chər ən ĭk sĕs/ə rēz] **59**
fuse box [fyōōz/ bäks/] **62**–13
fusion [fyōō/zhən] **218**–10
galaxy [găl/ək sē] **205**–15
gallbladder [göl/blăd/ər] **107**–44
gallon [găl/ən] **75**–5
game [gām]
    baseball game [bās/böl gām/] **44**–2
    board game [börd/ gām/] **232**–5
    game show [gām/ shō/] **236**–8
    video game console [vĭd/ē ō gām/ kän/sōl] **232**–3
    video game control [vĭd/ē ō gām kən trōl/] **232**–4
Games [gāmz] **59**
GAMES [gāmz] **232**–233
gang violence [găng/ vī/ə ləns] **142**–4
garage [gə räzh/, –räj/] **47**–14, **124**–1
    garage door [gə räzh/ dör/] **53**–7
Garage [gə räzh/, –räj/] **50**

GARAGE SALE [gə räzh/ sāl/] **102**–103
garbage [gär/bĭj]
    garbage can [gär/bĭj kăn/] **53**–24
    garbage disposal [gär/bĭj dĭ spō/zəl] **54**–7
    garbage truck [gär/bĭj trŭk/] **127**–22
garden [gär/dn]
    botanical garden [bə tăn/ə kəl gär/dn] **222**–3
    roof garden [rōōf/ gär/dn] **50**–4
    vegetable garden [vĕj/tə bəl gär/dn] **53**–27, **177**–14
garden [gär/dn] **53**–B
gardener [gär/dn er, gärd/nər] **167**–28
gardenia [gär dēn/yə] **211**–18
gardening [gärd/nĭng]
    gardening crew [gärd/nĭng krōō/] **176**–1
    gardening crew leader
        [gärd/nĭng krōō lēd/ər] **176**–4
GARDENING [gärd/nĭng] **176**
gargle [gär/gəl] **109**–L
garlic [gär/lĭk] **69**–30
    garlic bread [gär/lĭk brĕd/] **81**–28
    garlic press [gär/lĭk prĕs/] **78**–11
Garment Factory [gär/mənt făk/tə rē, fäk/trē] **98**
garment worker [gär/mənt wür/kər] **167**–29
garter [gär/tər]
    garter belt [gär/tər bĕlt/] **91**–16
    garter snake [gär/tər snāk/] **213**–39
gas [găs] **218**–3
    gas gauge [găs/gāj/] **159**–31
    gas meter [găs mē/tər] **62**–14
    gas pedal [găs pĕd/l] **159**–46
    gas shut-off valve [găs/ shŭt/öf vălv/] **146**–4
    gas station [găs stā/shən] **125**–10
    gas station attendant
        [găs stā/shən ə tĕn/dənt] **162**–3
    gas tank [găs tăngk/] **158**–10
gate [gāt] **50**–16, **53**–9, **161**–8
Gate [gāt] **161**
gauge [gāj]
    blood pressure gauge [blŭd/ prĕsh/ər gāj/] **118**–9
    gas gauge [găs/gāj/] **159**–31
    oil gauge [oyl/gāj/] **159**–29
    temperature gauge [tĕm/prə chər gāj/] **159**–30
gauze [göz] **117**–8
gear shift [gîr/ shĭft/] **159**–47
gel [jĕl] **108**–2, **108**–16
GEOGRAPHY AND HABITATS
    [jē äg/rə fē ən hă/bə tăts/] **204**
Geometric Solids [jē/ə mĕ/trĭk säl/ədz] **193**
geometry [jē äm/ə trē] **192**–17
geothermal energy [jē/ō thür/məl ĕn/ər jē] **218**–7
get [gĕt]
    get a job [gĕt/ ə jäb/] **40**–F
    get a learner's permit
        [gĕt/ ə lürn/ərz pür/mĭt] **137**–F
    get a library card [gĕt/ ə lī/brĕr ē kärd/] **133**–A
    get a loan [gĕt/ ə lōn/] **49**–J
    get an electric shock [gĕt/ ən ĭ lĕk/trĭk shäk/] **116**–F
    get a speeding ticket [gĕt/ ə spē/dĭng tĭk/ət] **162**–C
    get bed rest [gĕt/ bĕd/ rĕst/] **114**–B
    get change [gĕt/ chānj/] **26**–A
    get dressed [gĕt/ drĕst/] **38**–D
    get elected [gĕt/ ĭ lĕk/təd] **139**–C

get engaged [gĕt/ ĭn gājd/] **41**–J
get feedback [gĕt/ fēd/băk/] **191**–K
get frostbite [gĕt/ fröst/bĭt/] **116**–G
get good grades [gĕt/ gŏŏd/ grādz/] **10**–H
get hired [gĕt/ hīrd/] **173**–L
get home [gĕt/ hōm/] **39**–R
get immunized [gĕt/ ĭm/yə nīzd] **114**–I
get into [gĕt/ ĭn/tōō] **153**–E
get lost [gĕt/ löst/] **162**–B
get married [gĕt/ măr/ēd] **41**–K
get off [gĕt/ öf/] **153**–J
get on [gĕt/ än/, ön/] **153**–I
get out of [gĕt/ owt/ əv] **153**–F
get the title [gĕt/ dhə tīt/l] **157**–E
get up [gĕt/ ŭp/] **38**–B
get your license [gĕt/ yər lī/səns] **137**–I
Getting Your First License
    [gĕt/ĭng yər fürst/ lī/səns] **137**
Get Well [gĕt/ wĕl/] **114**
gift [gĭft] **94 ✦, 240**–3
gift shop [gĭft/ shäp/] **130 ✦, 184**–5
gills [gĭlz] **212**–2
giraffe [jə răf/] **217**–32
girder [gür/dər] **178**–3
girdle [gür/dl] **91**–15
girl [gürl] **31**–10
give [gĭv] **15**–F, **122**–B, **148**–A,
glad [glăd] **44**–5
glass [glăs] **53**–18, **83**–22, **83**–23
    glass cleaner [glăs klē/nər] **61**–14
glasses [glăs/əz] **92**–10, **115**–7, **179**–10
    sunglasses [sŭn/glăs/əz] **90**–27
global positioning system (GPS) [glō/bəl
    pə zĭ/shə nĭng sĭs/təm] / [jē/pē/ĕs/] **155**–11
gloves [glŭvz] **90**–6, **231**–17
    disposable gloves [dĭ spō/ zə bəl glŭvz/] **93**–27
    glove compartment [glŭv/ kəm pärt/mənt] **159**–44
    latex gloves [lā/tĕks glŭvz/] **93**–34
    rubber gloves [rŭb/ər glŭvz/] **61**–4
    surgical gloves [sür/jĭ kəl glŭvz/] **121**–39
    work gloves [würk/ glŭvz/] **92**–17, **179**–17
glue [glōō] **183**–33
    glue stick [glōō/ stĭk] **232**–11
go [gō]
    go back [gō/ băk/] **11**–M
    go for [gō/ fər] **157**–J
    go on [gō/ än] **173**–K
    go over [gō/ ō/vər] **153**–B
    go past [gō/ păst/] **155**–E
    go straight [gō/ strāt/] **155**–A
    go through [gō/ thrōō/] **160**–D
    go to an employment agency
        [gō/ tə ən ĭm ploy/mənt ā/jən sē] **173**–E
    go to bed [gō/ tə bĕd/] **39**–Y
    go to college [gō/ tə käl/ĭj] **41**–I
    go to jail [gō/ tə jāl/] **141**–G
    go to prison [gō/ tə prĭz/ən] **141**–G
    go to school [gō/ tə skōōl] **38**–J
    go to sleep [gō/ tə slēp/] **39**–Z
    go to the grocery store
        [gō/ tə dhə grōs/rē stör/, grösh/rē] **38**–L
    go to the next line [gō/ tə dhə nĕkst/ līn] **196**–D
    go to work [gō/ tə würk/] **38**–I
    go under [gō/ ŭn/dər] **153**–A
    to-go box [tə gō/ bäks/] **82**–5
GO [gō] **222**–**223**
goat [gōt] **215**–5
goggles [gäg/əlz] **179**–11
goldfish [gōld/fĭsh/] **215**–16
golf [gälf, gölf] **228**–8
    golf club [gälf/ klŭb/] **231**–1
good [gŏŏd] **23**–17
Goods [gŏŏdz] **73**
goose [gōōs] **214**–13
gopher [gō/fər] **215**–19
gorilla [gə rĭl/ə] **217**–29
gospel [gäs/pəl] **237**–30
Government [gŭ/ vərn mənt] **138**–**139**
GOVERNMENT AND MILITARY SERVICE
    [gŭ/ vərn mənt ən mĭ/ lə tër ē sür/vəs]**138**–**139**
governor [gŭ/ vər nər] **139**–20, **139**–21
gown [gown] **206**–8
    evening gown [ēv/nĭng gown/] **89**–18
    hospital gown [häs/pĭ tl gown/] **121**–19
    nightgown [nīt/gown/] **91**–25
    surgical gown [sür/jə kəl gown/] **93**–37, **121**–38
GPS (global positioning system) [jē/pē/ĕs/] /
    [glō/bəl pə zĭ/shə nĭng sĭs/təm] **155**–11
grab bar [grăb/ bär/] **57**–9
grades [grādz] **10**–4
graduate [grăj/ōō āt/] **40**–D
graduated cylinder [grăj/ōō ā/təd sĭl/ən dər] **195**–38
GRADUATION [grăj/ōō ā/shən] **206**–**207**
graffiti [grə fēt/tē] **148**–1
grandchild [grăn/chīld/, grănd/–] **34 ✦**
granddaughters [grăn/dö/tərz] **34 ✦**
grandfather [grăn/fä/dhər, grănd/–] **34**–2
grandmother [grăn/mŭdh/ər, grănd/–] **34**–1
Grandparents [grăn/për/ənts, grănd/–] **34**
grandson [grăn/sŭn/, grănd/–] **34 ✦**
grapefruit [grāp/frōōt/] **68**–6
grapes [grāps] **68**–3
graph [grăf] **192**–15
graphic designer [grăf/ĭk dĭ zī/nər] **167**–30
grasshopper [grăs/häp/ər] **214**–24
grate [grāt] **77**–G
grater [grā/tər] **78**–2
gray [grā] **24**–15
    gray hair [grā hër/] **33**–13
grease [grēs] **77**–B
green [grēn] **24**–5
    green card [grēn/ kärd/] **40**–2
    green onions [grēn/ ŭn/yənz] **69**–20
greet [grēt] **3**–G, **171**–M, **174**–H
GREETING [grē/tĭng] **2**–**3**
greeting card [grē/tĭng kärd/] **134**–15
grill [grĭl] **53**–17
grilled [grĭld/]
    grilled cheese sandwich
        [grĭld/ chēz/ săn/wĭch, –sănd/–] **80**–10
grilled fish [grĭld/ fĭsh/] **81**–29
grilled ribs [grĭld/ rĭbz/] **76**–2
grocery [grōs/rē, grösh/rē]
    grocery bag [grōs/rē băg/] **67**–13
    grocery clerk [grōs/rē klürk/] **72**–4
Grocery Products [grōs/rē präd/ŭkts] **72**
GROCERY STORE [grōs/ rē stör/] **72**–**73**
ground [grownd]
    ground beef [grownd/ bēf/] **70**–4
    ground post [grownd/ pōst/] **134**–6
    playground [plā/grownd/] **50**–3
group [grōōp] **115**–15
grower [grō/ər] **177**–13
guard [gärd] **141**–3
    Coast Guard [kōst/ gärd/] **138**–18
    lifeguard [līf/gärd/] **225**–19
    lifeguard station [līf/gärd/ stā/shən] **225**–21
    National Guard [nă/shə nəl gärd/] **138**–19
    security guard [sĭ kyŏŏr/ə tē gärd/] **132**–5, **169**–55
    shin guards [shĭn/ gärdz/] **231**–13
guest [gĕst] **184**–10
    guest room [gĕst/ rōōm/] **184**–13
    guest services [gĕst/ sür/vəs əs] **130**–12
    guest speaker [gĕst/ spē/kər] **206**–4
guinea pig [gĭn/ē pĭg/] **215**–14
guitar [gĭ tär/] **238**–9
gums [gŭmz] **106**–6
    gum disease [gŭm/ dĭ zēz/] **119**–11
gun [gŭn] **142**–13, **181**–21
gurney [gür/nē] **121**–33
gutter [gŭt/ər] **53**–4
gym [jĭm] **5**–19, **126**–10, **184**–24
gymnastics [jĭm năs/tĭks] **228**–9
gynecologists [gī/nə kăl/ə jĭsts] **120 ✦**
habitat [hă/bə tăt/] **194**–12
HABITATS [hă/bə tăts/] **204**
hacksaw [hăk/sö/] **180**–5
hail a taxi [hāl/ ə tăx/ē/] **152 ✦**
hailstorm [hāl/störm/] **13**–21
hair [hër] **104**–2
    black hair [blăk/ hër/] **33**–16
    blond hair [bländ/ hër/] **33**–17
    brown hair [brown/ hër/] **33**–18
    curly hair [kür/lē hër/] **33**–11
    gray hair [grā/ hër] **33**–13
    hair clip [hër klĭp/] **108**–19
    hairdresser [hër/drĕs/ər] **167**–31
    hair gel [hër jĕl/] **108**–16
    hairnet [hër nĕt/] **93**–25
    hair salon [hër sə län/] **131**–18
    hair spray [hër sprā/] **108**–12
    hair stylist [hër stī/lĭst] **167**–31
    long hair [löng/ hër/] **33**–3
    red hair [rĕd/ hër/] **33**–15
    short hair [shört/hër/] **33**–1
    shoulder-length hair [shōl/dər lĕnth/ hër/] **33**–2
    straight hair [strāt/ hër/] **33**–9
    wavy hair [wā/vē hër/] **33**–10
HAIR [hër] **33**

half [hăf]
half bath [hăf/ băth/] **57** ✦
half brother [hăf/ brŭdh/ər] **35**–28
1/2 cup [hăf/ kŭp/] **75**–9
half dollar [hăf/ däl/ər] **26**–5
half past one [hăf/ păst/ wŭn/] **18**–11
half sister [hăf/ sĭs/tər] **35**–27
half slip [hăf/ slĭp/] **91**–23
halibut steak [hăl/ə bət stāk/] **71**–6
hall [höl] **124**–8
hallway [höl/wā/] **5**–10, **184**–18
Hallway [höl/wā/] **51**
ham [hăm] **70**–9, **76**–5
hamburger [hăm/bür/gər] **79**–1
hammer [hăm/ər] **180**–1
jackhammer [jăk/hăm/ər] **178**–9
sledgehammer [slĕj/ hăm/ər] **178**–23
hammer [hăm/ər] **178**–D
hammock [hăm/ək] **53**–23
hamper [hăm/pər] **57**–1
hand [hănd] **105**–15, **177**–20
DMV handbook [dē/ĕm/vē/ hănd/bŏŏk] **136**–1
handbag [hănd/băg/] **87**–9, **94**–2
handbrake [hănd/ brāk/] **59**–48
handcuffs [hănd/kŭfs/] **141**–2
handsaw [hănd/sö/] **180**–4
handset [hănd/sĕt/] **14**–1
hand towel [hănd tow/əl] **57**–15
hand truck [hănd trŭk/] **175**–11
Hand [hănd] **106**
handicapped parking [hăn/dē kăpt pär/kĭng]
128–6, **154**–12
hand in [hănd/ ĭn/] **10**–O
hanger [hăng/gər] **101**–11
hang up [hăng/ ŭp/] **15**–D, **101**–H
happy [hăp/ē] **28**–6, **43**–31
hard [härd] **23**–5, **23**–24
hardboiled eggs [härd/boyld/ ĕgz/] **76**–8
hard drive [härd/ drīv/] **196**–6
hard hat [härd/ hăt/] **92**–1, **179**–9
hardware store [härd/wër/stör/] **148**–4
harmonica [här mä/ nĭ kə] **238**–21
harvest [här/vəst] **177**–B
hash browns [hăsh/ brownz/] **80**–3
hats [hăts] **90**–1, **95**–11
chef's hat [shĕfs/ hăt/] **93**–28
cowboy hat [kow/boy/ hăt/] **92**–18
hard hat [härd/ hăt/] **92**–1, **179**–9
ski hat [skē/ hăt/] **90**–11
straw hat [strö/ hăt/] **90**–23
have [hăv]
have a baby [hăv/ ə bā/bē] **41**–L
have a conversation [hăv/ ə kän/vər sā/shən] **11**–L
have a heart attack [hăv/ ə härt/ ə tăk/] **116**–D
have an allergic reaction
[hăv/ ən ə lür/jĭk rē ăk/shən] **116**–E
have a picnic [hăv/ ə pĭk/nĭk] **224**–D
have dinner [hăv/ dĭn/ər] **39**–S
have regular checkups
[hăv/ rĕg/yə lər chĕk/ups] **114**–H
Hawaii-Aleutian time [hə wī/ē ə lōō/shən tīm/] **19**–27

hay [hā] **177**–18
hazard [hăz/ərd] **186**–6
hazard lights [hăz/ərd līts/] **159**–36
Hazardous Materials [hăz/ər dəs mə tïr/ē əlz] **179**
hazardous waste [hăz/ər dəs wāst/] **218**–12
Hazards [hăz/ərdz] **179**
head [hĕd] **69**–32, **104**–1
headache [hĕd/āk/] **110**–1
headband [hĕd/bănd/] **90**–3
headboard [hĕd/börd/] **58**–10
head chef [hĕd/ shĕf/] **185**–7
headlight [hĕd/līt/] **158**–7
headline [hĕd/līn] **133**–7
headphones [hĕd/fōnz/] **6**–8, **234**–4
headset [hĕd/sĕt] **14**–13
headwaiter [hĕd/wā/tər] **185**–12
headwrap [hĕd/răp/] **90**–7
letterhead [lĕt/ər hĕd] **183**–42
overhead compartment
[ō/vər hĕd/ kəm pärt/mənt] **161**–13
overhead projector [ō/vər hĕd/prə jĕk/tər] **7**–16
wireless headset [wīr/ləs hĕd/sĕt] **14**–14
health [hĕlth] **167**–32
health history form [hĕlth/ hĭs/tə rē förm/] **118**–4
health insurance card
[hĕlth/ ĭn shŏŏr/əns kärd/] **118**–3
HEALTH [hĕlth] **114**–115
HEALTH FAIR [hĕlth/ fër/] **122**–123
Health Problems [hĕlth/ präb/ləmz] **115**
hear [hïr] **106**–B
hearing [hïr/ĭng]
hearing aid [hïr/ĭng ād/] **115**–10
hearing impaired [hïr/ĭng ĭm përd/] **32**–12
hearing loss [hïr/ĭng lös/] **115**–2
heart [härt] **107**–38, **116**–D, **239**–6
heart disease [härt/ dĭ zēz/] **111**–11
hearts [härts] **233**–31
heater [hē/tər] **159**–40
heating pad [hē/tĭng păd/] **113**–13
heat wave [hēt/ wāv/] **13**–13
heavy [hĕv/ē] **23**–13, **32**–7, **97**–27
hedge clippers [hĕj/ klĭp/ərz] **176**–11
heel [hēl] **94**–22, **106**–24
high heels [hī/ hēlz/] **89**–21, **95**–25
height [hīt] **17**–16, **32**–5
Height [hīt] **32**
Heimlich maneuver [hīm/lĭk mə nōō/vər] **117**–18
helicopter [hĕl/ə käp/tər] **151**–9
helmet [hĕl/mət] **93**–23, **231**–19
help [hĕlp] **8**–J, **147**–G
Help with Health Problems
[hĕlp/ wĭth/ hĕlth/ präb/ləmz] **115**
hem [hĕm] **100**–8
hen [hĕn] **215**–8
herbal tea [ür/bəl tē/, hür/bəl–] **81**–40
herbs [ürbz, hürbz] **84**–9
hibiscus [hī bĭs/kəs, hĭ–] **211**–12
hide [hīd] **240**–D
high [hī] **91**–12, **97**–32, **188**–3
high blood pressure [hī/ blŭd/ prĕsh/ər] **111**–14
high chair [hī/ chër/] **37**–6, **82**–3
high heels [hī/ hēlz/] **89**–21, **95**–25

high-rise [hī/ rīz/] **127**–13
high school [hī/ skōōl] **188**–4
highway [hī/wā] **155**–9
highway marker [hī/wā mär/kər] **154**–17
hiking [hī/kĭng] **226**–7
hiking boots [hī/kĭng bōōts/] **95**–31
hills [hĭlz] **204**–16
downhill skiing [down/hĭl/ skē/ĭng] **227**–1
hip hop [hĭp/häp] **237**–26
hippopotamus [hĭp/ə pät/ə məs] **217**–43
hire [hīr] **141**–B
hired hand [hīrd/ hănd/] **177**–20
Historical Terms [hĭs/tör/ə kəl türmz/] **199**
history [hĭs/tə rē] **118**–4, **189**–12
HISTORY [hĭs/tə rē] **198**–199
hit [hĭt] **230**–B
HIV (human immunodeficiency virus)
[āch/ī/vē/] / [hyōō/mən ĭm/yə nō
dĭ fĭsh/ən sē vī/rəs] **111**–17
Hi-Visibility safety vest [hī/vĭ/zə bĭl/ə tē vĕst/] **92**–4
HOBBIES AND GAMES [häb/ēz ən gāmz/] **232**–233
hockey [häk/ē] **229**–13
hockey stick [häk/ē stĭk/] **231**–11
hold [hōld] **36**–A
holder [hōl/dər]
candle holder [kăn/dl hōl/dər] **56**–21
cell phone holder [sĕl/ fōn/ hōld/ər] **94**–15
magazine holder [măg/ə zēn/ hōld/ər] **56**–23
pot holders [pät/ hōl/dərz] **78**–29
toothbrush holder [tōōth/brŭsh/ hōld/ər] **57**–22
holiday [häl/ə dā/] **22**–7, **22**–8
Holidays [häl/ə dāz/] **22**
HOLIDAYS [häl/ə dāz/] **239**
holly [häl/ē] **210**–19
home [hōm] **52**–7, **52**–12
home health care aide [hōm/ hĕlth/ kër ād] **167**–32
home improvement store
[hōm/ ĭm prōōv/mənt stör/] **127**–20
homemaker [hōm/mā/kər] **168**–33
homesick [hōm/sĭk/] **43**–20
HOME [hōm] **46**–47, **48**–49
honeybee [hŭn/ē bē/] **214**–25
hood [hŏŏd] **158**–4
Hood [hŏŏd] **158**
hoof / hooves [hŏŏf/] / [hŏŏvz/] **216**–17
hook [hŏŏk] **180**–39, **180**–40
hook and eye [hŏŏk/ ən ī/] **99**–27
hook and loop fastener
[hŏŏk/ ən lōōp/ fă/sən ər] **99**–29
horn [hörn] **159**–32, **216**–21, **238**–11
French horn [frĕnch/ hörn] **238**–13
horror story [hör/ər stör/ē, här/–] **237**–17
horse [hörs] **215**–4
horseback riding [hörs/băk rī/dĭng] **226**–9
horse racing [hörs/ rā/sĭng] **228**–19
seahorse [sē/hörs/] **212**–13
hose [hōz] **53**–21, **91**–18
hospital [häs/pĭ tl] **125**–9, **154**–18
hospital bed [häs/pĭ tl bĕd/] **121**–22
hospital gown [häs/pĭ tl gown/] **121**–19
HOSPITAL [häs/pĭ tl] **120**–121
Hospital Room [häs/pĭ tl rōōm/] **121**

Hospital Staff [häs/pǐ tl stäf/] **120**
hostess [hō/stəs] **82**–2
hot [hät] **13**–3, **42**–1
    hot cereal [hät sïr/ē əl] **80**–9
    hot dog [hät/ dög/] **79**–6
    hot water [hät/ wö/tər] **57**–8
    hot water bottle [hät/ wö/tər bät/l] **113**–15
hotel [hō tĕl/] **124**–3
A HOTEL [hō tĕl/] **184**
hour [ow/ər] **18**–1
house [hows]
    courthouse [kört/hows/] **125**–13
    dollhouse [däl/hows/] **59**–18
    housekeeper [hows/kē/pər] **168**–34, **184**–20
    housekeeping cart [hows/kē/pǐng kärt/] **184**–19
    House of Representatives
        [hows/ əv rĕp/rǐ zĕn/tə tǐvz] **138**–3
    house painter [hows/ pān/tər] **168**–46
    houseplant [hows/plänt/] **56**–4, **211**–27
    townhouse [town/hows/] **52**–6
    two-story house [tōō/stör/ē hows/] **52** ✦
    warehouse [wĕr/hows/] **175**–7
    White I louse [wīt/ hows/] **138**–7
House [hows] **49, 53**
A HOUSE AND YARD [hows/ən yärd/] **53**
HOUSEHOLD PROBLEMS AND REPAIRS
    [hows/hōld/ präb/ləmz ən rǐ pĕrz/] **62–63**
HOUSEWORK [hows/würk/] **60**
housing [how/zǐng] **52**–11
hubcap [hŭb/kăp/] **158**–9
hug [hŭg] **2**–E
human immunodeficiency virus (HIV)
    [hyōō/mən ǐm/yə nō dǐ físh/ən sē vī/rəs] /
    [ăch/ī/vē/] **111**–17
humid [hyōō/məd] **13**–15
humidifier [hyōō mǐd/ə fī/ər] **113**–11
humiliated [hyōō mǐl/ē ā/təd] **43** ✦
hummingbird [hŭm/ǐng bürd/] **214**–10
hump [hŭmp] **217**–51
hungry [hŭng/grē] **42**–5
hurricane [hür/ə kān/] **145**–14
hurt [hürt] **42**–16, **116**–C
husband [hŭz/bənd] **34**–13
    ex-husband [ĕks/ hŭz/bənd] **35** ✦
    former husband [för/mər hŭz/bənd] **35** ✦
hutch [hŭch] **55**–22
hybrid [hy/brǐd] **156**–3
hydrant [hī/drənt] **129**–27
hydroelectric power [hī/drō ǐ lĕk/trǐk pow/ər] **218**–5
hydrogen peroxide [hī/drə jən pə räk/sīd] **117**–9
hyena [hī ē/nə] **217**–30
HYGIENE [hy/jēn] **108–109**
hygienist [hī jē/nǐst, –jĕn/ǐst] **119**–3
hypertension [hī/pər tĕn/shən] **111**–14
hyphen [hy/fən] **190**–20
hypoallergenic [hī/pō ăl/ər jĕn/ǐk] **108** ✦
I beam [ī/ bēm/] **178**–3
ice [īs]
    ice cream [īs/ krēm/] **72**–26
    ice-cream cone [īs/ krēm/ kōn/] **79**–13
    ice cream shop [īs/ krēm/ shäp/] **131**–16
    ice hockey [īs/ häk/ē] **229**–13

ice pack [īs/ păk/] **117**–13
ice skates [īs/ skāts/] **231**–9
ice skating [īs/ skā/tǐng] **227**–4
iced tea [īst/ tē/] **79**–12
icy [ī/sē] **13**–22
ID [ī/dē/] **146**–19
identity theft [ī dĕn/tə tē thĕft/] **142**–9
ignition [ǐg nǐsh/ən] **159**–33
illegal drugs [ǐ lē/gəl drŭgz/] **142**–6
Illnesses and Childhood Diseases
    [ǐl/nə səz ən chīld/hŏŏd dǐ zēz/ əz] **111**
ILLNESSES AND MEDICAL CONDITIONS
    [ǐl/nə səz ən mĕd/ǐ kəl kən dǐsh/ənz] **111**
Immediate Family
    [ǐ mē/ dē ət făm/lē, –fă/məlē] **34**
immigrant [ǐm/ə grənt] **199**–19
immigrate [ǐm/ə grāt/] **40**–C
immigration [ǐm/ə grā/shən] **199**–18
immunization [ǐm/yə nə zā/shən] **114** ✦
immunodeficiency [ǐm/yə nō dǐ físh/ən sē] **111**–17
impaired [ǐm pĕrd/] **32**–11, **32**–12
important [ǐm pört/ənt] **146**–19
improvement [ǐm prōōv/mənt] **127**–20
in [ǐn] **25**–6
    be in shock [bē/ ǐn shäk/] **116**–B
    bubble in [bŭb/l ǐn/] **10**–K
    call in [käl/ ǐn/] **186**–A
    check in [chĕk/ ǐn/] **160**–A
    check-in kiosk [chĕk/ǐn kē/äsk/] **160**–2
    fall in love [fäl/ ǐn lŭv/] **40**–H
    fill in [fǐl/ ǐn/] **9**–O
    hand in [händ/ǐn/] **10**–O
    in fashion [ǐn făsh/ən] **88** ✦
    in front of [ǐn frŭnt/ əv] **24**–7
    in love [ǐn lŭv/] **42**–18
    in pain [ǐn pān/] **42**–11
    in style [ǐn stīl/] **88** ✦
    in the middle [ǐn dhə mǐd/l] **24**–2
    look in [lŏŏk/ ǐn] **173**–B
    move in [mōōv/ ǐn/] **48**–F
    send in [sĕnd/ ǐn/] **173**–H
    take in [tāk/ ǐn/] **100**–D
    turn in [türn/ ǐn/] **191**–M
    walk-in freezer [wäk/ǐn frē/zər] **185**–3
inch [ǐnch] **17**–15
indent [ǐn dĕnt/] **190**–D
independence [ǐn/də pĕn/dəns]
    Declaration of Independence
        [dĕk/lə rā/shən əv ǐn/də pĕn/dəns] **198**–5
    Independence Day [ǐn/də pĕn/dəns dā/] **22**–13
INDIVIDUAL SPORTS [ǐn/də vǐj/ōō əl spörts/] **228**
infant [ǐn/fənt] **31**–6
infection [ǐn fĕk/shən] **111**–3
infectious disease [ǐn fĕk/shəs dǐ zēz/] **111** ✦
influenza [ǐn/flōō ĕn/zə] **111** ✦
INFORMATION [ǐn/fər mā/shən] **4**
inhaler [ǐn hā/lər] **113**–33
injection [ǐn jĕk/shən] **114** ✦, **158**–17
injured [ǐn/ jərd] **116**–C
INJURIES [ǐn/jə rēz] **110**

ink [ǐnk]
    ink cartridge [ǐnk/ kär/trǐj] **183**–45
    inkjet printer [ǐnk/jĕt prǐn/tər] **183**–18
    ink pad [ǐnk/ păd/] **183**–46
inline [ǐn/lǐn/]
    inline skates [ǐn/lǐn/ skāts/] **231**–10
    inline skating [ǐn/lǐn/ skā/tǐng] **228**–10
inquire about benefits
    [ǐn kwīr/ ə bowt/bĕn/ə fǐts] **174** ✦
insects [ǐn/sĕkts] **209**–11
    insect bite [ǐn/sĕkt bīt/] **110**–11
    insect repellent [ǐn/sĕkt rǐ pĕl/ənt] **226**–23
Insects [ǐn/sĕkts] **214**
INSECTS [ǐn/sĕkts] **214**
insert [ǐn sürt/] **132**–D
INSIDE AND OUTSIDE THE BODY
    [ǐn/sīd/ ən owt/sīd/ dhə băd/ē] **106–107**
Inside the Car [ǐn/sīd/ dhə kär/] **159**
Inside the Kit [ǐn/sīd/ dhə kǐt/] **117**
Inside the Trunk [ǐn/sīd/ dhə trŭnk/] **158**
inspect [ǐn spĕkt/] **147**–N
install [ǐn stäl/] **176**–H, **178**–C
instructor [ǐn strŭk/tər] **6**–4
Instrument Panel [ǐn/strə mənt păn/əl] **159**
instruments [ǐn/strə mənts] **119**–4, **238**
insulation [ǐn/sə lā/shən] **178**–14
insurance [ǐn shŏŏr/əns] **118**–3, **136**–8
integers [ǐn/tə jərz] **192**–1, **192**–2
Integers [ǐn/tə jərz] **192**
intercom [ǐn/tər käm/] **50**–5
interest inventory [ǐn/trəst ǐn/vən tör/ ē] **172**–11
international call [ǐn/tər năsh/ə nəl köl/] **15**–35
Internet [ǐn/tər nĕt/]
    Internet listing [ǐn/tər nĕt/ lǐst/ǐng] **48**–1
    Internet map [ǐn/tər nĕt/ măp/] **155**–12
    Internet phone call [ǐn/tər nĕt/ fōn/ käl/] **14**–20
INTERNET [ǐn/tər nĕt/] **197**
internist [ǐn/tür/nǐst] **120**–1
internship [ǐn/türn shǐp/] **172**–6
interpreter [ǐn tür/prə tər] **168**–35
INTERSECTION [ǐn/tər sĕk/shən] **128–129**
INTERVIEW SKILLS [ǐn/tər vyōō/ skǐlz/] **174**
intestinal parasites [ǐn tĕs/tə nəl păr/ə sīts/] **111**–13
intestines [ǐn tĕs/tənz] **107**–42
In the Airline Terminal [ǐn dhə ĕr/lǐn tür/mə nəl] **160**
In the Examining Room
    [ǐn dhə ǐg zăm/ə nǐng rōōm/] **118**
In the Waiting Room [ǐn dhə wā/tǐng rōōm/] **118**
into [ǐn/tōō, –tə] **153**–E
intravenous drip (IV)
    [ǐn/trə vē/nəs drǐp/] / [ī/vē/] **121**–25
introduce [ǐn/trə dōōs/] **2**–C, **3**–I
introduction [ǐn/trə dŭk/shən] **190**–6
invention [ǐn vĕn/shən] **199**–12
inventor [ǐn vĕn/tər] **199**–13
inventory [ǐn/vən tör/ ē] **172**–11, **172**–12
invertebrates [ǐn vür/ tə brəts/] **194**–13
invitation [ǐn və tā/shən] **12**–I, **12**–J, **64**–9
invite [ǐn vīt/] **12**–H
iris [ī/rəs] **211**–16
iron [ī/ərn] **101**–13, **108**–17
iron [ī/ərn] **101**–G

ironed [ī/ərnd] **101**–20
ironing board [ī/ər nĭng börd/] **101**–14
irritated [ĭr/ə tā/təd] **64**–6
island [ī/lənd] **204**–8
IV (intravenous drip)
    [ī/vē/] / [ĭn/trə vē/nəs drĭp/] **121**–25
ivory [ī/vər ē] **24**–16
ivy [ī/vē] **210**–25
jack [jăk] **158**–24
jacket [jăk/ət] **90**–8
    chef's jacket [shĕfs/ jăk/ət] **93**–29
    down jacket [down/ jăk/ət] **90**–16
    leather jacket [lĕdh/ər jăk/ət] **90**–4
    sports jacket [spörts/ jăk/ət] **89**–14
jackhammer [jăk/ hăm/ər] **178**–9
jack-o'-lantern [jăk/ə lăn/tərn] **239**–10
janitor [jăn/ĭ tər] **182**–3
January [jăn/yōō ĕr/ē] **21**–25
jar [jär] **74**–2, **74**–14
jasmine [jăz/mən] **211**–22
jaw [jö] **106**–4
jay [jā] **214**–6
jaywalk [jā/wäk] **128**–C
jazz [jăz] **237**–24
jeans [jēnz] **86**–2, **92**–19
jellyfish [jĕl/ē fĭsh/] **212**–14
jewelry [jōō/əl rē]
    jewelry department [jōō/əl rē dĭ pärt/mənt] **95**–8
    jewelry store [jōō/əl rē stör/] **130**–2
jigsaw [jĭg/sö/] **180**–10
job [jäb] **172**–1, **172**–3, **172**–7
    job fair [jäb/ fër] **172**–13
JOB SAFETY [jäb/ sāf/tē] **179**
JOBS AND OCCUPATIONS
    [jäbz/ ən äk/yə pā/shənz] **166**–**169**
JOB SEARCH [jäb/ sürch/] **173**
JOB SKILLS [jäb/ skĭlz/] **170**
Job Training [jäb/ trān/ĭng] **172**
jockstrap [jäk/străp/] **91**–6
join [joyn] **143**–L
judge [jŭj] **141**–6
Judicial Branch [jōō dĭ/shəl brănch/] **138**
juice [jōōs] **73**–32
July [jōō lī/] **21**–31
jump [jŭmp] **230**–I
jumper cables [jŭm/pər kā/bəlz] **158**–21
jump rope [jŭmp/ rōp/] **224**–4
jumpsuit [jŭmp/sōōt/] **93**–24
June [jōōn] **21**–30
junior high school [jōōn/yər hī/ skōōl] **188**–3
junk mail [jŭnk/ māl/] **135** ✦
Jupiter [jōō/pə tər] **205**–5
jury [jŭr/ē] **141**–8
justices [jŭs/tə səz] **138**–12, **138**–13
kangaroo [kăng/gə rōō/] **217**–44
keep [kēp] **28**–B
ketchup [kĕch/əp, kăch/–] **79**–21
kettle [kĕt/l] **54**–21
key [kē] **51**–30, **155**–9
    key pad [kē/ păd/] **14**–5
    pound key [pownd/ kē/] **14**–7
    star key [stär/ kē/] **14**–6

keyboard [kē/börd/] **196**–14, **238**–18
Keyboarding [kē/börd/ĭng] **196**
kick [kĭk] **230**–E
kidney [kĭd/nē] **107**–43
kids' bedroom [kĭdz/ bĕd/rōōm/] **47**–9
KIDS' BEDROOM [kĭdz/ bĕd/rōōm/] **59**
king-size bed [kĭng/sīz/ bĕd/] **184**–15
kiosk [kē/äsk/] **131**–22, **160**–2
kiss [kĭs] **3**–K, **36**–P
kit [kĭt]
    doll making kit [däl/ mā/kĭng kĭt/] **232**–13
    first aid kit [fürst/ ād/ kĭt/] **117**–1, **146**–18
    model kit [mäd/l kĭt/] **232**–9
    woodworking kit [wŏŏd/wür/kĭng kĭt/] **232**–14
Kit [kĭt] **117**
kitchen [kĭch/ən] **46**–5, **83**–15
    kitchen timer [kĭch/ən tī/mər] **78**–18
A KITCHEN [ə kĭch/ən] **54**
Kitchen [kĭch/ən] **185**
KITCHEN UTENSILS [kĭch/ən yōō tĕn/səlz] **78**
kite [kīt] **225**–2
kitten [kĭt/n] **215**–10
kiwi [kē/wē] **68**–22
knee [nē] **106**–20
    knee highs [nē/hīz/] **91**–12
    knee pads [nē/pădz/] **179**–19
knife [nīf] **55**–4, **83**–30
    carving knife [kär/vĭng nīf/] **78**–12
    multi-use knife [mŭl/tē yōōs/nīf/, mŭl/tī–] **226**–20
    paring knife [për/ĭng nīf/] **78**–16
    steak knife [stāk/ nīf/] **83**–29
knit [nĭt] **233**–F
knitting needles [nĭt/ĭng nēd/lz] **233**–23
knit top [nĭt/ täp/] **88**–7
knob [näb] **194**–22, **194**–23
    doorknob [dör/näb/] **53**–12
knuckle [nŭk/l] **106**–17
koala [kō ä/lə] **217**–45
lab [lăb] **5**–15
    lab coat [lăb/ kōt/] **93**–33
Lab [lăb] **195**
label [lā/bəl]
    mailing label [mā/lĭng lā/bəl] **183**–41
    nutrition label [nōō trĭ/shən lā/bəl] **122**–8
    prescription label [prĭ skrĭp/shən lā/bəl] **112**–4
    warning label [wär/nĭng lā/bəl] **112**–8
label [lā/bəl] **9**–V
Labor Day [lā/bər dā/] **22**–14
lace [lās] **99**–9
    shoelaces [shōō/lā səz] **94**–24
ladder [lăd/ər] **178**–2
ladle [lā/dl] **78**–7
ladybug [lā/dē bŭg/] **214**–26
lake [lāk] **204**–13
lamb [lăm] **70**–14
    lamb chops [lăm/ chäps/] **70**–15
    lamb shanks [lăm/ shăngks/] **70**–13
Lamb [lăm] **70**
lamp [lămp] **56**–15, **58**–25
    lampshade [lămp/shād/] **56** ✦, **58**–26
land [lănd] **160**–K
landlord [lănd/lörd/] **51**–27

landmarks [lănd/märks/] **220**–1
landscape designer [lănd/skāp/ dĭ zī/nər] **176**–5
LANDSCAPING AND GARDENING
    [lănd/skā/pĭng ən gärd/nĭng] **176**
languages [lăng/gwĭ jəz] **189**–13
    language arts [lăng/gwĭj ärts/] **189**–9
lantern [lăn/tərn] **226**–22, **239**–10
laptop [lăp/täp/] **196**–16
large [lärj] **96**–4, **96**–5
laser printer [lā/zər prĭn/tər] **183**–19
lashes [lăsh/əz]
    eyelashes [ī/lăsh/əz] **106**–11
last [lăst]
    last name [lăst/ năm/] **4**–4
    last week [lăst/wēk/] **20**–18
late [lāt] **19**–24
latex gloves [lā/tĕks glŭvz/] **93**–34
laugh [lăf] **44**–A
laundromat [lön/drə măt/] **128**–1
laundry [lön/drē] **101**–1
    laundry basket [lön/drē băs/kət] **101**–2
    laundry detergent [lön/drē dĭ tür/jənt] **101**–8
LAUNDRY [lön/drē] **101**
Laundry Room [lön/drē rōōm/] **50**
lawn [lön] **53**–26
    lawn mower [lön/ mō/ər] **176**–6
lawyer [lö/yər] **168**–36
lay [lā] **178**–B
layer cake [lā/ər kāk] **81**–33
LCD projector [ĕl/sē/dē/ prə jĕk/tər] **6**–6, **235**–29
leader [lē/dər] **176**–4
leaf / leaves [lēf] / [lēvz] **210**–6, **211**–6
    leaf blower [lēf/ blō/ər] **176**–2
leaking [lē/kĭng] **62**–3
learn [lürn] **40**–E
Learning New Words [lür/nĭng nōō/ würdz/] **8**
lease [lēs] **48** ✦, **51**–28
leather [lĕdh/ər] **98**–6
    leather jacket [lĕdh/ər jăk/ət] **90**–4
leave [lēv] **11**–O, **38**–N, **82**–J, **160**–J, **171**–P
leaves / leaf [lēvz] / [lēf] **210**–6, **211**–6
    leaf blower [lēf/ blō/ər] **176**–2
lecture [lĕk/chər] **122**–9
left [lĕft] **25**–1, **154**–8, **155**–C
legal [lē/gəl]
    legal holiday [lē/gəl häl/ə dā/] **22**–8
    legal pad [lē/gəl păd/] **183**–38
Legal Holidays [lē/gəl häl/ə dāz/] **22**
LEGAL SYSTEM [lē/gəl sĭs/təm] **141**
Leg and Foot [lĕg/ ən fŏŏt/] **106**
leggings [lĕg/ĭngz] **90**–12
Legislature [lĕ/jəs lā/chər] **139**–23
legs [lĕgz] **70**–21, **105**–9
    leg of lamb [lĕg/ əv lăm/] **70**–14
lemonade [lĕm/ə nād/] **84**–2
lemons [lĕm/ənz] **68**–7
lend [lĕnd] **26**–C
length [lĕngkth] **17**–17, **96**–17
lengthen [lĕngk/thən] **100**–A
lens / lenses [lĕnz] / [lĕnz/əz] **115**–8, **235**–23
leopard [lĕp/ərd] **217**–34
let out [lĕt/ owt/] **100**–C

letter [lĕt/ər] **134**–13
   letter carrier [lĕt/ər kăr/ē ər] **134**–20
   letterhead [lĕt/ər hĕd/] **183**–42
lettuce [lĕt/əs] **69**–1
level [lĕv/əl] **172**–1, **180**–29
librarian [lī brër/ē ən] **133**–9
library [lī/brër ē] **5**–17, **125**–15
   library clerk [lī/brër ē klürk/] **133**–1
   library patron [lī/brër ē pā/trən] **133**–3
LIBRARY [lī/brër ē] **133**
license [lī/səns]
   driver's license [drī/vərz lī/səns] **40**–4, **136**–9
   driver's license number
      [drī/vərz lī/səns nŭm/bər] **136**–11
   license plate [lī/səns plāt/] **136**–12, **158**–12
   marriage license [măr/ĭj lī/səns] **41**–8
   renew a license [rĭ nōō/ ə lī/səns, –nyōō/–] **136** ✦
   taxi license [tăk/sē lī/səns] **152**–22
License [lī/səns] **137**
licensed practical nurse (LPN)
   [lī/sənst prăk/tə kəl nürs/] / [ĕl/pē/ĕn/] **120**–11
lid [lĭd] **78**–24
lieutenant governor [lōō tĕ/nənt gŭ/ vər nər] **139**–21
life [līf]
   lifeguard [līf/gärd/] **225**–19
   lifeguard station [līf/gärd/ stā/shən] **225**–21
   lifesaving device [līf/sā/vĭng dĭ vīs/] **225**–20
   life vest [līf/ vĕst/] **161**–25, **226**–14
   wildlife [wīld/ līf/] **220**–3
LIFE [līf] **212**–213
LIFE EVENTS AND DOCUMENTS
   [līf/ ĭ vĕnts/ ən dä/kyə mənts] **40**–41
lift [lĭft] **11**–E
light [līt] **23**–14, **97**–28
   brake light [brāk/ līt/] **158**–14
   daylight saving time [dā/līt/ sā/vĭng tīm/] **19**–25
   flashlight [flăsh/līt/] **146**–14
   hazard lights [hăz/ərd līts/] **159**–36
   headlight [hĕd/ līt/] **158**–7
   light blue [līt/ blōō/] **24**–11
   light bulb [līt/ bŭlb/] **56** ✦
   light fixture [līt/ fĭks/chər] **55**–18
   light source [līt/ sörs/] **194**–21
   light switch [līt/ swĭch/] **58**–27
   night light [nīt/ līt/] **37**–27
   porch light [pörch/ līt/] **53**–13
   streetlight [strēt/līt/] **148**–3
   string lights [strĭng/ lītz/] **239**–18
   tail light [tāl/ līt/] **158**–13
   traffic light [trăf/ĭk līt/] **128**–8
   work light [würk/ līt/] **181**–44
lightning [līt/nĭng] **13**–17
lily [lĭl/ē] **211**–26
limbs [lĭmz] **106** ✦, **210**–3
limes [līmz] **68**–8
limit [lĭ/mət] **154**–4
limo / limousine [lĭ/mō] / [lĭ/mə zēn] **156**–11
line [līn] **73**–11
   assembly line [ə sĕm/blē līn] **175**–6
   clothesline [klōz/līn/] **101**–9
   curved line [kürvd/ līn/] **193**–23
   headline [hĕd/līn/] **133**–7

line cook [līn/ kŏŏk/] **93, 185** ✦
line segment [līn/ sĕg/mənt] **193**–20
line supervisor [līn/ sōō/pər vī zər] **175**–4
   parallel lines [pă/rə lĕl līnz/] **193**–25
   perpendicular lines
      [pür/pən dĭk/yə lər līnz/] **193**–24
   straight line [strāt/ līn/] **193**–22
linen [lĭn/ən] **98**–2
   linen closet [lĭn/ən kläz/ət] **57** ✦
liner [lī/nər]
   eyeliner [ī/lī/nər] **109**–36
Lines [līnz] **193**
lingerie [län/zhə rā/, –jə–] **91** ✦
links [lĭnkz] **197**–10
lion [lī/ən] **213**–33, **216**–2, **217**–36
lip [lĭp] **106**–5
   lipstick [lĭp/stĭk/] **109**–38
Liquid Measures [lĭk/wəd mĕzh/ərz] **75**
liquids [lĭk/wədz] **61**–21, **179**–8
list [lĭst] **67**–14
listing [lĭst/ĭng] **48**–1
litter [lĭ/tər] **148**–2
litter [lĭ/tər] **219**–L
little [lĭt/l] **23**–1
Little League [lĭt/l lēg/] **229** ✦
live [lĭv] **140**–H
LIVE [lĭv] **52**
live music [lĭv/ myōō/zĭk] **84**–1
liver [lĭv/ər] **70**–7, **107**–40
livestock [lĭv/stäk/] **177**–15
living room [lĭv/ĭng rōōm/] **47**–12
LIVING ROOM [lĭv/ĭng rōōm/] **56**
lizard [lĭz/ərd] **213**–40
llama [lä/mə] **217**–25
load [lōd] **101**–C
loading dock [lō/dĭng däk/] **175**–15
loaf [lōf] **74**–10, **74**–22
   meatloaf [mēt/lōf/] **81**–31
loafers [lō/fərz] **95**–30
Lobby [läb/ē] **50**
lobster [läb/stər] **71**–10
local call [lō/kəl köl/] **15**–31
lock [läk] **51**–34, **159**–25
   locksmith [läk/smĭth/] **62**–11
lock [läk] **143**–E
locker [lä/kər] **5**–11, **50**–17
locket [läk/ət] **95**–35
Logging on and Sending Email
   [lög/ĭng än/ ən sĕnd/ĭng ē/māl, –ön–] **197**
lonely [lōn/lē] **42**–17
long [löng] **96**–18
   long distance call [löng/dĭs/təns köl/] **15**–32
   long hair [löng/ hër/] **33**–3
   long-sleeved [löng/slēvd/] **96**–14
   long underwear [löng/ ŭn/dər wër/] **91**–3
look [lŏŏk]
   look at [lŏŏk/ ăt/, –ət] **49**–H, **157**–A
   look for [lŏŏk/ för/] / [lŏŏk/ fər] **133**–B, **173**–C
   look in [lŏŏk/ ĭn] **173**–B
   look up [lŏŏk/ ŭp] **8**–A
loop [lōōp] **99**–29

loose [lōōs] **97**–30
lose [lōōz] **229** ✦
loss [lös] **115**–2
lost child [löst/ chīld/] **144**–1
lotion [lō/shən] **37**–13, **108**–9
loud [lowd] **23**–11
loungewear [lownj/wër/] **91** ✦
love [lŭv] **40**–H, **42**–18
   love seat [lŭv sēt/] **56**–1
low [lō] **97**–31
   low-cost exam [lō/köst ĭg zăm/] **122**–1
   low-cut socks [lō/kŭt/ säks/] **91**–10
   low-fat milk [lō/făt/ mĭlk/] **81**–42
lower back [lō/ər băk/] **107**–29
lozenges [läz/ən jəz] **113**–30
LPN (licensed practical nurse) [ĕl/pē/ĕn/] /
   [lī/sənst prăk/tə kəl nürs/] **120**–11
luggage [lŭg/ĭj] **161**–18
   luggage cart [lŭg/ĭj kärt/] **184**–8
lug wrench [lŭg/ rĕnch/] **158**–22
lumber [lŭm/bər] **178**–17
Lunch [lŭnch] **80**
lung [lŭng] **107**–39
machine [mə shēn/]
   answering machine [ăn/sər ĭng mə shēn/] **14**–17
   ATM (Automated Teller Machine) [ā/tē/ĕm/] /
      [ö/tə māt ĭd tĕ/lər mə shēn/] **132**
   fax machine [făks/ mə shēn/] **183**–21
   machine operator [mə shēn/ äp/ə rā tər] **168**–37
   machine screw [mə shēn/ skrōō/] **180**–32
   sewing machine [sō/ĭng mə shēn/] **98**–13
   sewing machine operator
      [sō/ĭng mə shēn/ äp/ə rā/tər] **98**–14
   stamp machine [stămp/ mə shēn/] **135**–11
   vending machine [vĕnd/ĭng mə shēn/] **152**–9
Machine [mə shēn/] **98, 132**
magazine [măg/ə zēn/, măg/ə zēn/] **133**–5
   magazine holder [măg/ə zēn/ hōl/dər] **56**–23
magnet [măg/nət] **195**–36
magnolia [măg nōl/yə] **210**–8
mail
   airmail [ër/māl/] **134**–5
   Certified Mail® [sür/tə fīd māl/] **134**–4
   Express Mail® [ĭk sprĕs/ māl/] **134**–2
   junk mail [jŭnk/ māl/] **135** ✦
   mailboxes [māl/bäk/səz] **50**–11, **53**–1, **128**–13,
      135–12
   media mail [mē/dē ə māl/] **134**–3
   overnight / next day mail
      [ō/vər nīt/ / nĕkst/ dā/ māl/] **135** ✦
   Priority Mail® [prī/ör ə tē māl/] **134**–1
mail [māl] **135**–D
mailer [mā/lər] **183**–40
mailing [mā/lĭng]
   mailing address [mā/lĭng ə drĕs/, ă/drĕs] **134**–22
   mailing label [mā/lĭng lā/bəl] **183**–41
main office [mān/ ö/fəs] **5**–12
MAINTAINING A CAR [mān/tā nĭng ə kär/] **157**
maintenance [mān/tn əns] **184**–23
maitre d' [mā/trə dē/] **185**–11
make [māk] **156** ✦

Index

make [māk]
make a deposit [māk/ ə dĭ päz/ət] **132**–B
make a disaster kit [māk/ ə dĭz/ăs tər kĭt/] **146**–B
make a mortgage payment
[māk/ ə mör/gəj pā/mənt] **49**–L
make an offer [māk/ ən ö/fər] **49**–I
make a wish [māk/ ə wĭsh/] **240**–B
make copies [māk/ käp/ēz] **171**–D
make dinner [māk/ dĭn/ər] **39**–Q
make eye contact [māk/ ī/ kän/täkt] **174**–J
make furniture [māk/ für/nĭ chər] **170**–G
make lunch [māk/ lŭnch/] **38**–F
make progress [māk/ prä/grəs] **10**–G
make small talk [māk/ smöl/tök] **12**–B
make the bed [māk/dhə bĕd/] **60**–F
maker [mā/kər]
dressmaker [drĕs/mā/kər] **100**–1
dressmaker's dummy [drĕs/mā/kərz dŭ/mē] **100**–2
homemaker [hōm/mā/kər] **168**–33
Makeup [māk/ŭp] **109**
makeup remover [māk/ŭp rĭ mōōv/ər] **109**–42
making [mā/kĭng] **232**–13
MAKING ALTERATIONS [māk/ĭng öl/tə rā/shənz] **100**
MAKING CLOTHES [māk/ĭng klōz/] **98–99**
Making an Emergency Call
[mā/kĭng ən ĭ mür/jən sē köl/] **15**
Making a Phone Call [mā/kĭng ə fōn/ köl] **15**
male [māl] **4**–17
mall [möl] **126**–7
MALL [möl] **130–131**
mallet [măl/ət] **180**–2
mammals [măm/əlz] **209**–10
Mammals [măm/əlz] **213**
MAMMALS [măm/əlz] **216–217**
manager [măn/ĭ jər] **50**–8, **72**–8
account manager [ə kownt/ măn/ĭ jər] **132**–9
office manager [ö/fəs măn/ĭ jər] **182**–8
Manager [măn/ĭ jər] **92**
mane [mān] **217**–49
maneuver [mə nōō/vər] **117**–18
mangoes [măng/gōz] **68**–21
manicurist [măn/nə kyōō/rĭst] **168**–38
man / men [măn] / [mĕn] **30**–1, **30**–4
doorman [dör/măn/] **184**–1
mantle [măn/təl] **56**–11
manual [măn/yōō əl] **117**–2
Manual Transmission [măn/yōō əl trănz mĭsh/ən] **159**
manufacture [măn/yə făk/chər] **175**–B
map [măp] **7**–12, **155**–12
Map [măp] **13**
maple [mā/pəl] **210**–12
Maps [măps] **155**
MAPS [măps] **155**
March [märch] **21**–27
margarine [mär/jər ən] **72**–20
marigold [măr/ə gōld/] **211**–13
MARINE LIFE, AMPHIBIANS, AND REPTILES
[mə rēn/ līf/ ăm fĭb/ē ənz ən rĕp/tīlz] **212–213**
Marines [mə rēnz/] **138**–17
mark [märk] **190**–12, **190**–13, **190**–15
postmark [pōst/märk/] **134**–24

markers [mär/kərz] **7**–17, **7**–24, **154**–17
market [mär/kət] **222**–6
supermarket [sōō/pər mar/kət] **127**–18
MARKET [mär/kət] **66–67**
marriage license [măr/ĭj lī/səns] **41**–8
married couple [măr/ēd kŭ/pəl] **35**–20
Mars [märz] **205**–4
martial arts [mär/shəl ärts/] **228**–11
Martin Luther King Jr. Day
[mär/tən lōō/thər-kĭng/ jōōn/yər dā/] **22**–10
mascara [mă skăr/ə] **109**–39
mashed potatoes [măsht/ pə tā/tōz] **81**–23
mask [măsk] **239**–9
catcher's mask [kăch/ərz măsk/] **231**–15
diving mask [dī/vĭng măsk/] **225**–6
face mask [fās/ măsk/] **93**–32
oxygen mask [äk/sĭ jən măsk/] **161**–24
particle mask [pär/tĭ kəl măsk/] **179**–14
ski mask [skē/ măsk/] **90**–15
surgical mask [sür/jĭ kəl măsk/] **93**–36
ventilation mask [vĕnt/əl ā/shən măsk/] **92**–7
masking tape [măs/kĭng tāp/] **181**–53
mat [măt] **57**–3, **57**–28
placemat [plās/măt] **55**–11
match [măch] **9**–T
matches [măch/əz] **146**–16, **226**–21
matching [mă/chĭng] **28**–3
Material [mə tïr/ē əl] **98**
materials [mə tïr/ē əlz] **98 ✦**, **179**–7
Materials [mə tïr/ē əlz] **179**
maternity [mə tür/nə tē]
maternity dress [mə tür/nə tē drĕs/] **88**–5
maternity store [mə tür/nə tē stör/] **131**–19
math [măth] **189**–10
MATHEMATICS [măth/ə măt/ĭks] **192–193**
Math Operations [măth/ äp/ə rā/shənz] **192**
Math Problem [măth/ präb/ləmz] **192**
mattress [mă/trəs] **58**–20
May [mā] **21**–29
mayonnaise [mā/ə nāz/, mā/ə nāz/] **79**–23
mayor [mā/ər] **139**–26
meadow [mĕd/ō] **204**–20
measles [mē/zəlz] **111**–5
measure [mĕzh/ər] **100**–17, **181**–45
measure [mĕzh/ər] **17**–C
Measurement [mĕzh/ər mənt] **17**
MEASUREMENTS [mĕzh/ər mənts] **17, 75**
Measures [mĕzh/ərz] **75**
Measuring Area and Volume
[mĕ/zhər ĭng ĕr/ē ə ən văl/yəm, –yōōm] **193**
meat [mēt] **66**–2
meatballs [mēt/bölz] **81**–27
meatloaf [mēt/lōf/] **81**–31
Meat [mēt] **70, 76**
MEAT AND POULTRY [mēt/ n pōl/trē] **70**
mechanic [mə kăn/ĭk] **166**–8
Mechanic [mə kăn/ĭk] **158**
media mail [mē/dē ə māl/] **134**–3
medical [mĕd/ĭ kəl] **121**–32
medical chart [mĕd/ĭ kəl chärt/] **121**–24
medical emergency bracelet
[mĕd/ĭ kəl ĭ mür/jən sē brās/lət] **117**–3

medical records technician
[mĕd/ĭ kəl rĕkərdz tĕk nĭsh/ən] **168**–39
medical waste disposal
[mĕd/ĭ kəl wāst/ dĭ spō/zəl] **121**–31
MEDICAL CARE [mĕd/ĭ kəl kër/] **118**
MEDICAL CONDITIONS [mĕd/ĭ kəl kən dĭsh/ənz] **111**
MEDICAL EMERGENCIES [mĕd/ĭ kəl ĭ mür/jən sēz] **116**
Medical Procedures [mĕd/ĭ kəl prə se/jərz] **118**
Medical Specialists [mĕd/ĭ kəl spē/shə lĭsts] **120**
Medical Technician [mĕd/ĭ kəl tĕk nĭsh/ən] **93**
Medical Warnings [mĕd/ĭ kəl wör/nĭngz] **112**
medication [mĕd/ə kā/shən] **112**–3, **112 ✦**,
113–18, **121**–20
Medication [mĕd/ə kā/shən] **113**
medicine cabinet [mĕd/ə sən kăb/ə nət] **57**–20
medium [mē/dē əm] **96**–3
meet [mēt] **222**–6
meet [mēt] **49**–G, **49**–R
meeting [mē/tĭng]
meeting place [mē/tĭng plās/] **146**–1
meeting room [mē/tĭng rōōm/] **184**–25
MEETING AND GREETING [mē/tĭng ən grē/tĭng] **2–3**
melons [mĕl/ənz] **68**–19
watermelons [wö/tər mĕl/ənz] **68**–18
membrane [mĕm/brān] **194**–6
Memorial Day [mə mör/ē əl dā/] **22**–12
memory card [mĕm/ə rē kärd/] **235**–20
men / man [mĕn] / [măn] **30**–1, **30**–4
doorman [dör/măn/] **184**–1
men's store [mĕnz/ stör/] **130 ✦**
Men's Underwear [mĕnz/ un/dər wër/] **91**
menu [mĕn/yōō] **82**–7, **197**–8
menu bar [mĕn/yōō bär/] **197**–1
MENU [mĕn/yōō] **80–81**
Mercury [mür/kyə rē] **205**–1
merge [mürj] **154**–10
mess [mĕs] **64**–8
message [mĕs/ĭj] **14**–18, **14**–19
messenger [mĕs/ən jər] **168**–40
meter [mē/tər] **62**–14, **129**–25, **152**–23
mice / mouse [mīs] / [mows] **63**–28, **196**–15, **215**–18
microphone [mī/krə fōn/] **234**–18
microprocessor [mī/krō prä/sĕ sər] **196**–4
Microscope [mī/krə skōp/] **194**
microwave [mī/krə wāv/] **77**–T
microwave oven [mī/krə wāv/ ŭv/ən] **54**–13
middle [mĭd/l] **25**–2
middle-aged [mĭd/l ājd/] **32**–2
middle initial [mĭd/l ĭ nĭsh/əl] **4**–3
middle school [mĭd/l skōōl/] **188**–3
mid-length [mĭd/lĕnth] **96**–17
midnight [mĭd/nīt/] **18**–21
Military [mĭ/lə tër ē] **138**
MILITARY SERVICE [mĭ/lə tër ē sür/vəs] **138–139**
milk [mĭlk] **66**–5, **81**–42
milkshake [mĭlk shāk/] **79**–14
milk [mĭlk] **177**–C
mini [mĭn/ē] **96**–15
mini-blinds [mĭn/ē blīndz/] **58**–8
minivan [mĭn/ē văn/] **156**–8
minister [mĭ/nə stər] **199**–7

minutes [mĭn/əts] **18**–2
mirror [mĭr/ər] **57**–16
    full-length mirror [fŏŏl/lĕnth mĭr/ər] **58**–6
    rearview mirror [rĭr/vyōō/ mĭr/ər] **159**–35
    sideview mirror [sĭd/vyōō/ mĭr/ər] **158**–3
misbehave [mĭs/bĭ hāv/] **44**–B
miss the bus [mĭs dhə bŭs/] **152** ✦
missing [mĭs/ĭng] **97**–40
mittens [mĭt/nz] **90**–10
mix [mĭks] **77**–R
mixed berries [mĭkst/ bĕr/ēz] **81**–36
mixer [mĭk/sər] **54**–25
mixing bowl [mĭk/sĭng bōl/] **54**–28, **78**–31
mobile [mō/bēl] **59**–5
    mobile home [mō/bəl hōm/] **52**–7
model [mäd/l] **156** ✦, **168**–41
    model kit [mäd/l kĭt/] **232**–9
    model trains [mäd/l trānz/] **233**–27
modern [mä/dərn] **199**–2
moist towelettes [moyst/ tow/əl ĕts] **146**–12
moisturizer [moys/chə rĭ/zər] **108**–9
mole [mōl] **32**–16
molecule [mäl/ĭ kyōōl/] **195**–27
monarch [mä/nərk, mä/närk/] **199**–4
Monday [mŭn/dā, –dē] **20**–9
MONEY [mŭn/ē] **26**
monitor [män/ə tər] **196**–11
    arrival and departure monitors
        [ə rī/vəl ən dĭ pär/chər män/ə tərz] **161**–7
    baby monitor [bā/bē män/ə tər] **59**–7
    vital signs monitor [vī/təl sīnz män/ə tər] **121**–26
monkey [mŭng/kē] **217**–26
month [mŭnth] **20**–3
Months of the Year [mŭnths/ əv dhə yĭr/] **21**
moon [mōōn]
    crescent moon [krĕs/ənt mōōn/] **205**–10
    full moon [fŏŏl/ mōōn/] **205**–12
    new moon [nōō/ mōōn/] **205**–9
    quarter moon [kwör/tər mōōn/] **205**–11
Moon [mōōn] **205**
moose [mōōs] **216**–1
mop [mäp] **61**–6
mop [mäp] **60**–D
morning [mör/nĭng] **18**–15
mosque [mäsk] **126**–5
mosquito [mə skē/tō] **214**–22
motel [mō tĕl/] **126**–12
moth [möth] **214**–21
mother [mŭdh/ər] **34**–3, **35**–22
    grandmother [grăn/mŭdh/ər, grănd/–] **34**–1
    motherboard [mŭdh/ər börd/] **196**–5
    mother-in-law [mŭdh/ər ĭn lö/] **34**–10
    stepmother [stĕp/mŭdh/ər] **35**–26
MOTION [mō/shən] **153**
motor [mō/tər] **124**–4
motorcycle [mō/tər sī/kəl] **150**–4
mountain [mown/tn]
    mountain biking [mown/tn bī/kĭng] **226**–8
    mountain lion [mown/tn lī/ən] **216**–2
    mountain peak [mown/tn pēk/] **204**–14
    mountain range [mown/tn rānj/] **204**–15
    Mountain time [mown/tn tīm/] **19**–30

mouse / mice [mows] / [mīs] **63**–28, **196**–15, **215**–18
mouth [mowth] **104**–7
    mouthwash [mowth/wäsh/, –wösh/] **109**–25
Mouth [mowth] **106**
move in [mōōv/ ĭn/] **48**–F
move out [mōōv/ owt/] **48** ✦
movement [mōōv/mənt] **199**–16
mover [mōō/vər] **168**–42
movies [mōō/vēz] **222**–2
    movie theater [mōō/vē thē/ə tər] **126**–6
Movies [mōō/vēz] **237**
Moving In [mōō/vĭng ĭn] **49**
moving van [mōō/vĭng văn/] **156**–18
mow [mō] **176**–A
mower [mō/ər] **176**–6
mozzarella cheese [möts/ə rĕ lə chēz/] **71**–29
MP3 player [ĕm/pē/thrē/ plā/ər] **234**–2
mudslide [mŭd/slīd/] **144**–6
muffin [mŭf/ən] **79**–16, **80**–5
muffler [mŭf/lər] **158**–16
muffs [mŭfs] **179**–16
mug [mŭg] **55**–7
mugging [mŭg/ĭng] **142**–11
multiply [mŭl/tə plī] **192**–C
multi-use knife [mŭl/tē yōōs/ nīf/, mŭl/tī–] **226**–20
mumps [mŭmps] **111**–7
murder [mŭr/dər] **142**–12
muscle [mŭs/əl] **107**–32
mushrooms [mŭsh/rōōmz/] **69**–27
music [myōō/zĭk] **64**–3, **189**–15
    live music [līv/ myōō/zĭk] **84**–1
    music store [myōō/zĭk stör/] **130**–1
    world music [würld/ myōō/zĭk] **237**–32
Music [myōō/zĭk] **237**
MUSIC [myōō/zĭk] **238**
musician [myōō zĭsh/ən] **168**–43
mussels [mŭs/əlz] **71**–13, **212**–17
mustache [mŭs/tăsh] **33**–5
mustard [mŭs/tərd] **79**–22
mystery [mĭs/tə rē] **237**–20
nachos [nä/chōz] **79**–7
nail [nāl] **180**–34
    fingernail [fĭng/gər nāl/] **106**–18
    nail clipper [nāl klĭp/ər] **109**–31
    nail polish [nāl päl/ĭsh] **109**–33
    nail salon [nāl sə län/] **130**–3
    toenail [tō/nāl/] **106** ✦
name [nām] **4**–1, **4**–2, **4**–4
    name tag [nām/ tăg/] **92**–15
napkin [năp/kĭn] **55**–10, **83**–26
narrow [năr/ō] **97**–35
nasal [nā/zəl]
    nasal congestion [nā/zəl kən jĕs/chən] **110**–7
    nasal spray [nā/zəl sprā/] **113**–32
National Guard [nă/shə nəl gärd/] **138**–19
NATIONAL PARKS [nă/shə nəl pärks/] **220**–221
Native Americans [nā/tĭv ə mĕr/ə kənz] **198**–3
natural [năch/rəl, năch/ər əl/]
    natural gas [năch/rəl găs/] **218**–3
    natural materials [năch/rəl mə tĭr/ē əlz] **98** ✦
NATURE CENTER [nā/chər sĕn/tər] **208**–209
nature program [nā/chər prō/grăm] **236**–7

Navigating a Webpage [nă/və gā/tĭng ə wĕb/pāj] **197**
Navy [nā/vē] **138**–15
navy blue [nā/vē blōō/] **28**–5
near [nĭr] **25** ✦
neck [nĕk] **96**–8, **96**–10, **104**–3
    crewneck [krōō/nĕk] **96**–7
    necklaces [nĕk/lə sĕz] **95**–10
    turtleneck [tür/tl nĕk/] **96**–9
needle [nēd/l] **98**–17, **100**–10, **210**–10, **233**–23
needle plate [nēd/l plāt/] **98**–18
negative integers [nĕ/gə tĭv ĭn/tə jərz] **192**–1
negotiate [nĭ gō/shē āt/] **157**–D
neighborhood [nā/bər hŏŏd/] **128** ✦
nephew [nĕf/yōō] **34**–19
Neptune [nĕp/tōōn] **205**–8
nervous [nür/vəs] **42**–10
nest [nĕst] **209**–12
net [nĕt] **226**–17
    hairnet [hër/nĕt/] **93**–25
network [nĕt/würk/] **173**–A
Neutral Colors [nōō/trəl kŭl/ərz] **24**
neutron [nōō/trän] **195**–32
new [nōō]
    new job [nōō/ jäb/] **172**–3
    new moon [nōō/ mōōn/] **205**–9
    New Year's Day [nōō/ yĭrz/ dā/] **22**–9
Newfoundland time [nōō/fən lənd tīm/, –fənd–] **19**–34
news [nōōz]
    newspaper [nōōz/pā/pər] **133**–6
    news program [nōōz prō/grăm] **236**–1
    newsstand [nōōz/stănd/] **128**–12
newt [nōōt] **212**–26
New Words [nōō/ würdz/] **8**
next [nĕkst]
    next day mail [nĕkst/ dā/ māl/] **135** ✦
    next to [nĕkst/ tōō, –tə] **24**–9
    next week [nĕkst/ wēk/] **20**–20
nickel [nĭk/əl] **26**–2
niece [nēs] **34**–18
night [nīt] **18**–20
    nightclub [nīt/klŭb/] **223**–12
    nightgown [nīt/gown/] **91**–25
    night light [nīt/lĭt/] **37**–27
    nightshirt [nīt/shürt/] **91**–28
    nightstand [nīt/stănd/] **58**–23
    night table [nīt/ tā/bəl] **58**–23
nine [nīn] **16**
nineteen [nīn/tēn/] **16**
nineteenth [nīn/tēnth/] **16**
ninetieth [nīn/tē əth] **16**
ninety [nīn/tē] **16**
    90° angle [nīn/tē də grē/ ăng/gəl] **193**–26
ninth [nīnth] **16**
nipple [nĭp/əl] **37**–2
no [nō]
    no left turn [nō/ lĕft/ türn] **154**–8
    no outlet [nō/ owt/lĕt, –lət] **154**–6
    no parking [nō/ pär/kĭng] **154**–11
noise [noyz] **64**–5
noisy [noy/zē] **23**–11
noon [nōōn] **18**–16
    afternoon [ăf/tər nōōn/] **18**–17

Index

north [nörth] **155**–1

NORTH AMERICA AND CENTRAL AMERICA
[nörth/ ə měr/ə kə ən sĕn/trəl ə měr/ə kə] **200–201**

nose [nōz] **104**–6, **110**–17

revolving nosepiece [rə väl/vĭng nōz/pēs] **194**–17

not [nät]

can't breathe [kănt/ brēdh/] **116**–N

do not drink [dōō/ nät/ drĭnk] **112**–F

do not enter [dōō/ nät/ ĕn/tər] **154**–2

do not operate [dōō/ nät/ äp/ər ăt/] **112**–E

do not take [dōō nät/ tāk/] **112**–D

don't be late [dōnt/ bē/ lāt/] **174**–E

don't litter [dōnt/ lĭt/ər] **219**–L

don't smoke [dōnt/ smōk/] **114**–G

not working [nät/ wür/kĭng] **62**–1

note [nōt] **183**–39

footnote [fŏŏt/nōt/] **190**–10

notebook [nōt/bŏŏk/] **7**–27

notebook paper [nōt/bŏŏk/ pāp/ər] **7**–28

spiral notebook [spī/rəl nōt/bŏŏk/] **7**–29

novel [nä/vəl] **133**–16

November [nō vĕm/bər] **21**–35

nuclear energy [nōō/klē ər ĕn/ər jē] **218**–8

nucleus [nōō/klē əs] **194**–7, **195**–29

numb [nŭm] **119**–C

number [nŭm/bər]

access number [ăk/sĕs/ nŭm/bər] **14**–16

apartment number [ə pärt/mənt nŭm/bər] **4**–6

cell phone number [sĕl/ fōn/ nŭm/bər] **4**–12

checking account number
[chĕk/ĭng ə kownt/ nŭm/bər] **132**–14

driver's license number
[drī/vərz lī/səns nŭm/bər] **136**–11

even numbers [ēv/ən nŭm/bərz] **192**–4

odd numbers [ŏd/ nŭm/bərz] **192**–3

phone number [fōn/ nŭm/bər] **4**–11, **15**–30

prescription number
[prĭ skrĭp/shən nŭm/bər] **112**–5

savings account number
[sā/vĭngz ə kownt/ nŭm/bər] **132**–11

SKU number [ĕs/kā/yōō/ nŭm/bər] **27**–5

Social Security number
[sō/shəl sĭ kyōōr/ə tē nŭm/bər] **4**–15

Numbers [nŭm/bərz] **16**

NUMBERS [nŭm/bərz] **16**

Numerals [nōō/mər əlz] **16**

numerator [nōō/mər ā/ tər] **192**–5

nurse [nürs] **118**–8, **168**–44

licensed practical nurse (LPN) [lī/sənst
prăk/tə kəl nürs/] / [ĕl/pē/ĕn/] **120**–11

nurse midwives [nürs/ mĭd/wīvz] **120** ✦

nurse practitioners [nürs/ prăk tĭ/shən ərz] **120** ✦

registered nurse (RN) [rĕj/ə stərd nürs/] / [är/ĕn/]
120–10

surgical nurse [sür/jĭ kəl nürs/] **120**–9

nurse [nürs] **36**–B

Nurse [nürs] **93**

nursery [nür/sə rē]

nursery rhymes [nür/sə rē rīmz/] **37**–22

nursery school [nür/sə rē skōōl/] **188**–1

nursing [nür/sĭng] **120**–12

nursing home [nür/sĭng hōm/] **52**–12

Nursing Staff [nür/sĭng stăf/] **120**

nutrition label [nōō trĭ/shən lā/bəl] **122**–8

nuts [nŭts] **73**–36, **180**–36

nylon [nī/län] **99**–12

oak [ōk] **210**–17, **210**–24

obey [ō bā/] **140**–C

objective [əb jĕk/tĭv] **194**–18

oboe [ō/bō] **238**–3

observatory [əb zür/və tör/ē] **205**–21

observe [əb zürv/] **195**–C

obstetrician [äb/stə trĭsh/ən] **120**–2

obtuse angle [äb/tōōs ăng/gəl] **193**–27

occupational therapist
[äk/yə pā/shən əl thĕr/ə pĭst] **168**–45

OCCUPATIONS [äk/yə pā/shənz] **166–169**

ocean [ō/shən] **204**–6, **225**–1

o'clock [ə kläk/] **18**–6

October [äk tō/bər] **21**–34

octopus [äk/tə pəs] **212**–9

odd numbers [ŏd/ nŭm/bərz] **192**–3

odometer [ō däm/ə tər] **159**–28

off [öf]

clear off [klĭr/ öf/] **10**–I

drop off [dräp/ öf/] **38**–G

gas shut-off valve [găs/ shŭt/öf välv/] **146**–4

get off [gĕt/ öf/] **153**–J

take off [tāk/ öf/] **109**–Q

turn off [türn/ öf/] **11**–P, **160**–I, **174**–G, **219**–G

offer [ö/fər] **12**–D

office [ö/fəs] **164**–3

main office [mān/ ö/fəs] **5**–12

office building [ö/fəs bĭld/ĭng] **124**–2

office manager [ö/fəs măn/ĭ jər] **182**–8

office supply store [ö/fəs sə plī/ stör/] **127**–21

post office [pōst/ ö/fəs] **125**–11

post office box (PO box) [pōst/ ö/fəs bäks/] /
[pē/ō bäks/] **135**–9

run for office [rŭn/ fər ö/fəs] **139**–A

Office [ö/fəs] **51**

OFFICE [ö/fəs] **134–135, 182–183**

Office Equipment [ö/fəs ĭ kwĭp/mənt] **183**

officer [ö/fə sər] **161**–17, **168**–48

Office Skills [ö/fəs skĭlz/] **171**

OFFICE SKILLS [ö/fəs skĭlz/] **171**

Office Supplies [ö/fəs sə plīz/] **183**

Office Visit [ö/fəs vĭ/zət] **119**

official [ə fĭsh/əl] **139**–32, **229**–6

oil [oyl] **73**–31, **218**–6

oil gauge [oyl/ gāj/] **159**–29

oil paint [oyl/ pānt/] **233**–19

oil spill [oyl/ spĭl/] **218**–17

ointment [oynt/mənt] **113**–24, **117**–10

OK [ō kā/] **154**–5

old [ōld] **31**–9, **31**–10

omelet [äm/lət, ä/mə lət] **76**–12

on [än, ön] **25**–11

get on [gĕt/ än, –ön] **153**–I

go on [gō/ än, –ön] **173**–K

on-the-job training [än dhə jäb/ trā/nĭng, –ön]
172–7

on the left [än dhə lĕft/, –ön] **25**–1

on the right [än dhə rīt/, –ön] **25**–3

on time [än tīm/, –ön] **19**–23, **16**–29

overdose on drugs [ō/vər dōs/ än drŭgz/] **116**–K

put on [pŏŏt/ än/, –ön/] **87**–B, **108**–D, **109**–P

try on [trī/ än/, –ön/] **95**–C

turn on [türn/ än/, –ön/] **11**–B

once a week [wŭns/ə wēk/] **20**–22

oncologist [ön/kö lə jĭst/] **120**–5

one [wŭn] **16**

five after one [fĭv/ ăf/ tər wŭn/] **18**–7

one billion [wŭn/ bĭl/yən] **16**

one eighth [wŭn/ ătth/, –āth/] **17**–5

one-fifteen [wŭn/fĭf/tēn/] **18**–9

one-forty [wŭn/för/tē] **18**–12

one-forty-five [wŭn/för/tē fĭv/] **18**–13

one fourth [wŭn/ förth/] **17**–4

one half [wŭn/ hăf/] **17**–2

one hundred [wŭn/ hŭn/drəd] **16**

one hundred dollars
[wŭn/ hŭn/drəd däl/ərz] **26**–12

one hundred one [wŭn/ hŭn/drəd wŭn/] **16**

100 percent [wŭn/ hŭn/drəd pər sĕnt/] **17**–8

one hundredth [wŭn/ hŭn/drəth] **16**

one hundred thousand
[wŭn/ hŭn/drəd thow/zənd] **16**

one million [wŭn/ mĭl/yən] **16**

one o'clock [wŭn/ ə kläk/] **18**–6

one-oh-five [wŭn/ō fĭv/] **18**–7

one-size-fits-all [wŭn/sīz fĭts/äl] **96**–6

one-ten [wŭn/tĕn/] **18**–8

one third [wŭn/ thürd/] **17**–3

one-thirty [wŭn/thür/tē] **18**–11

one thousand [wŭn/ thow/zənd] **16**

one thousandth [wŭn/ thow/zənth] **16**

one-twenty [wŭn/twĕn/tē] **18**–10

one way [wŭn/ wā/] **154**–3

one-way trip [wŭn/wā/ trĭp/] **152**–16

one whole [wŭn/hōl/] **17**–1

quarter after one [kwör/tər ăf/tər wŭn/] **18**–9

ten after one [tĕn/ ăf/tər wŭn/] **18**–8

twenty after one [twĕn/tē ăf/tər wŭn/] **18**–10

onions [ŭn/yənz] **69**–19, **69**–20

onion rings [ŭn/yən rĭngz/] **79**–4

online [än/līn/, ön–]

online catalog [än/līn/ kă/tə lög, ön–] **133**–11

online course [än/līn/ körs/, ön–] **172**–8

only [ōn/lē] **154**–7

On the Airplane [än/ dhe ĕr/plān/] **161**

open [ō/pən] **6**–G, **143**–F

opener [ō/pən ər] **54**–8, **78**–1, **146**–8

Opening an Account [ō/pə nĭng ən ə kownt/] **132**

opera [äp/rə] **223**–11, **236**–5

operate [äp/ə rāt/] **112**–E, **170**–H

Operating Room [äp/ə rā/tĭng rōōm/] **121**

operating table [äp/ə rā/tĭng tā/bəl] **121**–40

Operations [äp/ə rā/shənz] **192**

operator [äp/ə rā/tər] **14**–21, **98**–14, **168**–37

ophthalmologist
[äf/thəl mäl/ə jĭst, –thə mäl/–, äp/–] **120**–7

opinion [ə pĭn/yən] **44**–3

opossum [ə päs/əm, päs/əm] **216**–4

opponent [ə pō/nənt] **139**–30

optician [äp tĭsh/ən] **130**–9

optometrist [äp täm/ə trĭst] **115**–6
orange [ör/ənj, är/–] **24**–4
oranges [ör/ən jəz, är/–] **68**–5
orangutan [ə răng/ə tăng/, –tăn/] **217**–39
orchard [ör/chərd] **177**–10
orchid [ör/kĭd] **211**–19
order [ör/dər] **185**–1
   order puller [ör/dər poŏl/ər] **175**–10
order [ör/dər] **82**–D
orderly [ör/dər lē] **120**–16
Ordinal Numbers [ör/dn əl nŭm/bərz] **16**
organ [ör/gən] **238**–20
organic [ör gă/nĭk] **84**–2
organisms [ör/gə nĭzmz] **194**–1
organize [ör/gə nīz/] **171**–L, **191**–G
organizer [ör/gə nī/zər] **183**–49
ornament [ör/nə mənt] **239**–15
Orthodontics [ör/thə dän/tĭks] **119**
orthodontist [ör/thə dän/tĭst] **119**–5
orthopedists [ör/thə pē/dĭsts] **120** ✦
Other Instruments [ŭdh/ər ĭn/strə mənts] **238**
otter [ät/ər] **213**–35
ounce [owns] **75**–1, **75**–11
out [owt] **62**–2
   blow out [blō/ owt/] **240**–C
   check out [chĕk/ owt/] **133**–C
   cross out [krös/ owt/] **9**–R
   eat out [ēt/ owt/] **82** ✦
   fill out [fĭl/ owt/] **173**–J
   get out of [gĕt/ owt/ əv] **153**–F
   let out [lĕt/ owt/] **100**–C
   move out [mōōv/ owt/] **48** ✦
   outfit [owt/fĭt] **88** ✦
   out of focus [owt/ əv fō/kəs] **235**–33
   out-of-state contact [owt/əv stāt/ kän/tăkt] **146**–2
   run out of gas [rŭn/ owt/ əv găs/] **162**–E
   take out [tāk/ owt/] **9**–Y, **60**–Q, **82** ✦
   work out [würk/ owt/] **230**–N
OUTDOOR RECREATION [owt/dör rĕk/rē ā/shən] **226**
outlet [owt/lĕt, –lət] **58**–28, **154**–6, **159**–42
   outlet cover [owt/lĕt kŭv/ər] **181**–46
OUTSIDE THE BODY [owt/sīd/ dhe bä/dē] **106**–**107**
oven [ŭv/ən] **54**–15, **54**–20
   oven cleaner [ŭv/ən klē/nər] **61**–3
over [ō/vər] **76**–11, **153**–B
   overalls [ō/vər ölz/] **88**–6
   overcoat [ō/vər kōt/] **90**–2
   overexposed [ō/vər ĭk spōzd/] **235**–34
   overflowing [ō/vər flō/ĭng] **63**–17
   overhead compartment
      [ō/vər hĕd/ kəm pärt/mənt] **161**–13
   overhead projector [ō/vər hĕd/ prə jĕk/tər] **7**–16
   overjoyed [ō/vər joyd/] **43** ✦
   overnight mail [ō/vər nīt/ māl/] **135** ✦
   over-the-counter medication
      [ō/vər dhə -kown/tər mĕd/ə kā/shən] **113**–18
overdose [ō/vər dōs/, ō/vər dōs/] **116**–K
Over-the-Counter Medication
   [ō/vər dhə kown/tər mĕd/ə kā/shən] **113**
owl [owl] **214**–5
owner [ō/nər] **166**–11, **175**–1
oxfords [äks/fərdz] **95**–29

oxygen mask [äk/sĭ jən măsk/] **161**–24
oysters [oy/stərz] **71**–14
Pacific time [pə sĭf/ĭk tīm/] **19**–29
pacifier [păs/ə fi/ər] **37**–24
pack [păk] **74**–9, **117**–13, **235**–26
   backpack [băk/păk/] **94**–18, **226**–15
pack [păk] **49**–M, **162**–A
package [păk/ĭj] **74**–8, **74**–20, **134**–17
packaged food [păk/ĭjd fōōd/] **146**–10
PACKAGING [păk/ə jĭng] **74**
packer [păk/ər] **175**–18
packing tape [păk/ĭng tāp/] **183**–32
pad [păd]
   bumper pad [bŭm/pər păd/] **59**–4
   changing pad [chānj/ĭng păd/] **59**–2
   foam pad [fōm/ păd/] **226**–13
   heating pad [hē/tĭng păd/] **113**–13
   ink pad [ĭnk/ păd/] **183**–46
   knee pads [nē/ pădz/] **179**–19
   legal pad [lē/gəl păd/] **183**–38
   shoulder pads [shōl/dər pădz/] **231**–20
   steel-wool soap pads [stēl/wōōl/sōp/ pădz/] **61**–5
   sterile pad [stĕr/əl păd/] **117**–6
pail [pāl] **37**–7, **61**–7, **225**–8
pain [pān] **42**–11, **115**–3
   pain reliever [pān rĭ lē/vər] **113**–26
paint [pānt] **181**–25, **232**–10, **233**–19
   paintbrush [pānt/brŭsh/] **181**–22, **233**–20
   paint pan [pānt/ păn/] **181**–51
   paint roller [pānt/ rō/lər] **181**–23
paint [pānt] **49**–P, **178**–A, **233**–E
painter [pān/tər] **168**–46
Painter [pān/tər] **92**
painting [pān/tĭng] **56**–9
pair of scissors [për/ əv sĭz/ərz] **100**–16
paisley [pāz/lē] **96**–26
pajamas [pə jä/məz, –jä/–] **91**–24
pallet [pă/lət] **175**–13
palm [päm] **106**–15, **210**–14
pan [păn] **54**–24
   bed pan [bĕd/ păn/] **121**–28
   cake pan [kāk/ păn/] **78**–26
   dustpan [dŭst/ păn/] **61**–17
   frying pan [frī/ĭng păn/] **78**–5
   paint pan [pānt/ păn/] **181**–51
   pancakes [păn/kāks/] **80**–7
   pie pan [pī/ păn/] **78**–28
   roasting pan [rō/stĭng păn/] **78**–13
   saucepan [sös/păn/] **78**–25
pancreas [păng/krē əs] **107**–45
panda [păn/də] **217**–41
pane [pān] **178**–16
panel [păn/əl] **234**–7
Panel [păn/əl] **159**
panther [păn/thər] **217**–40
panties [păn/tēz] **91**–13
pants [pănts] **87**–12
   security pants [sĭ kyoŏr/ə tē pănts/] **93**–22
   training pants [trā/nĭng pănts/] **37**–11
   work pants [würk/ pănts/] **92**–5
panty hose [păn/tē hōz/] **91**–18
papayas [pə pī/əz] **68**–20

paper [pā/pər]
   construction paper [kən strŭk/shən pā/pər] **232**–12
   copies of important papers
      [kä/pēz əv ĭm pört/ənt pā/pərz] **146**–20
   newspaper [nōōz/pā/pər] **133**–6
   notebook paper [nōt/bōōk/ pā/pər] **7**–28
   paper clip [pā/pər klĭp/] **183**–31
   paper cutter [pā/pər kŭt/ər] **183**–22
   paper dolls [pā/pər dälz/] **233**–28
   paper shredder [pā/pər shrĕd/ər] **183**–24
   paper towels [pā/pər tow/əlz] **54**–3
   sandpaper [sănd/ pā/pər] **181**–56
   toilet paper [toy/lət pā/pər] **57**–17, **146**–13
   wallpaper [wäl/ pā/pər] **59**–8
parade [pə rād/] **239**–1
paragraph [păr/ə grăf/] **190**–3
parakeet [păr/ə kēt/] **215**–15
parallel lines [păr/ə lĕl/ līnz/] **193**–25
parallelogram [păr/ə lĕl/ə grăm/] **193**–33
paramedic [păr/ə mĕ/dĭk] **116**–2
parasites [păr/ə sīts/] **111**–13
parcel post [păr/səl pōst/] **134**–6
parentheses [pə rĕn/thə sēz/] **190**–19
PARENTING [păr/ən tĭng, për/–] **36**–**37**
Parents [păr/ənts, për/] **34**
parent-teacher conference
   [păr/ənt tē/chər kän/frəns, për/–] **22**–5
paring knife [për/ĭng nīf/] **78**–16
park [pärk] **223**–10
   park ranger [pärk/ rāng/jər] **220**–2
park [pärk] **129**–E
parka [pär/kə] **90**–9
PARK AND PLAYGROUND [pärk/ ən plā/grownd/] **224**
parking [pär/kĭng] **128**–6, **154**–11, **154**–12
   parking attendant [pär/kĭng ə tĕn/dənt] **184**–3
   parking garage [pär/kĭng gə räzh/, –räj/] **124**–1
   parking meter [pär/kĭng mē/tər] **129**–25
   parking space [pär/kĭng spās/] **50**–18, **128**–5
PARKS [pärks] **220**–**221**
parochial school [pə rō/kē əl skōōl/] **5** ✦
parsley [pär/slē] **69**–28
part [pärt] **33**–4
participate [pär tĭ/sə pāt/] **10**–B
particle [pär/tĭ kəl]
   particle board [pär/tĭ kəl börd/] **181**–20
   particle mask [pär/tĭ kəl măsk/] **179**–14
Partner [pärt/nər] **8**
parts [pärts] **175**–5
Parts of a Bird [pärts/ əv ə bürd/] **214**
PARTS OF A CAR [pärts/ əv ə kär/] **158**–**159**
Parts of a Fish [pärts/ əv ə fĭsh/] **212**
Parts of a Flower [pärts/ əv ə flow/ər] **211**
Parts of an Essay [pärts/ əv ən ĕs/ā] **190**
Parts of a Phone [pärts/ əv ə fōn/] **14**
Parts of a Sewing Machine
   [pärts/ əv ə sō/ĭng mə shēn/] **98**
Parts of a Tree [pärts/ əv ə trē/] **210**
party [pär/tē] **64**–2
pass [păs] **161**–20
   passbook [păs/bōōk/] **132**–10
   passport [păs/pört/] **41**–10
pass [păs] **10**–E, **137**–H, **230**–G

Index

passenger [păs/ən jər] **150–2, 161–15**
past [păst] **155–E**
pasta [päs/tə] **67–12**
    pasta salad [päs/tə săl/əd] **80–20**
paste [pāst]
    toothpaste [tōōth/pāst/] **109–23**
pastrami [pə strä/mē] **71–23**
path [păth] **208–3, 224–3**
Path [păth] **172**
patient [pā/shənt] **118–6, 121–18**
patio [păt/ē ō] **53–16**
    patio furniture [păt/ē ō für/nĭ chər] **53–19**
patron [pā/trən] **82–6, 133–3**
pattern [păt/ərn] **99–22**
PATTERNS [păt/ərnz] **96**
pause [pöz] **235–E**
paw [pö] **216–20**
pay [pā]
    paycheck [pā/chĕk/] **165–14**
    payroll clerk [pā/rōl klürk/] **165–10**
    pay stub [pā/ stŭb/] **165–11**
pay [pā]
    pay a late fine [pā/ ə lāt/ fīn/] **133–E**
    pay attention [pā/ ə tĕn/shən] **147–D**
    pay back [pā/ băk/] **26–D**
    pay cash [pā/ kăsh/] **27–A**
    pay for [pā/ för/, –fər] **27–G**
    pay phone [pā/ fōn/] **15–25, 129–23**
    pay taxes [pā/ tăks/əz] **140–B**
    pay the application fee
      [pā/ dhe ăp/lə kā/shən fē/] **137–D**
    pay the check [pā/ dhe chĕk/] **82–I**
    pay the rent [pā/ dhe rĕnt/] **48–E**
Pay [pā] **27**
PBX [pē/ bē/ ĕks/] **182–13**
peaceful assembly [pēs/fəl ə sĕm/blē] **140–1**
peaches [pē/chəz] **68–10**
peacock [pē/käk/] **214–14**
peak [pēk] **204–14**
pearls [pürlz] **95–39**
pears [përz] **68–4**
peas [pēz] **69–21**
pedal [pĕd/əl] **159–45, 159–46**
pedestrian [pə dĕs/trē ən] **128–14**
    pedestrian crossing [pə dĕs/trē ən krö/sĭng] **154–13**
pediatrician [pē/dē ə trĭsh/ən] **120–4**
peel [pēl] **77–K**
peeler [pē/lər] **78–15**
peephole [pēp/hōl/] **51–32**
pelvis [pĕl/vəs] **107–50**
pen [pĕn] **7–22**
pencil [pĕn/səl] **7–20, 109–34**
    pencil eraser [pĕn/səl ĭ rā/sər] **7–21**
    pencil sharpener [pĕn/səl shär/pə nər] **7–23, 183–26**
penguin [pĕng/wĭn] **214–11**
peninsula [pə nĭn/sə lə] **204–7**
penny [pĕn/ē] **26–1**
PEOPLE [pē/pəl] **32**
pepper [pĕp/ər] **55–13, 69–7, 69–29**
percent [pər sĕnt/]
    50 percent [fĭf/tē pər sĕnt/] **17–10**
    100 percent [wŭn/ hŭn/drəd pər sĕnt/] **17–8**

75 percent [sĕv/ən tē fīv/ pər sĕnt/] **17–9**
10 percent [tĕn/ pər sĕnt/] **17–12**
25 percent [twĕn/tē fīv/ pər sĕnt/] **17–11**
Percents [pər sĕnts/] **17**
Percussion [pər kŭsh/ən] **238**
perfume [pür/fyōōm/, pər fyōōm/] **108–6**
perimeter [pə rĭ/mə tər] **193–43**
period [pïr/ē əd] **190–11**
Period [pïr/ē əd] **198**
periodicals [pïr/ē äd/ĭ kəlz] **133–4**
periodic table [pïr/ē äd/ĭk tā/bəl] **195–26**
perm [pürm] **33–B**
peroxide [pə räk/ sīd] **117–9**
perpendicular lines [pür/pən dĭk/yə lər līnz/] **193–24**
person [pür/sən]
    appliance repair person
      [ə plī/əns rĭ për/ pür/sən] **166–4**
    assemblyperson [ə sĕm/blē pür/sən] **139–24**
    businessperson [bĭz/nəs pür/sən] **166–12**
    bus person [bŭs/ pür/sən] **185–13**
    congressperson [kän/grəs pür/sən] **138–4**
    councilperson [kown/səl pür/sən] **139–28**
    counterperson [kown/tər pür/sən] **79–17**
    delivery person [də lĭv/ə rē pür/sən] **167–21**
    electronics repair person
      [ĭ lĕk trän/ĭks rĭ për/ pür/sən] **167–24**
    repair person [rĭ për/ pür/sən] **62–10**
personal CD player [pür/sə nəl sē/dē/ plā/ər] **234–5**
PERSONAL HYGIENE [pür/sə nəl hī/jēn] **108–109**
PERSONAL INFORMATION
    [pür/sə nəl ĭn/fər mā/shən] **4**
pesticide poisoning [pĕs/tə sīd/ poy/zə nĭng] **218–16**
pests [pĕsts] **62 ✦**
pet [pĕt]
    pet food [pĕt fōōd/] **72–5**
    pet store [pĕt stör/] **130–6**
petals [pĕt/lz] **211–8**
petition [pə tĭ/shən] **148–5**
petroleum [pə trō/lē əm] **218–6**
Pets [pĕts] **215**
pharmacist [fär/mə sĭst] **112–1**
pharmacy [fär/mə sē] **128–4**
PHARMACY [fär/mə sē] **112–113**
Phase of the Moon [fāz/ əf dhə mōōn/] **205**
Phillips screwdriver [fĭl/ĭps skrōō/drī/vər] **180–31**
phlebotomist [flĭ bä/tə mĭst] **121–29**
phone [fōn]
    automated phone system
      [ö/tə māt ĭd fōn/ sĭs/təm] **14–23**
    cell phone holder [sĕl/ fōn/ hōl/dər] **94–15**
    cell phone kiosk [sĕl/ fōn/ kē/ösk] **131–22**
    cell phone number [sĕl/ fōn/ nŭm/bər] **4–12**
    cellular phone [sĕl/yə lər fōn/] **14–8**
    cordless phone [körd/ləs fōn/] **15–24**
    headphones [hĕd/ fōnz/] **6–8, 234–4**
    Internet phone call [ĭn/tər nĕt/ fōn/ käl/] **14–20**
    microphone [mī/krə fōn/] **234–18**
    pay phone [pā/ fōn/] **15–25, 129–23**
    phone bill [fōn/ bĭl/] **15–28**
    phone jack [fōn/ jăk/] **14–3**
    phone line [fōn/ līn/] **14–4**
    phone number [fōn/ nŭm/bər] **4–11, 15–30**
    smart phone [smärt/ fōn/] **15–27**

Phone [fōn] **14**
Phone Bill [fōn/ bĭl/] **15**
Phone Call [fōn/ köl/] **15**
photo [fō/tō] **58–3, 136–4**
    digital photo album [dĭ/jə təl fō/tō ăl/bəm] **235–32**
    funny photo [fŭn/ē fō/tō] **206–2**
    photo album [fō/tō ăl/bəm] **235–31**
    photocopier [fō/tə käp/ē ər] **183–23**
    serious photo [sïr/ē əs fō/tō] **206–3**
photographer [fə täg/rə fər] **206–1**
PHOTOGRAPHY [fə täg/rə fē] **234–235**
photosynthesis [fō/tō sĭn/thə səs] **194–10**
physical [fĭz/ĭ kəl]
    physical education [fĭz/ĭ kəl ĕ jə kā/shən] **189–17**
    physical therapist [fĭz/ĭ kəl thĕr/ə pĭst] **115–12**
    physical therapy [fĭz/ĭ kəl thĕr/ə pē] **115–11**
physically challenged [fĭz/ĭ klē chăl/ənjd] **32–10**
physician assistant [fĭz/ĭ shən ə sĭs/tənt] **168–47**
physicist [fĭz/ĭ sĭst/] **195–33**
Physics [fĭz/ĭks] **195**
pi (π) [pī] **193–46**
piano [pē ăn/ō] **238–14**
pick [pĭk] **108–15**
pickax [pĭk/ăks/] **178–21**
picker [pĭ/kər] **178–5**
pickle [pĭk/l] **80–11**
pick up [pĭk/ ŭp/] **6–I, 11–E, 38–M, 112 ✦**
pickup truck [pĭk/ŭp trŭk/] **156–12**
picnic [pĭk/nĭk] **224–D**
picnic table [pĭk/nĭk tā/bəl] **224–8**
picture [pĭk/chər]
    picture book [pĭk/chər bōōk/] **133–12**
    picture dictionary [pĭk/chər dĭk/shə nër ē] **7–31**
    picture frame [pĭk/chər frām/] **58–4**
pie [pī] **81–35**
    pie pan [pī/ păn/] **78–28**
pier [pïr] **225–18**
pierced [pïrst]
    pierced ear [pïrst/ ïr/] **32–17**
    pierced earrings [pïrst/ ïr/ĭngz] **95–36**
pig [pĭg] **215–2, 215–14**
pigeon [pĭj/ən] **214–15**
pile [pīl] **53–25**
pill [pĭl] **113–21**
pillow [pĭl/ō] **56–2, 58–11**
    pillowcase [pĭl/ō kās/] **58–14**
pilot [pī/lət] **161–11**
pin [pĭn] **95–38**
    bobby pins [băb/ē pĭnz/] **108–21**
    clothespin [klōz/ pĭn/] **101–10**
    pin cushion [pĭn/ kōōsh/ən] **100–13**
    pushpin [pōōsh/pĭn/] **183–35**
    rolling pin [rō/lĭng pĭn/] **78–30**
    safety pin [sāf/tē pĭn/] **37–9, 100–14**
    straight pin [strāt pĭn/] **100–12**
pine [pīn] **210–9**
    pinecone [pīn/kōn/] **210–11**
pineapples [pī/năp/əlz] **68–23**
pink [pĭnk] **24–7**
pint [pīnt] **75–3**
pipe [pīp] **158–15, 181–17**
    pipe wrench [pīp rĕnch/] **181–47**

pitch [pĭch] **230**–A
pizza [pēt/sə] **79**–10
place [plās] **146**–1
   fireplace [fīr/plās/] **56**–13
   placemat [plās/măt/] **55**–11
   place of birth [plās/ əv bürth/] **4**–14
   place setting [plās/ sĕt/ĭng] **83**–17
PLACES TO GO [plā/səz tə gō/] **222**–**223**
PLACES TO LIVE [plā/səz tə lĭv/] **52**
plaid [plăd] **96**–22
plain [plān] **97**–33
plains [plānz] **204**–19
plan [plăn] **186**–4
plan [plăn] **146**–A
plane [plān] **144**–3, **150**–8, **181**–57
Planets [plăn/əts] **205**
Planning a Career [plă/nĭng ə kə rēr/] **172**
plant [plănt] **176**–E, **177**–A, **219**–N
plants [plănts] **208**–5
   houseplant [hows/plănt/] **56**–4, **211**–27
Plants [plănts] **210**
PLANTS [plănts] **210**
plaque [plăk] **119**–12
plastic [plăs/tĭk]
   plastic storage bags [plăs/tĭk stör/ĭj băgz] **72**–25
   plastic storage container
      [plăs/tĭk stör/ĭj kən tā/nər] **78**–4
   plastic utensils [plăs/tĭk yōō tĕn/ səlz] **79**–19
   plastic wrap [plăs/tĭk răp/] **72**–24
plate [plāt] **55**–1
   bread-and-butter plate [brĕd/n bŭt/ər plāt/] **83**–19
   dinner plate [dĭn/ər plāt/] **83**–18
   license plate [lī/səns plāt/] **136**–12, **158**–12
   salad plate [săl/əd plāt/] **83**–20
   vanity plate [vă/nə tē plāt/]**136** ✦
platform [plăt/förm/] **152**–7
platter [plăt/ər] **55**–20
platypus [plăt/ĭ pəs, –pōōs/] **217**–46
play [plā] **223**–8
   play area [plā/ ër/ē ə] **130**–11
   playground [plā/grownd/] **50**–3
play [plā] **235**–B
   play an instrument [plā/ ən ĭn/strə mənt] **238**–A
   play cards [plā/ kärdz/] **233**–H
   play games [plā/ gāmz/] **232**–B
   play with [plā/ wĭth/] **36**–M
player [plā/ər] **229**–5
   CD player [sē/dē plā/ər] **159**–38
   DVD player [dē/vē/dē/ plā/ər] **56**–7, **234**–10
   MP3 player [ĕm/pē/thrē/ plā/ər] **234**–2
   personal CD player [pür/sə nəl sē/dē plā/ər] **234**–5
   portable cassette player
      [pör/tə bəl kə sĕt/ plā/ər] **234**–6
   portable DVD player
      [pör/tə bəl dē/vē/dē/ plā/ər] **234**–11
   video player [vĭd/ē ō plā/ər] **197**–11
PLAYGROUND [plā/grownd/] **224**
pliers [plī/ərz] **180**–7
plugs [plŭgz] **179**–15, **234**–16
plumber [plŭm/ər] **63**–20
plums [plŭmz] **68**–13
plunger [plŭn/jər] **181**–50

plywood [plī/wŏŏd/] **178**–18
p.m. [pē/ĕm/] **18**–5
pneumatic drill [nŏŏ măt/ĭk drĭl/] **178**–9
poached eggs [pōcht/ ĕgz/] **76**–9
PO box (post office box) [pē/ō băks/] /
   [pōst/ ö/fəs băks/] **135**–9
pocket [păk/ət] **100**–7
podium [pō/dē əm] **206**–5
poinsettia [poyn sĕt/ē ə, –sĕt/ə] **211**–24
point [poynt] **17**–7,
   endpoint [ĕnd/poynt/] **193**–21
pointer [poyn/tər] **197**–12
poison [poy/zən] **116**–J
   poison ivy [poy/zən ī/vē] **210**–25
   poison oak [poy/zən ōk/] **210**–24
   poison sumac [poy/zən sōō/măk, –shōō/–] **210**–23
poisoning [poy/zən ĭng] **218**–16
poisonous fumes [poy/zən əs fyōōmz/] **179**–3
poles [pōlz] **226**–18, **231**–25
police [pə lēs/]
   police officer [pə lēs/ ö/fə sər] **141**–1, **168**–48
   police station [pə lēs/ stā/shən] **124**–6
polish [päl/ĭsh] **61**–8, **109**–33
polish [päl/ĭsh] **60**–E, **109**–O
political [pə lĭ/tĭ kəl]
   political campaign [pə lĭ/tĭ kəl kăm pān/] **139**–29
   political movement [pə lĭ/tĭ kəl mōōv/mənt] **199**–16
   political party [pə lĭ/tĭ kəl pär/tē] **139** ✦
polka-dotted [pō/kə dät/əd] **96**–21
pollution [pə lōō/shən] **218**–11, **218**–14
Pollution [pə lōō/shən] **218**
polo [pō/lō] **229**–15
   polo shirt [pō/lō shïrt/] **92**–14
poncho [pän/chō] **90**–19
pond [pänd] **204**–21
pool [pōōl] **51**–22, **184**–22, **228**–2
   pool service [pōōl/ sür/vəs] **184**–21
   pool table [pōōl/ tā/bəl] **50**–14
pop [päp] **73**–34, **237**–25
   pop-up ad [păp/ŭp] **197**–9
porch light [pörch/ līt/] **53**–13
porcupine [pör/kyə pīn/] **216**–10
Pork [pörk] **70**
pork chops [pörk/ chäps/] **70**–10
porpoise [pör/pəs] **213**–30
port [pört] **196**–7
   airport [ër/pört/] **151**–10
portable [pör/tə bəl]
   portable cassette player
      [pör/tə bəl kə sĕt/ plā/ər] **234**–6
   portable DVD player
      [pör/tə bəl dē/vē/dē/ plā/ər] **234**–11
   portable TV [pör/tə bəl tē/ vē/] **234**–8
positive integers [pö/zə tīv ĭn/tə jərz] **192**–2
post [pōst] **134**–6
   post card [pōst/kärd] **134**–16
   postmark [pōst/märk/] **134**–24
   post office [pōst/ ö/fəs] **125**–11
   post office box (PO box) [pōst/ ö/fəs băks/] /
      [pē/ō băks/] **135**–9
postage [pō/stĭj] **135** ✦

postal [pō/stəl] **135**–10
   postal clerk [pō/stəl klürk/] **135**–7
   postal forms [pō/stəl förmz/] **134**–19
   postal scale [pō/stəl skāl/] **183**–27
   postal worker [pō/stəl wür/kər] **169**–49
POST OFFICE [pōst/ ö/fəs] **134**–**135**
pot [pät] **54**–16, **78**–6
   pot holders [pät hōl/dərz] **78**–29
   teapot [tē/pät/] **55**–16
potatoes [pə tā/tōz] **69**–17
   baked potato [bākt/ pə tā/tō] **81**–25
   mashed potatoes [măsht/ pə tā/tōz] **81**–23
   potato chips [pə tā/tō chĭps/] **73**–35
   potato salad [pə tā/tō săl/əd] **80**–19
   sweet potatoes [swēt/ pə tā/tōz] **69**–18
potty seat [pät/ē sēt/] **37**–12
pouch [powch] **217**–50
Poultry [pōl/trē] **70, 76**
POULTRY [pōl/trē] **70**
pound [pownd] **75**–12
   pound key [pownd/ kē/] **14**–7
pour [pör] **82**–C
powder [pow/dər] **37**–14, **108**–4, **109**–41
power [pow/ər] **218**–2, **218**–5
   power cord [pow/ər körd/] **196**–2
   power outlet [pow/ər owt/lĕt] **159**–42
   power sander [pow/ər săn/dər] **180**–11
pox [pöks] **111**–6
practical [prăk/tə kəl] **120**–11
prairie dog [prër/ē dög/] **215**–22
praise [prāz] **36**–J
pregnant [prĕg/nənt] **32**–15
preheat [prē/hēt/] **77**–A
preparation [prĕ/pə rā/shən] **185**–4
PREPARATION [prĕ/pə rā/shən] **76**–**77**
prepare [prĭ/për/] **174**–A
PREPOSITIONS [prĕp/ə zĭsh/ənz] **25**
PREPOSITIONS OF MOTION
   [prĕp/ə zĭsh/ənz əv mō/shən] **153**
preschool [prē/skōōl/] **188**–1
prescribe medication [prĭ skrīb/mĕd/ə kā/shən] **112** ✦
prescription [prĭ skrĭp/shən] **112**–2
   pick up a prescription
      [pĭk/ ŭp/ə prĭ skrĭp/shən] **112** ✦
   prescription label [prĭ skrĭp/shən lā/bəl] **112**–4
   prescription medication
      [prĭ skrĭp/shən mĕd/ə kā/shən] **112**–3
   prescription number [prĭ skrĭp/shən nŭm/bər]
      112–5
present [prĕz/ənt] **94** ✦, **240**–3
presentation [prĕ/zən tā/shən] **182**–6
president [prĕz/ə dənt] **138**–8, **199**–5
   first president [fürst/ prĕz/ə dənt] **198**–11
   Presidents' Day [prĕz/ə dənts dā/] **22**–11
   vice president [vīs/ prĕz/ə dənt] **138**–9
press [prĕs] **78**–11, **140**–4
press [prĕs] **15**–B, **15**–D
presser foot [prĕs/ər fŏŏt/] **98**–19
pressure [prĕsh/ər] **111**–14, **118**–9
pretend [prĭ tĕnd/] **233**–G
Prewriting [prē/rī/tĭng] **191**

price [prīs] **27**–2, **27**–3, **27**–7
   price tag [prīs tăg/] **27**–1
prime minister [prīm/ mĭn/ə stər] **199**–7
principal [prĭn/sə pəl] **5**–4
print [prĭnt] **96**–23
   fingerprint [fĭng/gər prĭnt/] **136**–5
print [prĭnt] **4**–C, **171**–I
printer [prĭn/tər] **169**–50, **196**–17
   inkjet printer [ĭnk/jĕt prĭn/tər] **183**–18
   laser printer [lā/zər prĭn/tər] **183**–19
Priority Mail® [prī ör/ə tē māl/, –är/–] **134**–1
prism [prĭz/əm] **195**–35
prisoner [prĭz/nər] **141**–15
private school [prī/vət skōōl/]**5** ✦
Problem [präb/ləm] **192**
problems [präb/ləmz] **115**–1, **192**–11
Problems [präb/ləmz] **115**, **119**
PROBLEMS [präb/ləmz] **62**–63
Procedures [prə sē/jərz] **117**, **118**
PROCEDURES [prə sē/jərz] **146**–147
Process [prä/sĕs] **191**
processor [prä/sĕ sər] **54**–26
Processor [prä/sĕ sər] **92**
produce section [prō/dōōs sĕk/shən] **72**–2
product [präd/ŭkt] **192**–9
Products [präd/ŭkts] **72**, **73**
program [prō/grăm]
   children's program [chĭl/drənz prō/grăm] **236**–9
   nature program [nā/chər prō/grăm] **236**–7
   news program [nōōz/ prō/grăm] **236**–1
   shopping program [shäp/ĭng prō/grăm] **236**–10
   sports program [spörtz/ prō/grăm] **236**–11
program [prō/grăm] **170**–I
Programs [prō/grămz] **236**
projector [prə jĕk/tər] **6**–6, **7**–16, **235**–29
promotion [prə mō/shən] **172**–4
proof of insurance [prōōf/ əv/ĭn shōōr/əns] **136**–8
proofread [prōōf/rēd/] **191**–I
prosecuting attorney
   [präs/ĭ kyōō/tĭng ə tür/nē] **141**–10
protect [prə tĕkt/] **143**–D
protector [prə tĕk/tər] **196**–1
proton [prō/tön] **195**–31
proud [prowd] **43**–21
prunes [prōōnz] **68**–26
pruning shears [prōō/nĭng shïrz/] **176**–11
psychiatrist [sī kī/ə trĭst, sə–] **120**–8
PUBLIC SAFETY [pŭb/lĭk sāf/tē] **143**
public school [pŭb/lĭk skōōl/] **5** ✦
PUBLIC TRANSPORTATION
   [pŭb/lĭk trăns/pər tā/shən] **152**
pull [pŏŏl] **119**–F, **224**–A
puller [pŏŏl/ər] **175**–10
pullover sweater [pŏŏl/ō/vər swĕt/ər] **88**–3
pulse [pŭls] **122**–A
pumps [pŭmps] **95**–26
Punctuation [pŭngk/chōō ā/shən] **190**
puppy [pŭp/ē] **215**–12
purchase [pür/chəs] **94**–A
purifier [pyŏŏ/rə fī/ ər] **113**–13
purple [pür/pəl] **24**–6
purses [pür/səz] **94**–2, **94**–14

push [pŏŏsh] **224**–B
pushpin [pŏŏsh/pĭn/] **183**–35
put [pŏŏt] **9**–X
put away
   [pŏŏt/ə wā/] **9**–Z, **60**–G
   put down [pŏŏt/ down/] **6**–J
   put in coolant [pŏŏt/ ĭn kōō/lənt] **157**–I
   put on [pŏŏt/ än/, –ön/] **87**–B, **108**–D, **109**–P, **135**–C
   put on hold [pŏŏt/ än hōld/, –ön] **171**–N
   put the utilities in your name
     [pŏŏt/ dhe yōō tĭl/ə tēz ĭn yər nām/] **49**–O
puzzle [pŭz/əl] **59**–17
pyramid [pïr/ə mĭd] **193**–39
quad [kwäd] **5**–1
quart [kwört] **75**–4
quarter [kwör/tər] **26**–4
   quarter after one [kwör/tər ăf/tər wŭn/] **18**–9
   1/4 cup [kwör/tər kŭp/] **75**–8
   quarter moon [kwör/tər mōōn/] **205**–11
   quarter to two [kwör/tər tə tōō/] **18**–13
   3/4 sleeved [thrē/ kwör/tər slēvd/] **96**–13
question mark [kwĕs/chən märk/] **190**–12
Quick and Easy Cake [kwĭk/ ən ē/zē kāk/] **77**
quiet [kwī/ət] **23**–12
quill [kwĭl] **216**–23
quilt [kwĭlt] **58**–16
   quilt block [kwĭlt/ bläk/] **232**–15
quilt [kwĭlt] **232**–C
quotation [kwōt tā/shən] **190**–9
   quotation marks [kwō tā/shən märks/] **190**–15
quotient [kwō /shənt] **192**–10
rabbit [răb/ət] **215**–13
race [rās] **230**–S
racing [rā/sĭng] **228**–19
rack [răk] **98**–16
   dish rack [dĭsh/ răk/] **54**–5
   roasting rack [rō/stĭng răk/] **78**–14
   towel rack [tow/əl răk/] **57**–13
racket [răk/ət] **231**–2
racquetball [răk/ət böl/] **228**–12
radiation [rā/dē ā/shən] **218**–15
radiator [rā/dē ā/tər] **158**–19
radio [rā/dē ō] **102**–6, **159**–37, **179**–22
radioactive materials
   [rā/dē ō ăk/tĭv mə tïr/ē əlz] **179**–7
radiologist [rā/dē äl/ə jĭst] **120**–6
radishes [răd/ĭ shəz] **69**–4
radius [rā/dē əs] **193**–35
rafting [răf/tĭng] **226**–2
rags [răgz] **61**–9
rail [rāl] **59**–10
railroad crossing [rāl/rōd krö/sĭng] **154**–14
rain [rān] **218**–13
   rain boots [rān/ bōōts/] **90**–20
   raincoat [rān/kōt/] **90**–18
   rain forest [rān/ för/əst, fär/–] **204**–1
raining [rā/nĭng] **13**–11
raise [rāz] **6**–A
raisins [rā/zənz] **68**–25
rake [rāk] **176**–8
rake [rāk] **176**–C

ranch [rănch] **52**–10
rancher [răn/chər] **177**–22
Ranch Hand [rănch hănd/] **92**
RANCHING [răn/chĭng] **177**
R&B [är/n bē/] **237**–28
range [rānj] **204**–15
ranger [rān/jər] **220**–2
rash [răsh] **110**–10
raspberries [răz/bĕr/ēz] **68**–15
rats [răts] **63**–27, **215**–17
rattle [răt/l] **37**–26
   rattlesnake [răt/l snāk/] **213**–38
raw [rö] **70**–24
ray [rā] **212**–11
razor [rā/zər] **109**–27
   razorblade [rā/zər blād/] **109**–28
reaction [rē/ăk shən] **116**–E
read [rēd]
   proofread [prōōf/rēd/] **191**–I
   read the card [rēd/ dhe kärd/] **135**–G
   read the definition [rēd/ dhe dĕ/fə nĭ/shən] **8**–B
   read the paper [rēd/ dhe pā/pər] **39**–V
   read to [rēd/ tōō] **36**–N
Reading a Phone Bill [rē/dĭng ə fōn/ bĭl/] **15**
reality show [rē ă lə tē shō/] **236**–6
rearview mirror [rïr/vyōō/ mïr/ər] **159**–35
receipt [rĭ sēt/] **27**–6
receive [rĭ sēv/] **135**–F
receiver [rĭ sē/vər] **14**–1
reception area [rĭ sĕp/shən ër/ē ə] **182**–15
receptionist [rĭ sĕp/shə nĭst] **118**–2, **164**–5,
   169–51, **182**–14
reclined seat [rĭ klīnd/ sēt/] **161**–27
record [rĭ körd/] **195**–D, **235**–A
records [rĕk/ərdz] **168**–39
RECREATION [rĕk/rē ā/shən] **226**
recreational vehicle (RV)
   [rĕk/rē ā/shən əl vē/ə kəl] / [är/vē/] **156**–10
Recreation Room [rĕk/rē ā/shən rōōm/] **50**
recruiter [rə krōō/tər] **172**–14
rectangle [rĕk/tăng/gəl] **193**–29
recycle [rē sī/kəl] **60**–B, **219**–C
recycling bin [rē sī/klĭng bĭn/] **61**–2
red [rĕd] **24**–1
   red hair [rĕd/ hër/] **33**–15
   redwood [rĕd/wŏŏd/] **210**–18
redecorate [rē dĕk/ə rāt/] **48** ✦
reduce [rĭ dōōs/] **219**–A
referee [rĕf/ə rē/] **229**–6
reference librarian [rĕf/rəns lī brër/ē ən] **133**–9
refrigerator [rĭ frĭj/ə rā/tər] **54**–9
refund [rē/fŭnd] **97** ✦
reggae [rĕ gā/] **237**–31
register [rĕj/ə stər] **73**–15
register [rĕj/ə stər] **140**–D, **157**–F
registered nurse (RN)
   [rĕj/ə stərd nürs/] / [är/ĕn/] **120**–10
registration [rĕj/ə strā/shən]
   registration sticker
     [rĕj/ə strā/shən stĭk/ər] **136**–13
   registration tag [rĕj/ə strā/shən tăg/] **136**–13
regular price [rĕg/yə lər prīs/] **27**–2

regulations [rĕ gyə lā/shənz] **164**–6
relatives [rĕ lə tĭvz] **44**–6
relax [rĭ lăks/] **39**–U
relieved [rĭ lēvd/] **42**–15
reliever [rĭ lēv/ər] **113**–26
religious holiday [rĭ lĭj/əs hăl/ə dā/] **22**–7
remain [rē/mān] **147**–E
remarried [rē măr/ēd] **35**–24
remote [rĭ mōt/] **234**–9
remove [rĭ mōōv/] **109**–Q, **132**–G
remover [rĭ mōō/vər] **109**–42
renew a license [rĭ nōō/ ə lī/səns, –nyōō/–] **136** ✦
rental agreement [rĕn/təl ə grē/mənt] **51**–28
Rental Office [rĕn/təl ö/fəs] **51**
Renting an Apartment [rĕn/tĭng ən ə pärt/mənt] **48**
repair [rĭ për/] **166**–4, **167**–24
　　repair person [rĭ për/ pür/sən] **62**–10
repair [rĭ për/] **170**–J
REPAIRS [rĭ përz/] **62**–63
repellent [rĭ pĕl/ənt] **226**–23
replace [rĭ plās/] **157**–K
report [rĭ pört/] **143**–J, **143**–K
reporter [rĭ pör/tər] **169**–52
representative [rĕ/prĭ zĕn/tə tĭv] **138**–3, **167**–20
Reptiles [rĕp/tĭlz] **213**
REPTILES [rĕp/tĭlz] **212**–**213**
request [rĭ kwĕst/] **12** ✦
Requirements [rĭ kwīr/mənts] **140**
rescue [rĕs/kyōō] **145**–20
　　rescue breathing [rĕs/kyōō brē/dhĭng] **117**–16
Resident Alien card [rĕz/ə dənt ā/lē ən kärd/] **40**–2
resource center [rē/sörs sĕn/tər] **172**–9
Resources [rē/sörs/səz, rĭ sör/səz] **219**
respirator [rĕs/pə rā/tər] **179**–13
Responding [rĭ spän/dĭng] **191**
Responsibilities [rĭ spän/sə bĭl/ə tēz] **140**
RESPONSIBILITIES [rĭ spän/sə bĭl/ə tēz] **140**
restaurant [rĕs/tə rənt, –ränt/] **125**–14, **128**–10
RESTAURANT [rĕs/tə rənt, –ränt/] **79**, **82**–83
Restaurant Dining [rĕs/tə rənt dī/nĭng, –ränt/] **185**
Restaurant Kitchen [rĕs/tə rənt kĭ/chən, –ränt/] **185**
restrooms [rĕst/ rōōmz/] **5**–10
results [rĭ zŭltz/] **139**–31
resuscitation [rĭ sə sə tā/shən] **117**–17
retail clerk [rē/tāl/ klürk/] **169**–53
retire [rĭ tīr/] **41**–O
return [rĭtürn/] **73**–16
　　return address [rĭ türn/ ə drĕs/, –ă/drĕs] **134**–21
return [rĭ türn/] **27**–H, **133**–D
REUNION [rē yōōn/yən] **44**–45
reuse [rē yōōz/] **219**–B
revise [rĭ vīz/] **191**–J
Revising [rĭ vī/zĭng] **191**
Revolutionary War [rĕ/və lōō/shə nër ē wör/] **198**–8
revolving [rĭ väl/vĭng]
　　revolving door [rĭ väl/vĭng dör/] **184**–2
　　revolving nosepiece [rĭ väl/vĭng nōz/pēs/] **194**–17
rewind [rē wīnd/] **235**–C
rewrite [rē rīt/] **191**–J
rhinoceros [rĭ näs/ər əs] **217**–28
ribbon [rĭ/bən] **99**–30

ribs [rĭbz] **70**–5, **76**–2
　　rib cage [rĭb/ kāj/] **107**–48
rice [rīs] **67**–10, **81**–30, **177**–1
ride [rīd] **129**–D
rider [rī/dər] **152**–3
riding [rī/dĭng] **226**–9
right [rīt] **25**–3, **155**–B, **198**–10
　　right angle [rīt/ ăng/gəl] **193**–26
　　right turn only [rīt/ türn/ ōn/lē] **154**–7
Rights [rīts] **140**
RIGHTS AND RESPONSIBILITIES
　　[rīts/ ən rĭ spän/sə bĭl/ə tēz] **140**
ring [rĭng] **37**–25, **79**–4, **95**–40
　　clip-on earrings [klĭp/än ïr/ïngz, –ön–] **95**–37
　　pierced earrings [pïrst/ ïr/ïngz] **95**–36
rinse [rĭns] **108**–F
ripe [rīp] **68**–30
ripped [rĭpt] **97**–41
ripper [rĭ/pər] **100**–18
rise [rīz] **127**–13
　　sunrise [sŭn/rīz/] **18**–14
river [rĭv/ər] **155**–10, **204**–3
RN (registered nurse) [är/ĕn/] / [rĕj/ə stərd nürs/]
　　120–10
road work [rōd/ würk/] **154**–16
Road Worker [rōd/ wür/kər] **92**
roast [rōst] **70**–1
　　roast beef [rōst bēf/] **71**–21
　　roast chicken [rōst chĭk/ən] **81**–22
　　roasted turkey [rō/stəd tür/kē] **76**–4
　　roasting pan [rō/stĭng păn/] **78**–13
　　roasting rack [rō/stĭng răk/] **78**–14
robe [rōb] **91**–29
robin [räb/ən] **214**–16
rock [räk] **36**–D
rock concert [räk/ kän/sərt] **222**–5
rocking chair [räk/ĭng chër/] **37**–21
rocks [räks] **208**–6, **237**–23
Rodents [rōd/nts] **215**
RODENTS [rōd/nts] **215**
rollers [rō/lərz] **33**–19, **181**–23
rolling pin [rō/lĭng pĭn/] **78**–30
rolls [rōlz] **74**–11, **74**–23, **80**–17
romance [rō măns/, rō/măns] **237**–16
Roman Numerals [rō/mən nōō/mər əlz] **16**
roof [rōōf] **46**–1
roof garden [rōōf/ gär/dn] **50**–4
roofer [rōō/fər] **62**–8
room [rōōm]
　　baby's room [bā/bēz rōōm/] **47**–10
　　ballroom [böl/ rōōm/] **184**–26
　　banquet room [băn/kwət rōōm/] **185**–14
　　bathroom [băth/rōōm/] **46**–4
　　bedroom [bĕd/rōōm/] **46**–2
　　conference room [kän/frəns rōōm/] **182**–4
　　dining room [dī/nĭng rōōm/] **82**–1
　　dining room chair [dī/nĭng rōōm/ chër/] **55**–8
　　dining room table [dī/nĭng rōōm/ tā/bəl] **55**–9
　　dish room [dĭsh/ rōōm/] **83**–13
　　guest room [gĕst/ rōōm/] **184**–13
　　kids' bedroom [kĭdz/ bĕd/rōōm/] **47**–9

living room [lĭv/ĭng rōōm/] **47**–12
meeting room [mē/tĭng rōōm/] **184**–25
roommates [rōōm/māts/] **64**–1
room service [rōōm/ sür/vəs] **184**–17
storeroom [stör/rōōm/] **185**–5
Room [rōōm] **50**, **118**, **121**
ROOM [rōōm] **56**
rooster [rōō/stər] **215**–7
roots [rōōts] **210**–5, **211**–3
rope [rōp] **224**–4, **226**–19
rose [rōz] **211**–15
rotary [rō/tə rē]
　　rotary card file [rō/tə rē kärd/ fīl/] **183**–44
　　rotary cutter [rō/tə rē kŭt/ər] **232**–16
rotten [rät/n] **68**–32
round trip [rownd/ trĭp/] **152**–17
route [rōōt] / [rowt]
　　bus route [bŭs/ rōōt, –rowt] **152**–1
　　escape route [ĕs/kāp rōōt, –rowt] **146**–3
　　evacuation route
　　　　[ĭ văk/yōō/ā shən rōōt, –rowt] **146**–5
　　U.S. route [yōō/ĕs/ rōōt, –rowt] **154**–17
router [row/tər] **180**–12
ROUTINES [rōō tēnz/] **38**–39
rubber [rŭb/ər]
　　rubber band [rŭb/ər bănd/] **183**–34
　　rubber gloves [rŭb/ər glŭvz/] **61**–4
　　rubber mat [rŭb/ər măt/] **57**–3
ruffle [rŭ/fəl] **58**–17
rug [rŭg] **58**–22
ruler [rōō/lər] **17**–13
rules [rōōlz] **64**–8
Rules [rōōlz] **190**
run [rŭn] **11**–D
　　run across [rŭn/ə krös/] **153**–G
　　run around [rŭn/ə rownd/] **153**–H
　　run for office [rŭn/ fər ö/fəs] **139**–A
　　run out [rŭn/owt/] **162**–E
runner [rŭ/nər] **185**–15
rural area [rōŏr/əl ër/ē ə] **52**–4
RV (recreational vehicle)
　　[är/vē/] / [rĕk/rē ā/shən əl vē/ə kəl] **156**–10
rye bread [rī/ brĕd/] **71**–20
sad [săd] **43**–19
safety [sāf/tē] **37**–19, **92**–4, **159**–53
　　safety boots [sāf/tē bōōts/] **179**–20
　　safety deposit box [sāf/tē dĭ päz/ət bäks/] **132**–7
　　safety glasses [sāf/tē glăs/əz] **92**–10, **179**–10
　　safety goggles [sāf/tē gäg/əlz] **179**–11
　　safety pin [sāf/tē pĭn/] **37**–9, **100**–14
　　safety rail [sāf/tē rāl/] **59**–10
　　safety regulations [sāf/tē rĕ/gyə lā/shənz] **164**–6
　　safety visor [sāf/tē vī/zər] **179**–12
Safety [sāf/tē] **76**
SAFETY [sāf/tē] **76**–77, **143**, **179**
Safety Equipment [sāf/tē ĭ kwĭp/mənt] **179**
Safety Hazards and Hazardous Materials
　　[sāf/tē hăz/ərdz ən hăz/ər dəs-mə tïr/ē əlz] **179**
sailboat [sāl/bōt/] **225**–3
sailing [sā/lĭng] **227**–8

salad [săl/əd]
    chef's salad [shĕfs/ săl/əd] **80**–14
    dinner salad [dĭn/ər săl/əd] **80**–15
    fruit salad [frōōt/ săl/əd] **80**–21
    pasta salad [päs/tə săl/əd] **80**–20
    potato salad [pə tā/tō săl/əd] **80**–19
    salad bar [săl/əd bär/] **79**–24
    salad fork [săl/əd förk/] **83**–27
    salad plate [săl/əd plāt/] **83**–20
    spinach salad [spĭ/nĭch săl/əd] **80**–13
Salad Dressings [săl/əd drĕ/sĭngz] **80**
Salads [săl/ədz] **80**
salamander [săl/ə măn/dər] **212**–27
salami [sə lä/mē] **71**–24
SALE [săl] **102**–**103**
sales [sălz]
    sale price [săl/ prīs/] **27**–3
    salesclerk [sālz/klürk/] **94**–3
    sales tax [sālz/ tăks/] **27**–8
Salesperson [sālz/pür/sən] **92**
salmon [săm/ən] **71**–3
    salmon steak [săm/ən stāk/] **71**–4
salon [sə lön/] **130**–3, **131**–18
salt and pepper shakers
    [sölt/ n pĕp/ər shā/kərz] **55**–13
same [sām] **23**–15
SAME AND DIFFERENT
    [sām/ ən dĭ/frənt, –dĭ fə rənt] **28**–**29**
samples [săm/pəlz] **84**–5
sand [sănd] **225**–23
    sandbox [sănd/bäks/] **224**–15
    sand castle [sănd kăs/əl] **225**–12
    sand dune [sănd dōōn/] **204**–5
    sandpaper [sănd/pā/pər] **181**–56
sandals [săn/dlz] **88**–9
sander [săn/dər] **180**–11
sandwich [săn/wĭch, –sănd/–] **79**–5, **80**–10, **80**–12
sanitation worker [săn/ə tā/shən wür/kər] **169**–54
satellite [săt/əl īt/] **205**–20
    satellite dish [săt/əl lĭt/ dĭsh/] **53**–6
satisfied [săt/ĭs fīd/] **42**–6
Saturday [săt/ər dā/, –dē] **20**–14
Saturn [săt/ərn] **205**–6
saucepan [sös/păn/] **78**–25
saucer [sö/sər] **83**–25
sausage [sö/sĭj] **70**–12, **80**–2
sauté [sö tā/, sō –] **77**–E
save [sāv] **219**–E
saving [sā/vĭng] **19**–25, **225**–20
savings account number
    [sā/vĭngz ə kownt/ nŭm/bər] **132**–11
saw [sö] **180**–9
    hacksaw [hăk/sö/] **180**–5
    jigsaw [jĭg/sö/] **180**–10
saxophone [săk/sə fōn/] **238**–5
say [sā] **2**–A, **3**–L, **4**–A
scaffolding [skăf/əl dĭng] **178**–4
scales [skālz] **57**–27, **72**–3, **135**–8, **155**–7, **195**–41, **212**–3
    postal scale [pō/stəl skāl/] **183**–27
scallions [skăl/yənz] **69**–20
scallops [skăl/əps, skäl/–] **71**–12, **212**–19

scan [skăn] **171**–H
scanner [skăn/ər] **183**–20
scared [skërd] **43**–23
scarf / scarves [skärf] / [skärvz] **95**–12
    winter scarf [wĭn/tər skärf/] **90**–5
scenery [sē/ nə rē] / [sēn/rē] **162**–3
schedule [skĕj/ōōl, –ōō əl] **152**–4
schedule [skĕj/ōōl, –ōō əl] **171**–J
school [skōōl] **126**–9
    adult school [[ə dŭlt/–, ăd/ŭlt skōōl/] **188**–8
    elementary school [ĕl/ə mĕn/trē skōōl/] **188**–2
    high school [hī/ skōōl/] **188**–4
    junior high school [jōōn/yər hī/ skōōl/] **188**–3
    middle school [mĭd/l skōōl/] **188**–3
    nursery school [nür/sə rē skōōl/] **188**–1
    parochial school [pə rō/kē əl skōōl/] **5** ✦
    preschool [prē/skōōl] **188**–1
    private school [prī/vət skōōl/] **5** ✦
    public school [pŭb/lĭk skōōl/] **5** ✦
    school bus [skōōl/ bŭs/] **156**–21
    school crossing [skōōl/ krö/sĭng] **154**–15
    technical school [tĕk/nĭ kəl skōōl/] **188**–5
    vocational school [vō kā/shə nəl skōōl/] **188**–5
SCHOOL [skōōl] **5, 10, 11**
School Registration Form
    [skōōl/ rĕj/ə strā/shən förm/] **4**
SCHOOLS AND SUBJECTS
    [sklōōz ən sŭb/jĭkts] **188**–**189**
science [sī/əns] **189**–11
SCIENCE [sī/əns] **194**–**195**
Science Lab [sī/əns lăb/] **195**
scissors [sĭz/ərz] **33**–20, **100**–16
scoop neck [skōōp/ nĕk/] **96**–10
score [skör] **10**–3, **229**–1
scorpion [skör/pē ən] **214**–30
scrambled eggs [skrăm/bəld ĕgz/] **76**–7
scraper [skrā/pər] **181**–52
screen [skrēn] **6**–2, **196**–11, **235**–30
    big-screen TV [bĭg/skrēn/ tē/ vē/] **50**–15
    fire screen [fīr/ skrēn/] **56**–12
    flat screen TV [flăt/ skrēn/ tē/vē/] **234**–7
    screen door [skrēn/ dör/] **53**–15
    sunscreen [sŭn/skrēn/] **108**–7, **225**–10
screener [skrēn/ər] **160**–5
screening area [skrē/nĭng ër/ē ə] **160**–4
screw [skrōō] **180**–32, **180**–33
    Phillips screwdriver [fĭl/ĭps skrōō/drī/vər] **180**–31
    screwdriver [skrōō/drī/vər] **180**–30
scroll bar [skrōl/bär/] **197**–15
scrub [skrŭb] **60**–K
scrubs [skrŭbz] **93**–31
    scrub brush [skrŭb/ brŭsh/] **61**–20
    surgical scrub cap [sür/jĭ kəl skrŭb/ kăp/] **93**–35
    surgical scrubs [sür/jĭ kəl skrŭbz/] **93**–38
scuba [skōō/bə]
    scuba diving [skōō/bə dī/vĭng] **227**–12
    scuba tank [skōō/bə tăngk/] **225**–5
sea [sē]
    sea anemone [sē/ ə nĕm/ə nē] **212**–24
    seahorse [sē/ hörs/] **212**–13
    sea lion [sē/ lī/ən] **213**–33
    sea otter [sē/ ät/ər] **213**–35

seashell [sē/ shĕl/] **225**–24
sea urchin [sē/ ür/chən] **212**–21
seaweed [sē/ wēd/] **225** ✦
Sea Animals [sē/ ăn/ə məlz] **212**
SEAFOOD AND DELI [sē/fōōd/ ən dĕ/lī] **71**
seal [sēl] **213**–34
Sea Mammals [sē/ măm/əlz] **213**
seam ripper [sēm/ rĭp/ər] **100**–18
search [sürch]
    search and rescue team
        [sürch/ ən rĕs/kyōō tēm/] **145**–20
    search box [sürch/ bäks/] **197**–5
    search engine [sürch/ ĕn/jən] **197**–6
SEARCH [sürch] **173**
SEASONAL CLOTHING [sē/zə nəl klō/dhĭng] **90**
Seasons [sē/zənz] **21**
seat [sēt]
    backseat [băk/ sēt/] **159**–54
    car safety seat [kär/ sāf/tē sēt/] **37**–19
    child safety seat [chīld/ sāf/tē sēt/] **159**–53
    front seat [frŭnt/ sēt/] **159**–51
    love seat [lŭv/ sēt/] **56**–1
    potty seat [pät/ē sēt/] **37**–12
    reclined seat [rĭ klīnd/ sēt/] **161**–27
    seat belt [sēt/ bĕlt/] **159**–52
    upright seat [ŭp/rīt/ sēt/] **161**–28
seat [sēt] **82**–B
second [sĕk/ənd] **16**
Second Floor [sĕk/ənd flör/] **50**
seconds [sĕk/əndz] **18**–3
section [sĕk/shən] **72**–2
security [sĭ kyŏŏr/ə tē]
    security camera [sĭ kyŏŏr/ə tē kăm/rə] **50**–19
    security gate [sĭ kyŏŏr/ə tē gāt/] **50**–16
    security guard [sĭ kyŏŏr/ə tē gärd/] **132**–5, **169**–55
    security pants [sĭ kyŏŏr/ə tē pănts/] **93**–22
    security screener [sĭ kyŏŏr/ə tē skrē/nər] **160**–5
    security shirt [sĭ kyŏŏr/ə tē shürt/] **93**–20
Security Checkpoint [sĭ kyŏŏr/ə tē chĕk/poynt/] **160**
Security Guard [sĭ kyŏŏr/ə tē gärd/] **93**
sedan [sə dăn/] **156**–1
see [sē] **106**–A
seed [sēd] **211**–1
    seedling [sēd/lĭng] **211**–4
seek [sēk] **114**–A, **147**–H
seesaw [sē/sö/] **224**–16
select [sə lĕkt/] **196**–B
self-checkout [sĕlf/ chĕk/owt/] **73**–10, **133**–10
sell [sĕl] **170**–K
semi [sĕm/ī] **156**–15
semicolon [sĕm/ē kō/lən] **190**–18
Senate [sĕn/ət] **138**–5
senator [sĕn/ə tər] **138**–6
    state senator [stāt/ sĕn/ə tər] **139**–25
send [sĕnd] **197**–I
    send in [sĕnd/ ĭn] **173**–H
Sending a Card [sĕn/dĭng ə kärd/] **135**
Sending Email [sĕn/dĭng ē/māl/] **197**
senior [sēn/yər]
    senior citizen [sēn/yər sĭt/ə zən] **30**–5
    senior housing [sēn/yər howz/ĭng] **52**–11
Senses [sĕn/səz] **106**

sentence [sĕn/tns] **190–2**
sentence [sĕn/tns] **141**–E
separate [sĕ/pə rāt/] **76**–B
September [sĕp tĕm/bər] **21–33**
sequins [sē/kwĭnz/] **99–33**
Serious Medical Conditions
[sïr/ē əs mĕd/ĭ kəl kən dĭsh/ənz] **111**
serious photo [sïr/ē əs fō/tō] **206–3**
serve [sürv] **139**–D, **230**–P
serve on a jury [sürv/ ăn ə jŏŏr/ē, –ön–] **140**–E
serve the meal [sürv/ dhə mēl/] **82**–F
Serve [sürv] **76**
server [sür/vər] **82**–8, **83**–9, **169**–56, **185**–8
service [sür/vəs]
customer service [kŭs/tə mər sür/vəs] **97** ✦
customer service representative
[kŭs/tə mər-sür/vəs rĕ/prə zĕn/tə tĭv] **167–20**
guest services [gĕst/ sür/vəs əz] **130–12**
pool service [pōōl/ sür/vəs] **184–21**
room service [rōōm/ sür/vəs] **184–17**
SERVICE [sür/vəs] **138–139, 185**
serving bowl [sür/vĭng bōl/] **55–21**
set [sĕt] **10**–A, **33**–C, **82**–A
set up [sĕt/ ŭp/] **173**–I
sunset [sŭn/sĕt/] **18–18**
setting [sĕ/tĭng] **83–17**
seven [sĕv/ən] **16**
seventeen [sĕv/ən tēn/] **16**
seventeenth [sĕv/ən tēnth/] **16**
seventh [sĕv/ənth] **16**
seventieth [sĕv/ən tē əth] **16**
seventy [sĕv/ən tē] **16**
75 percent [sĕv/ən tē fïv/ pər sĕnt/] **17–9**
sew [sō] **98**–A, **98**–B, **170**–L
sewing [sō/ĭng]
sewing machine [sō/ĭng mə shēn/] **98–13**
sewing machine operator
[sō/ĭng mə shēn/ äp/ə rā/ tər] **98–14**
Sewing Machine [sō/ĭng mə shēn/] **98**
Sewing Supplies [sō/ĭng sə plīz/] **100**
sex [sĕks] **4–16**
shade [shād] **225–13**
lampshade [lămp/shād/] **56** ✦, **58–26**
shadow [shă/dō/] **109–35**
shake [shāk]
milkshake [mĭlk/shāk/] **79–14**
shake [shāk] **3**–J, **174**–I
shakers [shā/kərz] **55–13**
shampoo [shăm pōō/] **108–10**
shanks [shănks] **70–13**
shaper [shā/pər] **91–15**
Shapes [shāps] **193**
share [shër] **8**–M
Sharing and Responding
[shër/ĭng ən rĭ spän/dĭng] **191**
shark [shärk] **212–4**
sharpener [shär/pən ər] **183–26**
shave [shāv]
aftershave [ăf/tər shāv/] **109–30**
shave [shāv] **109**–M
shaver [shā/vər] **109–26**
shaving cream [shā/vĭng krēm/] **109–29**

shears [shïrz] **176–9**
sheep [shēp] **215–6**
sheet [shēt]
cookie sheet [kŏŏk/ē shēt/] **78–27**
dryer sheets [drī/ər shēts/] **101–5**
fitted sheet [fĭt/əd shēt/] **58–12**
flat sheet [flăt/ shēt/] **58–13**
shelf [shĕlf] **54–2**
shell [shĕl]
seashell [sē/shĕl/] **225–24**
Shellfish [shĕl/fĭsh/] **71**
shelter [shĕl/tər] **52–13**
shield [shēld]
windshield [wĭnd/shēld/] **158–1**
windshield wipers [wĭnd/shēld wī/pərz] **158–2**
shift [shĭft] **159–49, 159–50**
shin [shĭn] **106–21**
shin guards [shĭn/ gärdz/] **231–13**
shingles [shĭng/gəlz] **178–20**
ship [shĭp] **175**–D
shipping clerk [shĭp/ĭng klürk/] **175–14**
shirt [shürt] **86–1**
nightshirt [nīt/shürt/] **91–28**
polo shirt [pō/lō shürt/] **92–14**
security shirt [sĭ kyŏŏr/ə tē shürt/] **93–20**
sports shirt [spörts/ shürt/] **88–4**
T-shirt [tē/shürt/] **86–4**
work shirt [würk/ shürt/] **92–2**
shock [shäk] **116**–B, **116**–F
shoes [shōōz] **86**–7, **87**–13, **95–32**
shoe department [shōō/ dĭ pärt/mənt] **95–7**
shoelaces [shōō/lās əz] **94–24**
shoe store [shōō/ stör/] **130–10**
SHOES AND ACCESSORIES
[shōōz/ ən ĭk sĕs/ə rēz] **94–95**
shoot [shōōt] **211–5**
shoot [shōōt] **230**–H
shop [shäp]
barbershop [bär/bər shäp/] **129–19**
beauty shop [byōō/tē shäp/] **130** ✦
coffee shop [kö/fē shäp/] **126–11**
donut shop [dō/nŭt shäp/] **129–17**
gift shop [gĭft/ shäp/] **130** ✦, **184–5**
ice cream shop [īs/ krēm shäp/] **131–16**
shop [shäp] **28**–A, **143**–H
Shop [shäp] **100**
SHOP [shäp] **80–81**
shoplifting [shäp/lĭf/tĭng] **142–8**
shopping [shäp/ĭng]
shopping basket [shäp/ĭng băs/kət] **73–9**
shopping list [shäp/ĭng lĭst/] **67–14**
shopping mall [shäp/ĭng mäl/] **126–7**
shopping program [shäp/ĭng mäl/] **236–10**
SHOPPING [shäp/ĭng] **27**
shore [shör] **204–12**
short [shört] **32**–6, **96–16**
short hair [shört/ hër/] **33–1**
short-order cook [shört/ör/dər kŏŏk/] **185–1**
short-sleeved [shört/slēvd/] **96–12**
shorten [shört/ən] **100**–B
shorts [shörts] **89–25, 91–4**

shoulder [shōl/dər] **105–13**
shoulder bag [shōl/dər băg/] **94–17**
shoulder blade [shōl/dər blād/] **107–28**
shoulder-length hair [shōl/dər lĕngkth/ hër/] **33–2**
shoulder pads [shōl/dər pădz/] **231–20**
shovel [shŭv/əl] **176–7, 178–22**
show [shō] **236**–4, **236**–6, **236**–8
show [shō] **137**–C, **160**–C
shower [show/ər]
shower cap [show/ər kăp/] **108–1**
shower curtain [show/ər kür/tn] **57–12**
shower gel [show/ər jĕl/] **108–2**
showerhead [show/ər hĕd/] **57–11**
stall shower [stöl/ show/ər] **57** ✦
shredder [shrĕ/dər] **183–24**
shrimp [shrĭmp] **71–11, 212–18**
shut [shŭt] **146–4**
shuttle [shŭt/l] **152–19, 205–19**
sick [sĭk] **42–12**
homesick [hōm/sĭk/] **43–20**
side [sīd] **76–10**
sideburns [sīd/bürnz/] **33–7**
sideview mirror [sīd/vyōō/ mïr/ər] **158–3**
Side Salads [sīd/ săl/ədz] **80**
sidewalk [sīd/wök/] **129–24**
sight impaired [sīt/ ĭm përd/] **32–11**
sign [sīn] **4**–D
street sign [strēt/ sīn/] **129–26**
vacancy sign [vā/kən sē sīn/] **50–7**
vital signs monitor [vīt/l sīnz/ män/ə tər] **121–26**
sign [sīn] **48**–D
signal [sĭg/nəl]
strong signal [sträng/ sĭg/nəl] **14–11**
turn signal [türn/ sĭg/nəl] **158–6, 159–34**
weak signal [wēk/ sĭg/nəl] **14–12**
signature [sĭg/nə chər] **4–19**
SIGNS [sīnz] **154**
silk [sĭlk] **98–5**
simmer [sĭm/ər] **77**–P
sing [sĭng] **36**–O, **238**–B
single [sĭng/gəl]
single father [sĭng/gəl fä/dhər] **35–23**
single mother [sĭng/gəl mŭdh/ər] **35–22**
sink [sĭnk] **54–4, 57–23**
Sirius [sĭr/ē əs] **205** ✦
sister [sĭs/tər] **34–5, 35–27**
sister-in-law [sĭs/tər ĭn lö/] **34–16**
stepsister [stĕp/sĭs/tər] **35–29**
sitcom (situation comedy)
[sĭt/käm/] / [sĭch/ōō ā/shən käm/ə dē] **236–2**
sit down [sĭt/ down/] **6**–F
site [sīt] **126–2**
sitter [sĭt/ər] **166–9**
situation comedy (sitcom)
[sĭch/ōō ā/shən-käm/ə dē] / [sĭt/käm/] **236–2**
six [sĭks] **16**
six-pack [sĭks/păk/] **74–9, 74–21**
6-year-old boy [sĭks/yïr ōld/boy/] **31–9**
sixteen [sĭks/tēn/] **16**
sixteenth [sĭks/tēnth/] **16**
sixth [sĭksth] **16**
sixtieth [sĭks/tē əth] **16**

sixty [sĭks/tē] **16**

Sizes [sī/zəz] **96**

skate [skāt] **230**–U

skates [skāts] **231**–9, **231**–10

skateboard [skāt/börd/] **224**–7

skateboarding [skāt/bör/dĭng] **228**–13

skating [skā/tĭng] **227**–4, **227**–5, **227** ✦, **228**–10

ski [skē] **230**–V

skiing [skē/ĭng] **227**–1, **227**–3

waterskiing [wö/tər skē/ĭng] **227**–7

skill inventory [skĭl/ ĭn/vən tör/ē] **172**–12

Skills [skĭlz] **171**

SKILLS [skĭlz] **170, 171, 174**

skin [skĭn] **107**–31

skinless [skĭn/ləs] **70** ✦

skirt [skürt] **87**–10

skis [skēz] **231**–24

ski boots [skē/ bōōts] **231**–26

ski hat [skē/ hăt/] **90**–11

ski mask [skē/ măsk/] **90**–15

ski poles [skē/ pōlz/] **231**–25

skull [skŭl] **107**–47

skunk [skŭngk] **216**–12

SKU number [ĕs/kā/yōō/ nŭm/bər, skyōō/] **27**–5

sky [skī] **209**–9

skycap [skē/kăp/] **160**–1

skyscraper [skī/skrā/pər] **127**–13

slacks [slăks] **87**–12

slaves [slāvz] **198**–4

sledding [slĕd/ĭng] **227**–6

sledgehammer [slĕj/hăm/ər] **178**–23

sleeper [slē/pər] **91**–27

sleeping bag [slē/pĭng băg/] **226**–12

Sleepwear [slēp/wër] **91**

SLEEPWEAR [slēp/wër] **91**

sleepy [slē/pē] **42**–3

sleeve [slēv] **100**–6

long-sleeved [löng/slēvd/] **96**–14

short-sleeved [shört/slēvd] **96**–12

sleeveless [slēv/ləs] **96**–11

3/4 sleeved [thrē/kwör/tər slēvd/] **96**–13

slender [slĕn/dər] **32**–9

slice [slīs] **77**–C

slide [slīd] **194**–3, **224**–13

mudslide [mŭd/slīd/] **144**–6

sliding glass door [slī/dĭng glăs/ dör/] **53**–18

sling [slĭng] **113**–19

slip [slĭp] **91**–22, **91**–23, **132**–4

slippers [slĭp/ərz] **91**–26

slippery floor [slĭ/pər ē flör/] **179**–6

slow [slō] **23**–4

small [smöl] **96**–1, **96**–2, **97**–37

small town [smöl/ town/] **52**–3

smart phone [smärt/ fōn/] **15**–27

smell [smĕl] **106**–C

smile [smīl] **2**–D

smock [smök] **93**–26

smog [smäg, smög] **218**–11

smoggy [smä/gē, smö/–] **13**–14

smoke [smōk] **114**–G

smoke detector [smōk/ dĭ tĕk/tər] **51**–29

smoked turkey [smōkt/ tür/kē] **71**–25

Snack Foods [snăk/ fōōdz/] **73**

snail [snāl] **212**–22

snake [snāk] **213**–39

rattlesnake [ră/təl snāk] **213**–38

snap [snăp] **99**–26

sneeze [snēz] **110**–B

snorkeling [snör/kə lĭng] **227**–11

snow [snō]

snowboard [snō/börd/] **231**–23

snowboarding [snō/bör/dĭng] **227**–2

snowstorm [snō/störm/] **13**–23

snowing [snō/ĭng] **13**–12

soap [sōp] **57**–24, **61**–5, **108**–3

soap dish [sōp/ dĭsh/] **57**–25

soap opera [sōp/ äp/rə] **236**–5

sober [sō/ bər] **143** ✦

soccer [säk/ər] **229**–12

soccer ball [säk/ər böl/] **231**–12

social [sō/shəl]

Social Security card

[sō/shəl sĭ kyŏŏr/ə tē kärd/] **40**–5

Social Security number

[sō/shəl sĭ kyŏŏr/ə tē nŭm/bər] **4**–15

social worker [sō/shəl wür/kər] **169**–57

socks [säks] **86**–6

ankle socks [ang/kəl säks/] **91**–7

crew socks [krōō/ säks/] **91**–8

dress socks [drĕs/ säks/] **91**–9

low-cut socks [lō/kŭt säks/] **91**–10

Socks [säks] **91**

soda [sō/də] **73**–34, **79**–11

sofa [sō/fə] **56**–18

sofa cushions [sō/fə kŏō/shənz] **56** ✦

soft [söft] **23**–6

softball [söft/böl/] **229**–10

softener [sö/fən ər] **101**–6

software [söft/wër/] **167**–18, **196**–10

soil [soyl] **208**–2

solar [sō/lər]

solar eclipse [sō/lər ĭ klĭps/] **205**–16, **205** ✦

solar energy [sō/lər ĕn/ər jē] **218**–1

Solar System and the Planets

[sō/lər sĭs/təm ən dhə plăn/əts] **205**

soldier [sōl/jər] **169**–58

sole [sōl] **94**–21

solid [säl/əd] **96**–19

Solids [säl/ədz] **193**

solution [sə lōō/ shən] **192**–14

solve [sölv] **170**–M

son [sŭn] **34**–15

grandson [grăn/sŭn/, grănd/–] **34** ✦

son-in-law [sŭn/ĭn lö/] **34** ✦

sore throat [sör/ thrōt/] **110**–6

sort [sört] **101**–A

soul [sōl] **237**–28

soup [sōōp] **72**–18, **80**–16

soup bowl [sōōp/ bōl/] **83**–21

soupspoon [sōōp/spōōn/] **83**–32

Soup [sōōp] **77**

sour [söw/ər] **84**–4

sour cream [sow/ər krēm/] **72**–21

Sources [sör/səz] **218**

sous chef [sōō/ shĕf/] **185**–6

south [sowth] **155**–3

soybeans [soy/bēnz/] **177**–3

space [spās] **50**–18, **128**–5

space shuttle [spās/ shŭt/əl] **205**–19

space station [spās/ stā/shən] **205**–18

Space [spās] **205**

Space Exploration [spās/ ĕk/splə rā/shən] **205**

spades [spādz] **233**–30

spaghetti [spə gĕt/ē] **81**–26

spare tire [spër/ tīr/] **158**–23

sparrow [spăr/ō] **214**–7

spatula [spăch/ə lə] **78**–19

speak [spēk] **170**–N

speakers [spē/kərz] **50**–5, **206**–4, **234**–14

Special [spĕ/shəl] **80**

Specialists [spĕsh/ə lĭsts/] **120**

speech [spēch] **140**–2

speed limit [spēd/ lĭm/ət] **154**–4

speedometer [spĭ däm/ə tər] **159**–27

speed skating [spēd/skā/tĭng] **227** ✦

spell [spĕl] **4**–B

sphere [sfĭr] **193**–42

spider [spī/dər] **214**–29

spill [spĭl] **218**–17

spinach [spĭn/ĭch] **69**–11

spinach salad [spĭn/ĭch săl/əd] **80**–13

spinal column [spī/nəl käl/əm] **107**–49

spiral notebook [spī/rəl nōt/bŏŏk/] **7**–29

splint [splĭnt] **117**–14

sponge [spŭnj] **61**–19

sponge mop [spŭnj/ mäp/] **61**–6

spoon [spōōn] **55**–5, **78**–9

soupspoon [sōōp/spōōn/] **83**–32

tablespoon [tā/bəl spōōn/] **75**–7

teaspoon [tē/spōōn/] **75**–6, **83**–31

spoon [spōōn] **77**–F

sports [spörts]

sports car [spörts/ kär/] **156**–4

sports coat [spörts/ kōt/] **89**–14

sports jacket [spörts/ jăk/ət] **89**–14

sports program [spörts/ prō/grăm] **236**–11

sports shirt [spörts/ shürt/] **88**–4

sport-utility vehicle (SUV) [spört/
yōō tĭl/ə tē vē/ĭ kəl] / [ĕs/yōō/vē/] **156**–7

SPORTS [spörts] **228, 229, 230, 231**

SPORTS EQUIPMENT [spörts/ ĭ kwĭp/mənt] **231**

SPORTS VERBS [spörts/ vürbz/] **230**

sprained ankle [sprānd/ ăng/kəl] **110**–18

spray [sprā] **108**–12, **113**–32

spray gun [sprā/ gŭn/] **181**–21

spray starch [sprā/ stärch/] **101**–12

spread [sprĕd]

bedspread [bĕd/sprĕd/] **59**–11

spring [sprĭng] **21**–37, **58**–19

sprinkler [sprĭng/klər] **53**–22

square [skwër] **193**–30

squash [skwäsh, skwösh] **69**–24

squeegee [skwē/jē] **61**–15

squid [skwĭd] **212**–7

squirrel [skwür/əl] **215**–21

stadium [stā/dē əm] **126**–1

staff [stăf] **185** ✦
Staff [stăf] **120**
stage [stāj] **194**–16
   stage clips [stāj/ klĭps/] **194**–24
stain [stān] **181**–24
stained [stānd] **97**–42
stairs [stërz] **50**–10
stairway [stër/wā/] **50**–10
stall shower [stöl/ show/ər] **57** ✦
stamps [stămps] **134**–18, **134**–23, **183**–47
   stamp machine [stămp/ mə shēn/] **135**–11
stand [stănd] **152**–18
   checkstand [chĕk/stănd/] **73**–12
   newsstand [nōōz/stănd/] **128**–12
   nightstand [nīt/stănd/] **58**–23
stand [stănd] **141**–D
   stand up [stănd/ ŭp/] **6**–D
standard time [stăn/dərd tīm/] **19**–26
staple [stā/pəl] **171**–F
stapler [stā/plər] **183**–28
staples [stā/pəlz] **183**–29
star [stär] **205**–13
   starfish [stär/fĭsh/] **212**–16
   star key [stär/ kē/] **14**–6
starch [stärch] **101**–12
start [stärt] **12**–A, **40**–B, **230**–R
starting point [stär/tĭng poynt/] **162**–1
starving [stär/vĭng] **43** ✦
state [stāt] **4**–8, **146**–2
   state capital [stāt kă/pət əl] **139**–22
   state senator [stāt sĕn/ə tər] **139**–25
state [stāt] **15**–G, **195**–A
State Government [stāt gŭ/ vərn mənt] **139**
statement [stāt/mənt] **132**–16
station [stā/shən]
   bus station [bŭs/ stā/shən] **124**–7
   fire station [fīr/ stā/shən] **125**–12
   gas station [găs/ stā/shən] **125**–10
   gas station attendant
      [găs/ stā/shən ə tĕn/dənt] **162**–3
   lifeguard station [līf/gärd/ stā/shən] **225**–21
   police station [pə lēs/ stā/shən] **124**–6
   space station [spās/ stā/shən] **205**–18
   station wagon [stā/shən wăg/ən] **156**–6
   subway station [sŭb/wā/ stā/shən] **151**–11
Station [stā/shən] **152**
stationery [stā/shə nër/ ē] **183**–42
stay [stā]
   stay away [stā ə wā/] **147**–I
   stay fit [stā fĭt/] **114**–E
   stay on the line [stā ön dhə līn/] **15**–H
   stay on well-lit streets [stā ön wĕl lĭt/ strēts/] **143**–B
Stay Well [stā wĕl/] **114**
steak [stāk] **70**–2, **81**–24
   broiled steak [broyld/ stāk/] **76**–3
   halibut steak [hăl/ə bŭt stāk/] **71**–6
   salmon steak [săm/ən stāk/] **71**–4
   steak knife [stāk/ nīf/] **83**–29
steal [stēl] **142** ✦
steam [stēm] **77**–D
steamed vegetables [stēmd/ vĕj/tə bəlz] **81**–32
steamer [stē/mər] **78**–3

steel [stēl]
   steel toe boots [stēl/ tō/ bōōts/] **92**–6
   steel-wool soap pads [stēl/wŏŏl/ sōp/ pădz/] **61**–5
steering wheel [stïr/ĭng wēl/] **159**–26
stems [stĕmz] **211**–9
step [stĕp]
   stepbrother [stĕp/brŭdh/ər] **35**–30
   stepdaughter [stĕp/dö/tər] **35** ✦
   stepfather [stĕp/fä/dhər] **35**–25
   stepladder [stĕp/lăd/ər] **61**–13
   stepmother [stĕp/mŭdh/ər] **35**–26
   steps [stĕps] **53**–3
   stepsister [stĕp/sĭs/tər] **35**–29
stereo system [stër/ē ō sĭs/təm] **56**–8
sterile [stër/əl]
   sterile pad [stër/əl păd/] **117**–6
   sterile tape [stër/əl tāp/] **117**–7
stethoscope [stĕth/ə skōp/] **118**–10
stewing beef [stōō/ĭng bēf/] **70**–3
stick [stĭk] **231**–11, **232**–11
   drumsticks [drŭm/stĭks/] **70**–23
   lipstick [lĭp/stĭk/] **109**–38
   stick shift [stĭk/ shĭft/] **159**–50
   yardstick [yärd/stĭk/] **181**–16
sticker [stĭk/ər] **102**–3, **136**–13
sticky notes [stĭk/ē nōts/] **183**–39
stir [stür] **77**–O
   stir-fried beef [stür/frīd/ bēf/] **76**–6
stitches [stĭch/əz] **117**–15
stock clerk [stäk/ klürk/] **169**–59
stockings [stäk/ĭngz] **91**–17
stomach [stŭm/ək] **107**–41
   stomachache [stŭm/ək āk/] **110**–4
stop [stäp] **129**–16, **151**–13, **154**–1
   stopover [stäp/ō/vər] **161** ✦
stop [stäp] **155**–D
Stop [stäp] **152**
stopped up [stäpt/ ŭp/] **63**–19
storage [stör/ĭj] **72**–25, **78**–4
   storage locker [stör/ĭj läk/ər] **50**–17
store [stör]
   bookstore [bŏŏk/stör/] **130**–4
   candy store [kăn/dē stör/] **131**–17
   card store [kärd/stör/] **130**–7
   convenience store [kən vēn/yəns stör/] **128**–3
   department store [dĭ pärt/mənt stör/] **131**–13
   electronics store [ē lĕk trän/ĭks stör/] **131**–20
   furniture store [für/nĭ chər stör/] **126**–8
   hardware store [härd/wër/ stör/] **148**–4
   home improvement store
      [hōm/ ĭm prōōv/mənt stör/] **127**–20
   jewelry store [jōō/əl rē stör/] **130**–2
   maternity store [mə tür/nə tē stör/] **131**–19
   men's store [mĕnz/ stör/] **130** ✦
   music store [myōō/zĭk stör/] **130**–1
   office supply store [ö/fəs sə plī/ stör/] **127**–21
   pet store [pĕt/ stör/] **130**–6
   shoe store [shōō/ stör/] **130**–10
   toy store [toy/ stör/] **130**–5
   video store [vĭd/ē ō stör/] **129**–20
Store [stör] **99**
STORE [stör] **72**–73

storeroom [stör/rōōm/] **185**–3
storm [störm] **13**–19
   hailstorm [hāl/störm/] **13**–21
   snowstorm [snō/störm/] **13**–23
   storm door [störm/ dör/] **53**–10
   thunderstorm [thŭn/dər störm/] **13**–16
story [stör/ē]
   action story [ăk/shən stör/ē] **237**–19
   adventure story [ăd vĕn/chər stör/ē] **237**–19
   horror story [hör/ər stör/ē, här/–] **237**–17
   science fiction story [sī/əns fĭk/shən stör/ē] **237**–18
   two-story house [tōō/stör/ē hows/] **52** ✦
stove [stōv] **54**–18, **226**–16
stow [stō] **160**–G
straight [strāt] **155**–A
   straight hair [strāt/ hër/] **33**–9
   straight line [strāt/ līn/] **193**–22
   straight pin [strāt/ pĭn/] **100**–12
strainer [strā/nər] **78**–22
straw [strö] **79**–18
   strawberries [strö/bër/ēz] **68**–14
   straw hat [strö/ hăt/] **90**–23
stream [strēm] **204** ✦
street [strēt] **150**–5, **155**–8
   streetlight [strēt/līt/] **148**–3
   street sign [strēt/ sīn] **129**–26
   street vender [strēt/ vĕn/dər] **129**–29
STREETS [strēts] **126**–127
strep throat [strĕp/ thrōt/] **111**–4
stress [strĕs] **115**–4
stretch [strĕch] **230**–M
stretcher [strĕch/ər] **121**–33
string [strĭng]
   string beans [strĭng/ bēnz/] **69**–8
   string lights [strĭng/ līts/] **239**–18
   string of pearls [strĭng/ əv pürlz/] **95**–39
Strings [strĭngz] **238**
striped [strīpt] **96**–20
stripper [strĭ/pər] **181**–42
stroller [strō/lər] **37**–18
strong signal [ströng/ sĭg/nəl] **14**–11
stub [stŭb] **165**–11
stucco [stŭk/ō] **178**–15
student [stōōd/nt] **6**–5
study [stŭ/dē] **10**–D, **137**–A
STUDYING [stŭ/dē ĭng] **8**–9
stuffed animals [stŭft/ ăn/ə məlz] **59**–15
style [stīl/] **88** ✦
Styles [stīlz] **96**
STYLES [stīlz] **96**
stylist [stī/lĭst] **167**–31
SUBJECTS [sŭb/jĭkts/] **188**–189
submit [səb mĭt/] **48**–C
substitute [sŭb/stə tōōt/] **79**–20
subtract [səb trăkt/] **192**–B
suburbs [sŭb/ürbz/] **52**–2
subway [sŭb/wā/] **151**–12
   subway car [sŭb/wā/ kär/] **152**–6
   subway station [sŭb/wā/ stā/shən] **151**–11
Subway Station [sŭb/wā/ stā/shən] **152**
Succeed [sək sēd/] **10**
SUCCEEDING IN SCHOOL [sək sē/dĭng ən skōōl/] **10**

suede [swād] **99**–8
sugar [shŏŏg/ər] **73**–30
   sugar bowl [shŏŏg/ər bōl/] **55**–14
   sugar-free [shŏŏg/ər frē/] **122**–7
   sugar substitute [shŏŏg/ər sŭb/stə tōōt/] **79**–20
suit [sōōt] **87**–11
   bathing suit [bā/dhĭng sōōt/] **90**–26
   business suit [bĭz/nəs sōōt/] **88**–11
   jumpsuit [jŭmp/sōōt/] **93**–24
   three piece suit [thrē/pēs/ sōōt/] **88** ✦
   wet suit [wĕt/ sōōt/] **225**–4
suite [swēt] **184**–16
sum [sŭm] **192**–7
sumac [sōō/măk] **210**–23
summer [sŭm/ər] **21**–38
sun [sŭn] **209**–8
   sunblock [sŭn/blăk/] **108**–8, **225**–0
   sunburn [sŭn/bürn/] **110**–14
   sunflower [sŭn/flow/ər] **211**–10
   sunglasses [sŭn/glăs/əz] **90**–27
   sunrise [sŭn/ rīz] **18**–14
   sunscreen [sŭn/skrēn/] **108**–7, **225**–10
   sunset [sŭn/ sĕt] **18**–19
Sunday [sŭn/dā, –dē] **20**–8
sunny [sŭn/ē] **13**–9, **76**–10
superintendent [sōō/prĭn tĕn/dənt, sōō/pər ĭn–] **50**–8
supermarket [sōō/pər/ mär/kət] **127**–18
supervise [sōō/pər vīz/] **170**–O
supervisor [sōō/pər vī/zər] **165**–8, **175**–4
Supplies [sə plīz/] **100, 183**
SUPPLIES [sə plīz/] **61, 180–181**
supply [sə plī/] **127**–21
   supply cabinet [sə plī/ kăb/ə nət] **182**–1
support [sə pört/] **179**–18
   support group [sə pört/ grōōp/] **115**–15
supporter [sə pör/tər] **91**–6
Supreme Court [sə prēm/ kört/] **138**–11
surfboard [sürf/börd/] **225**–16
surfer [sür/fər] **225**–15
surfing [sür/fĭng] **227**–9, **227**–10, **227** ✦
surgeon [sür/jən] **121**–36
Surgeon [sür/jən] **93**
surge protector [sürj/ prə tĕk/tər] **196**–1
surgical [sür/jĭ kəl]
   surgical cap [sür/jĭ kəl kăp/] **121**–37
   surgical gloves [sür/jĭ kəl glŭvz/] **121**–39
   surgical gown [sür/jĭ kəl gown/] **93**–37, **121**–38
   surgical mask [sür/jĭ kəl măsk/] **93**–36
   surgical nurse [sür/jĭ kəl nürs/] **120**–9
   surgical scrub cap [sür/jĭ kəl skrŭb/ kăp/] **93**–35
   surgical scrubs [sür/jĭ kəl skrŭbz/] **93**–38
Surgical Assistant [sür/jĭ kəl ə sĭs/tənt] **93**
surprised [sər prīzd/, sə–] **43**–30
suspenders [sə spĕn/dərz] **94**–1
suspense [sŭs/pĕns] **237**–20
SUV (sport-utility vehicle) [ĕs/yōō/vē/] /
   [spört/ yōō tĭl/ə tē vē/ĭ kəl] **156**–7
swallow [swäl/ō] **116**–J
swap meet [swäp/ mēt/] **222**–6
sweat [swĕt]
   sweatpants [swĕt/ pănts/] **89**–23
   sweatshirt [swĕt/ shürt/] **89**–22

sweater [swĕt/ər] **28**–2, **87**–14
   cardigan sweater [kär/də gən swĕt/ər] **88**–2
   pullover sweater [pōōl/ō/vər swĕt/ər] **88**–3
sweep [swēp] **60**–J
sweet potatoes [swĕt pə tā/tōz] **69**–18
sweets [swĕts] **84**–9
swim [swĭm] **230**–L
   swimsuit [swĭm/sōōt/] **90**–26
swimming [swĭm/ĭng]
   swimming pool [swĭm/ĭng pōōl/] **51**–22
   swimming trunks [swĭm/ĭng trŭngks/] **90**–22
swing [swĭng] **230**–Q
swings [swĭngz] **224**–11
Swiss cheese [swĭs/ chēz/] **71**–27
switch [swĭch] **58**–27
swollen finger [swō/lən fĭng/gər] **110**–16
swordfish [sörd/fĭsh/] **71**–5, **212**–10
symbol [sĭm/bəl] **155**–8
SYMPTOMS AND INJURIES
   [sĭmp/təmz ən ĭn/jə rēz] **110**
synagogue [sĭn/ə gäg/] **127**–16
synthetic materials [sĭn thĕ/tĭk mə tïr/ē əlz] **98** ✦
syringe [sə rĭnj/] **118**–12
syrup [sĭr/əp, sür/–] **113**–29
system [sĭs/təm]
   fuel injection system
      [fyōō/əl ĭn jĕk/shən sĭs/təm] **158**–17
   stereo system [stĕr/ē ō sĭs/təm] **56**–8
SYSTEM [sĭs/təm] **141**
tab [tăb] **197**–7
table [tā/bəl]
   bed table [bĕd/ tā/bəl] **121**–21
   changing table [chān/jĭng tā/bəl] **59**–1
   coffee table [kö/fē tā/bəl] **56**–19
   dining room table [dī/nĭng rōōm/ tā/bəl] **55**–9
   end table [ĕnd/ tā/bəl] **56**–14
   examination table [ĭg zăm/ə nā/shən tā/bəl] **118**–7
   folding card table [fōl/dĭng kärd/ tā/bəl] **102**–4
   night table [nīt/ tā/bəl] **58**–23
   operating table [äp/ə rā/tĭng tā/bəl] **121**–40
   periodic table [pïr/ē äd/ĭk tā/bəl] **195**–26
   picnic table [pĭk/nĭk tā/bəl] **224**–8
   pool table [pōōl/ tā/bəl] **50**–15
   tablecloth [tā/bəl klöth/] **55**–12
   tablespoon [tā/bəl spōōn/] **75**–7
   table tennis [tā/bəl tĕn/əs] **228**–14
   tray table [trā/ tā/bəl] **161**–21
   turntable [türn/tā/bəl] **234**–12
tablet [tăb/lət] **113**–22, **113**–27
tackle [tăk/əl] **230**–F
taco [tä/kō] **79**–8
tags [tăgz] **92**–15, **136**–13
tail [tāl] **216**–22
tail light [tāl/ līt/] **158**–13
tail pipe [tāl/ pīp/] **158**–15
tailor [tā/lər] **100**–3
take [tāk]
   do not take with dairy products
      [dōō nät/ tāk/ wĭth dër/ē präd/ŭkts] **112**–A
   take a bath [tāk/ ə băth/] **108**–B
   take a break [tāk/ ə brāk/] **11**–H
   take a citizenship test
      [tāk/ ə sĭt/ə zən shĭp tĕst/] **140**–I

take a driver education course
   [tāk/ ə drī/vərz ĕj/ə kā/shən körs/] **137**–B
take a driver's training course
   [tāk/ ə drī/vərz trā/nĭng körs/] **137**–G
take a message [tāk/ ə mĕs/ĭj] **171**–Q
take a nap [tāk/ ə năp/] **53**–A
take a picture [tāk/ ə pĭk/chər] **206**–B
take a seat [tāk/ ə sĕt/] **6**–F
take a shower [tāk/ ə show/ər] **38**–C, **108**–A
take a tour [tāk/ ə tōōr/] **220**–A
take a written test [tāk/ ə rĭt/ən tĕst] **137**–E
take care of children [tāk/ kër/ əv chĭl/drən] **170**–P
take cover [tāk/ kŭv/ər] **147**–J
take dictation [tāk/ dĭk/tā shən] **171**–K
take in [tāk/ ĭn] **100**–D
take medicine [tāk/ mĕd/ə sən] **114**–D
take notes [tāk/ nōts/] **10**–C
take off [tāk/ öf/] **109**–Q, **160**–J
take one hour before eating
   [tāk/ wŭn/ ow/ər bĭ för/ ē/tĭng] **112**–B
take out [tāk/ owt/] **9**–Y, **60**–Q, **82** ✦
take ownership [tāk/ ō/nər shĭp/] **49**–K
take temperature [tāk/ tĕm/prə chər] **118**–B
take the bus to school
   [tāk/ dhə bŭs/ tə skōōl/] **38**–H
take the car to a mechanic
   [tāk/ dhə kär/ tə dhə mə kăn/ĭk] **157**–C
take the children to school
   [tāk/ dhə chĭl/drən tə skōōl/] **38**–G
take the order [tāk/ dhē ör/dər] **82**–E
take with food [tāk/ wĭth fōōd/] **112**–A
take x-rays [tāk/ ĕks/rāz/] **119**–B
Taking a Flight [tā/kĭng ə flīt/] **160**
Taking a Test [tā/kĭng ə tĕst/] **10**
TAKING A TRIP [tā/kĭng ə trĭp/] **162–163**
Taking Care of Your Car [tā/kĭng kër/ əv yər kär/] **157**
TAKING CARE OF YOUR HEALTH
   [tā/kĭng kër əv yər hĕlth/] **114–115**
talk [tök]
   talk show [tök/ shō/] **236**–4
   talk therapy [tök/ thër/ ə pē] **115**–13
talk [tök]
   talk about [tök ə bowt/] **174**–L
   talk on the phone [tök/ ön dhə fōn/] **15**–C
   talk to friends [tök/ tə frĕndz/] **173**–A
   talk to the teacher [tök/ tə dhə tē/chər] **6**–B
tall [töl] **32**–4
tambourine [tăm/bə rēn/] **238**–17
tan [tăn] **24**–18
tangerines [tăn/jə rēnz/] **68**–9
tank [tăngk] **158**–10, **225**–5
   tank top [tăngk/ täp/] **89**–24
   tank truck [tăngk/ trŭk] **156**–20
tape [tāp]
   clear tape [klĕr/ tāp/] **183**–30
   correction tape [kə rĕk/shən tāp/] **183**–37
   duct tape [dŭkt/ tāp/] **181**–49
   electrical tape [ĭ lek/trĭ kəl tāp/] **181**–43
   masking tape [măs/kĭng tāp/] **181**–53
   packing tape [păk/ĭng tāp/] **183**–32
   sterile tape [stĕr/ əl tāp/] **117**–7
   tape measure [tāp mĕzh/ər] **100**–17, **181**–45

target [tär/gət] 231–7
taste [tāst] 106–D
tattoo [tă tōō/] 32–18
tax / taxes [tăks] / [tăks/əz] 27–8
taxi [tăk/sē] 150–3
  hail a taxi [hāl/ ə tăk/sē] 152 ✦
  taxi driver [tăk/sē drī/vər] 152–21
  taxi license [tăk/sē lī/səns] 152–22
  taxi stand [tăk/sē stănd/] 152–18
TB (tuberculosis) [tē/bē/] / [tōō bür/kyə lō/səs] 111–15
TDD [tē/dē/dē/] 15–26
tea [tē] 79–12, 81–39, 81–40
  teacup [tē/kŭp] 55–6
  tea kettle [tē/ kĕt/l] 54–21
  teapot [tē/pät/] 55–16
  teaspoon [tē/spōōn/] 75–6, 83–31
teach [tēch] 170–Q
teacher [tē/chər] 5–8, 6–4, 22–5
  teacher's aide [tē/chərz ād/] 5–16
team [tēm] 145–20, 229–3
TEAM SPORTS [tēm/ spörts/] 229
technical school [tĕk/nĭ kəl skōōl/] 188–5
technician [tĕk nĭsh/ən]
  computer technician
    [kəm pyōō/tər tĕk nĭsh/ən] 167–19, 182–12
  emergency medical technician (EMT)
    [ĭ mür/jən sē mĕd/ĭ kəl tĕk nish/ən] / [ē/ĕm/tē]
    121–32
  medical records technician
    [mĕd/ĭ kəl rĕk/ərdz tĕk nish/ən] 168–39
Technician [tĕk nĭsh/ən] 93
teddy bear [tĕd/ē bër/] 37–23
teen / teenager [tēn] / [tē/nā/jər] 31–11
teething ring [tē/dhĭng rĭng/] 37–25
teeth / tooth [tēth] / [tōōth] 106–7
  toothache [tōōth/āk/] 110–2
  toothbrush [tōōth/brŭsh/] 57–21, 109–22
  toothbrush holder [tōōth/brŭsh/ hōl/dər] 57–22
  toothpaste [tōōth/pāst/] 109–23
telemarketer [tĕl/ə mär/kə tər] 169–60
TELEPHONE [tĕl/ə fōn/] 14–15
Telephone Skills [tĕl/ə fōn/ skĭlz/] 171
telescope [tĕl/ə skōp/] 205–23
television / TV [tĕl/ə vĭzh/ən] / [tē/vē/] 56–6
  big-screen TV [bĭg/skrēn/ tē/vē/] 50–14
  flat panel TV [flăt/ păn/əl tē/vē/] 234–7
  flat screen TV [flăt/ skrēn/ tē/vē/] 234–7
  portable TV [pör/tə bəl tē/vē/] 234–8
teller [tĕl/ər] 132–1
Teller [tĕl/ər] 132
Telling Time [tĕ/lĭng tīm/] 18
temperature [tĕm/prə chər] 110–8
  temperature gauge [tĕm/prə chər gāj/] 159–30
Temperature [tĕm/prə chər] 13
ten [tĕn] 16
  ten after one [tĕn/ ăf/tər wŭn/] 18–8
  ten dollars [tĕn/ däl/ərz] 26–9
  10 percent [tĕn/ pər sĕnt/] 17–12
  ten thousand [tĕn/ thow/zənd] 16
  10-year-old girl [tĕn/yïr ōld/ gürl/] 31–10
tenant [tĕn/ənt] 50–6
TENANT MEETING [tĕn/ənt mē/tĭng] 64–65

tennis [tĕn/əs] 228–15
  table tennis [tā/bəl tĕn/əs] 228–14
  tennis court [tĕn/əs kört/] 224–6
  tennis racket [tĕn/əs răk/ət] 231–2
  tennis shoes [tĕn/əs shōōz/] 95–32
tent [tĕnt] 226–10
tenth [tĕnth] 16
Terminal [tür/mə nəl] 160
termites [tür/mīts] 63–22
term [türm] 139 ✦
Terms [türmz] 199
terrified [tĕr/ə fīd/] 43 ✦
test [tĕst] 121–30
  test booklet [tĕst/ bŏŏk/lət] 10–1
  testing area [tĕs/tĭng ër/ē ə] 136–2
  test tube [tĕst/ tōōb/] 195–42
Test [tĕst] 10
text [tĕkst]
  textbook [tĕkst/bŏŏk/, tĕks/-] 7–25
  text box [tĕkst/ bäks/, tĕks/-] 197–13
  text message [tĕkst/ mĕs/ĭj, tĕks/-] 14–19
thank [thăngk] 12–E, 174–N
Thanksgiving [thăngks gĭv/ĭng] 22–17
theater [thē/ə tər] 126–6, 127–23
theft [thĕft] 142–9
therapist [thër/ ə pĭst] 115–12, 115–14, 168–45
therapy [thër/ ə pē] 115–11, 115–13
thermal undershirt [thür/məl ŭn/dər shürt/] 91–2
thermometer [thər mäm/ə tər] 118–11
thick [thĭk] 23–7
thighs [thīz] 70–22, 106–19
thimble [thĭm/bəl] 100–15
thin [thĭn] 23–8, 32–9
THINGS [thĭngz] 23
think [thĭnk] 191–E
third [thürd] 16
Third Floor [thürd/ flör/] 50
thirsty [thür/stē] 42–2
thirteen [thür/tēn/] 16
  thirteen colonies [thür/tēn/ kä/lə nēz] 198–1
thirteenth [thür/tēnth/] 16
thirtieth [thür/tē əth] 16
thirty [thür/tē] 16
  35 mm camera
    [thür/tē fīv/ mĭl/ə mē/tər kăm/rə] 235–21
this week [dhĭs/ wēk/] 20–19
thorn [thörn] 211–29
thread [thrĕd] 99–23, 100–11
three [thrē] 16
  three piece suit [thrē/pēs/ sōōt/] 88 ✦
  3-ring binder [thrē/ rĭng/ bīn/dər] 7–27
  3/4 sleeved [thrē/kwör/tər slēv/] 96–13
  three times a week [thrē/ tīmz/ ə wēk/] 20–24
throat [thrōt] 107–35, 110–6, 111–4
  throat lozenges [thrōt/ lăz/ən jəz] 113–30
through [thrōō] 153–K
throw [thrō] 230–C
  throw away [thrō/ ə wā/] 11–N
  throw up [thrō/ ŭp/] 110–E
throw pillow [thrō/ pĭl/ō] 56–2
thumb [thŭm] 106–16
thunderstorm [thŭn/dər störm/] 13–16

Thursday [thürz/dā, –dē] 20–12
tick [tĭk] 214–27
ticket [tĭk/ət] 152–15, 161–19
  ticket agent [tĭk/ət ā/jənt] 160–3
  ticket window [tĭk/ət wĭn/dō/] 152–12
tidal wave [tīd/l wāv/] 145–17
tide [tīd] 225 ✦
tie [tī] 88–12, 89–16, 92–13, 229 ✦
tie [tī] 86–A
tiger [tī/gər] 217–37
tight [tīt] 97–29
tights [tīts] 91–19
tile [tīl] 57–10, 178–11, 178–D
time [tīm]
  Alaska time [ə lăs/kə tīm/] 19–28
  arrival time [ə rī/vəl tīm/] 161 ✦
  Atlantic time [ət lăn/tĭk tīm/] 19–33
  Central time [sĕn/trəl tīm/] 19–31
  daylight saving time [dā/līt/ sā/vĭng tīm/] 19–25
  departure time [dĭ pär/chər tīm/] 161 ✦
  Eastern time [ē/stərn tīm/] 19–32
  Hawaii-Aleutian time
    [hə wī/ē ə lōō/shən tīm/] 19–27
  Mountain time [mown/tn tīm/] 19–30
  Newfoundland time
    [nōō/fən lənd tīm/, –fənd–] 19–34
  on time [än/ tīm/, ön/ tīm/] 19–23, 161–29
  Pacific time [pə sĭf/ĭk tīm/] 19–29
  standard time [stăn/dərd tīm/] 19–26
  three times a week [thrē tīmz/ ə wēk/] 20–24
  time clock [tīm/ kläk/] 165–7
Time [tīm] 18
TIME [tīm] 18–19
timer [tī/mər] 78–18
Times of Day [tīmz/ əv dā/] 18
Time Zones [tīm/ zōnz/] 19
tire [tīr] 158–5, 158–23, 162–F
tired [tīrd] 43–32
title [tīt/l] 133–14, 190–5
toad [tōd] 212–28
toast [tōst] 80–4
toaster [tō/stər] 54–6
  toaster oven [tō/stər ŭv/ən] 54–15
today [tə dā/] 20–5
toddler [täd/lər] 31–8
toe [tō] 92–6, 94–23, 105–10
  toenail [tō/nāl/] 106 ✦
Tofu [tō/fōō/] 77
toggle bolt [täg/əl bōlt/] 180–38
to-go box [tə gō/ bäks/] 82–5
toilet [toy/lət] 57–19
  toilet brush [toy/lət brŭsh/] 57–18
  toilet paper [toy/lət pā/pər] 57–17, 146–13
token [tō/kən] 152–10
tomatoes [tə mā/tōz] 69–6
tomorrow [tə mär/ō, –mör/ō] 20–6
tongs [tängz, töngz] 78–23, 195–44
tongue [tŭng] 106–8
too [tōō]
  too big [tōō/ bĭg/] 97–38
  too expensive [tōō/ ĭk spĕn/sĭv/] 97–44
  too small [tōō/ smöl/] 97–37

tool belt [tool/ bĕlt/] **92**–3
TOOLS AND BUILDING SUPPLIES
   [toolz/ ən bĭl/dĭng sə plīz/] **180–181**
tooth / teeth [tooth] / [tēth] **106**–7
   toothache [tooth/āk/] **110**–2
   toothbrush [tooth/brŭsh/] 57–21, **109**–22
   toothbrush holder [tooth/brŭsh/ hōl/dər] **57**–22
   toothpaste [tooth/pāst/] **109**–23
top [täp] **88**–7, **89**–24
torn [törn] **97**–41
tornado [tör nā/dō] **145**–15
torso [tör/sō/] **106** ✦
tortoise [tör/təs] **213**–42
total [tōt/l] **27**–9
totebag [tōt/ băg/] **94**–19
touch [tŭch] **106**–E
towel [tow/əl]
   bath towel [băth/ tow/əl] **57**–14
   dish towel [dĭsh/ tow/əl] **61**–22
   hand towel [hănd/ tow/əl] **57**–15
   paper towels [pā/pər tow/əlz] **54**–3
   towel rack [tow/əl răk/] **57**–13
towelettes [tow/əl ĕts] **146**–12
tower [tow/ər] **196**–3
town [town] **52**–3
   town car [town/ kär/] **152**–20
   townhouse [town/hows/] **52**–6
tow truck [tō/ trŭk/] **156**–14
toy [toy]
   toy chest [toy/ chĕst/] **59**–16
   toy store [toy/ stör/] **130**–5
Toys and Games [toyz/ ən gāmz/] **59**
track [trăk] 5–21, **152**–14
   track and field [trăk/ ən fēld/] **228**–18
tractor [trăk/tər] **177**–9
   tractor trailer [trăk/tər trā/lər] **156**–15
traffic light [trăf/ĭk līt/] **128**–8
TRAFFIC SIGNS [trăf/ĭk sīnz/] **154**
tragedy [trăj/ə dē] **237**–14
trailer [trā/lər] 156–15, **156**–17
train [trān] 150–7, **233**–27
training [trā/nĭng] 172–2, 172–5, **172**–7
   training pants [trā/nĭng pănts/] **37**–11
Training [trā/nĭng] **172**
Train Station [trān/ stā/shən] **152**
transcribe [trăn skrīb/] **171**–C
transfer [trăns für/, trăns/fər] **152**–5
transfer [trăns für/, trăns/fər] **171**–O
translate [trănz/lāt] **8**–C
translator [trănz/lā/tər, trăns/–] **168**–35
Transmission [trănz mĭsh/ən, trăns–] **159**
Transportation [trăns/pər tā/shən] **152**
TRANSPORTATION [trăns/pər tā/shən] 150–151, **152**
trash [trăsh]
   trash bags [trăsh/ băgz/] **61**–24
   trash bin [trăsh/ bĭn/] **51**–23
   trash chute [trăsh/ shoot/] **51**–26
travel [trăv/əl] **41**–P
travel agency [trăv/əl ā/jən sē] **131**–14
tray [trā] 55–17, **83**–10
   tray table [trā tā/bəl] **161**–21
Tree [trē] **210**

trees [trēz] 208–1, **239**–16
TREES AND PLANTS [trēz/ ən plănts/] **210**
trench coat [trĕnch/ kōt/] **90**–21
trial [trī/əl] **140**–5
triangle [trī/ăng/gəl] **193**–32
tricycle [trī/sĭ kəl] **224**–12
trigonometry [trĭg/ə năm/ə trē] **192**–18
trim [trĭm] **176**–B
trip [trĭp] 152–16, **152**–17
tripe [trīp] **70**–8
tripod [trī/päd] **235**–25
trombone [trăm bōn/] **238**–10
trout [trowt] **71**–1
trowel [trow/əl] 176–10, **178**–13
truck [trŭk] **150**–5
   dump truck [dŭmp/trŭk/] **156**–19
   fire truck [fīr/ trŭk/] **144**–10
   garbage truck [gär/bĭj trŭk/] **127**–22
   hand truck [hănd/ trŭk/] **175**–11
   pickup truck [pĭk/ŭp trŭk/] **156**–12
   tank truck [tăngk/ trŭk/] **156**–20
   tow truck [tō/ trŭk/] **156**–14
   truck driver [trŭk/ drī/vər] **169**–61
TRUCKS [trŭks] **156**
trumpet [trŭm/pət] **238**–11
Trunk [trŭngk] **158**
trunks [trŭngks] 158–11, 210–4, **217**–47
   swimming trunks [swĭm/ĭng trŭngks/] **90**–22
try on [trī/ön] **95**–C
TSA agent [tē/ĕs/ā/ ā/jənt] **160**–5
T-shirt [tē/shürt/] **86**–4
tsunami [soo nä/ mē, tsoo–] **145**–17
tub [tŭb]
   bathtub [băth/tŭb/] **57**–2
tuba [too/bə] **238**–12
tube [toob] 74–12, 74–24, **195**–42
tuberculosis (TB)
   [too bür/kyə lō/səs] / [tē/bē/] **111**–15
Tuesday [tooz/dā, –dē] **20**–10
tulip [too/ləp] **211**–11
tuna [too/nə] 71–7, 72–19, **212**–8
tuner [too/nər] **234**–13
turbulence [tür/byə ləns] **161**–22
turkey [tür/kē] 70–17, **239**–14
   roasted turkey [rōs/təd tür/kē] **76**–4
   smoked turkey [smōkt/ tür/kē] **71**–25
turn [türn] 154–5, 154–7, **154**–8
   turn signal [türn/ sĭg/nəl] 158–6, **159**–34
   turnstile [türn/stīl/] **152**–8
   turntable [türn/tā/bəl] **234**–12
turn [türn]
   turn in [türn/ ĭn/] **191**–M
   turn left [türn/ lĕft/] **155**–C
   turn off [türn/ öf/] 11–P, 160–I, 174–G, **219**–G
   turn on [türn/ ön/, –än/] **11**–B
   turn right [türn/ rīt/] **155**–B
turnips [tür/nəps] **69**–16
turquoise [tür/koyz, –kwoyz] **24**–9
turtle [tür/tl] **213**–43
   turtleneck [tür/tl nĕk/] **96**–9
tusk [tŭsk] **217**–48
tuxedo [tŭk sē/dō] **89**–17

TV Programs [tē/vē/ prō/grămz] **236**
TV / television [tē/vē/] / [tĕl/ə vĭzh/ən] **56**–6
   big-screen TV [bĭg/skrēn/ tē/vē/] **50**–14
   flat panel TV [flăt/ păn/əl tē/vē/] **234**–7
   flat screen TV [flăt/ skrēn/ tē/ vē/] **234**–7
   portable TV [por/tə bəl tē/vē/] **234**–8
tweezers [twē/zərz] **117**–4
twelfth [twĕlfth] **16**
twelve [twĕlv] **16**
twentieth [twĕn/tē əth] **16**
twenty [twĕn/tē] **16**
   twenty after one [twĕn/tē ăf/tər wŭn/] **18**–10
   twenty dollars [twĕn/tē däl/ərz] **26**–10
   twenty-first [twĕn/tē fürst/] **16**
   twenty-five [twĕn/tē fīv/] **16**
   25 percent [twĕn/fīv/ pər sĕnt/] **17**–11
   twenty-four [twĕn/tē för] **16**
   twenty-one [twĕn/tē wŭn/] **16**
   twenty-three [twĕn/tē thrē/] **16**
   twenty to two [twĕn/tē tə too/] **18**–12
   twenty-two [twĕn/tē too/] **16**
twice a week [twīs/ ə wēk/] **20**–23
twig [twĭg] **210**–1
twins [twĭnz] **28**–1
two [too] **16**
   2-door car [too/dör kär/] **156**–2
   two-story house [too/stör/ē hows/] **52** ✦
   two-way radio [too/wā rā/dē ō] **179**–22
   2 x 4 (two by four) [too/ bī/ för/] **181**–19
type [tīp] 170–R, **196**–A
   type a letter [tīp/ə lĕt/ər] **171**–A
   type the message [tīp/ dhə mĕs/ĭj] **197**–E
   type the subject [tīp/ dhə sŭb/jĭkt] **197**–D
   type your password [tīp/ yər păs/würd/] **197**–A
Types of Health Problems
   [tīps/ əv hĕlth/ prăb/ləmz] **115**
Types of Job Training [tīps/ əv jäb/ trā/nĭng] **172**
Types of Material [tīps/ əv mə tïr/ē əl] **99**
Types of Math [tīps/ əv măth/] **192**
Types of Medication [tīps/ əv mĕd/ə kā/shən] **113**
Types of Movies [tīps/ əv moo/vēz] **237**
Types of Music [tīps/ əv myoo/zĭk] **237**
Types of TV Programs [tīps/ əv tē/vē/ prō/grămz] **236**
ugly [ŭg/lē] **23**–22
umbrella [ŭm brĕl/ə] 90–17, **225**–14
umpire [ŭm/pīr] **229** ✦
uncle [ŭng/kəl] **34**–8
uncomfortable [ŭn kŭmf/tə bəl, –tər–] **42**–9
unconscious [ŭn/kän/shəs] **116**–A
under [ŭn/dər] 25–10, **153**–A
   long underwear [löng/ ŭn/dər wër] **91**–3
   thermal undershirt [thür/məl ŭn/dər shürt] **91**–2
   underexposed [ŭn/dər ĭk spōzd/] **235**–35
   underpants [ŭn/dər pănts/] **91**–14
   undershirt [ŭn/dər shürt/] **91**–1
underline [ŭn/dər līn/] **9**–S
Under the Hood [ŭn/dər dhə hood/] **158**
Underwear [ŭn/dər wër/] **91**
UNDERWEAR AND SLEEPWEAR
   [ŭn/dər wër/ ən slēp/wër/] **91**
undress [ən drĕs/] **36**–E

unfurnished apartment
[ŭn/für nĭsht ə pärt/ mənt] **48**–4
uniform [yōō/nə förm/] **88**–10, **231**–16
Unisex Socks [yōō/nə sĕks/ säks/] **91**
Unisex Underwear [yōō/nə sĕks/ ŭn/dər wër] **91**
universal remote [yōō/nə vür/səl rĭ mōt/] **234**–9
UNIVERSE [yōō/nə vürs/] **205**
university [yōō/nə vür/sə tē] **188**–7
unload [ŭn lōd/] **101**–E
unpack [ŭn păk/] **49**–N
unraveling [ŭn răv/əl ĭng] **97**–43
unripe [ŭn rīp/] **68**–31
unscented [ŭn sĕn/təd] **108** ✦
unscramble [ŭn skrăm/bəl] **9**–W
up [ŭp]
    buckle up [bŭk/əl ŭp/] **36**–L
    clean up [klēn/ ŭp/] **147**–M
    cut up [kŭt/ ŭp/] **77**–I
    eggs sunny-side up [ĕgz/ sŭn/ē sīd/ ŭp/] **76**–10
    get up [gĕt/ ŭp/] **38**–B
    hang up [hăng/ ŭp/] **15**–D, **101**–H
    look up [lōōk/ ŭp/] **8**–A
    pick up [pĭk/ ŭp/] **6**–I, **11**–E, **38**–M
    pop-up ad [päp/ ŭp ăd/] **197**–9
    set up [sĕt/ ŭp/] **173**–I
    stand up [stănd/ ŭp/] **6**–D
    stopped up [stäpt/ ŭp/] **63**–19
    throw up [thrō/ ŭp/] **110**–E
    wake up [wāk/ ŭp/] **38**–A
    walk up [wök/ ŭp/] **153**–C
upright seat [ŭp/rīt/ sēt/] **161**–28
upset [ŭp sĕt/] **43**–28
upstairs [ŭp/stërz/] **51** ✦
Uranus [yōōr/ə nəs, yōō rā/nəs] **205**–7
urban area [ür/bən ër/ē ə] **52**–1
urchin [ür/chən] **212**–21
URL [yōō/är/ĕl/] **197**–4
U.S. [yōō/ĕs/]
    U.S. Capitol [yōō/ĕs/ kă/pət əl] **138**–1
    U.S. route [yōō/ĕs/ rōōt/, –rowt/] **154**–17
USB port [yōō/ĕs/ bē/ pört/] **196**–7
use [yōōz]
    use a cash register [yōōz/ə kăsh/ rĕj/ə stər] **170**–S
    use a credit card [yōōz/ə krĕ/dət kärd/] **27**–B
    use a debit card [yōōz/ə dĕ/bət kärd/] **27**–C
    use a gift card [yōōz/ ə gĭft/ kärd/] **27**–E
    use deodorant [yōōz/dē ō/dər ənt] **108**–C
    use energy-efficient bulbs
        [yōōz/ ĕn/ər jē ĭ fĭ/shənt bŭlbz] **219**–H
    use punctuation [yōōz/ pŭngk/chōō ā/shən] **190**–C
Used Car [yōōzd/ kär/] **157**
used clothing [yōōzd/ klō/dhĭng] **102**–2
U.S. HISTORY [yōō/ĕs/ hĭs/tə rē] **198**
U.S. NATIONAL PARKS
    [yōō/ĕs năsh/ə nəl pärks/] **220**–**221**
utensils [yōō tĕn/səlz] **79**–19
utility / utilities [yōō tĭl/ə tē] / [yōō tĭl/ə tēz]
    48–5, **156**–7
U-turn [yōō/türn/] **154**–5
vacancy sign [vā/kən sē sīn/] **50**–7
vacation [vā kā/shən] **22**–6
vaccination [văk/sə nā/shən] **114** ✦

vacuum [văk/yōōm]
    vacuum cleaner [văk/yōōm klē/nər] **61**–10
    vacuum cleaner attachments
        [văk/yōōm klē/nər ə tăch/mənts] **61**–11
    vacuum cleaner bag
        [văk/yōōm klē/nər băg/] **61**–12
vacuum [văk/yōōm] **60**–H
valley [văl/ē] **204**–17
valuables [văl/yə bəlz, –yə wə–] **132**–8
valve [vălv/] **146**–4
van [văn] **156**–13, **156**–18
vandalism [văn/də lĭz/əm] **142**–1
vanity plate [vă/nə tē plāt/]**136** ✦
variable [vër/ē ə bəl] **192**–12
vase [vās, vāz, väz] **55**–23
vault [völt] **132**–6
VCR [vē/sē/är/] **102**–7
veal cutlets [vēl/ kŭt/ləts] **70**–6
Vegetable [vĕj/tə bəl] **77**
vegetables [vĕj/tə bəlz] **66**–8, **72**–27, **81**–32
    vegetable garden [vĕj/tə bəl gär/dn] **53**–27, **177**–14
    vegetable peeler [vĕj/tə bəl pē/lər] **78**–15
VEGETABLES [vĕj/tə bəlz] **69**
vegetarian [vĕj/ə tër/ē ən] **70** ✦
vehicles [vē/ĭ kəlz] **124**–4, **156**–7, **156**–10
vein [vān] **107**–37
velvet [vĕl/vət] **99**–10
vending machine [vĕn/dĭng mə shēn/] **152**–9
vendors [vĕn/dərz] **84**–7, **129**–29
ventilation mask [vĕnt/əl ā/shən măsk/] **92**–7
Venus [vē/nəs] **205**–2
verdict [vür/dĭkt] **141**–14
vertebrates [vür/ tə brəts] **194**–13
vest [vĕst] **89**–15
    down vest [down/ vĕst] **90**–14
    Hi-Visibility safety vest
        [hī/vĭz/ə bĭl/ə tē sāf/tē vĕst] **92**–6
    life vest [līf/ vĕst/] **161**–25, **226**–14
Veterans Day [vĕt/ər ənz dā/] **22**–16
veterinarian [vĕt/ər ə nër/ē ən] **169**–62
vice president [vīs/ prĕz/ə dənt] **138**–9
victim [vĭk/təm] **142**–10
video [vĭd/ē ō]
    videocassette [vĭd/ē ō kə sĕt/] **133**–18
    video game console [vĭd/ē ō gām/ kän/sōl/] **232**–3
    video game control [vĭd/ē ō gām/ kän trōl/] **232**–4
    video player [vĭd/ē ō plā ər] **197**–11
    video store [vĭd/ē ō stör/] **129**–20
videotape [vĭd/ē ō tāp/] **240**–A
view [vyōō]
    rearview mirror [rĭr/vyōō/ mĭr/ər] **159**–35
    sideview mirror [sīd/vyōō/ mĭr/ər] **158**–3
village [vĭ/lĭj] **52**–3
vine [vīn] **210**–22
vineyard [vĭn/yərd] **177**–16
violence [vī/ləns, vī/ə–] **142**–4
violet [vī/ə lət, vī/lət] **24**–8, **211**–23
violin [vī/ə lĭn/] **238**–6
virus [vī/rəs] **111**–17
vise [vīs] **180**–26
vision [vĭ/zhən]
    vision exam [vĭ/zhən ĭg zăm/] **136**–6
    vision problems [vĭ/zhən präb/ləmz] **115**–1

Visit [vĭ/zət] **119**
visor [vī zər] **179**–12
vital signs monitor [vīt/l sīnz/ män/ə tər] **121**–26
vitamins [vī/tə mənz] **113**–17
v-neck [vē/nĕk/] **96**–8
vocational [vō kā/shə nəl]
    vocational school [vō kā/shə nəl skōōl/] **188**–5
    vocational training [vō kā/shə nəl trā/nĭng] **172**–5
voice message [voys mĕs/ĭj] **14**–18
volcanic eruption [väl kăn/ĭk ĭ rŭp/shən] **145**–16
volleyball [väl/ē böl/] **229**–14, **231**–3
Volume [väl/yəm, –yōōm] **75**, **193**
volunteer [väl/ən tïr/] **121**–17
volunteer [väl/ən tïr/] **41**–Q
vomit [väm/ət] **110**–E
vote [vōt] **140**–A
waffles [wä/fəlz, wö/–] **80**–8
wages [wā/jĭz] **165**–12
wagon [wă/gən] **156**–6
waist [wāst]
    waist apron [wāst/ ā/prən] **93**–30
    waistband [wāst/bănd/] **100**–5
wait [wāt] **94**–B, **128**–B, **170**–T
waiter [wā/tər] **82**–8
    headwaiter [hĕd/wā/tər] **185**–12
waiting area [wā/tĭng ër/ē ə] **182**–16
Waiting Room [wā/tĭng rōōm/] **118**
waitress [wā/trəs] **83**–9
wait staff [wāt/ stăf/] **185** ✦
wake up [wāk/ ŭp/] **38**–A
walk [wök] **53**–2
    crosswalk [krös/wök/] **128**–15
    walk-in freezer [wök/ĭn frē/zər] **185**–3
walk [wök]
    walk a dog [wök ə dög/] **129**–F
    walk down [wök/ down/] **153**–D
    walk to class [wök/ tə klăs/] **11**–C
    walk up [wök/ ŭp/] **153**–C
    walk with a friend [wök/ wĭth ə frĕnd/] **143**–A
walker [wö/kər] **113**–11
wall [wöl] **56**–10, **194**–5
    drywall [drī/wöl/] **178**–19
    wallpaper [wöl/pā/pər] **59**–8
wallet [wä/lət, wö/–] **94**–13
walrus [wöl/rəs] **213**–32
war [wör] **199**–10
    Revolutionary War [rĕ/və lōō/shə nër/ē wör/] **198**–8
warehouse [wër/hows/] **175**–7
warm [wörm] **13**–4
    warm clothes [wörm/ klōz/] **146**–6
warning label [wör/nĭng lā/bəl] **112**–8
Warnings [wör/nĭngz] **112**
wash [wäsh, wösh]
    mouthwash [mowth/wäsh/, –wösh/–] **109**–25
    washcloth [wäsh/klöth/, wösh/–] **57**–4
wash [wäsh, wösh]
    wash clothes [wäsh/ klōz/, wösh/–] **219**–K
    wash hair [wäsh/ hër/, wösh/–] **108**–E
    wash the dishes [wäsh/ dhə dĭsh/əz, wösh/–] **60**–M
    wash the windows
        [wäsh/ dhə wĭn/dōz, wösh/–] **60**–I
washer [wä/shər, wö/–] **50**–12, **101**–3, **180**–37
    dishwasher [dĭsh/wäsh/ər, –wö–] **54**–8, **185**–2

Index

washing [wä/shǐng, wö/–] **61**–21
wasp [wäsp, wösp] **214**–17
waste [wāst] **121**–31, **218**–12
　wastebasket [wāst/băs/kət] **57**–26
watch [wäch, wöch] **94**–16
watch [wäch, wöch] **39**–X, **147**–C
water [wö/tər] **209**–3, **225**–1
　body of water [băd/ē əv wö/tər] **204** ✦
　bottled water [bät/ld wö/tər] **146**–11
　cold water [kōld/ wö/tər] **57**–7
　hot water [hät/ wö/tər] **57**–8
　hot water bottle [hät/ wö/tər böt/l] **113**–15
　watercolor [wö/tər kŭl/ər] **233**–21
　waterfall [wä/tər föl/] **204**–2
　water fountain [wö/tər fown/tn] **224**–9
　water glass [wö/tər glăs/] **83**–22
　watermelons [wö/tər měl/ənz] **68**–18
　water pollution [wö/tər pə lōō/shən] **218**–14
　water polo [wö/tər pō/lō] **229**–15
　waterskiing [wö/tər skē/ǐng] **227**–7
water [wö/tər] **176**–F
WATER SPORTS [wö/tər spörts/] **227**
wave [wāv] **145**–17, **225**–17
wave [wāv] **2**–F
wavy hair [wā/vē hër/] **33**–10
way [wā]
　hallway [häl/wā] **184**–18
　one way [wŭn/ wā/] **154**–3
　one-way trip [wŭn/wā/ trǐp/] **152**–16
　two-way radio [tōō/wā/ rā/dē ō] **179**–22
　wrong way [röng/ wā/] **154**–2
Ways to Conserve Energy and Resources
　[wāz/ tə kən sürv/ ěn/ər jē n rē/sör/səz, –rǐ sör/səz] **219**
Ways to Get Well [wāz/ tə gět/ wěl/] **114**
Ways to Pay [wāz/ tə pā/] **27**
Ways to Serve Eggs [wāz/ tə sürv/ ěgz/] **76**
Ways to Serve Meat and Poultry
　[wāz/ tə sürv/ mět/ n pōl/trē/] **76**
Ways to Stay Well [wāz/ tə stā/ wěl/] **114**
Ways to Succeed [wāz/tə sək sēd/] **10**
weak signal [wěk/ sǐg/nəl] **14**–12
WEATHER [wědh/ər] **13**
Weather Conditions [wědh/ər kən dǐsh/ənz] **13**
Weather Map [wědh/ər măp/] **13**
webcam [wěb/kăm/] **196**–12
Webpage [wěb/pāg/] **197**
website address [wěb/sǐt ə drěs/] **197**–4
wedding [wě/dǐng] **22**–2
Wednesday [wěnz/dā, –dē] **20**–11
weed [wēd]
　seaweed [sē/ wēd/] **225** ✦
　weed eater [wēd/ ē/tər] **176**–12
　weed whacker [wēd/ wăk/ər] **176**–12
weed [wēd] **176**–G
week [wēk] **20**–15
　last week [lăst/ wēk/] **20**–18
　next week [někst/ wēk/] **20**–20
　once a week [wŭns/ ə wēk/] **20**–22
　this week [dhǐs/ wēk/] **20**–19
　three times a week [thrē/ tǐmz/ ə wēk/] **20**–24
　twice a week [twīs/ ə wēk/] **20**–23

weekdays [wēk/dāz/] **20**–16
　weekend [wēk/ěnd/] **20**–17
Week [wēk] **20**
weigh [wā] **75**–B
weight [wāt] **32**–8
Weight [wāt] **32, 75**
weightlifting [wāt/lǐf/tǐng] **228**–16
weights [wāts] **231**–22
WEIGHTS AND MEASUREMENTS
　[wāts/ ən mězh/ər mənts] **75**
welder [wěl/dər] **169**–63
well [wěl] **42**–14
Well [wěl] **114**
west [wěst] **155**–2
western [wěs/tərn] **237**–15
wet [wět] **101**–17
　wet suit [wět/ sōōt/] **225**–4
whacker [wăk/ər] **176**–12
whale [wāl] **213**–29
wheat [wēt] **177**–2
wheat bread [wēt/ brěd/] **71**–19
wheel [wēl] **159**–26
　wheelbarrow [wēl/băr/ō] **176**–3
　wheelchair [wēl/chër/] **113**–9
　wheel cover [wēl/ kŭv/ər] **158**–9
whisk [wǐsk] **78**–21
whiskers [wǐs/kərz] **216**–18
white [wīt] **24**–14
　whiteboard [wīt/börd/] **6**–3
　white bread [wīt/ brěd/] **71**–18
　White House [wīt/ hows/] **138**–7
whole salmon [hōl/ săm/ən] **71**–3
wide [wīd] **97**–36
widow [wǐd/ō] **41** ✦
widower [wǐd/ō ər] **41** ✦
width [wǐdth, wǐtth] **17**–19
wife [wīf] **34**–12
　ex-wife [ěks/ wīf/] **35** ✦
　former wife [för/mər wīf/] **35** ✦
wild [wīld] **215** ✦
wildlife [wīld/līf/] **220**–3
willow [wǐl/ō] **210**–13
win [wǐn] **229** ✦
wind [wǐnd]
　windbreaker [wǐnd/brā/kər] **90**–24
　wind power [wǐnd/ pow/ər] **218**–2
　windshield [wǐnd/ shēld/] **158**–1
　windshield wipers [wǐnd/shēld/wī/pərz] **158**–2
　windsurfing [wǐnd/sür/fǐng] **227**–10, **227** ✦
window [wǐn/dō] **47**–11, **56**–17, **136**–7
　drive-thru window [drīv/thrōō/ wǐn/dō] **128**–11
　ticket window [tǐk/ət wǐn/dō] **152**–12
　window pane [wǐn/dō pān/] **178**–16
windy [wǐn/dē] **13**–18
wine glass [wǐn/ glăs/] **83**–23
wing [wǐng] **70**–20, **214**–1
winter [wǐn/tər] **21**–40
　winter scarf [wǐn/tər/skärf/] **90**–5
WINTER AND WATER SPORTS
　[wǐn/tər ən wö/tər spörts/] **227**
wipe [wīp] **60**–O
wipers [wī/pərz] **158**–2

wipes [wīps] **37**–15, **61**–23
wire [wīr] **181**–13
　wire stripper [wīr/ strǐp/ər] **181**–42
　wireless headset [wīr/ləs hěd/sět] **14**–14
　wiring [wīr/ǐng] **186**–7
withdraw [wǐdh drö/, wǐth–] **132**–F
witness [wǐt/nəs] **141**–11
wolf [wŏŏlf] **216**–5
woman [wŏŏm/ən] **30**–2
women [wǐ/mən] **30**–3
Women's Socks [wǐ/mənz säks/] **91**
Women's Underwear [wǐ/mənz ŭn/dər wër/] **91**
wood [wŏŏd] **178**–18
　plywood [plī/wŏŏd] **178**–17
　redwood [rěd/wŏŏd] **210**–18
　wood floor [wŏŏd/ flör/] **58**–21
　woodpecker [wŏŏd/pěk/ər] **214**–8
　wood screw [wŏŏd/ skrōō/] **180**–33
　wood stain [wŏŏd/ stān/] **181**–24
　woodworking kit [wŏŏd/wür/kǐng kǐt/] **232**–14
wooden spoon [wŏŏd/n spōōn/] **78**–9
Woodwinds [wŏŏd/wǐndz/] **238**
wool [wŏŏl] **61**–5, **98**–3
word [würd] **190**–1
word problem [würd/ prä/bləm] **192**–11
Words [wördz] **8**
work [würk/] **121**–30, **154**–16
　workbook [würk/bŏŏk/] **7**–26
　work gloves [würk/ glŭvz/] **92**–17, **179**–17
　work light [würk/ lǐt/] **181**–44
　work pants [würk/ pănts/] **92**–5
　work shirt [würk/ shürt/] **92**–2
work [würk] **8**–I, **10**–J, **38**–K
WORK [würk] **186**–187
Work Clothes [würk/ klōz/] **88**
worker [wür/kər]
　careful worker [kër/fəl wür/kər] **179**–2
　careless worker [kër/ləs wür/kər] **179**–1
　childcare worker [chīld/kër wür/kər] **166**–16
　construction worker
　　[kən strŭk/shən wür/kər] **178**–1
　dockworker [däk/wür/kər] **167**–23
　factory worker [făk/tə rē wür/kər, –trē] **175**–3
　farmworker [färm/wür/kər] **177**–8
　food preparation worker
　　[fŏŏd/ prěp ə rā/shən wür/kər] **185**–4
　garment worker [gär/mənt wür/kər] **167**–29
　postal worker [pō/stəl wür/kər] **169**–49
　sanitation worker [săn/ə tā/shən wür/kər] **169**–54
　social worker [sō/shəl wür/kər] **169**–57
Worker [wür/kər] **92, 93**
working [wür/kǐng]
　not working [nät/ wür/kǐng] **62**–1
　woodworking kit [wŏŏd/wür/kǐng kǐt] **232**–14
Working with a Partner [wür/kǐng wǐth ə pärt/nər] **8**
Working with Your Classmates
　[wür/kǐng wǐth yər klăs/māts/] **8**
work out [würk/ owt/] **230**–N
WORKPLACE [würk/ plās/] **164**–165
WORKPLACE CLOTHING
　[würk/ plās/ klō/dhǐng] **92**–93

world [würld]
  world languages [würld/ lăng/gwĭ jəz] **189**–13
  world music [würld/ myoo/zĭk] **237**–32
WORLD MAP [würld/măp/] **202–203**
WORLD HISTORY [würld hĭs/tə rē] **199**
worm [würm] **212**–23
worried [wür/ēd] **42**–13
wrap [răp] **72**–24
wrap [răp] **240**–F
wrench [rěnch] **158**–22, **181**–47, **181**–48
wrestling [rěs/lĭng] **228**–17
wrinkled [rĭng/kəld] **101**–19
wrist [rĭst] **106**–14
  wristwatch [rĭst/wäch/, –wöch/] **94**–16
write [rīt]
  write a check [rīt/ ə chěk/] **27**–D
  write a cover letter [rīt/ ə kŭv/ər lět/ər] **173**–G
  write a final draft [rīt/ ə fī/nəl drăft/] **191**–L
  write a first draft [rīt/ ə fürst/ drăft/] **191**–H
  write a note [rīt/ ə nōt/] **135**–A
  write a resume [rīt/ ə rě/zə mā/] **173**–F
  write a thank-you note
    [rīt/ ə thăngk/ yoo nōt/] **174**–O
  write back [rīt/ băk/] **135**–H
  write on the board [rīt/ ön dhə börd/] **6**–E
writer [rī/tər] **169**–64
Writing and Revising [rī/tĭng ən rĭ vī/ zĭng] **191**
Writing Process [rī/tĭng prä/sěs] **191**
Writing Rules [rī/tĭng roolz] **190**
wrong way [röng/ wā/] **154**–2
xylophone [zī/lə fōn/] **238**–15
yard [yärd]
  courtyard [kört/ yärd/] **51**–21
  yardstick [yärd/stĭk/] **181**–16
YARD [yärd] **53**
yarn [yärn] **233**–22
year [yïr] **20**–4, **31**–9, **31**–10
Year [yïr] **21**
yellow [yěl/ō] **24**–2
yesterday [yěs/tər dā/, –dē] **20**–7
yield [yēld] **154**–9
yoga [yō/gə] **122**–4
yogurt [yō/gərt] **72**–22
young [yŭng] **32**–1
Your First License [yər fürst/ lī/səns] **137**
YOUR HEALTH [yər hělth/] **114–115**
zebra [zē/brə] **217**–33
zero [zïr/ō] **16**
ZIP code [zĭp/ kōd/] **4**–9
zipper [zĭp/ər] **99**–25
Zones [zōnz] **19**
zoo [zoo] **222**–1
zoom lens [zoom/ lěnz/] **235**–23
zucchini [zoo kē/nē] **69**–25

Geographical Index

Continents

Africa [ăf′rĭ kə] **202–5**
Antarctica [ănt ärk′tĭ kə, –är′tĭ–] **202–7**
Asia [ā′zhə] **202–4**
Australia [ö strāl′yə] **202–6**
Europe [yŏŏr′əp] **202–3**
North America [nörth′ ə mĕr′ə kə] **200–201, 202–1**
South America [sowth′ ə mĕr′ə kə] **202–2**

Countries and other locations

Afghanistan [ăf găn′ə stăn′] **203**
Albania [ăl bā′nē ə] **203**
Aleutian Islands [ə lōō′shən ī′ləndz] **200, 203**
Algeria [ăl jïr′ē ə] **203**
American Samoa [ə mĕr′ə kən sə mō′ə] **202**
Andaman Islands [ăn′də mən ī′ləndz] **203**
Angola [ăng gō′lə] **203**
Argentina [är′jən tē′nə] **202**
Armenia [är mē′nē ə] **203**
Austria [ö′strē ə] **203**
Azerbaijan [ăz′ər bī jän′] **203**
Azores [ā′zörz] **202**
Baffin Island [băf′ən ī′lənd] **200**
Bahamas [bə hä′məz] **200, 202**
Bahrain [bä rān′] **203**
Bangladesh [băng′glə dĕsh′, băng′–] **203**
Banks Island [băngks′ ī′lənd] **200**
Belarus [bē′lə rōōs′, byĕl′ə–] **203**
Belgium [bĕl′jəm] **203**
Belize [bə lēz′] **201, 202**
Benin [bə nïn′, –nēn′] **203**
Bermuda Islands [bər myōō′də ī′ ləndz] **200, 202**
Bhutan [bōō tän′] **203**
Bolivia [bə lĭv′ē ə] **202**
Bosnia [bäz′nē ə] **203**
Botswana [bät swä′nə] **203**
Brazil [brə zĭl′] **202**
Brunei [brōō nī′] **203**
Bulgaria [bŭl gĕr′ē ə] **203**
Burkina Faso [bər kē′nə fä′sō] **203**
Burma [bür′mə] **203**
Burundi [bōō rōōn′dē] **203**
Cambodia [kăm bō′dē ə] **203**
Cameroon [kăm′ə rōōn′] **203**
Canada [kăn′ə də] **200, 202**
Canary Islands [kə nĕr′ē ī′ ləndz] **203**
Cape Verde [kāp′ vürd′] **202**
Central African Republic
   [sĕn′trəl ăf′rĭ kən rĭ pŭb′lĭk] **203**
Chad [chăd] **203**
Chile [chĭl′ē] **202**
China [chī′nə] **203**
Colombia [kə lŭm′bē ə] **202**
Comoros [kăm′ə rōz] **203**
Congo [käng′gō] **203**
Cook Islands [kŏŏk′ ī′ləndz] **202**
Corsica [kör′sĭ kə] **203**
Costa Rica [kōs′tə rē′kə, käs′–] **201, 202**
Croatia [krō ā′shə] **203**
Cuba [kyōō′bə] **201, 202**
Cyprus [sī′prəs] **203**
Czech Republic [chĕk′ rĭ pŭb′lĭk] **203**

Democratic Republic of the Congo
   [dĕm′ə krăt′ĭk rĭ pŭb′lĭk əv dhə käng′gō] **203**
Denmark [dĕn′märk] **203**
Devon Island [dĕv′ən ī′lənd] **200**
Djibouti [jĭ bōō′tē] **203**
Dominican Republic [də mĭn′ĭ kən rĭ pŭb′lĭk] **201, 202**
Ecuador [ĕk′wə dör′] **202**
Egypt [ē′jĭpt] **203**
Ellesmere Island [ĕl′əs mïr′ ī′lənd] **200**
El Salvador [ĕl săl′və dör′] **201, 202**
Equatorial Guinea [ē′kwə tör′ē əl gĭn′ē, ĕk′wə–] **203**
Eritrea [ĕr′ə trē′ə] **203**
Estonia [ĕ stō′nē ə] **203**
Ethiopia [ē′thē ō′pē ə] **203**
Federated States of Micronesia
   [fĕ′də rā′təd stāts′ əv mī′krə nē′zhə] **203**
Fiji [fē′jē] **203**
Finland [fĭn′lənd] **203**
France [frăns] **203**
Franz Josef Land [fränz′ yō′səf länd′] **203**
French Guiana [frĕnch′ gē ăn′ə, –ä′nə] **202**
French Polynesia [frĕnch′ päl′ə nē′zhə] **202**
Gabon [gă bōn′] **203**
Galápagos Islands [gə lä pə gōs ī′ləndz] **202**
Gambia [găm′bē ə] **203**
Georgia [jör′jə] **203**
Germany [jür′mə nē] **203**
Ghana [gä′nə] **203**
Greater Antilles [grā′tər ăn tĭl′ēz] **201**
Greece [grēs] **203**
Greenland [grēn′lənd, –lănd′] **200, 202**
Guam [gwäm] **203**
Guatemala [gwä′tə mä′lə] **201, 202**
Guinea [gĭn′ē] **203**
Guinea-Bissau [gĭn′ē bĭ sow′] **203**
Guyana [gī ăn′ə] **202**
Haiti [hā′tē] **201, 202**
Hawaiian Islands [hə wī′ən ī′lənds] **200, 202**
Hispaniola [hĭs′pən yō′lə] **201**
Honduras [hän dŏŏr′əs] **201, 202**
Hong Kong [häng′ käng′] **203**
Hungary [hŭng′gə rē] **203**
Iceland [īs′lənd] **203**
India [ĭn′dē ə] **203**
Indonesia [ĭn′də nē′zhə] **203**
Iran [ĭ răn′, ĭ rän′] **203**
Iraq [ĭ răk′, ĭ räk′] **203**
Ireland [īr′lənd] **203**
Israel [ĭz′rē əl, –rā–] **203**
Italy [ĭt′l ē] **203**
Ivory Coast [īv′rē kōst′] **203**
Jamaica [jə mā′kə] **201, 202**
Japan [jə păn′] **203**
Jordan [jör′dn] **203**
Kazakhstan [kä′zäk stän′] **203**
Kenya [kĕn′yə, kēn′–] **203**
Kiribati [kĭr′ə bäs′] **203**
Kuwait [kōō wāt′] **203**
Kyrgyzstan [kïr′gĭ stän′, –stän′] **203**
Laos [lows, lä′ōs] **203**
Latvia [lăt′vē ə] **203**
Lebanon [lĕb′ə nən, –nän′] **203**

Lesotho [lə sō′tō, –sōō′tōō] **203**
Lesser Antilles [lĕ′sər ăn tĭl′ēz] **201, 202**
Liberia [lī bïr′ē ə] **203**
Libya [lĭb′ē ə] **203**
Lithuania [lĭth′ōō ā′nē ə] **203**
Luxembourg [lŭk′səm bürg′] **203**
Macedonia [măs′ə dō′nē ə] **203**
Madagascar [măd′ə găs′kər] **203**
Madeira Islands [mə dïr′ə ī′ləndz] **203**
Malawi [mə lä′wē] **203**
Malaysia [mə lā′zhə] **203**
Maldives [möl′dēvz, mäl′–] **203**
Mali [mä′lē] **203**
Malta [möl′tə] **203**
Marshall Islands [mär′shəl ī′ləndz] **203**
Mauritania [mör′ə tā′nē ə] **203**
Mauritius [mö rĭsh′əs] **203**
Mexico [mĕk′sĭ kō′] **200, 201, 202**
Moldova [möl dō′və, mäl–] **203**
Monaco [män′ə kō′] **203**
Mongolia [mäng gō′lē ə] **203**
Montenegro [män′tə nē′grō, –nĕ′–] **203**
Morocco [mə räk′ō] **203**
Mozambique [mō′zəm bēk′] **203**
Namibia [nə mĭb′ē ə] **203**
Nepal [nə pöl′, –päl′] **203**
Netherlands [nĕdh′ər ləndz] **203**
New Caledonia [nōō′ kăl′ə dō′nē ə] **203**
New Zealand [nōō′ zē′lənd] **203**
Nicaragua [nĭk′ə rä′gwə] **201, 202**
Niger [nī′jər, nē zhër′] **203**
Nigeria [nī jïr′ē ə] **203**
Northern Mariana Islands
   [nördh′ərn mär′rē ä′nə ī′ləndz] **203**
North Korea [nörth′ kə rē′ə] **203**
Norway [nör′wā] **203**
Oman [ō män′] **203**
Pakistan [păk′ə stän′] **203**
Palau [pə low′] **203**
Panama [păn′ə mä′] **201, 202**
Papua New Guinea [păp′yōō ə nōō′ gĭn′ē] **203**
Paraguay [păr′ə gwī′, –gwä′] **202**
Peru [pə rōō′] **202**
Philippines [fĭl′ə pēnz′, fĭl′ə pēnz′] **203**
Poland [pō′lənd] **203**
Portugal [pör′chə gəl] **203**
Puerto Rico [pwĕr′tə rē′kō, pör′tə–] **201, 202**
Qatar [kä′tär, kə tär′] **203**
Romania [rō mā′nē ə, rōō–] **203**
Russia [rŭsh′ə] **203**
Rwanda [rōō än′də] **203**
Samoa [sə mō′ə] **202**
Saudi Arabia [sow′dē ə rā′bē ə, sö′dē–] **203**
Senegal [sĕn′ə göl′, –gäl′] **203**
Serbia [sür′bē ə] **203**
Seychelles [sā shĕlz′, –shĕl′] **203**
Sierra Leone [sē ĕr′ə lē ōn′, –lē ō′nē] **203**
Singapore [sĭng′ə pör′] **203**
Slovakia [slō vä′kē ə] **203**
Slovenia [slō vē′nē ə] **203**
Society Islands [sə sī′ə tē ī′ləndz] **202**
Solomon Islands [säl′ə mən ī′ləndz] **203**

Somalia [sə mä/lē ə] **203**
South Africa [sowth/ ăf/rĭ kə] **203**
South Georgia [sowth/ jör/jə] **202**
South Korea [sowth/ kə rē/ə] **203**
Spain [spān] **203**
Sri Lanka [srē/ läng/kə, shrē/–] **203**
Sudan [sōō dăn/] **203**
Suriname [sŏŏr/ə nä/mə] **202**
Svalbard [sväl/bärd] **203**
Swaziland [swä/zē länd/] **203**
Sweden [swēd/n] **203**
Switzerland [swĭt/sər lənd] **203**
Syria [sĭr/ē ə] **203**
Tahiti [tə hē/tē] **202**
Taiwan [tī/wän/] **203**
Tajikistan [tä jĭk/ə stän/, –stän/] **203**
Tanzania [tăn/zə nē/ə] **203**
Tasmania [tăz mā/nē ə] **203**
Thailand [tī/lănd/, –lənd] **203**
Togo [tō/gō] **203**
Tonga [täng/gə] **202**
Tunisia [tōō nē/zhə] **203**
Turkey [tür/kē] **203**
Turkmenistan [türk měn/ə stän/, –stän/] **203**
Uganda [yōō găn/də] **203**
Ukraine [yōō/krān, yōō krän/] **203**
United Arab Emirates [yōō nī/təd ăr/əb ĕm/ər əts] **203**
United Kingdom [yōō nī/təd kĭng/dəm] **203**
United States of America
    [yōō nī/təd stāts/ əv ə mĕr/ə kə] **200, 202**
Uruguay [yŏŏr/ə gwī/, –gwā/] **202**
Uzbekistan [ŏŏz bĕk/ə stän/, –stän/] **203**
Vanuatu [vä/nōō ä/tōō] **203**
Venezuela [vĕn/ə zwā/lə] **202**
Victoria Island [vĭk/tör ē ə ī/lənd] **200**
Vietnam [vē/ĕt näm/, –năm/] **203**
Wake Island [wāk/ ī/lənd] **203**
Western Sahara [wĕs/tərn sə här/ə] **203**
Yemen [yĕm/ən] **203**
Zambia [zăm/bē ə] **203**
Zanzibar [zăn/zə bär] **203**
Zimbabwe [zĭm bäb/wā] **203**

Bodies of water
Arctic Ocean [ärk/tĭk ō/shən] **200, 203**
Atlantic Ocean [ət lăn/ tĭk ō/shən] **200, 202–203**
Baffin Bay [băf/ən bā/] **200, 202**
Baltic Sea [böl/tĭk sē/] **203**
Beaufort Sea [bō/fərt sē/] **200**
Bering Sea [bĕr/ĭng sē/, bĭr/–] **200**
Black Sea [blăk/ sē/] **203**
Caribbean Sea [kăr/ə bē/ən sē/, kə rĭb/ē ən–] **201**
Caspian Sea [kăs/pē ən sē/] **203**
Coral Sea [kör/əl sē/] **203**
Gulf of Alaska [gŭlf/ əv ə läs/kə] **200, 202**
Gulf of California [gŭlf/ əv kăl/ə förn/yə] **200**
Gulf of Mexico [gŭlf/ əv mĕk/sĭ kō/] **200, 202**
Hudson Bay [hŭd/sən bā/] **200, 202**
Indian Ocean [ĭn/dē ən ō/shən] **203**
Labrador Sea [lăb/rə dör/ sē/] **200**
Mediterranean Sea [mĕd/ə tə rā/nē ən sē/] **203**

North Atlantic Ocean [nörth/ ət lăn/tĭk ō/shən] **202**
North Pacific Ocean [nörth/ pə sĭf/ĭk ō/shən] **202, 203**
North Sea [nörth/ sē/] **203**
Pacific Ocean [pə sĭf/ĭk ō/shən] **200, 202, 203**
Philippine Sea [fĭl/ə pēn/ sē/] **203**
Red Sea [rĕd/ sē/] **203**
South Atlantic Ocean [sowth/ ət lăn/tĭk ō/shən] **203**
Southern Ocean [sŭdh/ərn ō/shən] **203**
South Pacific Ocean [sowth/ pə sĭf/ĭk ō/shən] **202, 203**

The United States of America
Capital: Washington, D.C. (District of Columbia)
    [wä/shĭng tən dē/sē/, wö/–] **200**

Regions of the United States
Mid–Atlantic States [mĭd/ət lăn/tĭk stāts/] **201-10**
Midwest [mĭd/wĕst/] **201-9**
New England [nōō/ ĭng/glənd] **201-11**
Pacific States [pə sĭf/ĭk stāts/] **201-7**
Rocky Mountain States [räk/ē mown/tn stāts/] **201-8**
South [sowth] **201-13**
Southeast [sowth/ēst/] **201-13**
Southwest [sowth/wĕst/] **201-12**
West Coast [wĕst/ kōst/] **201-7**

States of the United States
Alabama [ăl/ə băm/ə] **200**
Alaska [ə läs/kə] **200, 202**
Arizona [ăr/ə zō/nə] **200**
Arkansas [är/kən sö/] **200**
California [kăl/ə förn/yə] **200**
Colorado [käl/ə răd/ō, –ra/dō] **200**
Connecticut [kə nĕt/ĭ kət] **200**
Delaware [dĕl/ə wër/] **200**
Florida [flör/ə də, flär/–] **200**
Georgia [jör/jə] **200**
Hawaii [hə wī/ē] **200**
Idaho [ī/də hō/] **200**
Illinois [ĭl/ə noy/] **200**
Indiana [ĭn/dē ăn/ə] **200**
Iowa [ī/ə wə] **200**
Kansas [kăn/zəs] **200**
Kentucky [kən tŭk/ē] **200**
Louisiana [lōō ē/zē ăn/ə] **200**
Maine [mān] **200**
Maryland [mër/ə lənd] **200**
Massachusetts [măs/ə chōō/səts] **200**
Michigan [mĭsh/ĭ gən] **200**
Minnesota [mĭn/ə sō/tə] **200**
Mississippi [mĭs/ə sĭp/ē] **200**
Missouri [mə zŏŏr/ē, –zŏŏr/ə] **200**
Montana [män tăn/ə] **200**
Nebraska [nə brăs/kə] **200**
Nevada [nə văd/ə, –vä/də] **200**
New Hampshire [nōō/ hămp/shər] **200**
New Jersey [nōō/ jür/zē] **200**
New Mexico [nōō/ mĕk/sĭ kō/] **200**
New York [nōō/ yörk/] **200**
North Carolina [nörth/ kăr/ə lī/nə] **200**
North Dakota [nörth/ də kō/tə] **200**
Ohio [ō hī/ō] **200**
Oklahoma [ō/klə hō/mə] **200**
Oregon [ör/ĭ gən, –gän/, är/–] **200**

Pennsylvania [pĕn/səl vān/yə] **200**
Rhode Island [rōd/ ī/lənd] **200**
South Carolina [sowth/ kăr/ə li/nə] **200**
South Dakota [sowth/ də kō/tə] **200**
Tennessee [tĕn/ə sē/] **200**
Texas [tĕk/səs] **200**
Utah [yōō/tö, –tä] **200**
Vermont [vər mänt/] **200**
Virginia [vər jĭn/yə] **200**
Washington [wä/shĭng tən, wö/–] **200**
West Virginia [wĕst/ vər jĭn/yə] **200**
Wisconsin [wĭs kän/sən] **200**
Wyoming [wī ō/mĭng] **200**

Canada
Capital: Ottawa [ät/ə wə] **201**

Regions of Canada
British Columbia [brĭt/ĭsh kə lŭm/bē ə] **201-2**
Maritime Provinces [mër/ə tīm präv/ən səz] **201-6**
Northern Canada [nör/dhərn kăn/ə də] **201-1**
Ontario [än tër/ē ō/] **201-4**
Prairie Provinces [prër/ē präv/ən səz] **201-3**
Québec [kwĭ bĕk/] **201-5**

Provinces of Canada
Alberta [ăl bür/tə] **200**
British Columbia [brĭt/ĭsh kə lŭm/bē ə] **200**
Manitoba [măn/ə tō/bə] **200**
New Brunswick [nōō/ brŭnz/wĭk] **200**
Newfoundland and Labrador
    [nōō/fən lənd ən lă/brə dör/] **200**
Northwest Territories [nörth/wĕst/ tĕr/ə tör/ēz] **200**
Nova Scotia [nō/və skō/shə] **200**
Nunavut [nōō/nə vōōt/] **200**
Ontario [än tër/ē ō/] **200**
Prince Edward Island [prĭns/ ĕd/wərd ī/lənd] **200**
Québec [kwĭ bĕk/] **200**
Saskatchewan [să skăch/ə wən, –wän/] **200**
Yukon [yōō/kän] **200**

Mexico
Capital: Mexico (City) [mĕk/sĭ kō/ (sĭt/ē)] **201**

Regions of Mexico
Chiapas Highlands [chē ä/pəs hī/ləndz] **201-18**
Gulf Coastal Plain [gŭlf/ kō/stəl plān/] **201-16**
Pacific Northwest [pə sĭf/ĭk nörth/wĕst/] **201-14**
Plateau of Mexico [plă tō/ əv mĕk/sĭ kō/] **201-15**
Southern Uplands [sŭdh/ərn ŭp/ləndz] **201-17**
Yucatan Peninsula
    [yōō/kə tän/ pə nĭn/sə lə, yōō/kə tän/–] **201-19**

States of Mexico
Aguascalientes [ä/gwəs käl yĕn/täs] **201**
Baja California Norte [bä/hä kăl/ə förn/yə nör/tā] **200**
Baja California Sur [bä/hä kăl/ə förn/yə sŏŏr/] **200**
Campeche [kăm pā/chä, kăm pē/chē] **201**
Chiapas [chē ä/pəs] **201**
Chihuahua [chĭ wä/wä, –wə] **200**
Coahuila [kō/ə wē/lə] **200**
Colima Michoacán [kə lē/mə mē/chō ə kän/] **201**
Distrito Federal [dĭ strē/tō fĕd/ə räl/] **201**
Durango [dŏŏ răng/gō, –räng/–] **201**

Geographical Index

(금속•도기등의) 작은 상 **232**–1
(비키니) 팬티 **91**–13
(사슴의) 가지진 뿔 **216**–16
(성인) 남자 **30**–1
(성인) 여자 **30**–2
(손목) 시계 **94**–16
(연필) 지우개 **7**–21
(오버) 코트 **90**–2
(주택) 페인트공 **168**–46
(허리에 매는) 앞치마 **93**–30
"로그인"을 클릭한다 **197**–B
"안녕하세요"라고 말하기 **2**–A
"안녕히 가세요"라고 말하다 **3**–L
"잘 지내세요?"라고 묻기 **2**–B
"종료"를 누른다 **15**–D
"통화" 버튼을 누른다 **15**–B
1 달러 동전 **26**–6
1 센트 **26**–1
10 달러 **26**–9
10 센트 **26**–3
10 퍼센트 **17**–12
100 달러 **26**–12
100 퍼센트 **17**–8
10대 청소년 **31**–11
10세 소녀 **31**–10
10월 **21**–34
11월 **21**–35
12월 **21**–36
13개 식민지 **198**–1
18세 이상일 것 **140**–G
1시 10분 **18**–8
1시 15분 **18**–9
1시 20분 **18**–10
1시 30분 **18**–11
1시 40분 **18**–12
1시 45분 **18**–13
1시 5분 **18**–7
1월 **21**–25
1회용 기저귀 **37**–10
1회용 식도구 **79**–19
2 도어 자동차 **156**–2
2 x 4 **181**–19
20 달러 **26**–10
25 센트 **26**–4
25 퍼센트 **17**–11
2월 **21**–26
2인용 소파 **56**–1
2층 침대 **59**–9
35 mm 카메라 **235**–21
3링 바인더 **7**–27
3월 **21**–27
4 도어 자동차 **156**–1
4월 **21**–28
5 달러 **26**–8

5 센트 **26**–2
50 달러 **26**–11
50 퍼센트 **17**–10
5분간 전자레인지에 돌린다 **77**–T
5월 **21**–29
6개팩 탄산음료수 **74**–21
6개 들이 팩 **74**–9
6세 소년 **31**–9
6월 **21**–30
75 퍼센트 **17**–9
7부 바지 **88**–8
7부 소매 셔츠 **96**–13
7월 **21**–31
7월 4일 **22**–13
8월 **21**–32
90도 **193**–26
9월 **21**–33
가게 좀도둑질 **142**–8
가격 **27**–7
가격을 협상한다 **157**–D
가격표 **27**–1
가구 광택제 **61**–8
가구가 딸리지 않은 아파트 **48**–4
가구가 딸린 아파트 **48**–3
가구를 만들다 **170**–G
가구를 배치하다 **49**–Q
가구에 광을 내다 **60**–E
가구와 기타 살림 **59**
가구의 먼지를 털다 **60**–A
가구점 **126**–8
가글하다 **109**–L
가득 찬 잔 **23**–9
가디니아 **211**–18
가로등 **148**–3
가르마 **33**–4
가르치다 **36**–K, **170**–Q
가리비 **71**–12, **212**–19
가면 **239**–9
가뭄 **145**–11
가방 **161**–18
가방 카트 **184**–8
가방을 검사한다 **160**–B
가벼운 상자 **23**–14
가사 **60**
가설을 설명한다 **195**–A
가스 잠금 밸브 **146**–4
가스 페달 **159**–46
가스계량기 **62**–14
가스미터 **62**–14
가스펠 **237**–30
가슴 **104**–4, **107**–25
가슴살 **70**–19
가습기 **113**–12
가시 **211**–29

가연성 액체 **179**–8
가오리 **212**–11
가운 **91**–29
가위 **33**–20, **100**–16
가을 **21**–39
가자미 **212**–15
가재 **71**–10
가전 제품 수리공 **166**–4
가전제품을 수리하다 **170**–J
가정 내 가스, 보일러, 수도 등을
　점검한다 **147**–N
가제 **117**–8
가져오다 **240**–E
가족 **34**–35
가족 모임 **44**–45
가죽 **98**–6, **216**–19
가죽 자켓 **90**–4
가지 **69**–23, **210**–2
가축 **177**–15
가축 우리 **177**–17
가축과 설치류 동물 **215**
가터 벨트 **91**–16
각도 **193**
각뿔 **193**–39
각주 **190**–10
간 **70**–7, **107**–40
간단한 대화 나누기 **12**–B
간단한 메뉴 담당 요리사 **185**–1
간편한 케이크 만들기 **77**
간편화 **95**–30
간호 조무사 **120**–11
간호복 **93**–31
간호사 **36**–B, **118**–8, **120**, **168**–44
간호사 수술복 **93**–38
갈기 **217**–49
갈색 **24**–17
갈색 머리 **33**–18
갈색 스웨터는 오른쪽에 있습니다 **25**–3
갈퀴 **176**–8
감각 **106**
감기 **13**–6, **42**–4, **111**–1
감기용 정제약 **113**–27
감독자 **165**–8
감사의 뜻을 전하기 **12**–E
감옥에 들어 가다 **141**–G
감자 **69**–17
감자 샐러드 **80**–19
감자 칩 **73**–35
감자 튀김 **79**–2
감각 **42**–43
감각류 **71**
갓난 아기 **31**–6
강 **155**–10, **204**–3
강당 **5**–18

강도 **142**–2
강력 잠금장치 **51**–34
강모 비누 패드 **61**–5
강아지 **215**–12
강아지를 산책시키다 **129**–F
강의를 하다 **122**–B
강판 **78**–2
같은 색깔 **23**–15
개 **215**–11
개구리 **212**–25
개미 **63**–23
개미핥기 **217**–24
개인 수표를 쓴다 **27**–D
개인 스포츠 **228**
개인 위생 **108**–109
개인 CD 플레이어 **234**–5
개찰구 **152**–8
개코원숭이 **217**–31
객실 **184**–13
거들 **91**–15
거리 **150**–5, **155**–8
거미 **214**–29
거미류 **214**
거북 **213**–42
거북이 **213**–43
거스름돈을 받다 **26**–A
거실 **47**–12, **56**
거울 **57**–18
거위 **214**–13
거주자 **50**–6
거품기 **78**–21
건강 관리 **114**–115
건강 문제의 유형 **115**
건강 박람회 **122**–123
건강 보조 용품 **115**
건강에 좋은 음식을 먹는다 **114**–F
건강을 회복하는 방법 **114**
건강한 **42**–14
건설 작업자 **178**–1
건식벽 **178**–19
건전지 **146**–15, **158**–20
건조기 **50**–13, **101**–4
건조기에서 빨래를 꺼내다 **101**–E
건조기용 섬유 유연제 **101**–5
건초 **177**–18
건축 **178**
건축 자재 판매점 **127**–20
건축가 **166**–5
건축용 합판 **181**–20
건포도 **68**–25
건포도 1/2 컵 **75**–9
걸프 해안 평원 **201**–16
검사 **141**–10
검사실 **121**

검색 상자 197-5
검색 엔진 197-6
검안사 115-6
검은 머리 33-16
검정 24-13
검정색 스웨터는 흰색 스웨터 뒤에
　있습니다 25-8
검토 191-I
겁에 질린 43-23
게 71-9, 212-20
게시판 7-14
게이트 53-9, 161, 161-8
게임 쇼 236-8
게임을 하다 232-B
겨울 21-40
겨울용 스카프 90-5
격자 무늬 96-22
견과류 73-36
견인차 156-14
결과를 기록한다 195-D
결론 190-8
결론을 도출한다 195-E
결승점에 닿다 230-T
결핵 111-15
결혼 22-2
결혼 증서 41-8
결혼하다 41-K
결혼한 부부 35-20
경고문 112, 112-8
경고에 주의를 기울인다 147-D
경관 162-2
경마 228-19
경비원 132-5, 141-3, 169-55
경영진 182-5
경주하다 230-S
경찰관 141-1, 168-48
경찰서 124-6
계곡 204-18
계기판 및 장치 패널 159
계단 50-10, 53-3
계단을 내려오다 153-D
계단을 오르다 153-C
계단이 부서지다 62-7
계란 66-7
계란 교반기 78-20
계란 조리법 76
계모 35-26
계부 35-25
계산기 17-6, 183-25
계산대 73-12
계산원 73-13, 79-17, 166-15
계산하다 17-B, 82-I
계약자 186-5
계절 21

계절별 의복 90
계좌 담당 매니저 132-9
계좌 열기 132
고객 서비스 담당 직원 167-20
고객 서비스 센터 130-12
고구마 69-18
고기 66-2, 70
고기 썰기용 칼 78-12
고기잡이 그물 226-17
고대 199-1
고대기 108-17
고등학교 188-4
고래 213-29
고리 나사 180-40
고리 모양의 물리개 37-25
고릴라 217-29
고모 34-7
고무 매트 57-5
고무 밴드 183-34
고무 장갑 61-4
고무 젖꼭지 37-24
고속 앞으로 235-D
고속도로 155-9
고속도로로 진입하다 153-I
고속도로에서 빠져나오다 153-J
고슴도치 216-10
고양이 215-9
고용된다 173-L
고용주 164-4
고장나다 162-D
고장난 장비 179-4
고층 건물 127-13
고혈압 111-14
곡괭이 178-21
곡선 193-23
곤충 209-11, 214
곧은 머리 33-9
골목 51-24
골무 100-15
골반 107-50
골프 228-8
골프 채 231-1
곰 216-11
곰인형 37-23
곱 192-9
곱슬 머리 33-11
곱하기 192-C
공 59-12
공공 안전 143
공공 요금 지불자로 자신의 이름으로
　올리다 49-O
공구 및 건물 보수 용품 180-181
공구 벨트 92-3
공군 138-16

공기 여과 마스크 92-7, 93-32, 179-14
공기 정화기 113-14
공부하기 8-9
공사 현장 126-2
공상과학 237-18
공식 37-3, 195-34
공예를 하다 232-D
공원 관리인 220-2
공원과 놀이터 224
공인 간호사 120-10
공작 214-14
공장 126-3, 175
공장 근로자 175-3
공장 주인 175-1
공정한 재판의 권리 140-5
공제 165-13
공중 전화 15-25, 129-23
공책 7-27
공책 속지 7-28
공포물 237-17
공항 151-10, 160-161
공항 교통 수단 152
공해 218
과녁 231-7
과산화수소 117-9
과수원 177-10
과일 67-9, 68
과일 샐러드 80-21
과자를 사다 11-K
과학 189-11, 194-195
과학실 195
관리인 50-8
관심 분야 172-11
관절염 111-16
관찰한다 195-C
관측소 205-21
괄호 190-19
광고란을 본다 173-B
광고물 48-2
광고지 102-1
광원 194-19
광합성 194-10
교감 5-5
교과서 7-25
교내 시설 5
교사 5-8, 6-4
교실 5-7, 6-7
교실로 걸어가다 11-C
교실로 돌아가다 11-M
교실로 뛰어가다 11-D
교실에 들어가다 11-A
교실에서 나가다 11-O
교외 52-2
교육 172-2

교장 5-4
교정 191-I
교정과 119
교정기 119-6
교정치과의 119-5
교직원 5
교차로 128-129
교통 표지판 154
교환원 14-21
교환하다 27-I
교회 127-14
구 16
구강 위생사 119-3
구강 청정제 109-25
구강을 마치하다 119-C
구겨진 셔츠 101-19
구근 211-2
구급차 116-1, 121-34
구두끈 94-24
구명 조끼 161-25, 226-14
구부리다 230-O
구십 16
구운 감자 81-25
구운 닭고기 81-22
구운 생선 81-29
구인 광고 게시물을 찾아본다 173-C
구입하다 94-A
구장 224-1
구조대원 225-19
구조대원실 225-21
구체 193-42
구토하다 110-E
국가 번호 15-33
국기 239-8
국도/하이웨이 표지판 154-17
국자 78-7
국제 우편 134-5
국제 전화 15-35
국화 211-21
군 138
군대 199-11
군인 169-58
군주 199-4
굴 71-14
굴뚝 53-5
굴착기 178-8
굽기 77-H
굽기용 쇠선반 78-14
굽기용 팬 78-13
권리 140
권리장전 198-13
권투 228-4
귀 105-12
귀가먼 32-12

귀가리개 **90**–13, **179**–16
귀고리 **95**–36
귀뚜라미 **214**–23
귀를 뚫은 귀 **32**–17
귀마개 **179**–15
귀여운 **32**–14
귀중품 **132**–8
귀중품 보관함 **132**–7
귀화 증명서 **40**–6
규칙 **64**–7
귤 **68**–9
그네 **224**–11
그네를 밀다 **224**–B
그늘 **225**–13
그래프 **192**–15
그래픽 디자이너 **167**–30
그룹으로 공부한다 **8**–I
그릇을 치우다 **82**–G
그리다 **49**–P, **178**–A, **181**–25, **233**–E
그린카드 **40**–2
그릴 **53**–17
그릴 립 **76**–2
그릴 치즈 샌드위치 **80**–10
그림 **56**–9
그림 사전 **7**–31
그림에 이름을 붙이세요 **9**–V
그림을 그린다 **8**–H
그림책 **133**–12
극장 **126**–6, **127**–23
근무복 **88**
근육 **107**–32
금고 **132**–6
금관악기 **238**
금발 머리 **33**–17
금붕어 **215**–16
금성 **205**–2
금속판 절단 톱 **180**–5
금연한다 **114**–G
금요일 **20**–13
금잔화 **211**–13
금전 등록기 **27**–10, **73**–15
금전 등록기를 사용하다 **170**–S
금전 출납 계원 **132**–1
급여 담당 직원 **165**–10
급여 명세서 **165**–11
급여 수표 **165**–14
기계 나사 **180**–32
기계 작동자 **168**–37
기근 **145**–12
기내에서 **161**
기내휴대물을 보관함에 넣는다 **160**–G
기념일 **22**–3
기니피그 **215**–14
기름 유출 **218**–17

기름 한 컵 **75**–2
기름을 채운다 **157**–G
기름이 떨어지다 **162**–E
기린 **217**–32
기본 교통 수단 **150**–**151**
기본색 **24**
기쁜 **28**–6, **43**–31, **44**–5
기상 조건 **13**
기수 **16**
기술 분야 **172**–12
기술학교 **188**–5
기어 변속기 **159**–47
기어오르는 놀이 기구 **224**–14
기자 **169**–52
기저귀 가방 **37**–16
기저귀 갈이용 테이블 **59**–1
기저귀 갈이용 패드 **59**–2
기저귀 통 **37**–7
기저귀를 갈다 **36**–G
기중기 **178**–7
기차 **150**–7
기침시럽 **113**–29
기침하다 **110**–A
기타 **238**–9
기타 악기 **238**
기하 **192**–17
기하학석 입체 **193**
기호 **155**–5
긴 내의 **91**–3
긴 머리 **33**–3
긴 양말 **91**–8
긴 치마 **96**–18
긴급소집병 **198**–10
긴소매 셔츠 **96**–14
길 **208**–3
길을 건너다 **128**–A
길을 뛰어 건너다 **153**–G
길을 잃다 **162**–B
길이 **17**–17
깁스 **113**–20
깃대 **216**–23
깃털 **214**–4
깃털 총채 **61**–1
깊이 **17**–18
깍지콩 **69**–8
깔때기 **195**–40
깡통 따개 **78**–1, **146**–8
깨끗한 티셔츠 **101**–16
껍질 벗기는 칼 **78**–16
꼬리 **216**–22
꼭끼는 바지 **97**–29
꽃 **208**–7, **211**
꽃다발 **211**–28
꽃무늬 **96**–25

꽃밭 **53**–20
꽃병 **55**–23
꽃양배추 **69**–14
꽃의 각 부위 명칭 **211**
꽃잎 **211**–8
꿀벌 **214**–25
끈없는 가벼운 구두 **95**–26
꿀 **181**–55
나누기 **192**–D
나누다 **17**–A
나무 **208**–1
나무 숟가락 **78**–9
나무 울타리를 다듬다 **176**–B
나무를 심는다 **176**–E, **219**–N
나무메 **180**–2
나무와 식물 **210**
나무용 나사 **180**–33
나방 **214**–21
나비 **214**–19
나비 넥타이 **89**–16
나쁜 개 **23**–18
나이 **32**
나이트가운 **91**–25
나이트셔츠 **91**–28
나이트클럽 **223**–12
나일론 **99**–12
나초 **79**–7
낙상하다 **116**–O
낙서 **148**–1
낙심한 **43**–27
낙엽 송풍기 **176**–2
낙엽을 긁어 모으다 **176**–C
낙타 **217**–38
낚시 **226**–4
낚싯대 **226**–18
난류 **161**–22
난장판 **64**–8
난초 **211**–19
날개 **70**–20, **214**–1
날씨 **13**
날씨를 지켜본다 **147**–C
날씬한 **32**–9
날짜 **20**–1
남 **4**–17, **155**–3
남 아메리카 **202**–2
남극대륙 **202**–7
남녀공용 속옷 **91**
남녀공용 양말 **91**
남동부 **201**–13
남부 **201**–13
남부 고원 **201**–17
남색 **28**–5
남서부 **201**–12
남성용 속옷 **91**

남자 조카 **34**–19
남자 형제 **34**–6
남자들 **30**–4
남자용 지갑 **94**–13
남편 **34**–13
낮은 굽 **97**–31
낮은 신발 **95**–27
낮잠을 자다 **53**–A
내각 **138**–10
내과 의사 **120**–1
내다 보는 구멍 **51**–32
내복 **91**–2
내일 **20**–6
냄비 **54**–16, **78**–6
냄비 집게 **78**–29
냄새를 맡다 **106**–C
냅킨 **55**–10, **83**–26
냉각수를 넣는다 **157**–I
냉동 생선 **71**–17
냉동 식사 **72**–28
냉동 식품 **72**
냉동 야채 **72**–27
냉동 요거트 1 파인트 **75**–3
냉동고 **54**–10
냉수 **57**–10
냉장고 **54**–9
냉상하다 **76**–D
너구리 **216**–13
너무 비싸다 **97**–44
너무 작다 **97**–37
너무 크다 **97**–38
너비 **17**–19
너트 **180**–36
넓은 넥타이 **97**–36
넓적다리 **70**–22
네번째 **16**
네일 살롱 **130**–3
넥타이 **86**–A, **88**–12, **92**–13
년 **20**–4
노년의 **32**–3
노동절 **22**–14
노란색 스웨터는 왼쪽에 있습니다 **25**–1
노랑 **24**–2
노래를 부르다 **238**–B
노루발 **98**–19
노른자를 터트리지 않은 계란
　후라이 **76**–10
노예 **198**–4
노인 **30**–5
노인 거주 시설 **52**–11
노출 과다 **235**–34
노출 부족 **235**–35
노트에 필기한다 **10**–C
놀란 **43**–30

놀러갈 곳 222–223
놀이 틀 위를 기어오르다 224–C
놀이공간 130–11
놀이터 50–3
농구 코트 229–7
농구공 229–8, 231–4
농기구 177–12
농부 177–13
농사일과 목장일 177
농산물 시장 84–85
농산물 재배자 177–13
농산물 코너 72–2
농작물 177
농장 52–9
농장 노동자 177–8
농장 동물 215
높이 17–16, 32
뇌 107–34
누룩뱀 213–39
눈 105–11, 106
눈금실린더 195–38
눈꺼풀 106–10
눈보라 13–23, 145–13
눈사태 145–18
눈썹 106–9
눈썹 연필 109–34
눈을 검사하다 118–D
눈을 마주친다 174–J
눈이 오는 13–12
뉴스 236–1
뉴잉글랜드 201–11
뉴펀들랜드 표준시 19–34
느낌표 190–13
느릅나무 210–16
느린 운전사 23–4
늑대 216–5
늦은 19–24
니켈 26–2
니트 상의 88–7
다락방 47–8
다람쥐 215–21
다른 색깔들 23–16
다리 70–21, 105–9
다리 및 발 106
다리 아래로 가다 153–A
다리 위로 가다 153–B
다리미 101–13
다리미판 101–14
다린 셔츠 101–20
다섯번째 16
다시 쓴다 191–J
다양한 아이디어를 생각해 본다 191–F
다양한 주거 환경 52
다용도 칼 226–20

다음 주 20–20
다음 줄로 이동하다 196–D
다이빙 마스크 225–6
다이빙하다 230–K
다이아몬드 233–29
다이얼 911 15–E
다임 26–3
다진 쇠고기 70–4
다치다 116–C
다친 42–16
단 식품류 84–8
단락 190–3
단락의 첫 문장은 들여쓴다 190–D
단색 96–19
단순한 블라우스 97–33
단어 190–1
단어를 번역한다 8–C
단어를 베껴 쓴다 8–E
단어를 찾는다 8–A
단어식 문제 192–11
단어에 밑줄 치세요 9–S
단어에 줄을 그어 지우세요 9–R
단어의 철자 배열을 맞게
　고치세요 9–W
단열재 178–14
단위 17
단정하게 한다 174–C
단추 99–24
단추가 떨어지다 97–40
단풍나무 210–12
달걀 한 카톤 74–16
달래다 36–I
달러 26–7
달력 20–21
달팽이 212–22
닭 튀김 76–1
닭•오리 다리 70–23
닭고기 66–3, 70–16
닭고기 샌드위치 79–5
닭고기를 삶는다 77–M
닭고기를 자른다 77–I
담낭 107–44
담요 58–15, 146–7, 225–11
답 192–14
답안지 10–2
답에 동그라미 하세요 9–Q
답을 표시한다 10–K
답을 함께 생각해 본다 8–H
답장을 쓴다 135–H
당구 228–2
당구대 50–15
당근 69–3
당근 껍질을 벗긴다 77–K
당나귀 215–3

당뇨병 111–12
당선되다 139–C
당선된 공무원 139–32
당좌 계좌번호 132–14
당황스러운 43–28
당황한 43–24
대 96–4
대각선 193–31
대구 71–8, 212–5
대기 오염 218–11
대기실에서 118
대들보 178–3
대략 202
대머리 33–12
대물 렌즈 194–16
대법관 138–12
대법원 138–11
대법원장 138–13
대비책 146
대서양 표준시 19–33
대수 192–16
대양 204–6, 225–1
대중 교통 152
대추 68–28
대출 받다 49–J
대출 카운터 133–2
대통령 138–8, 199–5
대통령의 날 22–11
대패 181–57
대학 기숙사 52–8
대학 학위 41–7
대학교 188–7
대학에 들어가다 41–I
대합 조개 71–15
대형 손수건 92–16
대형스크린 TV 50–14
대화 시작하기 12–A
대화요법 115–13
대화하다 11–L
댄스 64–A
더러운 티셔츠 101–15
더블 베드 184–14
더운 13–3, 42–1
더하기 192–A
덕 테이프 181–49
던지다 230–A, 230–C
덜 익은 바나나 68–31
덤프 트럭 156–19
덧문 53–10
덩굴 210–22
덩굴옻나무 210–25
덩어리 74–10
데님 99–7
데스크 직원 184–11

데스크탑 컴퓨터 196
데이지 211–14
데이터를 입력하다 171–B
덱 240–2
도 13–8
도가니 집게 195–44
도끼 180–3
도넛 79–15
도넛가게 129–17
도로 공사 154–16
도로 표지판 129–26
도롱뇽 212–27
도마 54–27
도마뱀 213–40
도서관 5–17, 125–15, 133
도서관 서기 133–1
도서관 이용자 133–3
도서관 카드를 수령하다 133–A
도시 52–1
도어 체인 51–33
도어맨 184–1
도움을 요청한다 10–F
도착지 162–5
도착하다 160–K
도크 234–3
도형 193
도회 지역 52–1
독감 111–2
독립기념일 22–13
독립선언문 198–5
독립전쟁 198–8
독성 연기 179–3
독성분을 삼키다 116–J
독수리 214–9
독있는 오크 210–24
독있는 옻나무 210–23
독재자 199–6
돈을 갚다 26–D
돈을 빌려주다 26–C
돈을 빌리다 26–B
돌고래 213–31
돌고래 무리 213–30
동 155–4
동계 스포츠와 수중 스포츠 227
동굴 220–6
동맥 107–36
동물원 222–1
동상에 걸리다 116–G
동의하기 12–K
동의하지 않기 12–L
동일함과 상이함 28–29
동작 관련 전치사 153
동전 26
동전 지갑 94–14

돼지 215–2
돼지고기 70
되감다 235–C
두개골 107–47
두꺼비 212–28
두꺼비집–퓨즈 상자 62–13
두꺼운 재킷 97–27
두꺼운 책 23–7
두려워하는 43–23
두번째 16
두부를 얇게 썬다 77–C
두통 110–1
둔각 193–27
둔부 107–30
둘레 193–43
둥지 209–12
뒤로 단추 197–2
뒤로 젖힌 좌석 161–27
뒷마당 53
뒷좌석 159–54
드라마 236–12
드라이버 180–30
드럼 238–16
드롭다운 메뉴 197–8
드리블하다 230–J
드릴 비트 180–28
튼나 106–B
들것 121–33
들보 178–3
들소 216–6
들쥐 215–19
들통 61–7, 225–8
등 104–5, 107–29
등기 우편 134–4
등록 스티커 136–13
등록표 136–13
등산화 95–31
디너 샐러드 80–15
디너 접시 83–18
디너 포크 83–28
디자이너 175–2
디자인 175–A
디저트 쟁반 83–10
디지털 사진 앨범 235–32
디지털 카메라 235–19
따뜻한 13–4
따뜻한 옷 146–6
따옴표 190–15
딱따구리 214–8
딱딱한 의자 23–5
딱정벌레 214–18
딱풀 232–11
딸 34–14
딸기 68–14

딸랑이 37–26
떠나다 160–J
뚜껑 78–24
뜨개 바늘 233–23
뜨개실 233–22
뜻을 읽는다 8–B
라디에이터 158–19
라디오 159–37
라우터 180–12
라인 감독자 175–4
라임 68–8
라켓볼 228–12
라텍스 장갑 93–34
래프팅 226–2
랜턴 226–22
랩톱 196–16
러그렌치 158–22
런닝 셔츠 91–1
레게 237–32
레깅스 90–12
레모네이드 84–3
레몬 68–7
레슬링 228–17
레이스 99–9
레이저 프린터 183–19
레인코트 90–18
레프리 229–6
로마 숫자 16
로맨스 237–16
로비 50
로빈 214–16
로스트 70–1
로스트 비프 71–21
로스트 비프 1 파운드 75–12
로켓 목걸이 95–35
록 36–D, 208–6, 237–23
록 밴드 활동을 하다 238–D
록 콘서트 222–5
록키 산 주 201–8
롤 74–11, 80–17
롤러 33–19
룸 서비스 184–17
룸메이트 64–1
리무진 156–11
리본 99–30
리얼리티 쇼 236–6
립스틱 109–38
링크 197–10
마 98–2
마가린 72–20
마늘 69–30
마늘 압착기 78–11
마늘빵 81–28
마더보드 196–5

마루를 걸레질하다 60–D
마루를 쓸다 60–J
마루바닥 58–21
마른 32–9
마른 셔츠 101–18
마리타임 프로빈스 201–6
마스카라 109–39
마스킹 테이프 181–53
마시다 11–J
마요네즈 79–23
마운틴 표준시 19–30
마이크 234–18
마이크로프로세서 196–4
마취 전문의 121–35
마침표 190–11
마커 7–24
마틴 루터 킹 주니어 기념일 22–10
마흔번째 16
막다른 길 154–6
만 16, 204–9
만나서 인사하기 2–3
만날 장소 146–1
만들기 쉬운 닭고기 스프 77
만월 205–12
만족한 42–6
만지다 106–E
반화 236–3
말 215–4
말린 자두 68–26
말미잘 212, 212–24
말벌 214–17
말타기 226–9
맑음 13–9
맛보다 106–D
망고 68–21
망원경 205–23
망치 178–D, 180–1
맞는 답을 고르세요 9–P
맞는 항목끼리 짝지우세요 9–T
맞춤법을 검사한다 197–F
매니저 72–8
매니저에게 전화하다 48–A
매니큐어 미용사 168–38
매력적인 32–13
매시포테이토 81–23
매우 추운 13–7
매운 고추 69–29
매일 20–21
매트리스 58–20
매트리스 시트 58–12
매표소 152–12
매형 34–17
맥박을 검사하다 122–A
맹인 32–11

머리 104–1
머리 손질 33
머리 위 짐칸 161–13
머리감싸개 90–7
머리띠 90–3
머리를 감다 108–E
머리를 말리다 108–H
머리를 브러쉬로 빗다 108–I
머리를 빗다 108–G
머리를 세팅하다 33–C
머리를 염색하다 33–D
머리를 헹구다 108–F
머리카락 104–2
머리핀 108–20
머스타드 79–22
머플러 158–16
머핀 79–16
먹다 11–I
먹이다 36–C, 177–D
먼지 바람 13–19
먼지 방지용 프릴 58–17
멍 110–12
메기 71–2
메뉴 82–7
메뉴 표시줄 197–1
메뉴를 보고 주문하다 82–D
메뚜기 214–24
메모리 카드 235–20
메스꺼움을 느끼다 110–D
메시지를 기록하다 171–C
메시지를 남기다 171–P
메시지를 받아 적다 171–Q
메시지를 입력한다 197–E
메시지를 확인하다 171–R
메이컵 리무버 109–42
메일러 183–40
멕시코 고원 201–15
멕시코 지역 201
멜로 드라마 236–5
멜론 68–19
멜빵 94–1
멜빵 바지 88–6
면 98–1, 177–6
면도 후 바르는 로션 109–30
면도기 109–27
면도날 109–28
면도용 크림 109–29
면도하다 109–M
면적 및 부피 측정 193
면접 기술 174
면접 일정을 잡는다 173–I
면접관에게 감사 노트를 쓴다 174–O
면접관에게 감사의 뜻을 전한다 174–N
면접관에게 인사한다 174–H

면접을 본다 173-K
면접을 준비한다 174-A
면허증을 발급받는다 137-I
모 98-3
모기 214-22
모기지를 지불하다 49-L
모니터 196-11
모델 168-41
모델 기차 233-27
모래 225-23
모래 언덕 204-5
모래상자 224-15
모래성 225-12
모르는 사람에게 문을 열어주지
    않는다 143-F
모빌 59-5
모자 90-1, 95-11
모짜렐라 치즈 71-29
모텔 126-12
모퉁이 128-7
모퉁이를 돌아 뛰다 153-H
모퉁이에서 정지하다 155-D
모험 237-19
모형 키트 232-9
목 104-3, 107-35
목걸이 95-10
목공 키트 232-14
목관악기 238
목동 177-22
목마른 42-2
목발 113-10
목성 205-5
목수 62-12, 166-14
목알약 113-30
목없는 양말 91-10
목요일 20-12
목욕 시키다 36-F
목욕 파우더 108-4
목욕수건 57-16
목욕하다 108-B
목을 검사하다 118-E
목장 52-10
목재 178-17
목재용 염료 181-24
목표를 세운다 10-A
몫 192-10
몸을 숨긴다 147-J
못 180-34
묘목 211-4
묘지 127-15
무 69-4
무거운 상자 23-13
무게와 단위 75

무균 테이프 117-7
무균 패드 117-6
무단 횡단하다 128-C
무당 벌레 214-26
무릎 106-20
무릎 길이 96-17
무릎 높이까지 오는 양말 91-12
무릎 보호대 179-19, 231-13
무선 전화 15-24
무선 헤드셋 14-14
무설탕 122-7
무술 228-11
무스 216-1
무언가를 설명하기 12-M
무언가를 제공하기 12-D
무전기 179-22
무척추동물 194-13
무카페인 커피 81-37
무화과 68-27
문 46-3
문 손잡이 53-12
문명화 199
문서를 스캔하다 171-H
문서를 인쇄하다 171-I
문서를 팩스로 보내다 171-G
문신 32-18
문어 212-9
문을 잠근다 143-E
문자 메시지 14-19
문장 190-2
문장을 받아 쓴다 8-N
문장을 순서대로 놓으세요 9-X
문장의 첫자는 대문자로 표기한다 190-B
문제에 대해 토의한다 8-G
물 209-13, 225-1
물 한 병 74-13
물개 213-34
물건 담아주는 사람 73-14
물건을 수집하다 232-A
물고기 66-1, 71, 209-14
물리 195
물리치료 115-11
물리치료사 115-12
물리학자 195-33
물방울 무늬 96-21
물에 빠지다 116-I
물을 따르다 82-C
물을 아낀다 219-E
물을 주다 176-D
물음표 190-12
물이 새는 수도꼭지를 수리한다 219-F
물잔 83-22
물집 110-15

물티슈 37-15, 146-12
물품 183-42
미국 국도 표지판 154-17
미국 국립 공원 220-221
미국 동부 표준시 19-32
미국 역사 198
미국 중부 표준시 19-31
미국 지역 201
미국에서 5년 동안 거주 140-H
미국회의사당 138-1
미끄러운 마루바닥 179-6
미끄럼틀 194-3, 224-13
미끄럼판 98-18
미니 블라인드 58-8
미니 스커트 96-15
미니밴 156-8
미닫이 유리문 53-18
미드 애틀랜틱 주 201-10
미디어 우편 134-3
미세 조정 다이얼 194-22
미소 짓기 2-D
미술 189-15
미술관 223-9
미스터리 237-20
미아 144-1
미용사 167-31
미장원 131-18
미적분 192-19
미터기 152-23
미트로프 81-32
미트볼 81-27
믹스용 그릇 54-28, 78-31
민소매 셔츠 96-11
밀 177-2
밀가루 73-29
밀가루 1컵 75-10
밀가루 한 봉지 74-19
밀방망이 78-30
밀빵 71-19
밀짚모자 90-23
밀크쉐이크 79-14
밑단 100-8
밑단용 99
바구니 56-3
바나나 68-2
바나나 한 묶음 68-29
바느질 용품 100
바늘꽂이 100-13
바다 사자 213-33
바다 포유동물 213
바다생물 212
바다생물, 양서류 그리고
    파충류 212-213

바다코끼리 213-32
바닥 46-6
바디 로숀 108-9
바람이 부는 13-18
바로 세운 좌석 161-28
바르다 109-P
바베큐 76-2
바순 238-4
바이스 180-26
바이올린 238-6
바지 87-12
바지 길이를 늘리다 100-A
바지 길이를 줄이다 100-B
바지 품을 늘리다 100-C
바지 품을 줄이다 100-D
바코드 27-4
바퀴 달린 들것 121-33
바퀴벌레 63-26
박수치다 148-B
박쥐 216-7
반 친구를 도와준다 8-J
반 친구와 함께 학습하기 8
반납 처리기 133-10
반도 204-7
반바지 89-25
반소매 셔츠 96-12
반송 주소 134-21
반지 95-40
반지름 193-35
반창고 117-5
받아 적다 171-K
받침 193-45, 194-20
받침 접시 83-25
발 104-8, 216-20
발가락 94-23, 105-10
발굽 216-17
발권 담당 직원 160-3
발꿈치 94-22, 106-24
발등을 끈으로 매는 신사화 95-29
발명 199-19
발명가 199-18
발목 106-23
발목 길이 치마 96-17
발목까지 오는 양말 91-7, 91-11
발목을 삐다 110-18
발음을 확인한다 8-D
발진 110-10
발코니 51-20
발톱 214-2
발판 178-4
발한 억제제 108-5
밝은 청색 24-12
밤 18-20

방광 **107**–46
방독 마스크 **179**–14
방범용 바지 **93**–22
방범용 셔츠 **93**–20
방사능 **218**–15
방사능 물질 **179**–7
방사선과 의사 **120**–6
방울뱀 **213**–38
방위군 **138**–19
방정식 **192**–13
방충문 **53**–15
방충제 **226**–23
방취제 **108**–5
방취제를 사용하다 **108**–C
방향 **155**
방향 및 지도 **155**
방향 지시등 **158**–6, **159**–34
방화 **142**–7
밭 **5**–2, **177**–7
배 **68**–4
배고픈 **42**–5
배관공 **63**–20
배구공 **229**–14, **231**–3
배기관 **158**–15
배낭 **94**–18, **226**–15
배낭여행 **226**–6
배너 **44**–1
배달원 **167**–21
배드민턴 **228**–6
배변 연습 팬티 **37**–11
배부른 **42**–6
배선 **186**–7
배수구 **57**–7
배심원 **141**–8
배심원 임무를 수행하다 **140**–E
배우 **166**–2
배지 **93**–21
배터리 충전기 **235**–27
배터리 팩 **235**–26
백 **16**
백만 **16**
백미러 **159**–35
백발 **33**–13
백번째 **16**
백악관 **138**–7
백일 **16**
백합 **211**–26
백화점 **131**–13
버너 **54**–19
버드나무 **210**–13
버서(서빙 보조) **83**–12
버섯 **69**–27
버섯을 살짝 튀긴다 **77**–E

버스 **128**–9, **151**–14
버스 노선 **152**–1
버스정류장 **124**–7, **129**–16, **151**–13, **152**
버스를 타고 학교에 가다 **38**–H
버저 **51**–31
버클 **99**–28
버터 **66**–6
번개 **13**–17
번역사 **168**–35
번지 코드 **181**–15
번호판 **136**–12, **158**–12
벌금을 내다 **133**–E
벌레 **212**–23
벌레에게 물린 상처 **110**–11
벌새 **214**–10
범례 **51**–30, **155**–6
범용 리모콘 **234**–9
범죄 **142**
범죄를 보면 경찰에 신고한다 **143**–K
범퍼 **158**–8
법원 **125**–13
법원 속기사 **141**–12
법을 준수하다 **140**–C
법정 **141**–7
법정 간수 **141**–13
법정 공휴일 **22**, **22**–8
법성에 출두하다 **141**–C
법제도 **141**
벙어리 장갑 **90**–10
베개 **58**–11
베갯잇 **58**–14
베리 **210**–20
베리 칵테일 **81**–36
베이글 **73**–40
베이비 로션 **37**–13
베이비 파우더 **37**–14
베이스 **212**–6, **238**–8
베이지색 **24**–18
베이컨 **70**–11, **80**–1
베이킹 팬에 기름칠을 한다 **77**–B
벤 상처(자상) **110**–13
벤치 **224**–10
벨 캡틴 **184**–6
벨벳 **99**–10
벨보이 **184**–7
벨크로 테이프 **99**–29
벨트 **94**–6
벨트 버클 **94**–20
벨트를 채우다 **36**–L
벼룩 **63**–25
벼룩 시장 **222**–6
벽 **56**–10
벽난로 **56**–13

벽난로 선반 **56**–11
벽돌 **178**–12
벽돌공 **186**–8
벽돌을 쌓다 **178**–B
벽지 **59**–8
변기 **57**–21
변기 세척솔 **57**–20
변기가 막히다 **63**–19
변수 **192**–12
변호사 **168**–36
변호사를 고용하다 **141**–B
변화하다 **148**–C
별 **205**–13
별자리 **205**–14
별표 버튼 **14**–6
병 **74**–1
병 회수 **73**–16
병든 **42**–12
병력 기록 양식 **118**–4
병실 **121**
병원 **120**–121, **125**–9, **154**–18
병원 기록 관리직 **168**–39
병원 직원 **120**
병원 차트 **121**–24
병원 침대 **121**–22
보관하다 **28**–B
보관함 **50**–17
보기 흉한 광경 **23**–22
보닛 하부 **158**
보다 **106**–A
보도 **129**–24
보드게임 **232**–5
보라 **24**–8
보라색 스웨터는 회색 스웨터 옆에
  있습니다 **25**–10
보름달 **205**–12
보석 코너 **95**–8
보석상 **130**–2
보습제 **108**–9
보안 검사 구역에서 **160**
보안 검사원 **160**–5
보안 카메라 **50**–19
보안검사를 통과한다 **160**–D
보안용 문 **50**–16
보온 패드 **113**–13
보육 시설 **129**–30
보육원 **188**–1
보일러가 고장나다 **63**–15
보조 교사 **5**–16
보조원 **120**–16
보청기 **115**–10
보트타기 **226**–1
보풀 트랩을 청소하다 **101**–D

보행자 **128**–14
보험 가입 확인 증서 **136**–8
보험 카드 **118**–3
보호 안경 **92**–10, **179**–10
보호소 **52**–13
보호소를 찾는다 **147**–H
복도 **5**–10, **51**, **72**–6, **184**–18
복부 **107**–27
복사 센터 **129**–18
복사기 **183**–23
복사하다 **171**–D
복숭아 **68**–10
복용량 **112**–6
복장 **239**–11
복통 **110**–4
본론 **190**–7
볼 **106**–3
볼거리 **111**–7
볼링 **228**–3
볼링 볼 **231**–5
볼링장 **222**–4
볼터치 **109**–37
볼트 **180**–35
봄 **21**–37
봉우리 **211**–7
봉제 동물 완구 **59**–15
봉지 **74**–7
봉투 **134**–14, **183**–43
봉투에 주소를 쓴다 **135**–B
봉합 **117**–15
부동산 중개인을 만나다 **49**–G
부두 **225**–18
부두 근로자 **167**–23
부드러운 의자 **23**–6
부리 **26**, **214**–3
부리토 **79**–9
부목 **117**–14
부스 **82**–4, **122**–3
부어오른 손가락 **110**–16
부엌용 타이머 **78**–18
부주방장 **185**–6
부주의한 작업자 **179**–1
부지사 **139**–21
부츠 **95**–28
부통령 **138**–9
부품 **175**–5
부품을 조립하다 **170**–A
부호 **190**
부호를 사용하다 **190**–C
북 **155**–1
북아메리카 **202**–1
북아메리카 및 중앙
  아메리카 **200**–201

북 캐나다 **201**-1
분 **18**-2
분리하다 **76**-B
분말류 측정 **75**
분모 **192**-6
분쇄기 **183**-24
분수 **192**
분수대 **224**-5
분수와 소수 **17**
분자 **192**-5, **195**-27
분젠 가스 버너 **195**-37
분필 **7**-18
분홍 **24**-7
불 **144**-8
불가사리 **212**-16
불꽃 가리개 **56**-12
불도저 **178**-6
불법 마약 **142**-6
불안한 **42**-10
불을 끄다 **11**-P
불을 끈다 **219**-G
불을 켜다 **11**-B
불편한 **42**-9
뷔페 **55**-24, **185**-10
브라 **91**-20
브러쉬 **33**-22, **108**-14
브레이크 페달 **159**-45
브로일러 **54**-21
브로콜리 **69**-13
브로콜리를 찐다 **77**-D
브리티시 콜럼비아 **201**-2
브이넥 스웨터 **96**-8
블라우스 **87**-8
블랙베리 **68**-17
블레이저 **92**-12
블렌더 **54**-12
블록 **59**-19
블루베리 **68**-16
블루스 **237**-22
비 **13**-11
비극 **237**-14
비누 **57**-4, **108**-3
비누 받침대 **57**-3
비늘 **212**-3
비둘기 **214**-15
비드 **95**-34, **99**-32
비디오 가게 **129**-20
비디오 게임 조종기 **232**-4
비디오 게임기 **232**-3
비디오 촬영을 하다 **240**-A
비디오 카세트 **133**-18
비디오 플레이어 **197**-11
비밀번호를 입력한다 **197**-A

비버 **216**-9
비상 계단 **50**-2
비상 전화 걸기 **15**
비상구 **51**-25, **161**-14
비상구 안내 카드 **161**-26
비상등 **159**-36
비상사태와 천재지변 **144**-**145**
비스킷 **80**-6
비싼 반지 **23**-19
비용 **27**-7
비즈니스맨 **166**-12
비처방약 **113**, **113**-18
비치 가운 **90**-25
비치 파라솔 **225**-14
비커 **195**-39
비타민 **113**-17
비품 보관함 **182**-1
비행 지연 **161**-30
비행기 **150**-8
비행기 추락 **144**-3
비행기 타기 **160**
비행기를 조종하다 **170**-F
비행기에 탑승한다 **160**-E
빈 방 광고문 **50**-7
빈 잔 **23**-10
빈 칸을 채우세요 **9**-O
빈대 **63**-24
빈도 **20**
빗 **33**-21, **108**-13
빗자루 **61**-16
빠른 우편 **134**-1
빠른 운전사 **23**-3
빨간색 스웨터는 파란색 스웨터 위에
　있습니다 **25**-4
빨강 **24**-1
빨강 머리 **33**-15
빨대 **79**-18
빨래 **101**-1
빨래 바구니 **57**-1
빨래를 개다 **101**-F
빨래를 분류하다 **101**-A
빨래방 **128**-1
빨래집게 **101**-10
빨래통 **101**-2
빨랫줄 **101**-9
빵-버터용 접시 **83**-19
빵 **67**-11
빵 한 덩어리 **74**-22
빵바구니 **83**-11
빼기 **192**-B
뼈 **107**-33
뼈가 부러지다 **116**-P
뿌리 **210**-5, **211**-3

뿔 **159**-32, **216**-21
사 **16**
사각 팬티 **91**-4
사과 **68**-1
사과 받아들이기 **12**-G
사과 쥬스 **73**-32
사과하기 **12**-F
사다 **27**-G
사다리 **61**-13, **178**-2
사람 묘사하기 **32**
사람들에게 인사하다 **3**-G
사람을 관리하다 **170**-O
사랑에 빠지다 **40**-H
사랑에 빠진 **42**-18
사막 **204**-4
사망 증명서 **41**-11
사무 보조원 **182**-10
사무실 **51**, **164**-3, **182**-**183**
사무실 매니저 **182**-8
사무실 빌딩 **124**-2
사무실 용품 판매점 **127**-21
사무실 장비 **183**
사무실에서 필요한 기술들 **171**
사무용품 **183**
사무원 **5**-13, **166**-3, **182**-2
사물 묘사하기 **23**
사물함 **5**-11, **159**-44
사발 **55**-2
사법부서 **138**
사분의 일 **17**-4
사서함 **135**-9
사슴 **216**-14
사십 **16**
사업 경영자 **166**-11
사워크림 **72**-21
사이드 미러 **158**-3
사이즈 **96**
사이클링 **228**-5
사자 **217**-36
사전 **7**-30
사진 **58**-3, **136**-4
사진 앨범 **235**-31
사진사 **206**-1
사진을 찍다 **206**-A
사진을 첨부한다 **197**-G
사촌 **34**-9
사탕무 **69**-5
사포 **181**-56
사회 보장 카드 **40**-5
사회보장번호 **4**-15
사회사업 담당 직원 **169**-57
삭제하다 **196**-C
산과 의사 **120**-2

산딸기 **68**-15
산맥 **204**-15
산봉우리 **204**-14
산불 **144**-7
산성 비 **218**-13
산소 마스크 **161**-24
산악 자전거 타기 **226**-8
산호 **220**-5
살구 **68**-12
살라미 **71**-23
살인 **142**-12
살짝 삶은 계란 **76**-9
살찐 **32**-7
살충제 중독 **218**-16
삶은 계란 **76**-8
삶은 야채 **81**-32
삶은 햄 **76**-5
삼 **16**
삼각 팬티 **91**-5
삼각건 **113**-19
삼각대 **235**-25
삼각법 **192**-18
삼각형 **193**-32
삼분의 일 **17**-3
삼십 **16**
삼촌 **34**-8
삽 **176**-7, **178**-22
상담 교사 **5**-6
상대방 **139**-30
상대방 초대하기 **12**-H
상대방을 칭찬하기 **12**-C
상사 **164**-4
상아 **217**-48
상어 **212**-4
상원 **138**-5
상원 의원 **138**-6
상인 **84**-7
상자 **74**-6
상자 내용물 **117**
상추 **69**-1
상추 한 단 **69**-32
상추 한 봉지 **69**-31
상품 카드를 사용한다 **27**-E
상하가 붙은 작업복 **92**-8
상한 바나나 **68**-32
새 **208**-4, **214**
새끼 고양이 **215**-10
새로운 단어 학습 **8**
새로운 직업 **172**-3
새우 **71**-11, **212**-18
새해 첫날 **22**-9
색깔 **24**
색소폰 **238**-5

색종이 232–12
색종이 조각 239–3
색칠 공부책 59–13
샌들 88–9
샐러드 바 79–24
샐러드 접시 83–20
샐러드 포크 83–27
생 닭고기 70–24
생년월일 4–13
생명 징후 모니터 121–26
생물 194
생물 생선 71–16
생물 에너지 218–9
생물 자원 218–9
생물학자 194–2
생수 146–11
생수 1 갤런 75–5
생음악 84–1
생일 22–1
생일 파티 240–241
생쥐 63–28, 196–15, 215–18
샤워 커튼 57–14
샤워젤 108–2
샤워캡 108–1
샤워하다 38–C, 108–A
샤워헤드 57–13
샴푸 108–10
서 155–2
서랍 54–23, 58–2
서랍장 58–1, 59–6
서론 190–6
서류 가방 88–13
서류함 182–11
서른번째 16
서명 4–19
서명하다 4–D
서부영화 237–15
서빙 보조 185–13
서빙용 그릇 55–21
서빙하다 139–D, 230–P
서수 16
서스펜스 237–20
서식지 194–11
서양 장기 232–7
서양호랑가시나무 210–19
서점 130–4
서퍼 225–15
서프보드 225–16
서핑 227–9
서해안 201–7
석방되다 141–H
석유 218–6
석탄 218–4

섞은 재료를 휘젓는다 77–S
선 193
선거 139
선거 결과 139–31
선거에 출마하다 139–A
선글라스 90–27
선물 240–3
선물 가게 184–5
선반 54–2
선발 징병제에 등록하다 140–D
선분 193–20
선블락 108–8
선생님 6–4
선생님과 이야기하다 6–B
선수 229–5
선인장 210–21
선택하다 196–B
설거지하는 곳 83–13
설립자 198–7
설비 48–5
설치류 215
설탕 73–30
설탕 그릇 55–14
설탕 대체품 79–20
설탕 한 테이블스푼 75–7
섬 204–8
섬유 뉴연제 101–6
섭씨 13–2
성 4–4
성게 212–21
성난 64–6
성냥 146–16, 226–21
성명 4–1
성별 4–16
성에 제거 장치 159–41
성인용 보행 보조기 113–11
성인학교 188–8
성적 10–4
세계 지도 202–203
세계사 199
세관 직원 161–17
세관에서 161
세금을 납부하다 140–B
세다 84–A
세단 156–1
세면대 물이 넘치다 63–18
세면대를 닦다 60–K
세미 156–15
세미콜론 190–18
세발 자전거 224–12
세번째 16
세수 수건 57–6
세일가격 27–3

세제 61–18
세제를 넣다 101–B
세탁 세제 101–8
세탁기에 빨래를 넣다 101–C
세탁소 128–2
세탁하기 101
세포 194–4
세포막 194–6
세포벽 194–5
세포질 194–9
센티미터(cm) 17–14
셀러리 69–9
셀러리를 다진다 77–J
셀프 계산대 73–10
셔츠 86–1
셔틀 152–19
셰프 샐러드 80–14
소 96–2, 215–1
소고기 볶음 76–6
소금 한 티스푼 75–6
소금 후추통(식탁용) 55–13
소나무 210–9
소독용 물티슈 61–23
소매 100–6
소매없는 짧은 상의 89–24
소매점 직원 169–53
소방관 144–9, 167–26
소방서 125–12
소방차 144–10
소보조 테이블 56–14
소설 133–16
소수점 17–7
소스 냄비 78–25
소시지 70–12, 80–2
소식에 정통하다 140–F
소아과 의사 120–4
소울 237–28
소원을 말하다 240–B
소유권을 가지다 49–K
소음 64–5
소파 56–18
소포 134–17
소포 우편 134–6
소풍 224–D
소프트볼 229–10
소프트웨어 196–10
소형 핸드백 89–19
소화기 179–21
소화전 129–27
속눈썹 106–11
속도 위반 딱지를 떼다 162–C
속도계 159–27
속옷과 잠옷 91

손 105–15
손가락 105–16
손가락 마디 106–17
손님 72–1, 94–4, 132–2, 164–2, 184–10
손님 접대하다 170–T
손님을 도와주다 95–D
손님을 앉히다 82–B
손목 106–14
손으로 바느질하다 98–B
손을 들다 6–A
손잡이 57–11, 105–14, 194–23
손전등 146–14
손톱 106–18
손톱 광택제(매니큐어) 109–33
손톱 깎기 109–31
손톱에 매니큐어를 칠하다 109–O
손톱을 깎다 109–N
손톱줄 109–32
솔기 트는 기구 100–18
솔방울 210–11
송아지 고기 커틀렛 70–6
송어 71–1
쇠갈비 70–5
쇠고기 70
쇼크 상태에 있다 116–B
쇼핑 27
쇼핑 복록 67–14
쇼핑 바구니 73–9
쇼핑 백을 재사용한다 219–B
쇼핑 센터 126–7
쇼핑 프로그램 236–10
쇼핑센터 130–131
쇼핑하다 28–A
숄더 백 94–17
수갑 141–2
수건걸이 57–15
수구 229–15
수달 213–35
수도꼭지 57–8
수도꼭지가 새다 63–17
수동 변속 159
수동 변속 레버 159–50
수두 111–6
수레를 잡아당기다 224–A
수력 발전 218–5
수리공 62–10
수박 68–18
수분을 섭취한다 114–C
수상 199–7
수상스키 227–7
수상한 물건은 신고한다 143–J
수색구조팀 145–20
수석 웨이터 185–12

수석 주방장 **185**–7
수선 **100**
수선화 **211**–25
수성 **205**–1
수송 **175**–D
수술대 **121**–40
수술실 **121**
수술실 간호원 **120**–9
수술용 마스크 **93**–36
수술용 모자 **93**–35
수술용 장갑 **121**–39
수술용 캡 **121**–37
수신 상태 불량 **14**–12
수신 상태 양호 **14**–11
수업에 출석하다 **38**–J
수염 **216**–18
수영 팬츠 **90**–22
수영복 **90**–26
수영장 **51**–22, **184**–22
수영장 서비스 **184**–21
수영하다 **230**–L
수요일 **20**–11
수의사 **169**–62
수정 **191**–J
수정 테이프 **183**–37
수정액 **183**–36
수족관 **222**–7
수직선 **193**–24
수질 오염 **218**–14
수채화 물감 **233**–21
수탉 **215**–7
수통 **226**–24
수퍼마켓 **127**–18
수평기 **180**–29
수표 **132**–13
수표를 현금화하다 **132**–A
수표책 **132**–12
수하물 **161**–18
수하물 컨베이어 **161**–23
수학 **189**–10, **192**–193
수학 문제 **192**
수학 문제를 풀다 **170**–M
수학 연산 **192**
수학의 종류 **192**
수화기 **14**–1
수화기를 들고 기다린다 **15**–H
수화물 운반인 **160**–1
수화물을 찾는다 **160**–L
수확하다 **177**–B
숙모 **34**–7
숙제하다 **39**–T
순무 **69**–16
숟가락 **55**–5

술을 마시지 마십시오 **112**–F
술장식 **99**–34
숨다 **240**–D
숨을 못쉬다 **116**–N
숫송아지 **177**–21
숫자 **16**
숲 **204**–11
쉬다 **39**–U
쉬운 문제 **23**–23
쉰번째 **16**
쉼표 **190**–14
숫하다 **211**–5, **230**–H
스낵류 **73**
스냅 **99**–26
스노보드 **231**–23
스노보딩 **227**–2
스노클링 **227**–11
스마트폰 **15**–27
스모그 **218**–11
스모그 검사를 받으러 간다 **157**–J
스모그가 낀 **13**–14
스무번째 **16**
스물한번째 **16**
스웨이드 **99**–8
스웨터 **28**–2, **87**–14
스위스 치즈 **71**–27
스위트룸 **184**–16
스윙하다 **230**–Q
스카프 **95**–12
스캐너 **183**–20
스컹크 **216**–12
스케이트를 타다 **230**–U
스케이트보드 **224**–7, **228**–13
스쿠버 다이빙 **227**–12
스쿠버 탱크 **225**–5
스쿨 버스 **156**–21
스쿱넥 스웨터 **96**–10
스퀴지 **61**–15
스크레이퍼 **181**–52
스크롤 바 **197**–15
스크린 **6**–2, **235**–30
스키 **231**–24
스키 마스크 **90**–15
스키 모자 **90**–11
스키 폴 **231**–25
스키를 타다 **230**–V
스키화 **231**–26
스타일 **96**
스타킹 **91**–17
스탬프 **134**–23, **183**–47
스테레오 시스템 **56**–8
스테이션 웨곤 **156**–6
스테이크 **70**–2, **81**–24

스테이크용 넙치 **71**–6
스테이크용 연어 **71**–4
스테이크용 칼 **83**–29
스테이플 **183**–29
스테이플러 **183**–28
스테이플러로 찍다 **171**–F
스토브 **54**–18
스튜용 쇠고기 **70**–3
스트레스 **115**–4
스트레칭하다 **230**–M
스티커 **102**–3
스파게티 **81**–26
스페이드 **233**–30
스포츠 동사 **230**
스포츠 셔츠 **88**–4
스포츠 자켓 **89**–14
스포츠 카 **156**–4
스포츠 코트 **89**–14
스포츠 프로그램 **236**–11
스포츠용 잠바 **90**–24
스폰지 **61**–19
스폰지 대걸레 **61**–6
스프 **72**–18, **80**–16
스프 스푼 **83**–32
스프레이 총 **181**–21
스프레이 풀 **101**–12
스프링 노트 **7**–29
스프링클러 **53**–22
스프링클러를 설치하다 **176**–H
스프용 그릇 **83**–21
스피커 **50**–5, **234**–14
슬리퍼 **91**–26
슬리핑백 **226**–12
슬픈 **43**–19
습한 **13**–15
승객 **150**–2, **152**–3, **161**–15
승무원 **161**–12
승진 **172**–4
시 **4**–7
시 의회 **139**–27
시 정부 **139**
시가지 **126**–127
시각 **18**–1
시각 장애가 있는 **32**–11
시간 **18**–19
시간 말하기 **18**
시간대 **19**
시계 **7**–9
시계겸용 라디오 **102**–6
시골 **52**–4
시금치 **69**–11
시금치 샐러드 **80**–13
시끄러운 아이들 **23**–11

시내 **124**–125
시내 전화 **15**–31
시누이 **34**–16
시력 검사 **136**–6
시력 문제 **115**–1
시리얼 한 상자 **74**–18
시민권 시험 통과 **140**–I
시민권 요건 **140**
시민권과 의무 **140**
시민이 되다 **40**–G
시설 관리 **184**–23
시소 **224**–16
시식용 **84**–5
시아버지 **34**–11
시어머니 **34**–10
시연 **122**–6
시원한 **13**–5
시의원 **139**–28
시장 **139**–26
시장을 보고 돌아와서 **66**–67
시장을 보러 가다 **38**–L
시청 **124**–8
시침핀 **100**–12
시퀸 **99**–33
시트를 갈다 **60**–P
시트콤 **236**–2
시험 장소 **136**–2
시험 책자 **10**–1
시험관 **195**–42
시험에 통과한다 **10**–E
시험지를 제출한다 **10**–O
시험치기 **10**
식 **206**–6
식기 세척용 세제 **61**–21
식당 **82**–83
식당 **46**–7, **55**, **82**–1, **125**–14
식당 구역 **131**–15
식당 손님 **82**–6, **185**–9
식당 여직원 **82**–2
식당 주방 **185**
식당에서 식사 **185**
식도구 세팅 **83**–17
식료품 관련 제품 **72**
식료품 백 **67**–13
식료품점 **72**–73
식료품점 직원 **72**–4
식물 **208**–5, **210**
식물에 물을 주다 **176**–F
식물에 비료를 주다 **176**–D
식물원 **222**–3
식민지 시대 **198**
식민지 주민 **198**–2
식사하기 1시간 전에 복용하십시오 **112**–B

식탁 55-9
식탁 의자 55-8
식탁보 55-12
식탁을 차리다 82-A
식품 가공기 54-56
식품 안전 76
신고서 161-17
신맛 84-4
신문 133-6
신문 가판대 128-12
신문을 읽다 39-V
신문을 재활용하다 60-B
신발 87-13
신발 가게 130-10
신발 밑창 94-21
신발 코너 95-7
신발과 액세서리 94-95
신발을 신어보다 95-C
신분 도용 142-9
신분증과 신용 카드 사본 146-19
신분증을 제시한다 137-C
신상 정보 4
신용 카드를 사용한다 27-B
신월 205-9
신장 107-43
신정 22-9
신청료를 지불한다 137-D
신청서를 작성한다 173-J
신청서를 제출하다 48-C
신체 104-105
신체 내외부 106-107
신체 장애가 있는 32-10
신호등 128-8
신호등을 기다리다 128-B
실 99-23, 100-11
실내용 변기 121-23
실내화초 56-4, 211-27
실로폰 238-15
실망한 28-4
실크 98-5
실톱 180-10
실패 98-21
실핀 108-21
실험 195
실험복 93-33
실험을 실시한다 195-B
심각한 증상 및 질병 111
심다 177-A
심사 구역 160-4
심장 박동을 듣다 118-C
심장 전문의 120-3
심장마비를 일으키다 116-D
심장병 111-11

심판 229-6
십 16
십구 16
십만 16
십사 16
십삼 16
십억 16
십오 16
십육 16
십이 16
십일 16
십칠 16
십팔 16
싱크 54-4, 57-25
싼 반지 23-20
쌀 67-10, 81-30, 177-1
쌍둥이 28-1
썰매타기 227-6
쓰기 규칙 190
쓰기 순서 191
쓰레기 148-2
쓰레기 낙하장치 51-26
쓰레기 봉투 61-24
쓰레기를 내다놓다 60-Q
쓰레기를 버리다 11-N
쓰레기를 버리지 않는다 219-L
쓰레기를 줄인다 219-A
쓰레기차 127-22
쓰레기통 51-23, 53-24, 57-26
쓰레기통을 비우다 60-L
쓰레받기 61-17
씨 211-1
씻다 76-A
아가리가 넓은 병 74-2
아가미 212-2
아기 31-7
아기 모니터 59-7
아기 방 47-10
아기 봐주는 사람 166-9
아기 캐리어 37-17
아기를 낳다 41-L
아기용 유모차 37-20
아내 34-12
아들 34-15
아래턱 106-1
아랫단 100-9
아령 231-22
아르마딜로 216-8
아름다운 경치 23-21
아메리카 낙타 217-25
아메리카삼나무 210-18
아메리칸 치즈 71-26
아버지 34-4

아보카도 84-6
아스파라거스 69-26
아시아 202-4
아이들을 내려주다 38-G
아이들을 데려오다 38-M
아이들을 학교에 데려다 주다 38-G
아이디어를 정리한다 191-G
아이라이너 109-36
아이를 혼자 키우는 아빠 35-23
아이를 혼자 키우는 엄마 35-22
아이리스 211-16
아이보리 24-16
아이섀도우 109-35
아이스 스케이트 231-9
아이스 스케이팅 227-4
아이스 하키 229-13
아이스박스 225-9
아이스크림 72-26
아이스크림 가게 131-16
아이스크림 콘 79-13
아이스티 79-12
아침 18-15
아침 식사를 하다 38-E
아코디언 238-19
아크릴 페인트 232-10
아티초크 69-22
아파트 50-51
아파트 건물 50-1
아파트 임대하기 48
아파트 통로 51
아파트 호수 4-6
아포스트로피 190-16
아프리카 202-5
아픈 42-11
아홉번째 16
아흔번째 16
악기를 연주하다 238-A, 239-7
악수한다 3-J, 174-I
악어 213-36
안개 낀 13-20
안경 115-7
안경점 130-9
안과 의사 120-7
안내 182-14
안내판 131-24
안다 36-A
안도 42-15
안뜰 5-1, 51-21
안락의자 56-22
안아 주기 2-E
안약 113-31
안전 규정 164-6
안전 레일 59-10

안전 마스크 179-12
안전 벨트 159-52
안전 벨트를 맨다 160-H
안전 시트 37-19
안전 장비 179
안전 장화 179-20
안전모 92-1, 179-9
안전핀 37-9
안전한 웹사이트에서 쇼핑한다 143-H
안테나 14-9
앉다 6-F
알람 시계 58-24
알래스카 표준시 19-28
알레르기 111-8
알레르기 반응을 보이다 116-E
알루미늄 포일 72-23
알약 113-21
알파벳 7-13
암 111-10
암청색 24-10
암탉 215-8
압정 183-35
압축공기 드릴 178-9
앞 현관 53
앞마당과 주택 53
앞머리 33-8
앞면 193-44
앞문 53-11
앞유리 158-1
앞유리 와이퍼 158-2
앞유리 와이퍼를 교체한다 157-K
앞으로 단추 197-3
앞좌석 159-51
앞쪽 통로 53-2
앞치마 92-11
애벌레 214-20
애완동물 215
애완동물 가게 130-6
애완동물 식품 72-5
애플리케 99-31
액셀러레이터 159-46
액션 237-19
액션 인물 233-26
액자 58-4
액체류 측정 75
야간등 37-27
야구 경기 44-2
야구 모자 86-5
야구 방망이 231-14
야구 카드 232-2
야구공 229-9, 231-18
야드 자 181-16
야생 생물 220-3

야외 관람석 5-3
야외 활동 226
야자나무 106-15, 210-14
야채 66-8, 69
야채 껍질 제거기 78-15
야채를 첨가한다 77-N
약 121-20
약국 112-113, 128-4
약사 112-1
약속 22-4, 118-1
약을 과다 복용하다 116-K
약을 모두 복용하십시오 112-C
약을 복용한다 114-D
약의 종류 113
약품 수납장 57-22
약혼하다 41-J
얇은 재킷 97-28
얇은 책 23-8
양 215-6
양 다리 70-14
양 정강이 살 70-13
양고기 70
양고기찹 70-15
양궁 228-1
양동이 61-7, 225-8
양말 86-6
양배추 69-2
양보 154-9
양부분육 70-15
양서류 212
양성자 195-31
양손 전정 가위 176-11
양수 192-2
양식에 기입하기 4
양재사 100-1
양재용 마네킹 100-2
양치하다 109-J
양탄자 58-22
양파 69-19
양파를 잘게 썬다 77-L
양파링 79-4
양호박 69-25
어깨 105-13
어깨 닿을 정도의 머리 33-2
어깨 패드 231-20
어깨뼈 107-28
어댑터 234-15
어려운 문제 23-24
어른과 어린이 30-31
어린이 안전 시트 159-53
어린이 침실 47-9, 59
어린이 프로그램 236-9
어린이를 돌보다 170-P

어린이용 의자 37-6, 82-3
어머니 34-3
어부 167-17
어제 20-7
어지러움을 느끼다 110-C
언덕 204-16
언론의 자유 140-4
언어 189-9
얼굴 106
얼룩 다람쥐 215-20
얼룩말 217-33
얼룩지다 97-42
얼은 13-22
얼음 찜질팩 117-13
엄지 106-16
에그 스크램블 76-7
에너지 자원 218
에너지 효율성이 높은 전구를
  사용한다 219-H
에너지와 보존 218-219
에너지와 자원을 보존하는 방법 219
에세이 190-4
에세이 구성 190
에스컬레이터 131-23
에어로빅 122-5
에어백 159-43
에어컨 159-39
엔지니어 167-25
엔진 158-18
엔터테인먼트 236-237
엘리베이터 50-9, 131-21, 184-9
여 4-18
여과기 78-17
여권 41-10
여덟번째 16
여든번째 16
여름 21-38
여섯번째 16
여성용 속옷 91
여성용 양말 91
여우 216-15
여자 조카 34-18
여자 형제 34-5
여자들 30-3
여행사 131-14
여행을 하다 220-A
여행자 수표로 지불한다 27-F
여행하기 162-163
여행하다 41-P
역겨운 42-7
역도 228-16
역사 189-12
역사적 용어 199

연 225-2
연결 코드 181-14
연고 113-24
연기 탐지기 51-29
연단 206-5
연료 계기 159-31
연료 탱크 158-10
연료분사 장치 158-17
연립주택 52-6
연못 204-21
연방 정부 138
연석 129-21
연설을 하다 148-A
연습장 7-26
연어 구이 76-3
연어 한 마리 71-3
연필 7-20
연필 깎이 7-23
연필을 내려 놓다 6-J
연필을 들다 6-I
연회 요리 담당 185-16
연회장 184-26, 185-14
열 110-8
열기 13-13
열네번째 16
열다섯번째 16
열두번째 16
열번째 16
열세번째 16
열아홉번째 16
열여덟번째 16
열여섯번째 16
열일곱번째 16
열한번째 16
염려되는 42-13
염색체 194-8
염소 215-5
영 16
영국 군인 198-9
영수증 27-6
영양 217-35
영양 성분 표시 라벨 122-8
영양사 120-15
영원 212-26
영작문 190-191
영주권 40-2
영화관 222-2
영화의 종류 237
예각 193-28
예금 계좌번호 132-11
예방주사를 맞는다 114-I
예비 타이어 158-23
예산 186-3

예순번째 16
예술가 166-6
오 16
오거나이저 183-49
오늘 20-5
오디오북 133-17
오랑우탄 217-39
오렌지 68-5
오르간 238-20
오리 70-18, 214-12
오리구리 217-46
오리발 212-1, 225-7
오리털 자켓 90-16
오리털 조끼 90-14
오믈렛 76-12
오버헤드 프로젝터 7-16
오보에 238-3
오븐 54-20
오븐 클리너 61-3
오븐 토스터 54-15
오븐을 예열한다 77-A
오븐을 청소하다 60-C
오십 16
오이 69-10
오일 73-31, 218-6
오일을 점검한다 157-H
오전 18-4
오징어 212-7
오케스트라를 지휘하다 238-C
오크 210-17
오토바이 150-4
오페라 223-11
오한 110-9
오후 18-5, 18-17
옥상 정원 50-4
옥수수 69-12, 177-4
온도 13
온도 계기 159-30
온도를 조정한다 219-J
온라인 카탈로그 133-11
온라인 코스 172-8
온라인으로 은행 업무를 보다 132-C
온수 57-9
온수기가 고장나다 62-1
온타리오 201-4
올빼미 214-5
올이 풀리다 97-43
올케 34-16
옷 만들기 98-99
옷 수선 100
옷 수선점 100
옷 입다 38-D
옷걸이 98-16, 101-11

옷을 걸다 **101**–H
옷을 다림질하다 **101**–G
옷을 바느질하다 **170**–L
옷을 벗기다 **36**–E
옷장 **58**–5
옷핀 **100**–14
와셔 **50**–12, **101**–3, **180**–37
와이어 스트리퍼 **181**–42
와플 **80**–8
완충 패드 **59**–4
왕복 여행 **152**–17
외과 의사 **121**–36
외국어 **189**–13
외국어를 말하다 **170**–N
외로운 **42**–17
외양 **32**
요가 **122**–4
요거트 **72**–22
요금 **152**–2
요금 카드 **152**–11
요람 **59**–20
요리하다 **76**–C, **170**–C
요양원 **52**–12
요일 **20**, **20**–2
요통 **110**–5
요트 **225**–3, **227**–8
욕실 **57**
욕실용 매트 **57**–28
욕조 **57**–2
용기 **74**–5, **160**–6
용기와 포장 **74**
용의자를 체포하다 **141**–A
용접공 **169**–63
용지 순서를 맞추다 **171**–E
우림 **204**–1
우물정 버튼 **14**–7
우박을 동반한 폭풍 **13**–21
우산 **90**–17
우울증 **115**–5
우유 1 온스 **75**–1
우유 1 쿼트 **75**–4
우주 **205**
우주 정류장 **205**–18
우주비행사 **205**–17
우주선 **205**–19
우체국 **125**–11, **134**–**135**
우체국 소인 **134**–24
우체국 직원 **135**–7
우체부 **134**–20
우체통 **53**–1, **128**–13, **135**–12
우편 번호 **4**–9
우편 엽서 **134**–16
우편 주소 **134**–22

우편국 직원 **169**–49
우편물 기입 양식 **134**–19
우편물 라벨 **183**–41
우편물 저울 **183**–27
우편함 **50**–11
우표 1권 **134**–18
우표 판매기 **135**–11
우표를 붙인다 **135**–C
우회전만 허용 **154**–7
운동가 **199**–17
운동경기용 서포터 **91**–6
운동기구 **231**
운동복 **89**
운동을 한다 **114**–E
운동하다 **39**–P, **230**–N
운동화 **86**–7
운전 면허 번호 **136**–11
운전 면허국 **124**–4
운전 면허국(DMV) **136**–**137**
운전 면허증 **40**–4, **136**–9
운전석 **156**–16
운전을 배우다 **40**–E
운전자 교육 코스를 듣는다 **137**–B
운전자 훈련 코스를 듣는다 **137**–G
울다 **206**–B
울타리 **177**–19
웃다 **44**–A
원 **193**–34
원기둥 **193**–41
원뿔 **193**–40
원숭이 **217**–26
원자 **195**–28
원자력 에너지 **218**–8
원주 **193**–36
원주민 **198**–3
원피스 **36**–H, **86**–3
원형 재단기 **232**–16
원형 톱 **180**–9
월 **20**–3, **21**
월요일 **20**–9
웨이브가 있는 머리 **33**–10
웨이터 **82**–8, **169**–56, **185**–8
웨이트리스 **83**–9
웹 사이트 주소 **197**–4
웹 페이지 검색 **197**
웹캠 **196**–12
위 **70**–8, **107**–41
위생모 **93**–25
위성 **205**–20
위성방송 안테나 **53**–6
위에 소스를 숟가락으로 끼얹는다 **77**–F
위험 및 위험 물질 **179**
위험 폐기물 **218**–12

위험한 **186**–1
윈드서핑 **227**–10
유기농 **84**–2
유기체 **194**–1
유니폼 **88**–10, **231**–16
유대 교회 **127**–16
유량계 **159**–29
유럽 **202**–3
유리 클리너 **61**–14
유리창이 깨지다 **62**–5
유모차 **37**–18
유방 **107**–26
유아 **31**–8
유아용 변기 의자 **37**–12
유아용 책 **37**–22
유아용 침대 **59**–3
유원지 **223**–10
유자격 간호 보조원 **120**–12
유제품 **72**
유제품과 함께 복용하지 마십시오 **112**–D
유치원 **188**–1
유타칸 반도 **201**–19
유화 **233**–19
유효 기한 **112**–7, **136**–10
육 **16**
육군 **138**–14
육류 조리법 **76**
육면체 **193**–38
육상 경기 **228**–18
육상 우편 **134**–6
육십 **16**
육아 **36**–**37**
육체 노동을 하다 **170**–D
융합 **218**–10
은하계 **205**–15
은행 **124**–5, **132**
은행 명세서 **132**–16
음료대 **224**–9
음료수 **73**
음반 판매점 **130**–1
음성 메시지 **14**–18
음수 **192**–1
음식 또는 우유와 함께 복용하십시오 **112**–A
음식 무게를 달다 **75**–B
음식 서비스 **185**
음식 준비와 안전 **76**–**77**
음식물 쓰레기는 퇴비로 사용한다 **219**–M
음식을 서빙하다 **82**–F
음식찌거기 처리기 **54**–7
음악 **64**–3, **189**–16, **238**
음악가 **168**–43
음악의 종류 **237**
음주 운전 **142**–5

음주 운전을 하지 않는다 **143**–G
응급 상황 대비 절차 **146**–**147**
응급 상황 종료 후 **147**
응급 상황 중에 **147**
응급 상황에 대비한 계획을 세운다 **146**–A
응급 상황에 대해 설명한다 **15**–G
응급 의료 기술자 **121**–32
응급 의료 상황 **116**
응급 치료 **117**
응급 치료 상자 **117**–1, **146**–18
응급 치료 지침서 **117**–2
응급 호흡법 **117**–16
응급실 입구 **121**
응급치료 절차 **117**
응급환자 식별 팔찌 **117**–3
의견 **44**–3
의견을 들어본다 **191**–K
의료 보조자 **116**–2
의료 폐기물 처리기 **121**–31
의류 공장 **98**
의무 **140**
의복 묘사 **96**–**97**
의복 문제 **97**
의복 비교 **97**
의붓 자매 **35**–29
의붓 형제 **35**–30
의사 **118**–5
의사 보조원 **168**–47
의사의 수술복 **93**–37, **121**–38
의사의 지시를 따른다 **114**–J
의식을 잃다 **116**–A
의원 **139**–24
의자 **7**–11
의회 **138**–2
이 **16**
이동식 무대차 **239**–2
이동식 주택 **52**–7
이동식 크레인 **178**–5
이력서를 쓴다 **173**–F
이력서와 신분증을 가져간다 **174**–D
이력서와 자기 소개를
  제출하다 **173**–H
이륙하다 **160**–J
이른 **19**–22
이를 드릴하다 **119**–D
이를 뽑다 **119**–F
이름 **4**–2
이름을 말하다 **4**–A
이름을 말한다 **15**–F
이름을 쓰다 **4**–C
이름의 철자를 말하다 **4**–B
이름의 첫 글자는 대문자로
  표기한다 **190**–A

이름표 **92**–15
이마 **106**–2
이메일 로그온 및 발송 **197**
이메일 주소를 쓴다 **197**–C
이메일을 전송한다 **197**–I
이메일을 확인하다 **39**–W
이모 **34**–7
이민 **199**–12
이민자 **199**–13
이발 **33**–A
이발소 **129**–19
이번 주 **20**–19
이복 남자 형제 **35**–28
이복 여자 형제 **35**–27
이분의 일 **17**–2
이불 커버 **58**–13
이브닝 가운 **89**–18
이사짐 배달원 **168**–42
이사하다 **48**–F, 49
이삿짐 트럭 **156**–18
이상 전압 보호기 **196**–1
이십 **16**
이십 사 **16**
이십 삼 **16**
이십 오 **16**
이십 이 **16**
이십 일 **16**
이웃 감시 프로그램에 참가한다 **143**–L
이웃을 만나다 **49**–R
이유식 **37**–4
이젤 **233**–18
이주하다 **40**–C
이중 냄비 **78**–8
이착륙 모니터 **161**–7
이통 **110**–3
이혼한 부부 **35**–21
익은 바나나 **68**–30
인공 치관 **119**–9
인라인 스케이트 **231**–10
인라인 스케이팅 **228**–10
인명구조 기구 **225**–20
인생 경로 및 관련 문서 **40–41**
인용 **190**–9
인치(in) **17**–15
인터넷 **197**
인터넷 게시물 **48**–1
인터넷 구직 사이트를 확인한다 **173**–D
인터넷 전화 **14**–20
인터넷 지도 **155**–12
인터콤 **50**–5
인턴쉽 **172**–6
인형 **59**–21
인형 만드는 키트 **232**–13

인형집 **59**–18
인후통 **110**–6
일 **16**
일곱번째 **16**
일과 **38–39**
일광 절약 시간(서머타임) **19**–25
일기도 **13**
일꾼 **177**–20
일륜 수레 **176**–3
일몰 **18**–18
일방 통행 **154**–3
일상 회화 **12**
일시 정지 **235**–E
일식 **205**–16
일어 서다 **6**–D
일어나다 **38**–B
일요일 **20**–8
일정 관리 수첩 **183**–48
일정표 **152**–4
일주일에 두 번 **20**–23
일주일에 세 번 **20**–24
일주일에 한 번 **20**–22
일출 **18**–14
일하다 **38**–K
일회용 장갑 **93**–27
일흔번째 **16**
임금 **165**–12
임대 계약서 **51**–28
임대 계약서에 서명하다 **48**–D
임부복 상점 **131**–19
임산부용 원피스 **88**–5
임시 연습 허가증을 받는다 **137**–F
임신한 **32**–15
입 **104**–7, 106
입구 **50**, 164–1
입금 **132**–3
입금 용지 **132**–4
입금하다 **132**–B
입다 **87**–B
입법 부서 **138**
입술 **106**–5
입원과 직원 **120**–14
입주자 모임 **64–65**
잇몸 **106**–6
잇몸질환 **119**–11
잉글리쉬 머핀 **80**–5
잉꼬 **215**–15
잉크 카트리지 **183**–45
잉크 패드 **183**–46
잉크젯 프린터 **183**–18
잎 **210**–6, 211–6
자 **17**–13
자기 소개하기 **2**–C

자기소개서를 쓴다 **173**–G
자다 **39**–Z
자동 대출 **133**–10
자동 변속 **159**
자동 우편 센터 **135**–10
자동 응답 시스템 **14**–23
자동 응답기 **14**–17
자동 판매기 **152**–9
자동차 **150**–1
자동차 관리 **157**
자동차 광고를 본다 **157**–A
자동차 구입 및 유지관리 **157**
자동차 기술자 **166**–8
자동차 내부 **159**
자동차 딜러 **126**–4
자동차 부품 **158–159**
자동차 사고 **144**–2
자동차 클럽 카드 **162**–4
자동차 판매점에서 **158**
자동차를 등록한다 **157**–F
자동차를 정비공에게 가지고
　간다 **157**–C
자동차를 주차하다 **129**–E
자동차를 팔다 **170**–K
자동차와 트럭 **156**
자두 **68**–13
자랑스러운 **43**–21
자료를 정리하다 **171**–L
자리에 앉다 **6**–F
자몽 **68**–6
자물쇠 수리공 **62**–11
자물쇠가 고장나다 **62**–6
자석 **195**–36
자수 **233**–24
자신의 경력에 대해 말한다 **174**–L
자연 센터 **208–209**
자연 프로그램 **236**–7
자외선 차단제 **108**–7, 225–10
자외선 차단제를 바르다 **108**–D
자원 봉사자 **41**–Q, 121–17
자작나무 **210**–7
자장가를 부르다 **36**–O
자전거 **129**–22, 151–15
자전거 길 **224**–3
자전거 타는 사람 **224**–2
자전거를 타다 **129**–D
자정 **18**–21
자주 **24**–6
자주개자리 **177**–5
자주색 스웨터는 가운데 있습니다 **25**–2
자켓 **90**–8
작가 **169**–64
작곡 **199**–15

작곡가 **199**–14
작문을 제출한다 **191**–M
작업 셔츠 **92**–2
작업 안전 **179**
작업등 **181**–44
작업복 **93**–26
작업용 고글 **179**–11
작업용 바지 **92**–5
작업용 부츠 **92**–6
작업용 장갑 **92**–17, 179–17
작은 마을 **52**–3
작은 손 **23**–1
작은 타월 **57**–17
잔가지 **210**–1
잔고 **132**–17
잔디 **53**–26
잔디 깎는 기계 **176**–6
잔디를 깎다 **176**–A
잔해를 청소한다 **147**–M
잘 어울리는 **28**–3
잘못 표시한 것을 고친다 **10**–N
잘못 표시한 것을 지운다 **10**–M
잘못된 행동을 하다 **44**–B
잘자라고 키스하다 **36**–P
잠금용 **99**
잠수복 **225**–4
잠에서 깨다 **38**–A
잠옷 **91**
잠자리에 들다 **39**–Y
잡다 **230**–D
잡지 **133**–5
잡지 꽂이대 **56**–23
잡초 제거기 **176**–12
장 **107**–42
장갑 **90**–6, 231–17
장거리 전화 **15**–32
장난감 가게 **130**–5
장난감 상자 **59**–16
장난감과 게임 **59**
장난감을 치우다 **60**–G
장난스러운 사진 **206**–2
장내 기생충 **111**–13
장모 **34**–10
장미 **211**–15
장식 **239**–15, 240–1
장식용 전구 **239**–18
장식용 쿠션 **56**–2
장애 **32**
장애인 주차장 **128**–6, 154–12
장애인을 도와준다 **147**–G
장어 **212**–12
장인 **34**–11
장화 **90**–20

재료 준비 담당 **185**–4
재료를 섞는다 **77**–R
재료를 측량하다 **75**–A
재물대 **194**–17
재물대 고정 클립 **194**–21
재봉사 **100**–3, **167**–29
재봉틀 **98**–13
재봉틀 부품 **98**
재봉틀 사용자 **98**–14
재봉틀로 바느질하다 **98**–A
재생하다 **223**–8, **235**–B
재스민 **211**–22
재즈 **237**–24
재채기하다 **110**–B
재택 간병인 **167**–32
재판관 **141**–6
재판을 받다 **141**–D
재해 대책 키트를 만든다 **146**–B
재향군인의 날 **22**–16
재혼 **35**–24
재활용 제품을 구입한다 **219**–D
재활용 통 **61**–2
재활용한다 **219**–C
잭－오－랜턴 **239**–10
잭 **158**–24
잭해머 **178**–9
샘 한 병 **74**–14
쟁반 **55**–17
쟁반을 나르다 **82**–H
저가 검사 **122**–1
저녁 **18**–19
저녁 식사를 요리하다 **39**–Q
저녁을 먹다 **39**–S
저울 **195**–41
저자 **133**–15
저장소 **185**–5
저지방 우유 **81**–42
적재 도크 **175**–15
적절한 옷차림을 한다 **174**–B
전갈 **214**–30
전기 깡통 따개 **54**–14
전기 면도기 **109**–26
전기 믹서 **54**–25
전기 위험 **186**–6
전기 충격을 받다 **116**–F
전기 테이프 **181**–43
전기공 **62**–9
전기물 **133**–13
전동 드릴 **180**–8
전동 샌더 **180**–11
전동 연필깎이 **183**–26
전등 **58**–25
전등 스위치 **58**–27

전등갓 **58**–26
전몰장병 기념일 **22**–12
전문의 **120**
전선 **181**–13
전신 거울 **58**–6
전신 잠옷 **91**–27
전신용 슬립 **91**–22
전원 지역 **52**–4
전원 코드 **196**–2
전원이 나가다 **62**–2
전자 **195**–30
전자 승차권 **161**–19
전자 키보드 **238**–18
전자레인지용 볼에 계란 2개를
  깨뜨린다 **77**–Q
전자렌지 **54**–13
전자제품 가게 **131**–20
전자제품 수리공 **167**–24
전자제품과 사진 **234**–235
전쟁 **199**–10
전정 가위 **176**–9
전조등 **158**–7
전철역 **152**
전체 **17**–1
전축 **234**–12
전치사 **25**
선화 **14**–15
전화 걸기 **15**
전화 관련 기능 **171**
전화 교환기 **182**–13
전화 번호 **4**–11, **15**–30
전화 번호를 누른다 **15**–A
전화 요금 청구서 확인하기 **15**
전화 잭 **14**–3
전화 카드 **14**–15
전화로 병결을 알리다 **186**–A
전화를 건 사람에게 인사하다 **171**–M
전화를 건 사람을 기다리게 하다 **171**–N
전화를 끊는다 **15**–D
전화를 돌리다 **171**–O
전화번호 안내 **14**–22
전화선 **14**–4
전화요금 청구서 **15**–28
젊은 **32**–1
점 **32**–16
점수 **10**–3, **229**–1
점심을 만든다 **38**–F
점원 **94**–3
점적기 **195**–45
점퍼 케이블 **158**–21
점프수트 **93**–24
점프하다 **230**–I
점화 장치 **159**–33

접객원 **184**–4
접속 번호 **14**–16
접수 안내 구역 **182**–15
접수원 **118**–2, **164**–5, **169**–51
접시 **55**–1
접시 걸이 **54**–5
접시 닦는 행주 **61**–22
접시 매트 **55**–11
접시닦는 사람 **54**–8, **83**–14, **185**–2
접시를 닦다 **60**–M
접시를 말리다 **60**–N
접안 렌즈 **194**–14
접이식 의자 **102**–5
접이식 테이블 **102**–4
젓다 **77**–O
정강이 **106**–21
정기 간행물 **133**–4
정기 검사를 받는다 **114**–H
정답란을 확인하세요 **9**–U
정맥 **107**–37
정맥 주사 **121**–25
정보를 교환한다 **173**–A
정부 및 군 복무 **138**–139
정비소에서 **158**
정사각형 **193**–30
정상가 **27**–2
성수 **192**
정시에 **19**–23, **161**–29
정시에 도착한다 **174**–F
정신과 의사 **120**–8
정오 **18**–16
정원 **53**–B
정원 관리 책임자 **176**–4
정원사 **167**–28, **176**–1
정장 **87**–11, **88**–11, **89**
정장용 양말 **91**–9
정제 **113**–22
정지 **154**–1
정치 운동 **199**–16
정치 캠페인 **139**–29
젖꼭지 **37**–2
젖병 **37**–1
젖은 셔츠 **101**–17
젖을 짜다 **66**–5, **177**–C
제과류 **73**
제과점 **127**–19
제대로 알아 들었는지 확인하기 **12**–N
제동등 **158**–14
제목 **133**–14, **190**–5
제목을 쓴다 **197**–D
제비꽃 **211**–23
제빵 관련 제품 **73**
제빵사 **166**–10

제산제 **113**–28
제의하다 **49**–I
제조 **175**–B
제한 속도 **154**–4
조개 **225**–24
조건을 물어보다 **48**–B
조경 디자이너 **176**–5
조경 및 정원 관리 **176**
조끼 **89**–15
조동 나사 **194**–24
조리개 **194**–18
조리한 닭고기 **70**–25
조립 **175**–C
조립 라인 **175**–6
조립공 **166**–7
조명 기구 **55**–18
조부모가 되다 **41**–N
조용한 아이들 **23**–12
조정 가능한 렌치 **181**–48
조종사 **161**–11
조종실 **161**–10
졸린 **42**–3
졸업 **206**–207
졸업 가운 **206**–8
졸업 모자 **88**–1, **206**–7
졸업증서 **40**–3
솔업하나 **40**–D
좁은 넥타이 **97**–35
종교의 자유 **140**–3
종교적 휴일 **22**–7
종아리 **106**–22
종양학 전문의 **120**–5
종업원 **82**–8, **83**–9, **169**–56, **185**–8
종이 인형 **233**–28
종이 재단기 **183**–22
종이 타월 한 두루말이 **74**–23
종이 한 장을 빼세요 **9**–Y
종점 **193**–21
좋은 성적을 받는다 **10**–H
좌석을 찾는다 **160**–F
좌회전 금지 **154**–8
죄수 **141**–15
죄인 **141**–15
주 **4**–8, **20**–15
주 사무실 **5**–12
주 상원의원 **139**–25
주 정부 **139**
주걱 **78**–19
주기율표 **195**–26
주도 **139**–22
주말 **20**–17
주머니 **100**–7, **217**–50
주머니쥐 **216**–4

주문 담당자 **175**-10
주문원 **185**-15
주문을 받다 **82**-E
주방 **46**-5, **54**, **83**-15
주방 용품 **78**
주방장 **83**-16
주방장 가운 **93**-29
주방장 모자 **93**-28
주부 **168**-33
주사 **118**-12
주사위 **232**-6
주소 **4**-5
주어진 과제에 대해 생각해본다 **191**-E
주요 서류 사본 **146**-20
주위를 살펴본다 **143**-I
주유소 **125**-10
주유소 직원 **162**-3
주의 깊은 작업자 **179**-2
주의하여 경청한다 **174**-K
주의회 **139**-23
주지사 **139**-20
주차 공간 **50**-18, **128**-5
주차 금지 **154**-11
주차 미터 **129**-25
주차 직원 **184**-3
주차장 (옥내) **124**-1
주택과 정원 **53**
주택의 문제 및 수리 **62**-63
주행 기록계 **159**-28
주행 시험을 통과한다 **137**-H
주황 **24**-4
주황색 스웨터는 회색 스웨터 위에
　있습니다 **25**-9
죽다 **41**-R
줄 **73**-11, **226**-19
줄기 **211**-9
줄넘기 **224**-4
줄무늬 **96**-20
줄을 서서 기다리다 **94**-B
줄자 **100**-17, **181**-45
줌 렌즈 **235**-23
중 **96**-3
중간 이름 **4**-3
중간색 **24**
중고 의복 **102**-2
중고차 사기 **157**
중고품 시장 **222**-6
중국 배추 **69**-15
중년의 **32**-2
중서부 **201**-9
중성자 **195**-32
중이염 **111**-3
중장비를 운전하다 **170**-H

중학교 **188**-3
쥐 **63**-27, **215**-17
증거 **141**-9
증상 및 부상 **110**
증서 **41**-9
증인 **141**-11
지각을 하지 않는다 **174**-E
지갑을 지킨다 **143**-D
지게차 **175**-12
지구 **205**-3
지난 주 **20**-18
지도 **7**-12, **155**
지도책 **133**-8
지루한 **43**-25
지름 **193**-37
지문 **136**-5
지배인 **50**-8, **185**-11
지불 방법 **27**
지불하다 **27**-G
지붕 **46**-1
지붕 수리공 **62**-8
지붕널 **178**-20
지붕이 새다 **62**-3
지시를 따른다 **9**, **147**-F
지역 대학 **127**-17, **188**-6
지역 번호 **4**-10, **15**-29, **15**-34
지역사회 청소 **148**-149
지열 에너지 **218**-7
지우개 **7**-19
지우다 **109**-Q
지원 모임 **115**-15
지진 **144**-5
지팡이 **113**-16
지팡이 모양 캔디 **239**-17
지퍼 **99**-25
지퍼가 고장나다 **97**-39
지하 **47**-13, **50**
지하철 **151**-12
지하철 역 **151**-11, **152**
지하철 전동차 **152**-6
지형 및 서식지 **204**
지형지물 **220**-1
직각 **193**-26
직물점 **99**
직불 카드를 사용한다 **27**-C
직사각형 **193**-29
직선 **193**-22
직업 **166**-169
직업 교육의 종류 **172**
직업 박람회 **172**-13
직업 소개소에 간다 **173**-E
직업 정보 센터 **172**-9
직업 찾기 **173**

직업 치료사 **168**-45
직업 훈련 **172**-5
직업별 의복 **92**-93
직업상의 기술 **170**
직업학교 **188**-5
직원 **120**-13, **165**-9
직원 선발자 **172**-14
직장 **164**-165
직장에서의 불운한 하루 **186**-187
직장을 구하다 **40**-F
진공 청소기 **61**-10
진공 청소기 부품 **61**-11
진공 청소기 주머니 **61**-12
진드기 **214**-27
진로 경로 **172**
진로 계획 **172**
진로 계획하기 **172**
진로 상담원 **172**-10
진료 **118**
진료 절차 **118**
진료대 **118**-7
진료소 **186**-2
진료소를 방문한다 **114**-A
진료실에서 **119**
진열장 **94**-5
진입 금지 **154**-2
진주 목걸이 **95**-39
진지한 표정의 사진 **206**-3
진통제 **113**-26
진통제 **113**-26
진흙 사태 **144**-6
질문에 대답한다 **8**-L
질문을 한다 **8**-K
질문한다 **174**-M
질병과 건강 상태 **111**
질식하다 **116**-L
짐을 싸다 **49**-M, **162**-A
짐을 풀다 **49**-N
집 **46**-47
집 구매 하기 **49**
집 구하기 **48**-49
집게 **78**-23
집다 **11**-E
집안일 **60**
집에 도착하다 **39**-R
집에 오다 **39**-R
집에서 공부한다 **10**-D
집을 보다 **49**-H
집을 사다 **41**-M
집을 청소하다 **39**-O
집주인 **51**-27
짜다 **233**-F
짝과 함께 공부하기 **8**
짝수 **192**-4

짧은 구레나룻 **33**-7
짧은 머리 **33**-1
짧은 치마 **96**-16
찜통 **78**-3
찢어지다 **97**-41
차 **81**-38, **192**-8
차 또는 중장비를 운전하지
　마십시오 **112**-E
차 스푼 **83**-31
차 주전자 **54**-17, **55**-16
차 통행로 **53**-8
차가 터널 밑을 지나가다 **153**-K
차가운 물로 세탁한다 **219**-K
차고 **47**-14
차고 문 **53**-7
차고 세일 **102**-103
차다 **230**-E
차로 출근하다 **38**-I
차문 잠금 장치 **159**-25
차에 탄 채 주문하고 음식을 받아가는
　(식의) 식당 **128**-11
차장 **152**-13
착륙하다 **160**-K
착한 개 **23**-17
찬장 **54**-1, **55**-22
참고도서 사서 **133**-9
참새 **214**-7
참치 **71**-7, **72**-19, **212**-8
찻잔 **55**-6
창고 **175**-7
창고원 **169**-59
창구 **47**-11, **56**-17, **136**-7
창문에서 떨어져 있는다 **147**-I
창문을 닦다 **60**-I
창유리 **178**-16
찾아보다 **102**-B
채소밭 **53**-27, **177**-14
채혈 전문의 **121**-29
책상 **6**-7, **182**-9
책상 위를 치운다 **10**-I
책을 같이 본다 **8**-M
책을 나르다 **11**-F
책을 덮다 **6**-H
책을 들다 **11**-E
책을 반납하다 **133**-D
책을 빌리다 **133**-C
책을 읽어주다 **36**-N
책을 전달하다 **11**-G
책을 찾아보다 **133**-B
책을 치우세요 **9**-Z
책을 펴다 **6**-G
책장 **7**-10
처남 **34**-17

처방 번호 112-5
처방약 112-3
처방약 정보 라벨 112-4
처방전 112-2
처음 면허 따기 137
척추 107-49
척추동물 194-12
천 16
천 종류 98-99
천 한 필 98-15
천둥 13-16
천문학자 205-22
천번째 16
천식 111-9
천연 가스 218-3
천왕성 205-7
천천히 끓인다 77-P
철도 건널목 154-14
철물점 148-4
첫번째 16
첫번째 달과 마지막 달 임대료를
　지불하다 48-E
청각 장애가 있는 32-12
청각 장애자용 전화기 15-26
청력 손실 115-2
청력 전문의 115-9
청록 24-9
청록색 스웨터는 상자 안에 있습니다 25-6
청바지 86-2, 92-19
청소 용품 61
청소 카트 184-19
청소부 182-3
청소용 솔 61-20
청원서 148-5
청진기 118-10
체 78-22
체다 치즈 71-28
체리 68-11
체스 232-8
체온계 118-11
체온을 재다 118-B
체육 189-17
체육관 5-19, 126-10, 184-24
체인 95-33, 180-41
체조 228-9
체중 32, 75
체중이 많이 나가는 32-7
체크 무늬 96-24
체크인 데스크 160-2
첼로 238-7
초 18-3, 56-20
초대 64-9
초대 거절하기 12-J

초대 대통령 198-11
초대 받아들이기 12-I
초대형 냉동고 185-3
초등학교 188-2
초록 24-5
초록색 스웨터는 분홍색 스웨터
　사이에 있습니다 25-12
초보적인 직업 172-1
초빙 연사 206-4
초승달 205-10
초안을 쓴다 191-H
초원 204-20
초인종 53-14
초코렛 바 73-37
촛대 56-21
촛불을 불다 240-C
촛점이 안맞다 235-33
총 142-14
총액 27-9
촬영하다 235-A
최종안을 쓴다 191-L
최초의 의회 198-6
추수감사절 22-17
축구 229-12
축구공 231-12
축제 239-13
축석 57-27, 72-3, 135-8, 155-7
축하하다 206-C
출구 없음 154-6
출근하다 38-I
출발점 162-1
출발하다 160-J, 230-R
출생 증명서 40-1
출생지 4-14
출하담당 계원 175-14
출혈하다 116-M
충격 완충 모자 92-9
충전기 14-10, 234-17
충전재 119-8
충치 119-7
충치를 메우다 119-E
췌장 107-45
취미와 게임 232-233
측량치를 환산하다 75-C
측정 17
측정하다 17-C
층계 50-10
층층나무 210-15
치과 119
치과 보조원 119-2, 167-22
치과 장비 119-4
치과 진료 119
치과 질환 119

치과의사 119-1
치다 230-B
치료사 115-14
치료소 186-2
치마 87-10
치매 111-18
치석 119-12
치솔 57-23, 109-22
치솔 꽂이 57-24
치수 17
치실 109-24
치실을 사용하다 109-K
치아 106-7
치아를 닦다 119-A
치아파스 고지 201-18
치약 109-23
치약 튜브 하나 74-24
치장 벽토 178-15
치즈 66-4
치즈 1 온스 75-11
치즈 두부 야채 케서롤 77
치즈 케이크 81-34
치즈를 간다 77-G
치즈버거 79-3
치통 110-2
친구들과 얘기한다 173-A
친구를 소개 하다 3-I
친구와 같이 걷는다 143-A
친척 44-6
칠 16
칠면조 70-17, 239-14
칠면조 구이 76-4
칠십 16
칠판 6-1
칠판에 쓰다 6-E
침 122-2
침대 58-9
침대 머리판 58-10
침대 박스 스프링 58-19
침대 옆 작은 탁자 121-21
침대 조절기 121-27
침대 틀 58-18
침대를 정돈하다 60-F
침대보 59-11
침상에서 휴식을 취한다 114-B
침상엽 98-17, 100-10, 210-10
침실 46-2, 58
침실용 탁자 58-23
침착한 42-8
침착함을 유지한다 147-E
침팬지 217-27
칭찬하다 36-J
카네이션 211-20

카누 타기 226-3
카드 134-15, 239-5
카드 가게 130-7
카드 보내기 135
카드놀이를 하다 233-H
카드를 받는다 135-F
카드를 배달한다 135-E
카드를 보낸다 135-D
카드를 빼다 132-G
카드를 읽는다 135-G
카드에 글을 쓴다 135-A
카디건 스웨터 88-2
카메라 케이스 235-28
카우보이 모자 92-18
카운터 54-22
카운터를 닦다 60-O
카운티 페어 223-13
카톤 74-4
카트 72-7, 129-28,
카티지치즈 한 통 74-17
카페트 56-24
카페트를 진공 청소하다 60-H
카풀을 한다 219-I
칵테일 드레스 89-20
칸막이 182-7
칼 55-4, 83-30
칼라 100-4
캐나다 지역 201
캐미솔 91-21
캐시미어 98-4
캐주얼 복장 88
캐주얼, 근무복 및 정장 88-89
캐처 마스크 231-15
캔 74-3
캔 식품 72, 146-9
캔디 239-12
캔디 가게 131-17
캔버스 233-17
캠코더 235-24
캠퍼스 5
캠프파이어 226-11
캠핑 226-5
캠핑 스토브 226-16
캠핑카 156-9
캡슐 113-23
캥거루 217-44
커서 197-14
커튼 56-16, 58-7
커플 239-4
커피 73-33, 81-37
커피 숍 126-11
커피 숍 메뉴 80-81
커피 탁자 56-19

커피메이커 **54**–11
커피잔 **55**–7
컨디셔너 **108**–11
컨버터블 **156**–5
컨베이어 벨트 **175**–9
컨벤션 센터 **127**–24
컨츄리 **237**–27
컬럼버스 기념일 **22**–15
컴퓨터 **7**–15, **183**–17
컴퓨터 기술자 **167**–19, **182**–12
컴퓨터 소프트웨어 엔지니어 **167**–18
컴퓨터로 체크인한다 **160**–A
컴퓨터를 프로그램하다 **170**–I
컴퓨터실 **5**–15
컵 **83**–24
케서롤 접시 **78**–10
케이블 **196**–13
케이크 **73**–39, **81**–33
케이크팬 **78**–26
케찹 **79**–21
코 **104**–6
코 스프레이 **113**–32
코끼리 **217**–42
코끼리 코 **158**–11, **210**–4, **217**–47
코듀로이 **99**–11
코드 **14**–2
코막힘 **110**–7
코미디 **237**–13
코바늘뜨기 **233**–25
코브라 **213**–41
코뿔소 **217**–28
코알라 **217**–45
코요테 **216**–3
코울슬로우 **80**–18
코치 **5**–20, **229**–2
코코넛 **68**–24
코피가 나다 **110**–17
콘도 **52**–5
콘드 비프 **71**–22
콘로 **33**–14
콘센트 **58**–28, **159**–42
콘센트 커버 **181**–46
콘크리트 **178**–10
콘택트 렌즈 **115**–8
콜론 **190**–17
콜롱 **108**–6
콧수염 **33**–5
콩 **69**–21, **72**–17, **177**–3
콩 한 캔 **74**–15
쿠거 **216**–2
쿠키 **73**–38
쿠키 판 **78**–27
쿠키 한 봉지 **74**–20

쿠페 **156**–2
쿠폰 **67**–15
쿼터 **26**–4
퀘벡 **201**–5
퀼트 조각 **232**–15
퀼트를 하다 **58**–16, **232**–C
크레용 **59**–14
크로스컨트리 스키 **227**–3
크로커스 **211**–17
크로코다일 **213**–37
크루넥 스웨터 **96**–7
크리스마스 **22**–18
크리스마스 트리 **239**–16
크림 **81**–41, **113**–25
크림 그릇 **55**–15
크림색 **24**–16
큰 가지 **210**–3
큰 동굴 **220**–7
큰 손 **23**–2
큰 쇠망치 **178**–23
큰 접시 **55**–20
큰어치 **214**–6
클라리넷 **238**–2
클래식 **237**–21
클래식 콘서트 **223**–14
클러치 **159**–49
클럽 **233**–32
클럽 샌드위치 **80**–12
클립형 귀고리 **95**–37
키가 작은 **32**–6
키가 큰 **32**–4
키보드 **196**, **196**–14
키스하다 **3**–K
키위 **68**–22
키친 타월 **54**–3
키패드 **14**–5
킹 사이즈 베드 **184**–15
타악기 **238**
타운카 **152**–20
타워 **196**–3
타이어 **158**–5
타이어 펑크가 나다 **162**–F
타이어에 공기를 넣는다 **157**–L
타이츠 **91**–19
타일 **57**–12, **178**–11
타일에 금이 가다 **62**–4
타일을 설치하다 **178**–C
타임 클록 **165**–7
타자를 치다 **170**–R, **196**–A
타주 연락책 **146**–2
타주 연락책에 전화한다 **147**–L
타코 **79**–8
탁구 **228**–14

탁아소 직원 **166**–16
탄력 붕대 **117**–12
탄산음료수 **73**–34, **79**–11
탈출 경로 **146**–3
탐험 **199**–8
탐험가 **199**–9
탑승 구역 **161**–9
탑승권 **161**–20
탑승권과 신분증을 제시한다 **160**–C
태산목 **210**–8
태양 **209**–8
태양 에너지 **218**–1
태양계 및 행성 **205**
태어나다 **40**–A
태클하다 **230**–F
태평양 북서부 **201**–14
태평양 연안주 **201**–7
태평양 표준시 **19**–29
택배원 **168**–40
택시 **150**–3
택시 면허 **152**–22
택시 승차장 **152**–18
택시 운전사 **152**–21
택시를 타다 **153**–E
택시에서 내리다 **153**–F
탬버린 **238**–17
탭 **197**–7
탱크 트럭 **156**–20
터틀넥 스웨터 **96**–9
턱 **106**–4
턱받이 **37**–5
턱수염 **33**–6
턱시도 **89**–17
털 **216**–19
테니스 **228**–15
테니스 라켓 **231**–2
테니스 코트 **224**–6
테니스화 **95**–32
텍스트 상자 **197**–13
텐트 **226**–10
텔레마케팅을 하는 사람 **169**–60
텔레비전 **56**–5, **56**–6
텔레비전을 보다 **39**–X
토글 볼트 **180**–38
토끼 **215**–13
토네이도 **145**–5
토론하다 **139**–B
토마토 **69**–6
토성 **205**–6
토스터 **54**–6
토스트 **80**–4
토요일 **20**–14
토크 쇼 **236**–4

토큰 **152**–10
토트 백 **94**–19
토하다 **110**–E
톱 **180**–4
톱날 **180**–27
통역사 **168**–35
통장 **132**–10
통증 **115**–3
통화 한다 **15**–C
퇴근하다 **38**–N
퇴비 더미 **53**–25
퇴직하다 **41**–O
투명 테이프 **183**–30
투표하다 **140**–A
튜너 **234**–13
튜바 **238**–12
튜브 **74**–12
튤립 **211**–11
트랙 **5**–21, **126**–1, **152**–14
트랙터 **177**–9
트랙터 트레일러 **156**–15
트럭 **150**–6
트럭 기사 **169**–61
트럭을 운전하다 **170**–E
트럼펫 **238**–11
트렁크 내부 **158**
트레이 테이블 **161**–21
트레이닝 바지 **89**–23
트레이닝 윗도리 **89**–22
트레일러 **156**–17
트렌치 코트 **90**–21
트롬본 **238**–10
특급 우편 **134**–2
특대 **96**–5
특매가 **27**–3
특소 **96**–1
틀니 **119**–10
티셔츠 **86**–4
티켓 **152**–15
팀 **229**–3
팀 스포츠 **229**
팁을 놓다 **82**–J
파 **69**–20
파괴 행위 **142**–1
파도 **2**–F, **225**–17
파란색 스웨터는 빨간색 스웨터 아래에
　있습니다 **25**–5
파랑 **24**–3
파리 **214**–28
파마하다 **33**–B
파스타 **67**–12
파스타 샐러드 **80**–20
파슬리 **69**–28

파우더 109–41
파이 81–35, 193–46
파이 팬 78–28
파이프 181–17
파이프 렌치 181–47
파이프가 얼다 63–16
파인애플 68–23
파일 폴더 183–50
파일을 첨부한다 197–H
파자마 91–24
파충류 213
파카 90–9
파티 64–2
파티오 53–16
파티오 가구 53–19
파파야 68–20
판다 217–41
판매세 27–8
판매자로부터 소유권 증서를 받는다 157–E
판매자에게 자동차에 대해 물어본다 157–B
판초 90–19
팔 16
팔, 손 및 손가락 106
팔꿈치 106–12
팔뚝 106–13
팔분의 일 17–5
쌀십 16
팔찌 95–9
팝 237–25
팝 음악 237–32
팝업 광고물 197–9
패스트 푸드 식당 128–10
패스트 푸드점 79
패스하다 230–G
패턴 96, 99–22
팩스기 183–21
팬 54–24, 55–19, 229–4
팬케이크 80–7
팬티 91–14
팬티 스타킹 91–18
퍼레이드 239–1
퍼센트 17
퍼즐 59–17
페니 26–1
페리 220–4
페이즐리 무늬 96–26
페이지 19
페이퍼 클립 183–31
페인트 롤러 181–23
페인트 브러쉬 181–22, 233–20
페인트 팬 181–51
펜 7–22
펜싱 228–7

펜치 180–7
펭귄 214–11
편도 여행 152–16
편의점 128–3
편지 134–13
편지를 타이프하다 171–A
평결 141–14
평균 신장 32–5
평균 체중 32–8
평면 TV 234–7
평면도 186–4
평상복 86–87
평원 204–19
평일 20–16
평행사변형 193–33
평행선 193–25
평화적인 집회 140–1
폐 107–39
포도 68–3
포도원 177–16
포도주 잔 83–23
포스트잇 183–39
포유동물 209–10, 216–217
포인세티아 211–24
포인터 197–12
포장 74–8
보상 용기 82–5
포장 테이프 183–32
포장된 식품 146–10
포장하는 사람(기계) 175–8
포장하다 240–F
포켓볼 228–2
포크 55–3, 237–29
폭력 강도 142–11
폭력단 폭력 142–4
폭발 144–4
폭찹 70–10
폭포 204–2
폭행 142–3
폴로 셔츠 92–14
폼 패드 226–13
표백제 101–7
표범 217–34, 217–40
표시한 답을 확인 한다 10–L
표준 시간 19–26
표현의 자유 140–2
푸주한 166–13
풀 183–33
풀오버 스웨터 88–3
풋볼 헬멧 231–19
풋볼공 229–11, 231–21
풍력 218–2
풍선 44–4

프런트 데스크 184–12
프레리 도그 215–22
프레리 프로빈스 201–3
프레젠테이션 182–6
프렌치 혼 238–13
프리 사이즈 96–6
프리즈비 231–27
프리즘 195–35
프린터 169–50, 196–17
프린트 무늬 96–23
플라스틱 랩 72–24
플라스틱 저장 용기 78–4
플라스틱 저장백 72–25
플래시 드라이브 196–8
플랫폼 152–7
플러그 234–16
플런저 181–50
플로리스트 130–8, 167–27
플로어 램프 56–15
플루트 238–1
피겨 스케이팅 227–5
피고 141–5
피고에게 유죄를 선고하다 141–E
피고에게 판결을 내리다 141–F
피고측 변호사 141–4
피곤한 43–32
씨난 경로 146–5
피드 독 98–20
피드 바 98–20
피를 뽑다 118–F
피망 69–7
피복이 벗겨진 코드 179–5
피부 107–31
피아노 238–14
피자 79–10
피크 108–15
피크닉 테이블 224–8
피클 80–11
피팅 181–18
피해자 142–10
픽업 트럭 156–12
핀 95–38
핀셋 117–4, 195–43
필기 시험을 본다 137–E
필름 235–22
필름 카메라 235–21
필립스 드라이버 180–31
하늘 209–9
하늘색 24–11
하드 드라이브 196–6
하루 중의 때 18
하마 217–43
하모니카 238–21

하와이－알류샨 표준시 19–27
하원 138–3
하원 의원 138–4
하의용 슬립 91–23
하이브리드 156–3
하이비스커스 211–12
하이에나 217–30
하이킹 226–7
하이폰 190–20
하이힐 89–21, 95–25, 97–32
하임 리크 처치법 117–18
하키 스틱 231–11
하트 107–38, 233–31, 239–6
하현달 205–11
학교 5, 126–9
학교 등록 양식 4
학교 및 과목 188–189
학교 생활 잘하기 10
학교 생활을 잘하는 방법 10
학교 식당 5–14
학교 횡단보도 154–15
학교를 다니기 시작하다 40–B
학교에서의 하루 일과 11
학급 활동에 참여한다 10–B
학부모회 22–5
학생 6–5
한번만 뒤집어 살짝 익힌 계란 후라이 76–11
한시 18–6
한시 사십분 18–12
한시 사십오분 18–13
한시 삼십분 18–11
한시 십분 18–8
한시 십오분 18–9
한시 오분 18–7
한시 이십분 18–10
할머니 34–1
할아버지 34–2
함께 놀아주다 36–M
합계 192–7
합류 차선 154–10
합판 178–18
핫 씨리얼 80–9
핫도그 79–6
핫팩 113–15
항공사 터미널에서 160
항생연고제 117–11
항히스타민 크림 117–10
해결책을 함께 생각해 본다 8–H
해군 138–15
해당 지역을 빠져 나간다 147–K
해마 212–13
해먹 53–23
해바라기 211–10

해변 **204**–10, **225**
해변용 의자 **225**–22
해병 **138**–17
해산물 및 가공 식품 **71**
해쉬 브라운 **80**–3
해안 **204**–12
해안 경비대 **138**–18
해왕성 **205**–8
해일 **145**–17
해충 구제업자 **63**–21
해파리 **212**–14
해프 달러 **26**–5
핵 **194**–7, **195**–29
핸드 브레이크 **159**–48
핸드 트럭 **175**–11
핸드백 **87**–9, **94**–2
핸드북을 공부한다 **137**–A
핸들 **159**–26
햄 **70**–9
햄버거 **79**–1
햇볕에 타다 **110**–14
행사 **22**
행상인 **129**–29
행정 부서 **138**
향상시킨다 **10**–G
향수 **108**–6
향수병에 걸린 **43**–20
허리 보호 벨트 **179**–18
허리띠 **100**–5
허리케인 **145**–14
허벅지 **106**–19
허브 **84**–9
허브차 **81**–40
헌법 **198**–12
헐거운 바지 **97**–30
헐렁한 바지 **97**–30
헛간 **177**–11
헝겊 **61**–9, **181**–54
헝겊 기저귀 **37**–8
헤드라인 **133**–7
헤드셋 **6**–8, **14**–13, **234**–4
헤어 드라이기 **33**–23, **108**–18,
헤어 디자이너 **167**–31
헤어 스프레이 **108**–12
헤어 클립 **108**–19
헤어스타일 묘사하기 **33**
헤어젤 **108**–16
헬리콥터 **151**–9
헬멧 **93**–23
혀 **106**–8
현관등 **53**–13
현금 자동 출납기 카드 **132**–15
현금과 동전 **146**–17

현금으로 지불한다 **27**–A
현금을 인출하다 **132**–F
현대 **199**–2
현미경 **194**
현악기 **238**
현장 교육 **172**–7
혈압계 **118**–9
혈압을 재다 **118**–A
혈액 검사 **121**–30
협곡 **204**–17
형광색 안전 조끼 **92**–4
혜성 **205**–24
호랑이 **217**–37
호밀빵 **71**–20
호박 **69**–24
호수 **204**–13
호스 **53**–21
호주 **202**–6
호출 단추 **121**–28
호텔 **124**–3, **184**
호텔 객실 청소부 **168**–34, **184**–20
호흡 마스크 **179**–13
혹 **217**–51
혼 **238**–11
혼란스러운 **43**–26
혼자서 문제를 푼다 **10**–J
홀수 **192**–3
홈통 **53**–4
홍수 **145**–19
홍역 **111**–5
홍합 **71**–13, **212**–17
화가 난 **43**–29
화단의 잡초를 뽑다 **176**–G
화려한 블라우스 **97**–34
화면 **196**–11
화물 밴 **156**–13
화물 운반대 **175**–13
화산 폭발 **145**–16
화살 **231**–8
화상을 입다 **116**–H
화성 **205**–4
화씨 **13**–1
화요일 **20**–10
화운데이션 **109**–40
화이트보드 **6**–3
화이트보트용 마커 **7**–17
화장 **109**
화장실 **5**–9, **46**–4
화장지 **57**–19, **146**–13
화폐 **26**
화학 **195**
화학자 **195**–25
환경미화원 **169**–54

환불하다 **27**–H
환산하다 **17**–D
환승 **152**–5
환자 **118**–6, **121**–18
환자를 보조하다 **170**–B
환자복 **121**–19
환한 길로 간다 **143**–B
활 **3**–H, **231**–6
활강 스키 **227**–1
황새치 **71**–5, **212**–10
황색 괘선지철 **183**–38
황제 **199**–3
회계사 **166**–1
회교사원 **126**–5
회사 로그 인쇄 용지 **183**–42
회색 **24**–15
회색 스웨터는 주황색 스웨터 아래에
　있습니다 **25**–11
회의 일정을 잡다 **171**–J
회의실 **182**–4, **184**–25
회전 카드 파일 **183**–44
회전문 **184**–2
회전식 대물렌즈대 **194**–15
횡단보도 **128**–15, **154**–13
후두염 **111**–4
후드(보닛) **158**–4
후라이팬 **78**–5
후미등 **158**–13
훅 **180**–39
훅단추 **99**–27
훈제 쇠고기 **71**–23
훈제 칠면조 **71**–25
휠 커버 **158**–9
휠체어 **113**–9
휴가 **22**–6
휴대 전화 **4**–12
휴대 전화 판매소 **131**–22
휴대 전화 홀더 **94**–15
휴대 전화를 끄다 **160**–I, **174**–G
휴대용 카세트 플레이어 **234**–6
휴대용 DVD 플레이어 **234**–11
휴대용 TV **234**–8
휴대폰 **14**–8
휴식을 취하다 **11**–H
휴일 **239**
흉곽 **107**–48
흉내를 내다 **233**–G
흐린 **13**–10
흑설탕 1/4 컵 **75**–8
흔들 의자 **37**–21
흔한 병 및 어린이 질병 **111**
흙 **208**–2
흙손 **176**–10, **178**–13

흡입기 **113**–33
흥분한 **43**–22
흥정하다 **102**–A
흰 빵 **71**–18
흰개미 **63**–22
흰색 **24**–14
흰색 스웨터는 검정색 스웨터 앞에
　있습니다 **25**–7
히터 **159**–40
힙합 **237**–26
ATM (자동 현금 인출기) **132**
ATM 카드를 넣다 **132**–D
C–클램프 **180**–6
CD 플레이어 **159**–38, **234**–1
CD를 듣다 **6**–C
CPR (심폐기능 소생법) **117**–17
CPU **196**–4
DJ **64**–4
DMV 직원 **136**–3
DMV 핸드북 **136**–1
DVD **133**–19
DVD 및 CD–ROM 드라이브 **196**–9
DVD 플레이어 **56**–7, **234**–10
Elm St.에서 직진하다 **155**–A
ESL **189**–14
ESOL **189**–14
First St.으로 한 블록 가다 **155**–F
GPS (글로벌 위치확인 시스템) **155**–11
HIV (인체 면역 결핍 바이러스) **111**–17
LCD 프로젝터 **6**–6, **235**–29
Main St.를 지나다 **155**–E
MP3 선수 **234**–2
Oak St.에서 좌회전하다 **155**–C
PIN 번호를 노출시키지 않는다 **143**–C
PIN 번호를 입력하다 **132**–E
Pine St.에서 우회전하다 **155**–B
R&B **237**–28
RV **156**–10
SKU 번호 **27**–5
SUV (스포츠 유틸리티 카) **156**–7
TSA 직원 **160**–5
TV 프로그램 종류 **236**
U 턴 허용 **154**–5
URL **197**–4
USB 포트 **196**–7
VCR **102**–7
x선 촬영을 하다 **119**–B

Research Bibliography

The authors and publisher wish to acknowledge the contribution of the following educators for their research on vocabulary development, which has helped inform the principals underlying OPD.

Burt, M., J. K. Peyton, and R. Adams. *Reading and Adult English Language Learners: A Review of the Research*. Washington, D.C.: Center for Applied Linguistics, 2003.

Coady, J. "Research on ESL/EFL Vocabulary Acquisition: Putting it in Context." In *Second Language Reading and Vocabulary Learning*, edited by T. Huckin, M. Haynes, and J. Coady. Norwood, NJ: Ablex, 1993.

de la Fuente, M. J. "Negotiation and Oral Acquisition of L2 Vocabulary: The Roles of Input and Output in the Receptive and Productive Acquisition of Words." *Studies in Second Language Acquisition* 24 (2002): 81–112.

DeCarrico, J. "Vocabulary learning and teaching." In *Teaching English as a Second or Foreign Language,* edited by M. Celcia-Murcia. 3rd ed. Boston: Heinle & Heinle, 2001.

Ellis, R. *The Study of Second Language Acquisition*. Oxford: Oxford University Press, 1994.

Folse, K. *Vocabulary Myths: Applying Second Language Research to Classroom Teaching*. Ann Arbor, MI: University of Michigan Press, 2004.

Gairns, R. and S. Redman. *Working with Words: A Guide to Teaching and Learning Vocabulary*. Cambridge: Cambridge University Press, 1986.

Gass, S. M. and M.J.A. Torres. "Attention When?: An Investigation Of The Ordering Effect Of Input And Interaction." *Studies in Second Language Acquisition* 27 (Mar 2005): 1–31.

Henriksen, Birgit. "Three Dimensions of Vocabulary Development." *Studies in Second Language Acquisition* 21 (1999): 303–317.

Koprowski, Mark. "Investigating the Usefulness of Lexical Phrases in Contemporary Coursebooks." *Oxford ELT Journal* 59(4) (2005): 322–32.

McCrostie, James. "Examining Learner Vocabulary Notebooks." *Oxford ELT Journal* 61 (July 2007): 246–55.

Nation, P. *Learning Vocabulary in Another Language*. Cambridge: Cambridge University Press, 2001.

National Center for ESL Literacy Education Staff. *Adult English Language Instruction in the 21st Century*. Washington, D.C.: Center for Applied Linguistics, 2003.

National Reading Panel. *Teaching Children to Read: An Evidenced-Based Assessment of the Scientific Research Literature on Reading and its Implications on Reading Instruction*. 2000. http://www. nationalreadingpanel.org/Publications/summary.htm/.

Newton, J. "Options for Vocabulary Learning Through Communication Tasks." *Oxford ELT Journal* 55(1) (2001): 30–37.

Prince, P. "Second Language Vocabulary Learning: The Role of Context Versus Translations as a Function of Proficiency." *Modern Language Journal* 80(4) (1996): 478-93.

Savage, K. L., ed. *Teacher Training Through Video - ESL Techniques: Early Production*. White Plains, NY: Longman Publishing Group, 1992.

Schmitt, N. *Vocabulary in Language Teaching*. Cambridge: Cambridge University Press, 2000.

Smith, C. B. *Vocabulary Instruction and Reading Comprehension*. Bloomington, IN: ERIC Clearinghouse on Reading English and Communication, 1997.

Wood, K. and J. Josefina Tinajero. "Using Pictures to Teach Content to Second Language Learners." *Middle School Journal* 33 (2002): 47–51.